COASTAL AND RIVER TRADE IN PRE-INDUSTRIAL ENGLAND

The history of Bristol in the seventeenth and eighteenth centuries, the widely acknowledged 'Golden Age' of the port, has tended to be read through extended narratives of overseas trade. Internal trade has been largely overlooked. *Coastal and River Trade in Pre-Industrial England* addresses this omission by providing full case studies and fresh, critical analysis of the coastal trade of Bristol and its domestic hinterland, extending a new interpretation of Bristol's role in its core domestic markets.

Making use of data derived from the Coastal Port Books, a source hitherto under-used, David Hussey argues that Bristol, in this period, did not stand alone but operated as part of a functioning regional system. The extensive coastal and river network that served the city provided a vital link in the organisation of the pre-industrial economy of the city and its domestic hinterland—the ports of the Bristol Channel and Severn Valley, south-west England, the central and west Midland counties, the Welsh Borderlands and south and south-west Wales.

David Hussey is Senior Lecturer in History and Director of the Portbooks Programme at the University of Wolverhampton.

EXETER MARITIME STUDIES

General Editors: Michael Duffy and David J. Starkey

COASTAL AND RIVER TRADE IN PRE-INDUSTRIAL ENGLAND

BRISTOL AND ITS REGION
1680–1730

David Hussey

UNIVERSITY
of
EXETER
PRESS

To my mother and father

First published in 2000 by
University of Exeter Press
Reed Hall, Streatham Drive
Exeter, Devon EX4 4QR
UK
www.ex.ac.uk/uep/

British Library Cataloguing in Publication Data
A catalogue record for this book is available from the British Library

ISBN 0 85989 617 X

Typeset in 11/12.5pt Garamond by Exe Valley Dataset, Exeter

Printed in Great Britain by
Short Run Press Ltd, Exeter

CONTENTS

TABLES, FIGURES, MAPS AND PLATES

Tables

Figures

Maps

Plates

(following page xvi)

PREFACE

This book is inspired by two main concerns. Firstly, whilst completing my doctoral thesis, it struck me that in many ways, the coastal and river trade of pre-industrial England and Wales has remained the eternal bridesmaid, the 'forgotten sector' of British economic history and that some revision of T.S. Willan's seminal work was long overdue. Secondly, my interests in my native city, Bristol, led me to reconsider its role in the organisation of early modern trade. As my researches progressed, I became increasingly aware that although the great narratives of Bristol's overseas trades had been painstakingly described by generations of historians, scant attention had been paid to either the city's core internal trades, or the commercial linkages it fostered with a wide and productive domestic hinterland. The book is an attempt to fuse these themes into a coherent analysis.

In undertaking the research for this book, I have many debts to acknowledge. In terms of financial support, the *Economic and Social Research Council* and the *Leverhulme Trust* provided the main funding for the Portbooks Programme, the pioneering, computer-based historical research group within which this project was conceived and nurtured. In addition, the History Research Committee of the University of Wolverhampton must be thanked for recognising the worth of this work and granting me the sustained periods of sabbatical leave from teaching, without which completion would have been severely delayed.

Naturally, I am greatly indebted to my colleagues at Wolverhampton in general and those associated with the Portbooks Programme in particular. Amongst these, Malcolm Wanklyn and Nancy Cox deserve special mention for their consistently helpful suggestions and sound criticisms, and Peter Wakelin and Barrie Trinder were invaluable in offering knowledge and support in the early incarnations of the project. In the course of my research, I have also been fortunate to benefit from the generous advice of many historians and scholars in the field. For both their formal and informal comments and suggestions, I wish to thank: Jonathan Barry; Maxine Berg;

Angela Brown; Peter Claughton; Chris Evans; David Hey; Pat Hudson; Walter Minchinton; Kenneth Morgan; Michael Power; Jon Press; Michael Price; Richard Rodger; Göran Rydén; Marie Rowlands; Geoff Timmins; Peter Wardley; and Joyce Youings.

I would also like to express my gratitude to the archivists and staff of the record offices and libraries listed in the bibliography. Their gracious responses to my many requests, even the most banal and facile, have greatly aided this work. Similarly, Hugh Conway-Jones and the team of volunteer transcribers based at Gloucester (in particular, Jane Bradshaw; Josie Collings; Pam Daw; Jean and Reg Edwards; Johanne Lewis; Jim Simmonds; and Len Vear) were central to the processing of much of the Bristol Channel port book data. Sue Giles and Sheena Stoddard, respectively Curator of Ethnography and Curator of Fine Art at Bristol City Museum and Art Gallery, David Hopkins, Librarian of The Ironbridge Gorge Museum Trust, Tim Bridges, Collections Manager at the Worcester City Art Gallery and Museum and Tony Carr of the Shropshire Records and Research Unit procured the illustrations with much courtesy and good humour, despite the rather forced time schedule and my slightly garbled stream of messages. At Wolverhampton, Marek Paul and Mike Griffiths were the main avenues of technical and computer support for a project that was demanding on both time and resources; Simone Clarke undertook additional, last minute work at the PRO; and Martin Roberts applied a much-needed geographer's sense of spatial awareness in digitising the maps from my crude sketchings. At the University of Exeter Press, Simon Baker, Rosemary Rooke, Anna Henderson and Genevieve Davey have provided much enthusiasm, patience and help throughout the writing and delivery of the book.

My final thanks go to my mother, father, brothers and friends for their unstinting support. I am eternally grateful to the blue half of Bristol for times of both sublime inspiration and abject disappointment that have uncannily mirrored the shifting fortunes of undertaking long-term research in not always supportive conditions. In this last respect, I owe a huge debt of gratitude, as well as much love, to my partner, Lisa Taylor, for her encouragement and her belief in the realization of this work. However, my greatest thanks are for my colleague and friend, Penny Robson. She has not only spared much of her own research time in casting an admirably critical eye over the various drafts of this book, but she has also provided many positive suggestions of both an academic and stylistic nature and much needed moments of levity along the way. Any faults that remain are entirely my own.

David Hussey
September 2000

INTRODUCTION

By the late seventeenth century Bristol was a vibrant mercantile centre with a long and illustrious maritime past and a seemingly boundless age of commercial opportunity stretching out before it.[1] Situated at the heart of a wide and productive hinterland, the city dominated regional trade and its burgeoning overseas interests permeated the very fabric of the transoceanic world.

Bristol was a major player in a vast 'Empire of goods', second only to the capital in the value and range of its trade.[2] Indeed, as Defoe intimated, the city, alone amongst domestic ports, traded 'with a more entire independency upon London than any other town in Britain'.[3] Yet the remarkable feature of Bristol's development was its heterogeneity. Bristol was 'not more a commercial than a manufacturing town'.[4] The industrial spin-offs from the Atlantic trades, notably the processing and redistribution of tobacco and sugar, vied for commercial and physical space with a host of domestic enterprises. The large-scale production of iron, lead, brass, glass and soap flourished alongside the brewing, distilling and ceramics industries in the early years of the eighteenth century. By this time, Bristol's population had risen to around 20,000–25,000 souls, outstripping Norwich as the largest provincial town.[5] To be sure, the improvement of the city lagged behind commercial opportunity: for much of the period trade, industry and society were still uncomfortably and somewhat uneasily crammed into the old medieval core of the town. None the less, the jostling press of commerce and humanity, the 'strange mixture of seamen, women, children, loaded Horses, Asses, and Sledges with Goods dragging along' that choked the quays, backs and famously narrow streets of the city,[6] was beginning to be transformed by the gradual addition of enhanced commercial and civic amenities.

Given the maritime experience of the city, it is perhaps understandable that the history of Bristol is inextricably linked to the development of overseas commerce. A persistent symbiosis exists between the chronicled fortunes of the great western city and its control of vital sectors of foreign trade in this period. Just as deliberately and in many ways as laboriously and conservatively as the port was reshaped to keep pace with expanding levels of trade, so has the historiography of Bristol been fashioned piece by piece from the weighty narratives of overseas commerce. The progressive capitalisation of Bristol's trade, in particular the aggressive commercial exploitation of the colonial markets of the north American seaboard and the West Indies, has occupied generations of historians and filled many pages of academic and more popular literature. Historical attention has focused upon not only describing these trades, but also charting the impact of transoceanic commerce upon the port's merchant oligarchy and the wider economic, social and cultural development of the town.[7] The lustrous 'Golden Age' of Bristol thus rests squarely upon an extended discourse of overseas trade. In this view Bristol was the 'Gateway of Empire', the jumping-off point to brave new worlds and unlimited mercantile fortunes. In return, the city acted as a provincial 'navel of the world': a great centre where a plethora of foreign goods and exotica were brought back, the profits of which were reinvested in domestic business and nascent financial services, or laundered into suburban estates and Clifton's leafy parades.[8]

The association between civic development, mercantile wealth and overseas trade was not lost on contemporary observers. As the seventeenth century progressed, the image of the sober, substantial Bristol merchant of Pepys's time gave way to North's more ambivalent portrait of energetic speculation in a range of trades including human cargoes.[9] By the eighteenth century, the prevailing consensus was that Bristol, for all its commercial prowess, was, as Walpole memorably described, 'the dirtiest great shop', populated by insatiable, low-born creatures of mammon.[10] Even the clergy, it was reported, 'talk of nothing but trade and how to turn a penny . . . all are in a hurry, running up and down with cloudy looks and busy faces'.[11] Unlike their London counterparts, Bristol merchants were roundly condemned as oafish hogs disporting themselves in the tawdry swill of commerce. Yet, however caustic such comments may appear, they were shot through with a veiled admiration, an awe at the extent and almost obsessive activity generated by trade.

No matter how seductive or indeed entertaining these constructs appear to modern eyes, the emphasis on foreign trade has conspired to obscure the full picture of Bristol's commerce. As Jackson has stressed, overseas trade, 'the sort that involved the merchants, made the money, and gained the prestige', has monopolised critical analysis.[12] But it is surely crass to suggest that we can read the development of Bristol, or indeed other major port cities, solely in the most conspicuous aspects of external trade. If Bristol can be seen as an 'open gateway', a dual portal through which commercial and cultural stimuli were filtered, the city's domestic trade needs to be studied in much greater depth.

To an extent, historical accounts have always been aware of a domestic perspective to Bristol's more high-profile trades: they merely have not been afforded much weight. Most work has tended to return to Professor Minchinton's brief exposition of Bristol's role as a 'quasi-metropolis' of the west.[13] Minchinton's main argument was that eighteenth-century Bristol formed both the cohesive and the dynamic element to provincial trade. As a result of its physical situation, unchallenged dominance in key overseas goods, and the demographic and industrial growth of the city itself, Bristol imposed a vital polarity upon a wide hinterland, stretching from the Midlands and the Welsh borderlands to the south-west of England and south Wales. In this model, a kind of debased commodity peonage was played out: the fragmented and localised economies of the hinterland were progressively subjugated to Bristol, the dominant regional centre of commerce and consumption.[14] In turn, the hinterland became increasingly dependent upon Bristol for high-quality producer and consumer wares; overseas goods; sources of capital and finance; and, rather more vicariously, diluted forms of 'metropolitan' cultural experience.[15]

The durability of Minchinton's work is testimony to its breadth of vision and conception. However, whilst it would be churlish to deny the profound impact the metropolitan model has had upon subsequent analyses of Bristol, it is equally not difficult to unravel many of its premises. Primarily, there is a distinct lack of hard data relating Bristol to its core hinterland. As a consequence, the assumptions underpinning the study become increasingly attenuated. Similarly, the emphasis upon the centrality of Bristol above and beyond the regional periphery has necessarily polarised discussion around models of control and dependence.[16] Yet, if the full extent of Bristol's regional hegemony and, by implication, its wider economic prosperity is to be grasped, research must be embedded in a far more comprehensive critique of the internal trade not only of Bristol, but also of its nominally subordinate hinterland.

The aim of this book is to cast new light upon these issues by subjecting the coastal trade of Bristol and its surrounding region to fresh analysis. This has been facilitated by integrating quantitative data derived from the Exchequer coastal port books for a period between 1680 and 1730 with more illustrative and, in many ways, more elusive evidence gleaned from merchant accounts and commercial papers. In so doing, the study reasserts the importance of sensitively-applied quantitative approaches, recently and somewhat unhelpfully dismissed as 'more useful for pathology than for diagnosis'.[17]

The analysis is divided into five chapters, each addressing a central aspect of the trade of Bristol and its domestic hinterland. Chapter 1 describes the main features of the regional basis to the study, providing an outline of the principal methodological and interpretative issues underpinning the main body of port book data rendered available for this and, hopefully, further research. In chapter 2, the spatial patterns of trade are identified and analysed in more depth. Voyages are mapped according to their direction and frequency and a comparative functional hierarchy of commercial activity amongst regional ports is constructed. The chapter concludes by gauging the impact of such variables as seasonality, war, weather and marketing strategies upon the major patterns of trade. Chapter 3 provides an insight into the extent and range of goods traded, arguing that bulk staples—coal, for example—did not dominate trade as fully or completely as has been implied elsewhere.[18] Chapter 4 discusses the level of mercantile organisation, crewing, boat provision and operation. The pervasive thesis that Bristol merchants, particularly those involved in overseas trade, were prepared to leave the business of organisation to provincial operatives is examined more rigorously, and the physical provision of trade in terms of the number and location of regional coasters and their operatives is also subject to fresh critical appraisal. The discussion outlined above is brought into sharp relief in the final chapter. Here port book data are combined with the accounts and correspondence of Hoare and Company and William Alloway, two important regional merchant houses. The chapter analyses the development and organisation of the trade in a wide range of commodities, and pieces together the patterns of finance, shipping, factorage and distribution that bound regional systems of trade into a coherent commercial network. In 1712, William Goldwin published a laboured if earnest *Poetical Description of Bristol*. Naturally, trade figured prominently in his eulogistic verses to this most commercial of cities. To Goldwin, the old conceit that Bristol was but London writ small was not enough to communicate the majesty of his subject. Whilst London still had half an eye fixed on the old European and Mediterranean trades, it was Bristol that was the truly dynamic centre,

> Whose Oozy Banks with two great Streams inlaid
> And Naval Strength alternately convey'd
> Command[ed] the Staple of the *Western* Trade.[19]

Although Goldwin was rhapsodising on overseas commerce, his assessment has perhaps even greater resonances for the city's core internal trades. Yet, hamstrung by the obscurity and impenetrability of the sources, research has been conspicuously limited in describing these western staples. This book, by teasing out the full spectrum of trade within Bristol's coastal and riparian hinterland, seeks to invert the centrality of foreign commerce. If this study encourages a re-interpretation of Bristol based not so much upon the grand discourses of overseas trade, but upon the city's domestic arena, it will have satisfied its major objective.

Plate 1

James Millerd, *An Exact Delineation of the Famous Cittie of Bristol,* 1671

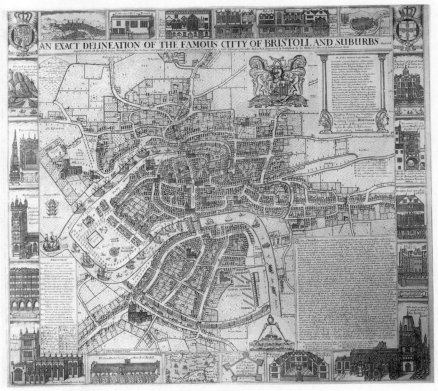

Plate 2

S. and N. Buck, *The North West Prospect of the City of Bristol*, 1734

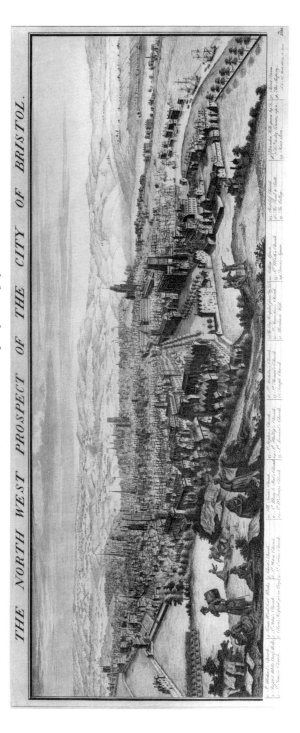

THE NORTH WEST PROSPECT OF THE CITY OF BRISTOL.

Plate 3

S. and N. Buck, *The South East Prospect of the City of Bristol*, 1734

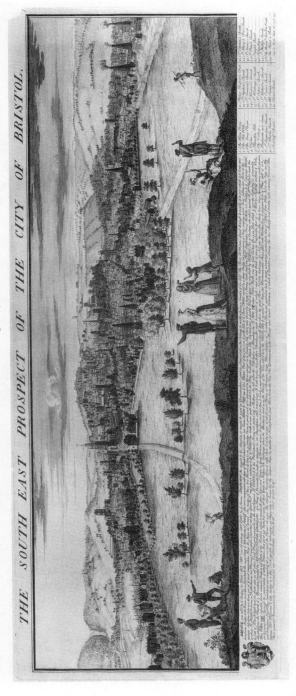

THE SOUTH EAST PROSPECT OF THE CITY OF BRISTOL.

Plate 4

Nicholas Pocock, *View of St Mary Redcliffe from Sea Banks*, 1785

Pocock's View shows the bustling, yet largely unimproved port of Bristol thronged with overseas and coastal vessels riding at anchor on the river Avon. In the centre of the picture, a small market boat, characteristic of many that plied the Bristol Channel in the early eighteenth century, prepares to sail; note the goods stacked on its deck.

Plate 5

An engraving of the Iron Bridge, Shropshire, *c.* 1790

A late depiction of the river Severn at the newly-constructed Iron Bridge. In the foreground a loaded packhorse team shares the towpath with a gang of four bowhauliers, pulling a heavily-laden single-masted Severn trow upstream. Two further trows await downstream.

Plate 6

George Robertson, engraved by James Fittler, 1788, *Lincoln Hill and the Iron Bridge from the river Severn*

Fittler's engraving shows three Severn trows and a much smaller barge awaiting cargoes under the shadow of Lincoln Hill, Shropshire. In the eighteenth century, the area was a major exporter of iron and ironware to Bristol.

One

Bristol, coastal trade and the Bristol Channel region

As many commentators remarked, the key to Bristol's development was to be found in the 'most advantagious situation' of the port.[1] Based upon two rivers, the Avon and the Frome, and connected to the open sea via a somewhat tortuous navigation, Bristol was both favoured and constrained by its urban port site and western aspect. The large tidal range of the Avon that served to swell the busy quays and backs, yet reduce the commercial centre of Bristol to but a 'rill slow creeping through a world of mud', mirrored the dramatic, if relative, rise, stagnation and decline of the city in the seventeenth and eighteenth centuries.[2] In our period, however, the problems of over-crowding, insufficient capacity and lack of access remained distant concerns, acknowledged but not yet serious enough to impinge upon the continued viability of the port. Indeed, the extent of maritime activity and commercial well-being is stressed in two very different representations of the city that frame this period: James Millerd's *Exact Delineation of the Famous Cittie of Bristoll* (Plate 1) first published in 1671 with subsequent revisions thereafter, and Samuel and Nathaniel Buck's *Prospects,* published in 1734 (Plates 2 and 3).

Millerd's naive and curiously descriptive topography of the city shows the town on the verge of expansion. Bristol was still oriented around its four central streets, Wine Street, Broad Street, Corn Street and High Street. This zone, deliberately emphasised by the alignment of the map, marked out the central business and administrative quarter from the open space and piece-meal development across the bridge in St Thomas and Redcliffe parishes and the eastwards extension of St Philip and St Jacob. Yet, Millerd's map is, despite its overblown title, less an exact delineation and more an exercise in the iconography of power. This was displayed in a highly traditional way. The prominence of Bristol's parish churches and the extensively realised St Augustine's, probably the meanest cathedral in the country, give formal and

1

loyally orthodox substance to the city. Moreover, the intact town walls and gates demonstrate the independent nature of civic authority, and represent a cultural and juridic *cordon sanitaire* demarcating the city from its surroundings.[3] Apart from these antiquarian trappings, Millerd's Bristol was undeniably an outward-looking commercial and maritime city. The quay and the back winding past the unimproved Marsh with its rather forlorn bowling green represent the focus of activity. Here ride a number of artlessly executed, but none the less largely accurate depictions of sailing craft. Three and four masted ocean-going vessels crowd the quay, whilst more conservatively rigged trows and coastal sloops are dotted along the back towards Bristol Bridge and yet more barges, lighters and rowing boats ply the upper Avon.[4]

In comparison, Samuel and Nathaniel Buck's *Prospects* present studiedly 'accurate' perspectives, snapshots even, of a city overspilling with commerce, industry and shipping. Amidst the fashionable cultural references—the bucolic, *rus in urbe* setting of the increasingly industrial town, and the inclusion of the black servant, itself surely a transparent allusion to the grounding of Bristol's bourgeois wealth—the *Prospects* show a far more complex and more intense cityscape. New additions, in particular the distant but still noteworthy brass works and the numerous glass cones, now compete with the established ecclesiastical monuments in dominating the skyline. Similarly, the development of St Michael's Hill, the beginnings of salubrious lodgings around the Long Room at the Hotwell and the newly laid out Queen's Square offer some welcome relief from the functional artisan dwellings massed to the south and east of the city. However, it is clear that Bristol's importance is unequivocally mercantile: the emphasis laid on the Society of Merchant Venturers' unassuming hall is testament to the ideo-logical underpinnings of both the city and its wider impact. Moreover, a sea of shipping is visible. In the *North-West Prospect,* two ocean-going vessels are being towed up the Avon, another waits at the entrance to the Frome, whilst the quay, quayhead and backs are thronged with overseas and coastal craft. In the *South-East Prospect,* the tail of this tangle of vessels is seen entering the Avon, whilst a solitary barge clears downstream on the newly improved navigation to Bath.[5]

Both Millerd's *Delineation* and the Bucks' panoramas show an important, self-consciously maritime Bristol, to which the prominent display of the city's insignia makes explicit reference. At the same time, the vistas offered by the Bucks, suggest a wider regional perspective: the navigation to Bath and the Avon Gorge open up inviting avenues to extra-urban commerce, and it is not hard to read the interaction of town and country and the diffusion of trade in the stylised human foregrounds. In effect, pre-industrial Bristol is depicted as something greater than a mere assemblage of physical features. Its importance stretched beyond the bounds of the city.[6]

In essence, these representations reflect contemporary views of Bristol. It was widely recognised that the city stood at the centre of an extensive domestic hinterland. Undoubtedly, this was not a wholly cohesive bloc: rival centres of population, marketing, communications and commerce developed later in the period, and exerted limiting, centrifugal pressures upon the peripheral areas of the hinterland. However, the pivotal role Bristol played in the economic and spatial organisation of its region remained a largely unchallenged commercial factor in this period.[7] The dominance Bristol exerted over this region served as an extended metaphor of the wider power and prestige of the city. Alongside its overseas ventures, Bristol's domestic ascendancy was an emblematic source of local pride. Bristol, as Campbell opined with more than a little civic chauvinism, was 'without a rival' in terms of domestic trade,

> for by the Avon she draws unto herself commodities from Warwickshire; by the help of the Teem, she receives those of Herefordshire and Shropshire; the Wye also brings her some part of the tribute of the former of those counties, and of Radnorshire; and if there be any thing yet left in Herefordshire and Shropshire, the Lugg drains them both: Monmouthshire and the adjacent parts of Wales send their supplies by the Uske; and a great part of Somersetshire communicates both goods and manufactures by the Ivel, the Parrot and Tone; and Cornwall sends hither its tin and copper for the pewter and brass wire and copper company manufactories.[8]

The geography may have been a little askew, and Campbell seems to have utterly forgotten about the Severn, but the conclusions were emphatic. Although Bristol drove an important overland trade with 'all the principal countries and towns from Southampton in the south, even to the banks of the Trent',[9] its core hinterland remained fundamentally coastal and riparian. In essence, the integrity of the region was inextricably linked to water transport and the distinct cost advantages it conferred upon the movement of goods.[10] By the later seventeenth century, improvements to the navigation of the major regional river systems and advances in the operational efficiency of coastal and river craft stressed these benefits.[11] The region, depicted in map 1.1, thus formed a distinct economic enclave, characterised by enclosed, navigationally 'safe' waters.[12] At its centre, four ports—Bristol, Gloucester, Chepstow and Cardiff—formed the principal focus of trade. This area, bounded to the west by Steep Holm and Flat Holm,[13] encompassed the most sheltered coastal waters accessible to the trows and barges of the Severn and Wye and the smaller vessels of the Usk and the Taff. Here Bristol found ready markets and consistent sources of supply. The river Severn, navigable to Pool Quay near Welshpool, linked Bristol to the agriculturally diverse areas of the Midland plain and the Vale of Evesham, the industrialising core of the Severn Gorge and west Midlands, and the

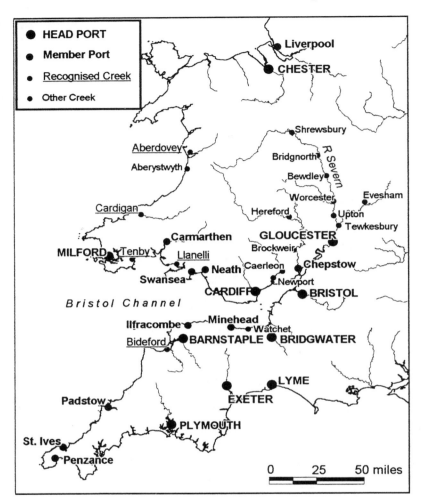

Map 1.1
The Bristol Channel region, *c.*1700.

major urban markets of the Severn valley and Warwickshire Avon.[14] Trade
was dependent upon the tidal zone and the consequent limitations this
imposed upon river craft. Negotiating the Bristol Avon was hazardous and
navigating the middle and upper reaches of the Severn largely reliant on the
impetus of the spring tide. Even then the river above Tewkesbury was only
passable to flat-bottomed trows. Such vessels were generally constrained to
the navigation proper and the stretch of sheltered littoral water bounded by
the Holms, although they occasionally ventured along the coasts of south

Wales and south-west England. For transport further afield, transhipment at Bristol was the norm.[15]

On the west bank, Chepstow acted as an entrepôt for goods brought down the Wye from the corn lands, pastures and orchards of Herefordshire, the industries of the Forest of Dean and local metal-producing and collection centres such as Brockweir and Redbrook.[16] Cider, hops, timber-stuff, wooden ware, millstones, iron and ironwares, copper and wire formed Chepstow's staple coastal trades. In contrast, Cardiff and its main creeks, Newport and Caerleon, remained minor places of trade. Coastal exports were dominated by agricultural goods and rural crafts emanating from the Vale of Glamorgan.

Below the Holms, western Glamorganshire and south-west Wales formed an 'outer region' markedly less well developed and dominated by agrarian production.[17] The area was divided between a more densely settled and agriculturally advanced lowland and coastal 'pale' which extended from the Severnside wetlands and the Vale of Glamorgan to the 'Englishries' of the Gower peninsula and Pembrokeshire, and a sparsely populated swathe of marginal pasturage and barren upland to the north.[18] Agricultural surpluses were geared to either the Bristol provisions market or the urban centres of the south-west and north-west of England and the small ports of north and west Wales.[19] Coal, however, remained the defining trade of this area. With plentiful supplies and ready markets, all the major ports of south and south-west Wales were adapted to shipping large quantities of coal. Swansea, Neath, South Burry, Newton and Llanelli traded mainly bituminous coals, whilst smaller, anthracitic culm was dispatched from Milford and Tenby.[20] Despite the relative abundance of fuel, industrial development continued to be comparatively retarded until the later eighteenth century, although interests in copper and lead smelting were established around Neath in the 1690s.[21]

Access to the Bristol Channel also brought the northern districts of Somerset, Devon and Cornwall within the wider commercial ambit of Bristol.[22] Bridgwater and Minehead provided the principal centres of trade, giving access to the mixed pastoral grounds of the lower Quantock and Brendon Hills and the prosperous arable economy of the Vale of Taunton Deane. In addition, the substantial meadow and pasture land of the Somerset Levels, increasingly used for new 'industrial' crops and market vegetables, and the upper reaches of the Exe valley were drawn into the local hinterland of the Somerset ports.[23] Here, trade was focused upon a central corridor of more intensive land use, industrial activity and nucleated settlement which established a vital connection between the Bristol Channel and Exeter through a radial network of packhorse roads. It was also the means by which the clothing districts of south and east Devon were supplied with Irish and domestic wool and also a range of other merchandises after the closing of Exeter as a staple port in 1693.[24]

The Taw–Torridge basin, an extensive, sheltered deepwater anchorage set in a fertile lowland plain and centred upon the customs ports of Barnstaple and Bideford, formed the second focus of trade. Both ports maintained a flourishing trade in tobacco, and possessed substantial interests in the Newfoundland cod and domestic herring fisheries.[25] In these trades, Bideford had outstripped Barnstaple, although the head port maintained its role as an inland entrepôt and market centre.[26] Even so, the hinterland of both ports remained severely limited in terms of markets and industries. Only vernacular earthenware and local ball clay enjoyed a sizeable regional and overseas trade, supplementing basic agricultural, fishery and mineral staples.[27] The smaller south-western ports were less important. Ilfracombe served a parochial hinterland constricted by upland Exmoor to the east and the Taw–Torridge basin to the south. Its harbour was, however, of some significance as a convenient landing place, and as a major centre of the herring trade.[28] The trade of the north Cornish ports was also limited. Navigational difficulties and the excessive silting of the river Camel severely undermined the utility of Padstow in all but local and Irish trade, and the exposed harbour of St Ives was accessible only to smaller coasters.[29] Both ports remained redistributive centres for the local economy with an erratic coastal trade in copper ore, tin and hilling stones.

Land's End and St David's Head served as the effective parameters to the region, although consistent demand for certain basic goods—Cheshire salt, south Wales coal and culm, and, to a lesser extent, Cornish copper and tin— encouraged a degree of long-distance coasting. To the north, Cardigan and Aberdovey maintained a minor trade in lead and lead ore with south Wales and Bristol. However, the minor ports of Cardigan Bay and north Wales were more firmly drawn into the trading hinterland of Chester, Liverpool and Ireland.[30] Land's End also formed a distinct if not impassable barrier to sea-borne trade. Freight charges reflected the prohibitive nature of rounding Land's End, especially during winter, and the compressed geography and limited economic means of the south-western peninsula encouraged the use of overland routes and the ports of the Exe estuary.[31] Throughout the period, the trade of Penzance and the ports of south Cornwall gravitated towards Exeter, Plymouth and London, rather than Bristol.

Coastal trade, customs and the ports of the Bristol Channel: some problems and definitions

The coastal trade of Bristol and its hinterland, and indeed internal trade in general, has suffered from a lack of quantitative material. Compared to the overseas trades, where statistical and more illustrative material survives in comparative abundance, the dearth of a coherent body of data has impeded research.[32] This is not the place to rehearse the mechanisms by which the major source for the study of internal trade, the Exchequer coastal port books, can be utilised to throw light onto what has been hitherto a rather murky historical backwater. Indeed, the many surveys of the source have adequately described the most salient areas of research.[33] Moreover, the selective and largely anecdotal uses of port books in studies of port economies, maritime development and the trade in a range of staple goods, have also highlighted the principal strengths and weaknesses of the data.[34] However, it is important to outline here the major avenues of inquiry and to lay to rest some rather persistent spectres regarding the integrity, application and interpretation of the coastal port books.

Between 1565 and 1799, port books were kept at 122 maritime centres collectively responsible for the coastline of England and Wales.[35] The records were primarily fiscal devices instituted to police the collection of customs duties on goods traded to and from overseas and to enforce the provisions of the Navigation Acts regarding boat construction, crew composition and the carriage of enumerated commodities.[36] Overseas port books were kept severally by three main patent officers, the customer, comptroller and surveyor, attached to each major port. The coastal records, maintained jointly by the customer and comptroller, underpinned revenue collection by providing full details of voyages passing between domestic ports. As Crouch intimated, officers were required to note 'the Name of the Ship, the Master, the Goods, the Port of Landing, and the Date of the Certificate of Return . . . not only where the Goods are all landed at one Port, but likewise where the Vessels discharge at several Ports; and to enter together in one Part of the [coastal port] Book, all Goods *going out*, and in the other Part, all Goods *going in*'.[37] The main purpose of the books was to ensure that goods were not traded overseas under colour of coastal movement, or that dutiable overseas goods were not passed off as purely coastal consignments, or disguised within legitimate domestic cargoes. Customs officers were charged to inspect the craft of suspect traders and to confiscate suspicious goods. In 1739, the Cardiff customs administration reported that for many years it had been common practice to place officers on coasters arriving from Devon and Cornwall in order to deter petty frauds: 'for when they're loaden wth tile, stones and earthenware their cargoes being of that nature that they can't be rummaged or easyly unloaden, they have a greater oportunity of running any little thing they may have on board unless there is an officer boarded upon [th]em'.[38] A substantial bond, returnable on the domestic completion of the voyage, together with an elaborate mechanism of cross-checking shipments and, ultimately, formal indictment and prosecution provided the legal and financial teeth to the system.[39]

Despite the comprehensive nature of these checks and balances, the system did not always transfer smoothly into a consistent body of records. On one level, the customs system was notoriously venal, a factor which severely compromised recording standards.[40] Undoubtedly, systematic under-recording, dilatory record-keeping and evasion, undertaken both surrep-titiously and with the active connivance of officials, were commonplace.[41] For many of the smaller ports, the burden of administration and the complexity of the customs system encouraged negligence and the survival of idiosyncratic and to the customs commissioners unacceptably unstandard local practices. In 1737, the beleaguered Cardiff customs officers reported that they were 'never put to the expense' of remitting coastal port books to the Exchequer annually, as they were required to do by law, but still held 'three years' Books from Xmas 1730 to Xmas 1733 now by us ready filled', along with 'the Books and Bonds from Cardiff, Swanzey and Chepstow'.[42] Moreover, the customs administration with its links of kinship and shared commercial outlook with local mercantile interests offered opportunities for petty malfeasance and, in the case of Bristol, downright financial impropriety.[43] Such frauds clearly riddled the records of overseas trade, especially in high-duty commodities like rum, tobacco and tea which were run with what appears to be impunity.[44] In 1718, for example, the collector, deputy comptroller and the tide surveyor at Bristol were indicted for conspiring to 'alter the Books highly to the prejudice of the Revenue'.[45] However, the impact of such practices on the coastal port books was limited. As no direct customs dues were liable on domestic trade, and administration and port fees were largely incidental, it was in the interests of the coastal merchant to submit cargoes to full and precise record. Through such means, traders avoided having to account for duties that had already been secured on importation.[46]

In practice, the recording of trade was indivisible from the wider operation of the customs system. By the late seventeenth century, 22 discrete customs jurisdictions partitioned the coastline of England and Wales into a three-tiered hierarchy of ports. The main customs house and the three patent officers were based at a central head port, which exercised effective supervision over all subordinate centres within its jurisdiction. At member ports, coastal and overseas trade were lawfully permitted and recorded in separate port books under the authority of deputy officers. In turn, head and member ports oversaw the trade of lesser creeks, landing places and havens. At these centres, overseas trade could not be conducted without the especial sufferance of the immediately superior customs house, but coastal trade, under the supervision of minor officials, had been permitted time out of mind.[47]

Table 1.1 describes the tripartite division of ports as it existed in the Bristol Channel region in 1700. The table distinguishes between head ports, member ports and substantial creeks, places like Tenby or Newnham where trade and a customs presence were long established, and a host of formally unrecognised landing places, coves, inlets and harbours. Historians have argued that such port lists were ossified administrative structures obscuring the tensions that occurred between economically buoyant subordinate creeks and commercially depressed head ports.[48] However, the table depicts a relatively flexible and organic system. For example, in 1672, control of the north Devon ports passed from Exeter and Dartmouth to the newly created head port of Barnstaple.[49] As a result, Barnstaple exercised authority over the rather isolated member port of Ilfracombe and retained direct supervision over a number of local creeks, the largest and most commercially important of which was Bideford. Yet Bideford's development, particularly in the transoceanic and Newfoundland trades, called its subordinate status into question.[50] By 1707, Bideford customs house was sending up its own port books to London.[51]

None the less, the rapid administrative development of the north Devon seaboard caused problems. Much confusion existed as to the status of the host of minor creeks of the Taw–Torridge estuary assigned to the head port or to Bideford. Clovelly, a small but locally important port nominally within the limits of Bideford, was recorded without distinction amongst the Bideford returns. Between 1695 and 1704, Clovelly boats accounted for some 4 per cent of all voyages listed at Bideford.[52] However, trade bound for Fremington and Braunton was recorded within Barnstaple's entries, whilst the trade of Northam, Instow and Appledore was split between the rival administrations of Barnstaple and Bideford. Of these ports, Northam possessed considerable harbour facilities, a flourishing coastal trade in mostly coal and culm, and a large resident population of boat masters and associated mariners.[53] Similarly, both Barnstaple and Bideford claimed the strategic port of Appledore at the mouth of the Torridge and fought a protracted and somewhat fractious legal battle to assert their supremacy.[54] From internal evidence, Appledore boats generally proceeded to Bideford customs house for official ratification.

The relation between smaller creeks and head and member ports responsible for the keeping of coastal port books is central to the analysis of the coastal trade. Failure to distinguish between the trade of individual ports that collectively constituted a given port book can lead to confusion and misinterpretation. For example, as Andrews discovered, the extensive coastal trade of Margate in the late seventeenth century was contained in and subsumed under the official records of Faversham. Although Margate was far larger than the smaller creeks of the Taw–Torridge estuary, this procedure

Table 1.1

Customs ports, creeks and landing places in the Bristol Channel, c.1700

Head port	Member port	Creek with separate section	Other creeks
BRISTOL			Pill[1]
			Uphill/Axe[2]
			Beachley
GLOUCESTER			Severn/Avon Ports[3]
		Newnham	
		Berkeley[4]	
BRIDGWATER			Combwich[5]
			Highbridge
	Minehead		Watchet
			Porlock
BARNSTAPLE			Braunton
			Fremington
		Bideford	Clovelly
			Northam
			Appledore
	Ilfracombe		Combe Martin
			Lynmouth[6]
PLYMOUTH & FOWEY[7]	Padstow		Boscastle
			Port Isaac
			Wadebridge
	St Ives		St. Agnes
	Mount's Bay		Penzance
MILFORD			Pembroke
			Haverfordwest
	Carmarthen[8]	Llanelli	
		Tenby	
		Cardigan	
		Aberdovey	Aberystwyth
CARDIFF			Newport[9]
			Aberthaw[10]
			Caerleon
			Penarth
			Sully
	Swansea & Neath		Oystermouth
			Port Eynon
			The Mumbles
		South Burry[11]	
		Newton[12]	
	Chepstow[13]		Wye ports[14]

has significant implications for the north Devon ports.[55] Similarly, as table 1.1 reveals, many Bristol Channel ports, often little more than sheltered inlets, were not contained within the official organisation of head, member and recognised creek. Although these ports remained important to local economies and often possessed highly developed port functions and installations, trade could and often did go unrecorded. Even where records were kept, the accounts of such minor ports could be absorbed within the port books of nominally superior centres, causing problems in distinguishing the trade of constituent ports. For example, in the early eighteenth century, the trade of Newton was only very occasionally separated from that of the much larger customs port of Swansea.

The relation of creek to superior port can best be studied where local petty customs exist alongside formal Exchequer port books. Such records provide a corroborative and occasionally more comprehensive account of trade.[56] The ports of Porlock and Watchet are a case in point. Although these ports were attached to Minehead, they conducted a vigorous and independent coastal trade in south Wales coal and, in the case of Watchet, groceries, overseas goods and consumables from Bristol. By the early eighteenth century, both ports had invested heavily in harbour improvement

---

Notes to Table 1.1:

1 Crouch, *Complete View*, p. 247. Pill was traditionally the berth of Bristol pilots: Farr, 'Bristol Channel pilotage'. There is no evidence of any direct trade to or from Pill, although both Kingroad and Hungroad, deep-water anchorages in the mouth of the Bristol Avon, are occasionally mentioned in the coastal port books. See Williams, 'Bristol port plans', pp. 141–4, for a concise description of the port of Bristol.

2 Crouch, Complete View, p. 247. The Axe was 'navigable as far up as Axbridge . . . for coal vessels and other small craft' at this time: Knight, *Sea-board of Mendip*, pp. 263, 271. Uphill was a very minor port, although evidence exists for it transhipping overseas goods to Bristol in 1696 (PRO C104/12 Pt. 1, f. 5v) and receiving cargoes of livestock and agricultural goods from Wales: Bettey, 'Livestock trade'; Jones and Scourfield, 'Sully', pp. 135–6

3 See Wakelin, 'Pre-industrial trade', pp. 35–6, and Cox, Hussey and Milne, eds, *Gloucester port books database*, for a discussion of the various ports.

4 The first separate record for Newnham and Berkeley was in 1673. The ports were only consistently recorded as discrete sections in the Gloucester coastal port books from 1704.

5 Traditionally the pilots' harbour at the mouth of the Parrett.

6 Often recorded under Minehead.

7 The customs port of Plymouth and Fowey also held jurisdiction over Helston, Penryn, Truro and Looe: Williams, *Descriptive list*. By 1725, the growth of Falmouth was recognised by the provision of member port status: Crouch, *Complete View*, p. 249; Whetter, 'Rise of the port of Falmouth', pp. 1–32.

8 The port of Carmarthen contained within its own boundaries other sizeable landing places such as Laugharne and St Clears in the Taf estuary.

9 Endowed with the status of creek by 1732: MGRO B/C CH2 pp. 83, 107, 164–5, 169, 173.

10 Recorded in separate sections in the Swansea and Neath records between 1673 and 1682.

11 Not consistently recorded as a separate section until 1701.

12 Not consistently recorded as a separate section until 1702.

13 Detached in 1700–1: Andrews, 'Chepstow', pp. 97–107.

14 The main Wye ports were Tintern (Abbey Tintern), Brockweir, Redbrook, Monmouth, Ross and Hereford. Willan, *River navigation*, pp. 53–4.

schemes, and Watchet petitioned, unsuccessfully, for the status of an independent staple wool port.[57] However, an analysis of the Minehead port books indicates that the trade of Porlock and Watchet is collated with that of the superior port. In most analyses this distinction has not been appreciated, with the result that the commerce of Minehead has tended to be exaggerated at the expense of its subject creeks.[58]

A rough approximation of Watchet's trade can be made by reconstructing voyages recorded in the port books of other centres. However, owing to patchy survival and inconsistent local practice, such a composite record provides an inconsistent index of trade.[59] Moreover, even with the aid of remote computerised analysis, piecing together each shipment would be prohibitively time-consuming. Similarly, an idea of Watchet and Porlock cargoes embedded within the Minehead record can be gauged by assessing the number of boats 'of' each 'home' port.[60] For example, between Mid-summer 1699 and Midsummer 1700, 475 voyages were recorded in the Minehead Books of which 194 were undertaken by vessels 'of' Watchet, by far the largest of the home ports, 51 by craft 'of' Minehead, and 22 specifying Porlock as the home port. Whilst this may indicate the provenance or direction of some shipments, it remains a largely arbitrary method of assessing the commerce of creeks obscured within the record of superior ports.[61] However, detailed accounts of shipping paying port dues at Watchet, levied to fund extensive but ultimately abortive harbour improvement, survive from 1708.[62] From Lady Day 1709 to Michaelmas 1719, when the dues were transferred to private farm,[63] a total of 1,729 vessels were recorded as entering or clearing Watchet, of which 40 were in ballast and 6 were carrying overseas cargoes. The mean of 153 coastal shipments per year, even accounting for purely local consignments within the port bounds, represents around a third of the recorded entries in the coastal port books of Minehead in this period. Clearly, Watchet was trading on a major scale, comparable even to Minehead itself. In such cases, it is clear that port book data refer to the trade of an area, and not that of a port nucleus.

Similarly, the economic and commercial conditions that underpinned the compilation of the coastal port books must be recognised if misinter-pretation is to be avoided.[64] For example, when the port of Cardiff was established in 1559, it exercised control over the coast from the river Wye to Worms Head, with deputy administrations set up at Chepstow and at the joint member port of Swansea and Neath. However, by the later seventeenth century, Cardiff's jurisdiction was residual; both member ports had far outgrown the commercially stagnant centre.[65] In 1700, Chepstow 'being a growing place in trade' was separated from its erstwhile head port,[66] and by 1735 Swansea and Neath had split away, the Cardiff customer noting somewhat poignantly that Cardiff was the 'most inconsiderable port for trade' in south Wales and that both Chepstow and Swansea and Neath had 'ten times the trade we have'.[67] Behind such changes lay the persistent problem as to which customs house creeks within the Cardiff administration 'belonged'. Swansea held administrative sway over Oystermouth, The Mumbles and Port Eynon, the very limited trade of which was undifferentiated in the port books.[68] Cardiff itself exerted control over the ports of the Usk,[69] a number of coastal inlets including Penarth and Sully,[70] and Aberthaw, which maintained a steady if unremarkable trade in livestock and agricultural goods with the south-west of England.[71] At such centres, deputy coastwaiters, itinerant riding officers, and local boatmen were maintained to oversee and record coastal trade.[72] However, such is the paucity of entries in the coastal books of Cardiff, it appears that most voyages emanating from the lesser creeks, and, most damagingly, Newport, Caerleon and Aberthaw, were simply not recorded. In order to gain an impression of this trade, records from corresponding ports must be consulted.[73]

In addition, there is some confusion as to whether shipments passing between head port, member port and creek contained within the jurisdiction of a single port were consistently recorded.[74] At Gloucester, for example, the authority of the port stretched from Tidenham on the north bank of the Severn estuary to Aust on the south bank, and included not only the river Severn and the Warwickshire Avon, but also two important estuarine creeks, Newnham and Berkeley. Trade that remained within these geographical limits escaped record.[75] In contrast, as map 1.2 demonstrates, the 'extent, bounds and limits' of the neighbouring Bristol port administration were far more compact, which, given the extent of the city's trade, was perhaps more prudent.[76] In 1724, Bristol's jurisdiction encompassed an area from

> the westernmost parts of the [Bristol] Channell eastwards to Aust in the county of Gloucester and from the said Holmes [Steep Holm and Flat Holm] southwarde athwart the Channell to a place called Uphill which is included and from thence along the coast or shoar eastwards in the county of Gloucester hath been for many years past a creek place called Holes Mouth in King Road up the river Avon to the said city of Bristoll, together with the severall pills lying upon the said river. And we doe further certifye that a place called Bechesley [Beachley] scituate on the north side of the river Severne in the country of Gloucester hath been for many years past a creek and belonging to the said port of Bristoll.[77]

Thus, ensconced in their recently built and rather elegant customs house, the grandees of Bristol's customs administration oversaw the city's main urban quays and backs, as well as the deep-water anchorages of Kingroad and Hungroad, where goods were often transhipped from large ocean-going vessels to lighters; the pilots' haven at Crockerne Pill; a speculatively constructed wet dock at Sea Mills which was far too distant from town to

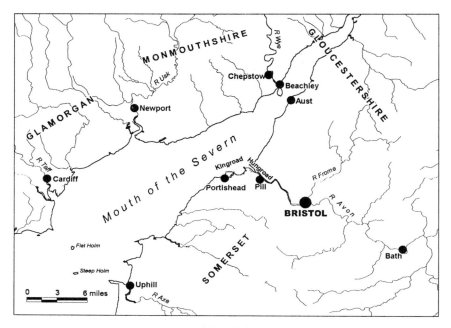

Map 1.2
The port of Bristol, *c.*1724.

be of much use; and two open-water creeks.[78] Beachley, the terminal point of the Old Passage to Aust, hence its retention by Bristol, was a geographical and administrative aberration. A remnant of Bristol's earlier control of the entire lower Severn estuary,[79] the creek had no customable commerce although it is likely that a limited trade in livestock was maintained alongside the regular passenger services to Aust.[80] Similarly, Uphill was merely a small inlet with an even smaller trade in Welsh coal and livestock.[81] Isolated from the main centre of Bristol's administration, a factor exploited by unscrupulous traders in the 1730s, Uphill remained largely dependent upon the customs houses of Bridgwater and Minehead throughout the period.[82]

Trade between creeks was not a common feature at Bristol, where port administration was fairly cohesive and dominated by a central commercial focus. However, in the more dispersed jurisdictions of the region, inter-port trade was a regular occurrence. When boats passed between ports under the same jurisdiction, the shipment was recorded *as long as* the boat moved between discrete record-keeping centres. Thus, shipments from Barnstaple, the head port, to Ilfracombe, a member port endowed with its own independent administration, were regularly recorded. However, shipments between Barnstaple and Northam, for example, were omitted, because, like Gloucester, the shipment did not traverse the bounds of the record-keeping customs house. In the case of Carmarthen, a member port of Milford exercising superintendence over Llanelli, Tenby, Cardigan, Aberdovey, and Aberystwyth, shipments between the five creeks and the superior port were habitually recorded within the same port book. In such instances the record is particularly full and the integrity of the port book from section to section can be readily assessed.

A final consideration involves the internal consistency of the port books. Most coastal trade progressed under coquet and bond, a system whereby formal customs documentation, legally underwritten by monetary securities pegged at the customs value of the cargo if exported, was issued at the port of lading and ratified at the port of discharge. All high-value goods, commodities bearing excise, and other substantial cargoes traded coastwise required this form of highly structured certification on pain of forfeiture and prosecution. These formal transactions were more or less recorded fastidiously and formed the basis to the official port books dispatched to the Exchequer at the end of each year.[83] However, smaller cargoes and goods of low unit value or little dutiable worth were often allowed to proceed 'without security' under inferior customs devices known as letpasses, transires, warrants or sufferances.[84] Letpasses and their equivalents were mostly confined to petty items of cargo and were then only issued when these goods were not part of a larger coquet-bearing shipment. Yet, as there was no legal requirement to record this trade, responsibility was assigned to the discretion of individual customs jurisdictions. Consequently, letpass traffic appears very inconsistently in the formal record of certain ports.[85]

The letpass trade had important repercussions for Bristol and the ports of the Bristol Channel. As Bristol, Gloucester, the ports of north Cornwall, and Cardiff and its member ports, Chepstow, Swansea and Neath, only recorded coquets, data obtained for these ports are likely to be underestimates of the totality of coasting.[86] At Bristol, the level of letpass trade was generally small, but none the less significant. Where data permit comparative analysis, around 9 per cent of coastal clearances appear to have been conducted under letpass, with single shipments of glass and glassware forming the principal item of cargo. Similarly, it is only possible to reconstruct certain important trades of south Wales, most notably the shipment of livestock, by either casual references in allied customs documents, or the painstaking examination of the more complete records of the ports of Somerset and north Devon.[87] At Chepstow, grindstones, millstones and timber, considerable staples of the Wye trade, were under-recorded at least until 1700 when customs clerks appear to have noted selected letpass cargoes. At the Cornish ports, large quantities of stone and fish were also routinely omitted. For example, in

1697, Mount's Bay, a noted centre of pilchard fishing, recorded only 17 voyages in all, the majority of which were imports of dutiable (thus coquet-bearing) cargoes of coal from south Wales and charcoal from Southampton.[88] Quantitative assessments of the trade in hilling stones and rags, roofing materials quarried from around Boscastle, have also suffered from the omission of letpass traffic, although this has not been widely recognised in statistical projections of the trade.[89] Hilling stones were entirely absent from Padstow's coastal record in 1696, whereas the contemporary Bridgwater books recorded 50,000 stones and 40 hilling rags imported in five letpass shipments. In 1703, 313,000 hilling stones and 100 hilling rags unrecorded in the Padstow books were noted entering Bridgwater in 13 letpass consignments mostly in small open boats.

The major implication of non-coquet trade was at Gloucester. Gloucester was somewhat of a commercial anomaly: although granted full customs status in 1584, its coastal trade remained overshadowed by that of the nominally subordinate ports of the river Severn.[90] Unlike the ports of the Humber estuary, transhipment from river vessels to coastal craft was not a regular feature of the trade at Gloucester. Instead, long-distance through-shipments conducted in up-river trows formed the basis of trade, with the central customs house merely acting as an administrative filter. For much of the period, letpasses at Gloucester were confined to the minor Severn trades: salt trows returning from Somerset occasionally carried small items of back cargo under letpass, and it is likely, though unquantifiable, that a proportion of vessels clearing Bristol for Gloucester ostensibly in ballast carried the kind of petty letpass goods that escaped official record.[91] However, the redrawing of the official limits of the river Severn had severe implications for customs practice at Gloucester. From 1730, it was declared that for customs purposes, the mouth of the Severn would terminate not at Gloucester but at the Holms.[92] As vessels travelling between ports above the 'cardinal point' of the Holms were not passing into 'open sea', and thereby the potential horizons of illicit overseas export, the 'belt and braces' security of the coquet and bond system was not required and transires, warrants and letpasses would suffice for all but the most noteworthy of cargoes.[93] As such devices were not habitually registered at the 'above-Holms' ports, levels of recorded trade plummeted not only at Gloucester and Bristol, but also at Chepstow and Cardiff, in the latter case causing some impoverishment to the small and overstretched customs administration.[94] Although this virtual deregulation of trade has been recognised by historians, erratic and limited data from the post-1730 period continues to be used to impute commercial change at the major ports of the region.[95]

Port book data and the trade of the Bristol Channel

Despite the criticisms of the source, the most intractable problem facing historians is one of logistics and resources. Quite simply, the coastal port books are far too voluminous to be handled satisfactorily by traditional, manual methods of research alone. In the late seventeenth century, for example, over 500 coastal voyages cleared the port of Bristol each year. For every one of these voyages details of the dates, ports, boats, merchants, boat masters and cargoes associated with the shipment were recorded. In total, around 30,000 discrete segments of information are listed for coastal exports alone in a single year. A further 900 voyages describing perhaps another 30,000 data attributes entered Bristol each year.[96] Given this explosion of information, it is hardly surprising that port book data have been restricted to impressionistic overviews and even the most comprehensive of works have tended to rely on chronologically dispersed samples. Indeed, without the kind of advanced, computer-aided techniques of storage and analysis available to more recent researchers, Willan's dismissive side-swipe at the miscellaneous, 'unstatistical' nature of Bristol's coastal trade appears wholly understandable.[97]

Computerisation has liberated the source. The port books have been rendered into electronic datasets using recognised standards of data standardisation, exchange and transfer.[98] Through such means, the source can be mined for the rich seams of quantitative data it contains. The period chosen for this study is in part the product of the extancy and integrity of the records. From the early 1680s, the supervision of the coastal trade was progressively reformed and a concerted campaign was instituted to consolidate outport administration and eradicate erratic and corrupt practice.[99] Specimen entries detailing the precise way to record 'ships entring inward or clearing outward . . . from or to any other Country or Coastways' were dispatched to customs officials.[100] The principal patent officers were urged to note the 'number of Casks, bales or other packags of Goods and mentioning the Species as farr as you can from the masters reports inward and the total Quantity of the several Species at least of bulky Goods from the Cocquets of all Coasters or entry of other ships outward'. Failure to do so would result in summary dismissal and the appointment of 'some other Collector who is both able & willing to practice our directions for his Ma[ties] service & the advantage of the Revenue'.[101] A stream of further orders regulating the shipment of goods and standardising administrative practice in the regions greatly enhanced the reliability of the coastal port books as accurate accounts of trade at least until the gradual decay of the system in the later 1720s.[102] Tellingly, if rather surprisingly, it was not unknown for merchants in cases of commercial dispute to seek official confirmation of trade by consulting copies of port books held at local customs houses.[103]

Three basic strategies underpin the data used in this book. First, work has focused upon the full series of Gloucester records extant for the period from 1680 to 1730.[104] The Gloucester data, outlined in appendix 1, provide both an important control and a central element of continuity to the study. As the entrepôt to the Severn valley, Gloucester gave access to arguably the most productive and densely settled area of Bristol's domestic hinterland. Throughout the period, the Severn was the focus of Bristol's coasting trade: between 1680 and 1730, over half of all shipments clearing Bristol were bound for Gloucester or ports under its jurisdiction, and around a third of voyages destined for the city emanated from the area. On a more prosaic level, as coastal imports were routinely omitted from the Bristol records after 1660, the Gloucester data supply an invaluable representation of the more long-term patterns that shaped Bristol's domestic trade.

Second, all surviving coastal port books for the 20 official customs ports of the Bristol Channel from Mount's Bay to Milford have been analysed over a more abbreviated, and more manageable, ten-year period from 1695 to 1704. This approach serves to contextualise the Gloucester series and provides the matrix through which wider aspects of Bristol's trade can be studied more fully. The temptation to use broad chronological samples, ripped from their administrative context, to construct models of long-term commercial change has been strenuously resisted.[105] Instead, the sample, outlined in appendix 2 and table 1.2, stresses the comparative importance of nominally lesser, subordinate ports previously only explored in *ad hoc* or tentative ways.[106] The sample is again record-driven. It combines the required geographical coverage with high levels of data extancy for the major ports. In comparison to the poor and discontinuous record of adjacent periods, at least one full year survives for all ports in the survey. Indeed, although the smaller Cornish ports present difficulties, over half the maximum number of coastal port books are available for each customs port in this period.[107]

A final strategy has been to emphasise a single, comparative 'sample year' of *c.*1699 taken from the period between the conclusion of the Anglo-French War in 1697 and the outbreak of the War of the Spanish Succession in 1702. This provides a snapshot of regional trade at its potentially most stable.[108] Details of the records accessed for the sample year are given in appendix 2. To aid coverage, selected data from ports beyond the immediate parameters of the region, principally Liverpool, Chester, north Wales, and the south coasts of Cornwall and Devon, have also been captured. Where records are not extant, as in the case of Swansea and Neath and the Cornish ports, the most proximate full year has been computerised. Although this necessarily renders some data chronologically discontinuous, it does not materially hamper the analysis of trade. Even where patchy survival has rendered the sample incomplete, the degree of intra-regional trade which

Table 1.2

Voyages clearing and entering regional ports, 1695–1704

	1695 Out	1695 In	1696 Out	1696 In	1697 Out	1697 In	1698 Out	1698 In	1699 Out	1699 In	1700 Out	1700 In	1701 Out	1701 In	1702 Out	1702 In	1703 Out	1703 In	1704 Out	1704 In	Total
Bristol	430	–	383	–	–	–	445	–	**491**	–	229	–	412	–	–	–	229	–	–	–	2,619
Gloucester	289	235	334	190	357	235	–	–	**332**	**294**	–	–	335	216	–	–	–	–	331	252	3,400
Bridgwater	55	382	56	282	55	442	55	321	**95**	**331**	–	–	73	345	–	–	70	360	40	173	3,135
Minehead	66	306	59	240	62	314	125	304	**127**	**348**	125	355	62	162	–	25	–	–	–	–	2,680
Ilfracombe	13	106	19	89	37	131	9	69	**43**	**132**	48	142	68	149	24	62	45	112	19	56	1,373
Barnstaple	28	289	24	215	37	282	22	134	**54**	**266**	61	259	45	138	58	235	–	–	23	141	2,311
Bideford	70	186	70	170	57	166	22	92	**72**	**225**	83	245	23	112	72	207	–	–	43	155	2,070
Padstow	19	95	29	117	**28**	**129**	–	–	–	–	–	–	–	–	–	–	5	129	–	–	551
St Ives	33	42	34	46	**43**	**51**	–	–	–	–	–	–	–	–	–	–	29	33	80	94	485
Mount's Bay	5	11	4	13	**4**	**13**	–	–	–	–	–	–	–	–	–	–	1	6	0	13	70
Milford	–	–	230	49	308	57	427	61	**452**	**54**	500	58	227	35	274	48	226	45	243	28	3,322
Carmarthen	36	53	38	28	–	–	3	8	**29**	**44**	20	32	22	33	24	37	21	30	49	46	553
Tenby	232	25	209	17	221	14	181	17	**176**	**10**	244	10	259	26	224	12	78	15	221	23	2,214
Llanelli	130	–	98	–	136	41	82	26	**78**	–	43	2	102	7	39	2	20	–	55	2	863
South Burry	–	–	–	–	–	–	–	–	18	–	32	–	**13**	–	57	–	77	–	46	–	243
Swansea	232	–	–	–	–	–	255	–	228	–	228	–	**531**	–	227	–	437	–	463	–	2,601
Neath	162	–	–	–	–	–	174	–	164	–	206	–	**437**	–	401	–	440	–	440	–	2,424
Newton	–	–	–	–	–	–	–	–	–	–	5	–	–	–	30	–	–	–	–	–	35
Cardiff	21	–	–	–	–	–	–	–	**31**	–	29	–	18	–	5	–	15	–	26	–	145
Chepstow	–	–	–	–	–	–	–	–	**345**	**65**	158	57	226	163	186	134	84	50	171	122	1761
Total	1,821	1,730	1,587	1,456	1,345	1,875	1,800	1,032	2,735	1,769	2,011	1,160	2,853	1,386	1,621	762	1,777	780	2,250	1,105	32,855

Note: Data for Swansea, South Burry and Newton in 1702 refer to the period from Christmas 1701 to June 1702 only. Bold indicates sample year.

Source: PRO E190 coastal port books.

took place in the confined coastal seaboard of the Bristol Channel renders an informed reconstruction of trade practicable. In total, 255 coastal port books, describing over 50,000 shipments and 2.5 million data attributes, have been utilised to examine the coastal and river trade of Bristol and its domestic region.[109]

Bristol, it was reported, was 'a place very early addicted to trade'. Both physically and metaphorically it swam in the waters of domestic commerce that daily lapped its quays and scoured the city.[110] The broad matrix of port book data outlined here enables this association to be studied in more depth. Much emphasis has been placed upon the interpretation of data and by implication the mechanistic ordering and sorting of information. Yet, the coastal port books are not merely a convenient quarry of easily plundered quantitative material awaiting the imposition of an advanced schema of computer-aided analysis. Computerisation can never do full justice to the intricacies of the source and to base conclusions solely upon the integrity of such methodologies would tell a very one-sided story. Indeed, techniques which neither convincingly examine the theoretical and practical conditions under which the records were compiled nor make allowances for the somewhat erratic standards of a pre-industrial age can be dangerously misleading. To overcome this the book has adopted a broad front by analysing regional patterns of coasting rather than linear models of growth and decline from the perspective of Bristol alone. Port books have, of course, been widely used to supply information about regional systems of coasting, but such studies have tended to be too selective in terms of the goods studied or too limited spatially to offer more than a cursory analysis of trade.[111] The extensive geographical sweep of this study and the methods taken to ensure the widest possible contextual background have been an attempt to correct these imbalances, themselves the partial result of handling a complex and sprawling source using manual research methods alone.

There is perhaps a danger with all data-centred research in elevating, in Professor Fogel's words, the 'methodological hall-marks' of technique above critique.[112] This book seeks to employ quantitative data sensitively and not to inhibit research by imposed methodological or 'statistical' constraints.[113] To do so would be to remove the collective and often chaotic human element from the study of coastal trade and commerce, an element that perhaps can only be gleaned from the more anecdotal forms of evidence that have always formed an integral part of economic history. As the following chapters demonstrate, the synthesis of port book data with such discursive sources allows a more coherent picture to be drawn of how the coastal trade of the 'metropolis of the west' and its hinterland was conducted.

Two

Voyages and connections in the Bristol Channel

For outsiders, Bristol in the late seventeenth and eighteenth centuries appeared to exist solely as a commercial machine. Like the 'filth and dirt' that contaminated the city's two rivers, the Avon and the Frome, the overweening attention to the hard laws of commerce obliterated any higher social or cultural pretensions. Despite a few ersatz nods to gentility, Bristol and Bristol's mercantile bourgeois, the 'sordid devotees of Plutos' as one commentator tartly remarked, were quite emphatically *trade*.[1] The sense that Bristol, a city which had constructed for itself a wholly spurious antiquity,[2] was a major *urbs* with but a shallow veneer of urbanity was emphasised by Alexander Pope during his brief stay in the city in 1739. Advised to visit the Hotwell, Bristol's apologetic attempt at a modish spa, Pope vented his spleen on the 'unpleasant' aspect of the city, the uncivilised nature of its merchant company, and the desperately backward, almost bucolic, Hotwell facility. None the less, he was struck by the vigour of commercial life. At the heart of this dynamic—at the heart of Bristol itself—was the town quay. Here Pope noted with some amazement how Bristol's maritime locus and commercial quarter blended together:

> . . . with houses on both sides, and in the middle of the street, as far as you can see, hundreds of Ships, their masts as thick as they can stand by one another, which is the oddest & most surprising sight imaginable. This street is fuller of them, than the Thames from London Bridge to Deptford, & at certain times only, the Water rises to carry them out; so that at other times, a Long Street full of Ships in the Middle & Houses on each side looks like a Dream.[3]

Behind this almost hallucinatory dreamscape lie important assumptions about the city of Bristol and its trade. To begin with, Pope's derogatory though humorous asides must be seen in context. His literary glosses on the tensions between commerce and society, between what were essentially capitalistic and aristocratised modes of production, were commonplace, Augustan-age set-pieces, and, as such, reveal more about the cultural arena in which Pope and his ilk operated than the structural realities of eighteenth-century Bristol.[4]

However, implicit in these comments is the emphasis on overseas trade. Put simply, most historical accounts have tended to associate the 'hundreds of ships' described by Pope with Bristol's high-profile foreign and, above all, transatlantic trades. Admittedly, passing reference has been made to the fact that 'the Bristol Avon was thronged with coastal craft, with market boats and with . . . river barges and trows' and much local work has advanced a rather limited description of the operation of the domestic side of port business in this period.[5] Indeed no assessment of Bristol in the early eighteenth century would be complete without at least a peripheral aware-ness of the fleets of regional craft clearing the Back or the large numbers of Severn trows discharging at the quay head.[6] However, apart from the highly anecdotal evidence of some contemporary observers, scant regard has been paid to the more basic trades that connected the city to its hinterland. Any attempt to quantify the number or frequency of shipments involved in the domestic trades as opposed to the various overseas branches of foreign commerce has been conspicuous only by its absence.[7] This chapter seeks to redress this position by charting the main connections and commercial vectors that wired Bristol into its domestic region. In so doing, it begins to peer between the forest of masts that clogged the port and start to make some long overdue distinctions between Bristol's long streets 'full of ships'.

The system of trade: coasting links in the Bristol Channel

In the late seventeenth century, the Bristol Channel was a major commercial highway. From small harbours and inlets to large corporate towns and river ports, a fleet of coastal craft, ketches, coal hoys, trows, barges, woodbushes and open boats plied a kaleidoscope of goods ranging from the mundane to the exotic. For many regional ports, servicing these coastal vessels formed the principal maritime experience and provided the backbone to the local economy. At these centres, if not at Bristol itself, domestic voyages and craft underpinned the operation of the port, paid most of the incidental dues and impositions levied on shipping, and occupied the majority of local port resources. At the Somerset port of Watchet, for example, over 97 per cent of the 1,729 craft paying quay and keelage duties between 1709 and 1719 were active coasters, mainly engaged in the coal trade with south Wales and the regular Bristol run.[8]

However, to understand how coasting operated, it is important to form a quantitative picture of the volume of traffic. This provides a connective matrix which outlines the principal arteries of commerce and the foundation upon which more complex analyses of coasting can be built.[9] The following figures present a series of sections through the commercial network that linked Bristol to the ports and creeks of the Bristol Channel. These data are ordered by two methodological constructs. Firstly, research has adopted the voyage as the standard unit of assessment.[10] In the data reproduced below, voyages have been used to demonstrate linkage not value: a single letpass shipment of herrings traded from Ilfracombe, for example, has the same representational weight as a large mixed cargo of high-cost goods and consumables clearing from Bristol. It is recognised that in such instances tonnage provides an alternative and arguably more indicative commercial standard.[11] However, burden tonnage was not regularly specified in the port books after *c.*1660, and although it is feasible to convert the multiple and irregular measures associated with coastal cargoes to a common tonnage equivalent, this would be prohibitively time-consuming for all vessels and all shipments.[12] None the less, given these caveats, an analysis of voyage patterns provides a flexible index of trade, in much the same way as historians of road transport have concentrated on the number and connectivity of metropolitan routes to estimate sectoral development.[13]

Second, the number of centres involved in coastal trade was extensive and enumerating every minor port that featured as either the destination or origin of voyages, or the named home port of coastal vessels, would obscure the main patterns of trade. For instance, between 1695 and 1704, 77 separate ports within the region were recorded as regular centres of trade, whilst beyond the Bristol Channel a further 74 ports stretching from Newcastle-upon-Tyne to Whitehaven were represented. In order to handle such a mass of data coherently, a 12 point geographical classification of ports has been devised. This is based upon the administrative subdivision of the coastline organised under the official customs head ports outlined in chapter 1. Thus, Gloucester, its creeks, Newnham and Berkeley, and the inland ports of the Severn and Warwickshire Avon have been grouped under a unitary 'Severn' category, coinciding with the extents, bounds and limits of the customs port of Gloucester. The other divisions correspond to the officially recognised ports of Bristol; Bridgwater (described as Somerset); Barnstaple (north Devon); Padstow, St Ives and Mounts Bay (collectively, north Cornwall); and Milford (Pembrokeshire and Carmarthenshire). All ports, whether member ports, sufferance creeks or 'unofficial' harbours, inlets and landing places under the jurisdiction of these major centres, have been included in each respective category. However, in the case of Cardiff, the diversity of trade recorded at the three constituent customs house ports—Swansea and Neath, Cardiff, and

Chepstow (notified as Wye)—has warranted discrete categories. A further 'cross-regional' category relates to voyages bound for destinations under the jurisdiction of more than one regional customs head port. Voyages undertaken to and from centres beyond the region and data omitted by customs clerks or too illegible to decipher have also been appointed separate categories.

Undoubtedly, the clumsy or insensitive application of such broad spatial groupings can lead to the erosion of the differences that existed between ports in terms of markets, supply, goods and such factors as ease of access and port facilities and infrastructure. In widely dispersed areas like Pembrokeshire, Carmarthenshire, or the extensive internal hinterland of the Severn navigation, the constituent coastal and river ports undertook markedly different types of trade and served very contrasting economic locales.[14] None the less, the division of ports under customs head port serves to prepare the data for more manageable analysis and presentation. Tables 2.1 and 2.2 analyse the voyages patterns of regional ports in the sample year. For both tables, data for Liverpool have been appended and ordered according to the regional categories outlined above. For these purposes, all voyages not associated with the Bristol Channel have been aggregated under 'extra-regional' shipments, although these were concerned with either the immediate coastal hinterland of Liverpool or long-distance salt and cheese trades to the south-coast of England and London.[15]

With regard to the number, frequency and inter-connection of voyages, the tables emphasise the four customs ports situated above Steep Holm and Flat Holm. This area was dominated by the trade of the major Severn and Wye navigations, and the demands of the Bristol market. For example, in the sample year, Cardiff traded only with Bristol, whilst at Chepstow, where the record is more complete, 295 shipments cleared for Bristol, 26 for Gloucester and the Severn ports, and a further 2 shipments proceeded to Cardiff. In total almost 94 per cent of coastal shipments from the Wye ports were contained in the above-Holms area, with agricultural goods, foodstuffs and metalwares traded to Bristol forming the major cargo items. However, Chepstow was less constrained by the physical capabilities of its vessels. Unlike the Severn, where the principal craft, the flat-bottomed river trow, was generally limited to the upper estuary and the proximate seaboard, Chepstow's access to deep-water anchorages encouraged a small but consistent trade with extra-regional ports, mostly Liverpool.

At Gloucester, trade beyond the region was negligible and almost solely confined to the activities of estuary craft operating out of the estuary ports, principally Newnham. In 1699, almost 85 per cent of coasters cleared Gloucester for Bristol, and a further 4 per cent of voyages were destined for Chepstow or Cardiff and its creeks. The only significant geographical grouping to which Severn ports traded outside the above-Holms area was

Table 2.1

Destinations of voyages clearing regional ports, sample year

	Bristol	Severn	Somerset	N. Devon	N. Cornwall	Pembroke/ Carmarthen	Swansea/ Neath	Cardiff	Wye	Cross regional	Extra regional	Unknown	Total
Bristol	–	231	50	27	15	29	19	29	23	–	59	9	491
Gloucester	281	–	26	6	–	2	–	5	10	–	–	2	332
Bridgwater	34	15	4	5	1	2	10	–	4	–	20	–	95
Minehead	64	9	6	7	–	6	20	4	3	–	7	1	127
Ilfracombe	16	–	7	5	4	–	1	–	–	–	9	1	43
Barnstaple	17	4	3	6	–	6	9	1	2	1	5	–	54
Bideford	15	–	6	2	2	8	16	1	–	–	19	3	72
Padstow	23	–	–	–	–	–	1	–	2	–	2	–	28
St Ives	5	–	–	1	–	–	1	–	31	–	5	–	43
Mount's Bay	–	–	–	–	–	–	–	–	–	–	4	–	4
Milford	18	1	19	142	2	4	1	–	–	–	255	10	452
Carmarthen	9	1	–	–	–	–	2	–	1	–	15	1	29
Tenby	5	2	102	42	–	2	2	4	–	–	9	8	176
Llanelli	–	–	–	–	–	–	–	–	–	–	–	78	78
South Burry	–	–	–	11	–	–	–	–	–	–	–	3	14
Neath	16	2	208	108	39	–	–	7	–	–	53	4	437
Swansea	6	3	70	70	93	–	2	2	8	–	223	54	531
Cardiff	31	–	–	–	–	–	–	–	–	–	–	–	31
Chepstow	295	26	9	1	–	2	–	2	1	3	5	1	345
Total	835	294	510	433	156	61	84	55	85	4	690	175	3,382
Liverpool	34	1	28	20	10	18	1	–	–	1	193	–	306

Source: PRO E190 coastal port books.

Table 2.2

Voyages entering regional ports by ports of clearance, sample year

	Bristol	Severn	Somerset	N. Devon	N. Cornwall	Pembroke/ Carmarthen	Swansea/ Neath	Cardiff	Wye	Cross regional	Extra regional	Unknown	Total
Gloucester	225	–	17	–	–	5	7	8	31	–	–	1	294
Bridgwater	31	20	4	7	8	47	179	–	11	–	24	–	331
Minehead	56	11	–	3	3	99	133	22	11	–	10	–	348
Ilfracombe	8	2	9	9	1	32	46	–	4	–	21	–	132
Barnstaple	13	1	4	–	5	111	83	–	1	–	12	36	266
Bideford	11	–	2	1	3	89	75	–	2	–	20	22	225
Padstow	6	–	–	2	–	8	106	–	–	–	7	–	129
St Ives	6	–	–	–	–	1	37	–	–	–	7	–	51
Mount's Bay	–	–	–	–	–	1	5	–	–	–	6	1	13
Milford	14	3	3	3	1	4	3	–	1	–	21	1	54
Carmarthen	14	2	1	4	3	6	3	1	2	–	7	1	44
Tenby	5	–	1	–	–	1	–	–	–	–	1	2	10
Chepstow	21	10	–	–	10	2	5	6	–	–	10	1	65
Total	410	49	41	29	34	406	682	37	63	0	146	65	1,962
Liverpool	8	2	15	8	13	35	–	1	4	–	117	–	203

Source: PRO E190 coastal port books.

Somerset. Here, the ports of Bridgwater and Minehead accounted for around 8 per cent of voyages. Trade pivoted upon the demand for Droitwich salt. In the early 1690s, the fisheries of the south-west were severely hit by a combination of war and embargo which drastically reduced the quality and quantity of Biscay salt entering the region. Instead, regional users turned to Droitwich and Cheshire salt, increasingly preferring cheaper Droitwich supplies obtained through Gloucester. The main river ports, Worcester and Bewdley, figured strongly in this trade, although salt was also carried by Tewkesbury and Upton-on-Severn boats which specialised in longer-distance coasting and, in particular, the less-frequented ports of south Wales. The cumulative effect of the demand for salt was to encourage independent through-trade and thus bypass the hitherto more regular practice of tran-shipping Severn goods onto regional packet services at Bristol.[16]

The wider commercial profile of Gloucester in the early eighteenth century reflects the importance of salt, not only as a primary commodity, but also in establishing fresh commercial opportunities for other Severn goods.[17] Figures 2.1 and 2.2 compare the total number of voyages clearing and entering Gloucester between 1680 and 1728 with shipments to and from Bristol.[18] The figures indicate that salt-inspired trade to Somerset (principally Bridgwater), south-west Wales (notably Swansea, Neath and Carmarthen) and Chepstow, where iron and glass were also important cargoes, assumed a larger share of trade in the latter half of the period. Bristol's share of coastal exports dropped from a high of over 90 per cent of all shipments in 1691 and 1692 to around 75 per cent of trade by 1718. This was in part occasioned by the constrictions of war in the early 1690s which tended to curtail the less regular routes and funnel trade into Bristol.[19] In addition, the erratic recording of voyages at Newnham and Berkeley, which tended to trade beyond Bristol, cannot be discounted for the earlier period.[20] Even so, the data emphasise the central importance of Bristol. For most Severn ports, and especially the up-river ports like Shrewsbury and Bridgnorth which were constrained by the size and navigational capability of their craft, Bristol remained in effect the sole focus of trade.[21] The inwards trade reveals a very similar picture. Over the period, around 80 per cent of all inwards voyages emanated from Bristol. However, the proportion of Bristol shipments declined over time as both Chepstow and the south Wales ports developed as important metal-working centres, and recording practice at the minor Severn estuary creeks improved.

Viewed from the perspective of Bristol, it is also apparent that the above-Holms sector provided the principal area of trade. Between 1695 and 1703, over 60 per cent of all shipments clearing Bristol were bound for Gloucester, Chepstow, or Cardiff and its creeks.[22] However, in comparison to the confined commercial horizons of the river ports, Bristol's entrepôt functions

Figure 2.1

Voyages clearing Gloucester, 1680–1728

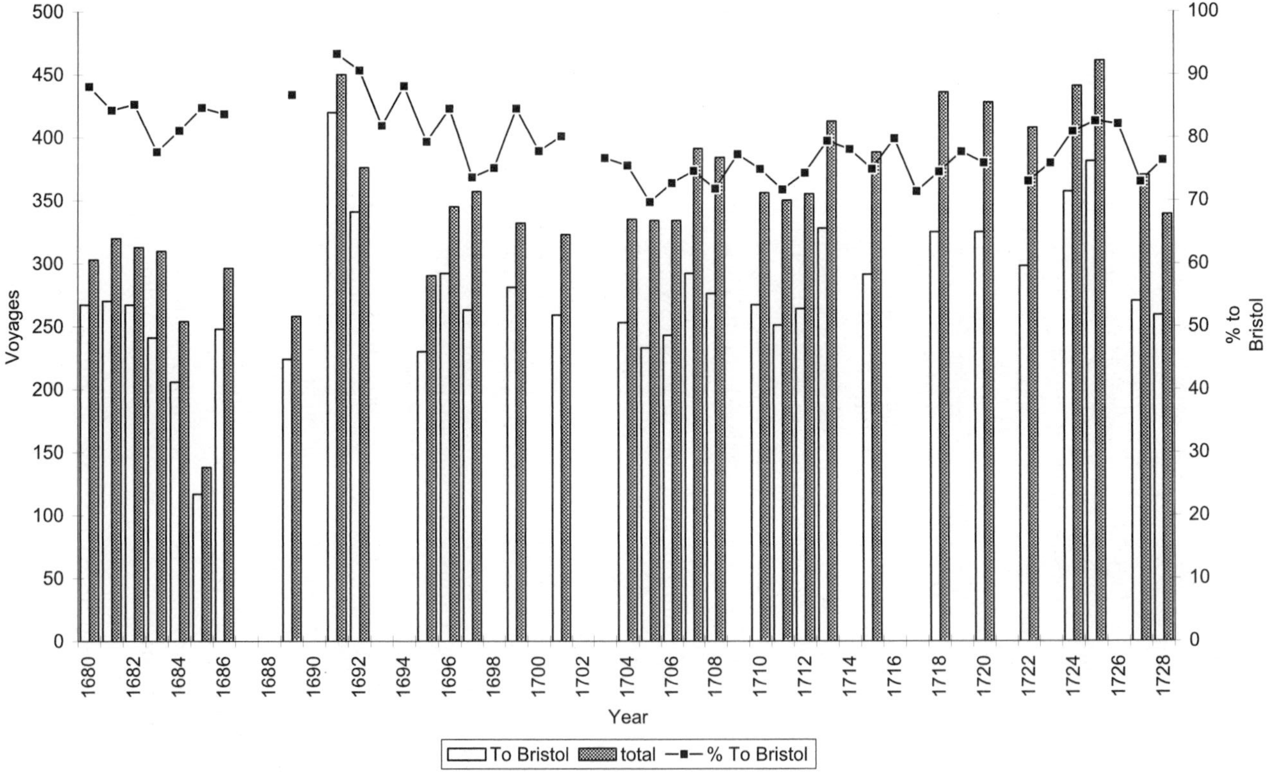

Source: Cox, Hussey and Milne, eds, *Gloucester port books database.*

Figure 2.2

Voyages entering Gloucester, 1680–1728

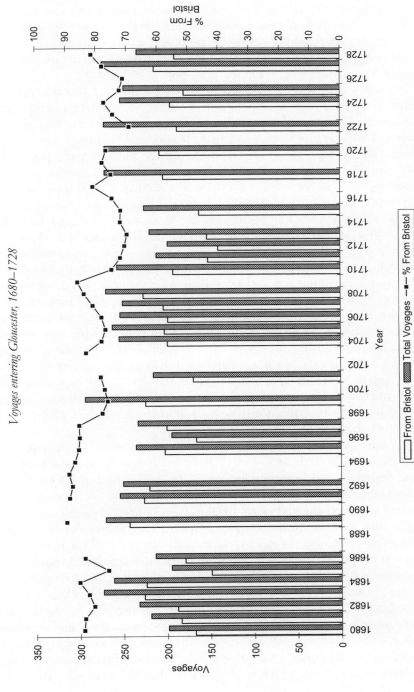

Source: Cox, Hussey and Milne, eds, *Gloucester port books database.*

and its control over a range of domestic and overseas goods ensured that trade was conducted on a much more extensive scale. In 1699, for example, 140 voyages connected the city to the ports and creeks of the lower Bristol Channel. Similarly, 59 voyages cleared for extra-regional ports with the rival metropolises of London, Exeter and Liverpool prominent.[23]

The shipping patterns outlined in tables 2.1 and 2.2 reveal a cyclical exchange mechanism in operation, with shuttle services linking Bristol to the principal regional ports. This was largely a consequence of the very general nature of the cargoes dispatched from Bristol and also the more diffuse demand for the types of goods that could only be acquired through the city. As chapter 3 emphasises, voyages clearing from Bristol carried very similar assemblages of overseas and domestic wares, no matter what their intended destination. Apart from such bulk staples as iron and metal wares, Bristol dispatched the sort of easily merchantable 'shop goods' not directly available to consumers in the region. The number of shipments was therefore dependent upon the ability of each regional grouping and its hinterland to absorb high-value goods emanating from the 'metropolis of the west'. For many ports, ballasting was a characteristic of the out-leg of many Bristol voyages.[24] The exceptions to this pattern were at Bideford and Barnstaple. In this period, both ports maintained a relatively small but none the less profitable stake in overseas trade. Consequently, links with Bristol were structured rather differently. For a start, consignments like tobacco, wine or train oil, staple goods which were imported directly from overseas, did not figure greatly in incoming shipments. None the less, Bristol-supplied goods still furnished an extensive trade, with domestic iron, ironwares and strong waters, the latter probably for overseas export, forming the major cargoes dispatched to north Devon.[25]

The bipolar nature of Bristol's relation to its hinterland is clearly indicated through the trade of the *Agreement* of Bideford. Between 1695 and 1704, the vessel was employed almost exclusively as the local Bristol–Bideford packet, undertaking between five and six round trips a year, occasionally being diverted into supplementary local freights. For example, alongside the Bristol service, the *Agreement* picked up a coal freight from Swansea in 1695 and a small letpass shipment for Barnstaple *en route* to Bristol in 1700. In the main, the cargoes carried by the *Agreement* were remarkably standard. From Bristol, the vessel was loaded with iron and a range of bulk iron goods and iron-mongers' wares; strong waters and English spirits in quantities large enough to suggest industrial use; and a rather motley assortment of haberdashery goods, textiles, leather and skins, hats, wearing apparel, Baltic and domestic timber; and basic foodstuffs like cheese. In return, copper, copper ore and tobacco pipe clay formed the principal customs-worthy cargoes, although earthenware and small amounts of agricultural goods were also sent up to

Bristol, often under the authority of letpasses and transires. In the early years, the *Agreement* was mastered by William Harris. By 1701, however, Harris had eased into a rather more executive, mercantile or quasi-shipowning role, leaving the physical business of coasting to such lesser operatives as Robert Pick and Samuel Dennard.[26] In effect, Harris and his associates were providing space within a regular transport. On 19 September 1701, for example, the *Agreement* under Dennard cleared for Bideford with a fairly typical Bristol cargo. Amongst this was a parcel of iron compiled by George Bartlett for William Sealey of Bridgwater. When the vessel discharged at Bideford on 5 December 1701, Sealey's iron was consigned to George Strange, a prominent local trader, who organised freightage costs, storage and ultimately disposal of the goods in south Devon.[27]

The central importance of Bristol as a regional focus of trade is also demonstrated in the figures for the ports of the south-west. Bristol was the single most important destination for coastal vessels clearing Bridgwater, Minehead, Ilfracombe, Barnstaple and Padstow, although in the case of Padstow the absence of letpasses has overemphasised the Bristol-bound coquet trade. In comparison, the trade of the letpass-recording ports ranged more widely. Bridgwater, for example, traded heavily with Gloucester and Liverpool, venturing small cargoes of non-customable goods in returning salt vessels. This explains the high proportion of extra-regional voyages recorded at Bridgwater and, conversely, the apparent absence of incoming Somerset trade at Gloucester, a port which did not habitually record letpasses. In 1699, for example, of the 20 shipments that cleared Bridgwater for Gloucester, 9 proceeded by letpass and were consequently not noted in the corresponding Gloucester records. With Liverpool, 14 shipments departed Bridgwater in 1699, picking up substantial loadings of salt in return. In practice, vessels like the *Bonadventure* of Liverpool, mastered by William Cragg, the *Crown* of Bridgwater, under John Murren, and the Bridgwater vessels the *Hannah* and the *Lively*, part-owned by Robert Reid and Joseph Tibbs respectively, were effectively constant coasters plying the long-distance salt routes. Despite high freight charges, occasionally onerous incidental dues and wages, and recurrent delays at Frodsham and Liverpool, these vessels regularly managed three or four round trips a year: relatively long-haul voyages that compare favourably with Ville's later estimates for the east-coast trade.[28] The importance of Cheshire salt, and indeed the importance of coasting, in opening up dispersed markets is also apparent in the consistently large numbers of voyages linking extra-regional centres to Minehead, St Ives, and, especially, Bideford, where boats from London and the ports of south Cornwall were also well represented.[29] At Ilfracombe, a port mainly concerned with the inshore herring fishery, south-coast centres were wholly responsible for voyages beyond the region.

A further area of trade comprised voyages from the south-west to the Welsh coal ports carrying mainly small items of cargo under letpass, transire or sufferance. At Minehead and Bideford this assumed fairly substantial levels, with over a third of all coastal clearances from Bideford in 1699 being letpass voyages to ports under the jurisdiction of either Swansea and Neath or Milford. Apart from Mount's Bay, where recorded coastal voyages were too sporadic to imply any major shipping patterns, the outstanding feature of the south-western ports was the number of voyages clearing St Ives for Chepstow. In the sample year, almost two-thirds of shipments from St Ives were bound for the Wye. Again the lack of recorded non-coquet trade affects these figures, although the importance of the trade in copper ore and tin cannot be underestimated for the economies of either area.[30]

However, these were minor trades compared to the frequency and size of coal shipments. The large number of voyages recorded at Swansea, Milford, Neath, and, to a lesser extent, Tenby and Llanelli almost entirely proceeded from the ability of the region's industries and hearths to consume regular supplies of coal and culm.[31] Yet, behind such a simple supply-led equation lay important differences in both the geographical groupings served by each coal-exporting port and the specific centres to which voyages were made. Thus, at Milford, over three-quarters of the voyages destined for the Bristol Channel region in the sample year were bound for Barnstaple, Bideford, Ilfracombe and their creeks. On the other hand, Tenby was principally oriented towards Somerset: only a quarter of its voyages discharged in north Devon. At Swansea, whilst the ports of Somerset and north Devon both received 70 voyages, 93 shipments cleared in the rather smaller boats of and for north Cornwall. In comparison, Neath was largely tied to supplying Somerset: almost half its voyages cleared for ports under Bridgwater's jurisdiction, whereas only a quarter were destined for north Devon and a mere 9 per cent discharged for Padstow, St Ives or Mount's Bay and their subordinate ports. All 11 voyages from South Burry which indicated destinations were bound for north Devon, and where the erratic record of Llanelli shipments can be reconstructed, a further 60 voyages cleared for the Taw–Torridge estuary.[32]

A more complex picture of this trade is presented in table 2.3 where coal voyages are broken down by the port of destination. Clearly, within the broad geographical parameters outlined above, Bridgwater was the most prominent regional centre, the bulk of its supply coming from Neath. However, cumulatively, Minehead and, in particular, its formally unrecognised creek, Watchet, outstripped the head port in terms of voyages clearing from Swansea and Tenby. With regard to the north Devon ports, the figures are overshadowed by the number of voyages recorded in the Milford port books as bound solely for Barnstaple. In fact, comparison with the inwards sections of the

Table 2.3

Coal shipments from regional ports, sample year

Area	Port	Neath	Swansea	South Burry	Tenby	Milford	Severn	Bristol	Total
				Coal exporting centre					
Somerset	Bridgwater	139	34	–	40	11	1	–	225
	Combwich	2	–	–	–	–	–	–	2
	Minehead	64	21	–	11	–	–	–	96
	Watchet	3	15	–	39	7	–	–	64
	Porlock	–	–	–	12	–	–	–	12
North Devon	Lynmouth	–	–	–	4	–	–	–	4
	Ilfracombe	26	23	–	25	1	–	–	75
	Barnstaple	28	8	4	7	121	–	–	168
	Bideford	34	21	2	2	10	–	–	69
	Northam	19	7	5	–	–	–	–	31
	Clovelly	1	11	–	3	1	–	–	16
North Cornwall	Padstow	32	45	–	–	2	–	–	79
	Boscastle	–	1	–	–	–	–	–	1
	Port Isaac	–	9	–	–	–	–	–	9
	St Ives	5	30	–	–	–	–	–	35
	St Agnes	–	1	–	–	–	–	–	1
	Penzance	2	7	–	–	–	–	–	9
Other regional	Bristol	9	1	–	4	1	14	–	29
	Cardiff	–	2	–	4	–	–	–	6
	Carmarthen	–	–	–	2	1	–	–	3
	Wye	–	8	–	–	–	5	1	14
	Severn	2	1	–	2	–	–	63	68
	Laugharne	–	–	–	–	1	–	–	1
	Oystermouth	–	1	–	1	–	–	–	2
	South Burry	–	1	–	–	–	–	–	1
Extra–regional (south)	Gweek	5	–	–	–	–	–	–	5
	Falmouth	4	32	–	–	2	–	1	39
	Penryn	1	–	–	–	–	–	–	1
	Truro	11	14	–	–	12	–	–	37
	Fowey	7	8	–	–	4	–	–	19
	Looe	4	13	–	–	3	–	–	20
	Plymouth	3	75	–	–	24	–	–	102
	Dartmouth	–	17	–	–	36	–	–	53
	Teignmouth	–	4	–	–	–	–	–	4
	Topsham	1	23	–	4	–	–	–	28
	Exeter	9	8	–	–	95	–	–	112
	Lyme	–	1	–	–	–	–	–	1
	Weymouth	–	–	–	–	5	–	–	5
	Poole	–	–	–	–	2	–	–	2
	Southampton	1	2	–	–	–	–	–	3
	Portsmouth	–	–	–	–	1	–	–	1
	Cowes	1	–	–	–	–	–	1	2
	Brighton	–	3	–	–	–	–	–	3
	London	–	–	–	3	9	–	–	12
	Dunwich	–	–	–	–	1	–	–	1
	Yarmouth	–	–	–	–	6	–	–	6
	Wells	–	–	–	–	1	–	–	1
Extra–regional (north)	Cardigan	–	–	–	–	1	–	–	1
	Aberdovey	–	–	–	–	3	–	–	3
Channel Islands	Guernsey	2	11	–	–	–	–	–	13
	Jersey	–	2	–	–	–	–	–	2
Ireland	Dublin	1	–	–	–	–	–	–	1
	Cork	1	–	–	–	–	–	–	1
Unknown/ unspecified		5	55	–	6	3	–	–	69
Total		422	515	11	169	364	20	66	1,567

Source: PRO E190 coastal port books.

Barnstaple and Bideford port books emphasises that this reflected recording practice at Milford more than the precise destination of colliers. Voyages from Neath were roughly divided between Barnstaple, Bideford, Northam and Ilfracombe. Ilfracombe, an exposed port and one which operated much smaller coasters on a rather more frequent basis than other south-western ports, was engaged in a vigorous trade with Swansea and Tenby. In contrast, Padstow and St Ives, the only substantial ports of north Cornwall, monopolised what trade cleared Swansea and Neath for the area.

Intra-regional voyages represented only a part of the shipments clearing the south Wales ports. Milford culm, widely praised for its range of industrial uses, could be delivered more competitively than inferior grade Tenby or Saundersfoot culm or even Glamorganshire bituminous coals at the south-coast ports. Although longer-distance coasting posed logistical problems, Milford's peripheral location in relation to the Bristol Channel ensured that its culm traded at an advantage over other coal-exporting ports.[33] Consequently, trade conducted with external centres overshadowed the regional market. In 1699, Milford dispatched 255 voyages for ports beyond the region, with almost two-thirds bound for the principal commercial centres of south Cornwall and Devon. Exeter, Dartmouth and Plymouth took the bulk of this trade. None the less, the quality of Milford culm ensured that regular links were maintained with such far-flung centres as London and Yarmouth. Likewise, Swansea coal found important extra-regional markets. In the sample year, almost 90 per cent of the 223 voyages clearing beyond the Bristol Channel were bound for south Devon and Cornwall, with Plymouth, Falmouth and Exeter/Topsham the main centres. At Neath, where only 53 voyages cleared for more remote markets, most shipments were controlled by the ports of south Devon and Cornwall. Truro, which was sending large quantities of copper ore to Mackworth's works at Neath, and Exeter were the main promoters of this trade.

In comparison, trade recorded at Gloucester and Bristol was negligible. With supplies of variable quality coal nearby, Bristol was less dependent upon the regular mineral shipments that formed the lifeblood of London, for example. Moreover, the output of the Shropshire collieries was generally confined to the immediate hinterland of the Severn navigation.[34] The absence of a large collier fleet servicing Bristol and the kind of potentially exploitable empty tonnage returning to the region effectively capped the levels of coasting operating from the city.[35] In 1699, for instance, Bristol received 14 coal shipments via Gloucester and dispatched 63 voyages to the Severn ports. Given the odd shipment of Neath coals and Tenby culm to Bristol in this period, it is probable that some of these vessels carried coal transhipped from the south Wales ports. It is also clear that much of Bristol's meagre coal trade was confined to the exchange of specialist grades of mineral rather than bulk carriage: the Severn coal trows and barges that cleared Bristol for up-river destinations rarely carried more than 19 tons and, like the *John* of Tewkesbury, were often limited to single 8–12 ton consignments.

The numbers of voyages entering regional ports roughly confirm the broad patterns of trade described above. For this reason, it is not proposed to reiterate in depth the coastal connections of the Bristol Channel from the perspective of importing centres. However, a comparison between coastal clearances and entrances throws an important light upon the economic underpinnings of the coastal trade: the procuring of return cargo. Evidently it was in the interests of shippers and merchants to secure sufficient back cargo to cover at least the expenses of the crew, victuals and port charges. As chapter 5 shows, acquiring a return freight was often a laborious and fractious process involving large networks of merchants and factors and dependent upon such variables as availability of goods and the ability to sell the same at the port of discharge: the port books often note speculative cargoes returned 'for want of sale'. Ports with small populations and constricted hinterlands, like Penzance or Milford, had low commercial thresholds, and in such cases returning to port in ballast or obtaining freightage to other ports were often the only practical and economic options open to local merchants.

Table 2.4 illustrates the issue of return cargoes by comparing the number of recorded voyages undertaken between 13 regional ports with three important sources of coastal supply, Bristol, Liverpool, and the main south Wales coal ports. In this no attempt has been made to conflate figures from different records to balance potentially imperfect datasets.[36] With regard to trade with the south Wales ports and, to a lesser extent, Liverpool, the bulk shipment of coal and salt was the overriding commercial factor. However, trade with Bristol was more complex and not wholly 'one-way', to use Willan's rather inappropriate expression: Bristol was as dependent upon goods sent coastways from the region as the latter relied upon the high-value commodities clearing Bristol.[37] Most vessels involved in these trades were 'constant coasters' regularly plying the same course. In this respect, table 2.4 provides an indication of the percentage of voyages that either entered from Bristol or cleared for the south Wales coal staithes or for Liverpool in ballast. This presupposes that voyages were cyclical or followed established and consistent routes. This was certainly the case for most colliers and the packet-type vessels tied into short-haul Bristol services, but may not have always pertained to vessels in the Liverpool trade. Yet, as in the case of Bridgwater's long-distance salt vessels, it is clear that the trade to and from the north-west was highly organised and involved a core number of regular craft operating on generally fixed routes. Port book evidence suggests that similar patterns were in place at most salt-importing regional ports.

Table 2.4

Return voyages: Bristol, Liverpool and south Wales coal ports, sample year

	Bristol			Liverpool			South Wales coal ports		
	To	From	% return in ballast	From	To	% clear in ballast	From	To	% clear in ballast
Bridgwater	34	31	9	20	14	30	226	12	95
Minehead	64	56	14	4	0	100	232	26	89
Ilfracombe	16	8	50	10	0	100	78	1	99
Barnstaple	17	13	24	3	1	67	194	15	92
Bideford	15	11	27	9	7	22	164	24	85
Padstow	23	6	74	7	2	71	114	1	99
St Ives	5	6	0	7	5	29	38	1	97
Mount's Bay	0	0	0	0	1	0	6	0	100
Milford	16	12	25	6	24	0	7	5	29
Carmarthen	9	13	0	6	13	0	9	2	56
Tenby	5	4	20	0	2	0	1	4	0
Chepstow	295	21	93	1	5	0	7	2	71
Gloucester	281	225	20	0	0	0	11	2	82

Source: PRO E190 coastal port books.

The major feature of table 2.4 is the almost complete absence of return voyages to south Wales. This was a result of the economics of the coal trade and the commercially undeveloped nature of the south Wales hinterland. In the Bristol Channel low unit costs prevailed: voyages were usually short, crew and overheads were minimal, and the coal itself involved little capital outlay.[38] What is more, the proximate, ready markets in the south-west of England encouraged quick turn-around times. For example, when pressed to describe shipping conditions at Bridgwater in 1673, John Tiver, a former boatman, argued that 'if the winde and weather prove good, a barke or trough may make her voyage from Bridgwater . . . into Wales and there be loaden and returned to Bridgwater againe with her loadinge and the coles and culme where with it is loaden be conveyed from thence to Ham Mills [the highest navigable port on the river Parrett] . . . in the space of a weeke and ordinarily in a fortnight'.[39] In return, however, south Wales did not offer extensive opportunities for the sale of industrial goods or foodstuffs produced in the south-west. Consequently, most colliers returned to south Wales in ballast, with only the ship's provisions on board. Thus, on 30 December 1696, Hoare and Company's regular collier, the *William and Richard* of Bridgwater, mastered by Philip Richards, returned to Swansea from Bridgwater with a non-dutiable loading of beef, pork, turnips and carrots, peas, bread and beer worth £2 18s 8d. It discharged its usual coal cargo at Bridgwater 15 days later.[40] The only exceptions to this general pattern were the few voyages that carried letpass goods to Wales from Bideford and Minehead, and also a very minor exchange trade in different grades of coal which existed between the south Wales ports. In this sense, the more enclosed dynamic of the Bristol Channel trade contrasts sharply with the east-coast coal trade. Although supply was still the paramount factor, the greater distance and cost involved in coasting the less sheltered waters of the North Sea appear to have encouraged colliers either to risk higher value and more merchantable return cargoes from London, as Dietz has indicated, or, alternatively, to ply goods between the intermediary coastal ports.[41]

A rather different structural basis can be distinguished in trade of the south-western ports with Liverpool. The south-west was dependent on salt sent coastwise from Liverpool for much of the supplies required for industrial and domestic purposes and, in particular, the inshore and Newfoundland fisheries. Although by 1699 Droitwich white salt had captured a large share of this lucrative market, Cheshire white and rock salt remained an important commodity.[42] A substantial and regular return trade was maintained between the salt-importing centres of the region and the north-west: Bridgwater consistently dispatched small consignments of agricultural goods; Bideford sent earthenware and tobacco pipe clay; and St Ives sent copper ore and tin. Such patterns were more emphasised in the trade of the south Wales ports. Milford, Carmarthen, Tenby and even Chepstow were net coastal exporters to Liverpool. Indeed, Liverpool can be seen to be rather more reliant upon Pembrokeshire and Carmarthenshire grain than the south Wales seaboard had need for large shipments of Cheshire salt. Chepstow's involvement was mainly the result of enterprising Bridgwater salt vessels collecting cinders, corn and cider. Three of Hoare and Company's boats, the *Exchange*, the *Fly*, and the *Two Sisters*, received consignments from Alexander Phillips of Brockweir on the return leg to Liverpool in 1699. This partially explains the shortfall in voyages recorded clearing Bridgwater for the north-west.[43] The one vessel discharging salt at Swansea in 1699, the *Phoenix* of Swansea, also picked up a return cargo of agricultural goods at Chepstow. In contrast, Minehead, Ilfracombe, Barnstaple and Padstow dispatched only a fraction of the trade discharging from Liverpool. Similarly, whilst Bristol received 34 salt shipments in 1699, only 8 returned with customable cargo. In the case of Bristol and Minehead, return voyages may have been directed to Ireland and thence to Liverpool. In November 1702, for instance, the rather inappropriately named *Plain Dealing* of Minehead under George Priest delivered Cheshire salt to the Somerset port, before discharging in ballast to Milford to pick up a culm freight for Dublin. Delayed by contrary winds, Priest dumped his culm cargo at Bridgwater in January 1703 intending to return to Milford and thence Dublin, although his commissioning merchant, William Sealey of Bridgwater, doubted his probity and seamanship. The *Plain Dealing* with Priest on board finally cleared Liverpool for Minehead in April 1703 with a cargo of mostly rock salt.[44]

The data relating to Bristol outline a contrasting commercial arrangement with inward-bound voyages outweighing clearances. Bristol sucked in more coastal trade than it dispensed, reflecting a greater demand for goods at Bristol, often shipped up in small consignments, than there was regional demand for the more costly wares characteristic of many Bristol cargoes. This pattern was most apparent at Chepstow where over 90 per cent of voyages to Bristol returned in ballast or with goods of little customable worth. Similarly, around a fifth of all Severn trows returned to Gloucester in 1699 unladen or carrying non-coquet goods. As the longer sample of data reveals, trade at Gloucester was imbalanced towards clearances. Although some trows may well have cleared Bristol with petty non-customable letpass cargoes, it is apparent that many up-river vessels completed their home legs solely in ballast. Indeed ballasting was likely to have been a commercial necessity for trow owners based in the Severn ports, especially when back-cargo was not readily available: at Bristol port dues and incremental costs could quickly mount up for idle tonnage and port officials were strictly charged to alleviate the city's overworked and congested facilities by rapidly turning round coasters.[45]

At the other regional centres, a small discrepancy between coastal imports and exports was recorded. At the Somerset and north Devon ports, outwards trade to Bristol was conducted mainly under letpasses, transires and sufferances, the absence of which probably explains the excessively low figures for coastal clearances at the coquet-ports, Padstow and St Ives. However, the centripetal pattern of coastal supply was reversed at the periphery of the region. Both St Ives and Carmarthen received more shipments from Bristol than were dispatched. This suggests that the trade of these ports operated on a more strict cycle involving regular craft and organised by regular merchants. For example, the local packet vessel, the *John* of St Ives, undertook all 11 of the recorded voyages between St Ives and Bristol in the sample year. Three of the vessel's inward voyages were undertaken in the name of Edward Crofts, a major tin and copper merchant.[46] In the case of Carmarthen, the figures may have been distorted by vessels which cleared to Bristol from other south Wales centres discharging at Carmarthen on return. In a localised way, Carmarthen thus acted as the economic hub and coastal redistributor of Bristol goods to a more limited economic and geographical hinterland.[47]

On a more prosaic level, the analysis of inward voyages can begin to restore the 'holes' in imperfect datasets. At Bristol, Cardiff, Swansea and Neath this approach fleshes out the commercial profile of ports at which only coastal clearances were recorded. The south Wales ports were dominated by coal exports to such an extent that coastal imports were all but vestigial. However, at Bristol, where inwards traffic was considerable, the reconstruction of this 'lost' data allows the commercial use of the port to be examined in a more critical light. Table 2.5 compares voyages and tonnage engaged in Bristol's coastal and overseas trades ordered by areas of activity.[48] In the coastal figures, data from the regional sample are combined with a wider trawl of centres. In cases where the record of extra-regional ports is neither complete nor extant, it has been assumed that clearances from Bristol were accompanied by a reciprocal in-voyage. The data presented here are more illustrative than substantive assessments of the various branches of trade. They are derived from very different sources and are also discontinuous in terms of chronology. Equally, it is uncertain whether the overseas assessments measure ships or voyages. In the long-distance, transoceanic trades the extended voyage times makes this distinction somewhat academic. In a given year, it is unlikely, although not inconceivable, that more than one round trip would be completed. However, in the short-haul European and Irish trades, the latter being little more than an extension to coasting, turn-around times were much quicker. As a result, far greater numbers and tonnages should be expected for these sectors if vessels and not voyages are listed.

Given these interpretational difficulties, the implications of table 2.5 are still dramatic. Clearly, the number of voyages and the tonnage involved in Bristol's coastal trade in the late seventeenth and early eighteenth centuries was considerable. Although we are perhaps used to stressing overseas trade, the numerical ascendancy of coasting reflects a correlation revealed by other sources for eighteenth-century trade and a host of impressionistic evidence.[49] Yet, what is most remarkable is the extent of coasting, given that the figures for *c.*1699 clearly under-represent important sectors of Bristol's domestic trade, most notably shipments proceeding under letpass.[50] Thus, at the turn of the seventeenth century, Bristol was very much a coastal metropolis: coastal vessels, river trows, barges and ketches crowded the city's quays and backs. With this in mind, it is perhaps a salutary experience for historians dazzled by the lustre of overseas commerce to reflect on the fact that at the dawn of its 'Golden Age', the most regular, and indeed the most common maritime trade at Bristol was fundamentally local and coastal.

Cycles and seasons: coastal voyages and shipping patterns in the Bristol Channel, 1680–1730

Despite Willan's unflattering picture of regional coasting as chaotic and unstructured, it is clear from the preceding discussion that coastal voyages in the Bristol Channel followed distinctive and regular patterns.[51] This is not to

Table 2.5

Trade to and from Bristol, coastal and overseas

	Coastal, c.1699[1]			Overseas inward: June 1699–June 1700[2]				Overseas inward: Dec. 1699–Dec. 1700[3]			Overseas outward: Dec. 1686–Dec. 1688[4]		
	Out	In	Burden Tonnage[5]		Out	Burden	Average		Out	Burden[6]		In	Burden[7]
Severn	231	281	20,480	Virginia	29	4,270	147	Virginia	12	1,767	Virginia[8]		0
Somerset	50	98	4,144	West Indies[9]	55	5,170	94	West Indies	50	4,700	West Indies	56	5,264
N. Devon	27	48	2,100	Iberia[10]	22	1,450	66	Iberia[11]	28	1,845	Iberia[12]	30	1,977
N. Cornwall	15	28	1,204	France	8	195	24	France	5	122	France	47	1,146
Pemb./Carm.	29	32	1,708	N. Europe[13]	31	4,075	131	N. Europe[14]	9	1,183	N. Europe[15]	17	2,235
Swansea/Neath	19	22	1,148	N. America[16]	9	390	43	N. America[17]	21	910	N. America[18]	18	780
Cardiff	29	31	1,680	Mediterranean[19]	18	2,100	117	Mediterranean[20]	3	350	Mediterranean[21]	1	117
Wye	23	295	8,904	Ireland	68	2,228	33	Ireland	83	2,719	Ireland	60	1,966
Extra-regional[22]	59	85	4,032	Others				Others[23]	12	996	Others[24]	11	913
Unknown	9		252										
Total	491	920	45,652	Total	240	19,878	83	Total	225	14,593	Total	240	14,397

Notes to Table 2.5:

1. As tables 2.1. and 2.2 above: Hussey, 'Coastal trade', pp. 70–7.
2. Based on BM Add. MSS 9764, ff. 115–16 quoted in Minchinton, ed., *Trade of Bristol*, p. 5. Figures corrected as per original.
3. Based on PRO E190/1158/1 in McGrath, ed., *Merchants*, p. 281.
4. Reproduced from McGrath, ed., *Merchants*, p. 280.
5. A standard, and very conservative estimate based on Barrett's anachronistic figures for tonnage (*History and antiquities*, pp.189–90) and burden tonnage figures taken from the early Gloucester port books, 1575–1647. See Hussey, 'Coastal trade', pp. 226–30; Hussey et al., *Gloucester coastal port books*, pp. 50–2.
6. Compiled from Minchinton, ed., *Trade of Bristol*, p. 5. See also Morgan, *Bristol*, pp. 13–15.
7. As above, note 2.
8. Included in N. America.
9. Antigua, Nevis, Montserrat and St Kitts 28; Jamaica 18; Barbados 9.
10. Lisbon; Bilbao; St Sebastian; Oporto; Faro; Canaries.
11. Madeira 2; Portugal 5; Spain 20; Tenerife 1.
12. Canaries 2; Madeira 1; Portugal 2; Spain 25.
13. Hamburg and Rotterdam 16; Baltic 5; Norway and Gothenburg 10.
14. Hamburg 3; Rotterdam 5; Stockholm, 1.
15. Hamburg 6; Norway 1; Rotterdam 9; Stockholm 1.
16. Carolina; Newfoundland; New England; Bermuda.
17. Carolina 3; New England 1; New York 1; Pennsylvania 7; Newfoundland 9.
18. America 14; Newfoundland 4.
19. Cadiz; St Lucar; Malaga; Straits and beyond.
20. Leghorn 3.
21. Genoa 1.
22. Voyages to/from ports beyond the Bristol Channel. Inwards shipments data are taken from port books where extant. Where this has not been possible, it has been assumed that voyages from Bristol returned with cargo to the port.
23. Channel Islands 2; Scotland 7; Guinea 3.
24. Others 10; Scotland 1.

imply that uniform levels of coasting existed: the sample year outlined in tables 2.1 and 2.2 represents data of optimum stability in which contingent factors such as war, excessively inclement weather, and the worst of the region's periodic and, in some localities, severe harvest failure and dearth were absent.[52] However, in an age dominated by primary production, external variables had important repercussions upon how trade was conducted. This was largely expressed in the choice exercised by producers, merchants and wholesalers between complementary forms of transport.[53] It is, therefore, important to subject the wider series of data to further analyses in order to determine whether the structural underpinnings of regional trade were affected by variation and to what extent the main patterns of coasting were determined by seasonal or more *ad hoc* factors.

As we have seen, the number of voyages recorded at regional ports fluctuated markedly from year to year. Evidently, some shifts in local economies were expressed through subtle adjustments in the trade in specific goods. However, more general factors can be detected. War, or even the threat of impending hostility, disturbed an always tenuous commercial equilibrium. The 1688–97 conflict with France, for example, provoked extensive maritime stoppage and economic disruption. In 1689 and 1690, the Bristol Channel was closed to coasters—an embargo, in part occasioned by domestic considerations, which threatened to curtail normal trading and seriously disrupt Bristol's fairs, 'upon wch', the Merchant Venturers exclaimed, 'not only the trade of this city, but of the adjacent countryes & Wales doe principally depende'.[54] Fresh hostilities in 1702 caused disruption to the staple fish and wine trades with the Iberian peninsula, and to the overseas convoys transporting much of the region's supply of sugar, tobacco, dyestuffs and other transoceanic comestibles.[55] In 1715, unsubstantiated rumours of the Pretender's actions were enough to unsettle Bristol's jittery merchant community.[56]

International disputes had tangible short-term repercussions for coasting. Warfare heightened the operation of the press, which remained an intermittent blight on regional coasters, particularly those dealing with the larger ports or engaged in voyages beyond the Bristol Channel. In 1696, Hoare and Company's newly acquired Swedish-built barque, the *Fortune*, was stripped of all its crew bar the commander, Valentine Francis, a carpenter and a boy *en route* from North Shields to Bridgwater.[57] However, the most serious local problem was the threat privateering posed to the conduct of long-distance coasting.[58] In 1692, at the height of the French action, coasters were ransacked off the coast of Ilfracombe,[59] and as late as 1697 most long-haul coasting vessels would not move without convoy. Philip Cockrem, master and part-owner of the *Exchange* of Bridgwater, writing from Liverpool in June 1696, complained that he was unavoidably delayed in delivering his cargo of salt, 'finding the French fleet laid up in Brest, inferr that theire condition compels them to infest our coasts & chanels with theire privateers'. Indeed, 'some masters belonging to this town' had already encountered '2 French men of war & 15 privateers at the north of Ireland and the adjacent partes'. Further information filtering through to Cockrem was equally distressing: 'letters from Penzant', he warned, 'advise the privateers are seen daily and from Exon they advise their M[aste]rs not to come out to sea with out convoy & from Watchett it is writ [that] the French privateers [are] as high as the Homes [Holms]'.[60] Cockrem's hysteria was well founded; a year earlier William Alloway and John Wheddon, merchants of Bridgwater and Watchet, suffered the loss of their coaster, the *Satisfaction* of Bridgwater, to one such privateer.[61]

The effects of these factors upon the patterns of regional coasting were profound. Figures 2.3 and 2.4 indicate the fluctuating levels of trade undertaken by eight principal Bristol Channel ports with centres from beyond the region between 1695 and 1704. In this all extant port books, including half-years, have been used and the data are expressed as a percentage of total annual voyages to account for variations between the relative size and importance of the coastal ports. The figures address the widely held assumption that war shackled the coastal trade.[62] Undoubtedly, privateering made long-distance coasting both more hazardous and arduous by the delay and expense involved in travelling in convoy, where this was available. In such conditions, one would expect coasting to be limited to the more secluded waters of the Bristol Channel. This was certainly the case with Bristol, which, because of its more easterly position, was more affected by disruption to long-distance routes and also more able to switch to its established network of overland carriers. In 1695 and 1696 voyages to centres beyond the region numbered only four and ten respectively, with Liverpool the main destination. By 1698, the first full peace year available, 45 voyages were bound for extra-regional centres. London, Topsham and the exposed south coast of England received 36 of these shipments.[63] This had risen to 59 voyages in 1699 and 51 in 1701. In both years shipments were focused on London. Between 1699 and 1701, therefore, 12–14 per cent of coastal clearances from Bristol were long-distance voyages. By the second half of 1703, only 12 voyages were recorded clearing for beyond the region, although freak weather conditions certainly played a part: the Great Storm flooded over a third of the city and severely disrupted the operation of the port wrecking both the *Abundance* of London and the *Primrose* of St Ives which had both cleared for the capital.[64] Nevertheless, it appears that Bristol's long-distance coastal voyages were largely dependent upon the safety of south-coast shipping lanes and that in times of maritime distur-bance Land's End acted as an effective south-western parameter to trade.

Figure 2.3

Extra-regional voyages recorded at south-west of England ports, percentage of annual voyages, 1695–1704

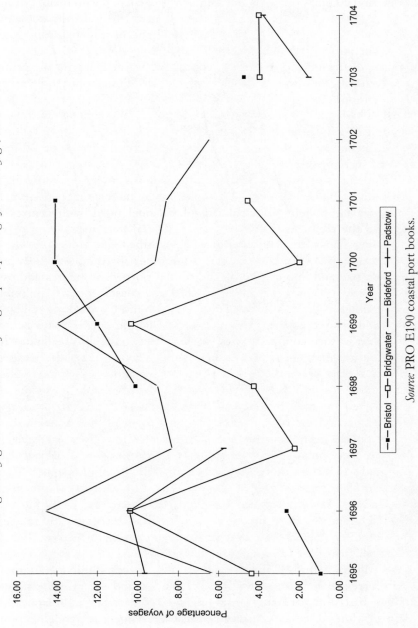

Year

Percentage of voyages

—■— Bristol   —□— Bridgwater   —— Bideford   —+— Padstow

Source: PRO E190 coastal port books.

Figure 2.4

Extra-regional voyages recorded at south Wales ports, percentage of annual voyages, 1695–1704

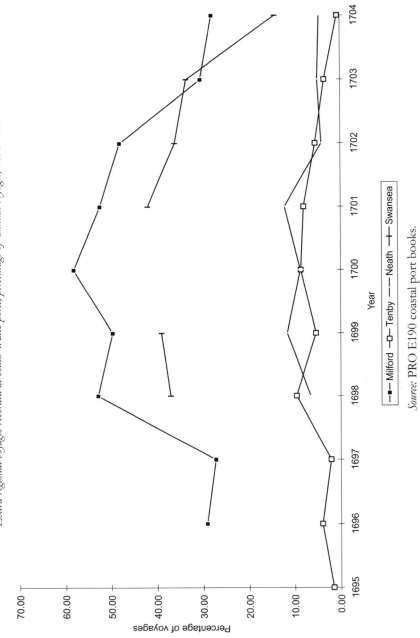

Source: PRO E190 coastal port books.

At Neath, data from the half-years for 1699 and 1700 confirm a broadly similar picture. Between 1698 and 1701, the ports of south Cornwall, south Devon and London formed the principal 'external' domestic market for Neath coal, accounting for no less than 87 per cent of extra-regional clearances. By 1702, however, such shipments had declined dramatically, with more voyages destined for Aberdovey. In part this reflected Sir Humphrey Mackworth's development of lead mining in Cardiganshire and smelting in Neath: Mackworth's vessel, the *Mine Adventurer*, was increasingly employed in ferrying coal to Aberdovey in exchange for lead ore destined for the Melin Cryddan smelter.[65] At Swansea and Milford, ports far more tied to supplying the south coast, extra-regional voyages fell away from a distinct peak between 1698 and 1702. Although the erratic recording of destinations at Swansea prevents a full comparison of shipping patterns over the period, it is clear that around 37 per cent of all voyages cleared to centres beyond the region in 1699, rising to 42 per cent of shipments in 1701. There was then a swift and marked decline. In 1704, only 66 of the 463 recorded shipments traded beyond Land's End or St David's Head. Similarly, extra-regional trade at Milford accounted for less than 30 per cent of shipments in 1696 and 1697, rising to around half of all voyages in the boom years of 1700 and 1701, before falling away to levels obtained earlier in the sample. Here, the decline in the representation of extra-regional trade was accompanied by a direct fall in the total number of shipments. At Tenby, where regional systems of coasting dominated the trade of the port, the peacetime hiatus between 1698 and 1701/2 also saw proportionally greater trade conducted with the south-coast centres, mainly Plymouth, London, Topsham/Exeter and even Yarmouth.

The port books for Swansea, Neath and Bristol only contain data for coastal clearances, and Tenby and Milford were so dominated by the coastal export of culm as to render the inwards trade numerically insignificant. However, there is reason to suggest that inwards shipments, especially the bulk trade in Cheshire salt, was less affected by the rigours of privateering than trade with the south coast.[66] If data for Bridgwater, Bideford and Padstow are examined, a distinct peak in extra-regional voyages is shown in 1696. This was almost wholly the result of salt imported coastally from Liverpool and, to a much lesser extent, Chester.[67] Evidence also suggests that for regional ports below the Holms, Cheshire white and rock salt enjoyed a near monopoly of trade, greatly enhanced by the embargo on French supplies. By 1697, competition from restored overseas imports and Droitwich salt, which could be delivered more cheaply, substantially reduced coastal shipments from Liverpool.[68] With these factors in mind, Bideford and Bridgwater show some similarity to the wider sample of ports. In particular, extra-regional voyages peaked in 1699, representing over 14 per cent and 10 per cent of all voyages respectively. What is more, although trade with

Liverpool remained the single most important long-distance route, other centres, especially London and a ring of south-western ports from Falmouth to Exeter, assumed a far larger share of trade, notably so at Bideford.

The Bideford data also indicate that war may have been decisive in influencing the diversion of certain high-value coastal cargoes to overland routes.[69] Table 2.6 gives an account of tobacco traded domestically from the port between 1695 and 1704. In this, data from the half-years 1698, 1701 and 1704 have been used to provide an indication of the comparative levels of overland and coastal traffic if not a chronologically complete reconstruction of trade. The data show that in both 1695 and 1696 overland routes were preferred to coastal voyages: 72 per cent and 91 per cent of all tobacco moved in these years was taken by land carriage, mainly to Exeter and Plymouth. In 1695, 25,570 lb of tobacco was carried to Exeter, mostly on the account of John Smith, and eight wagon journeys accounted for the 19,578 lb dispatched by George Buck to Plymouth. In 1696, Smith, Buck, George Strange and John Wadland were responsible for 22,962 lb of tobacco sent to Exeter in ten overland consignments, whilst Smith merchanted two further tobacco entries 'per land carriage' to Penryn (3,590 lb) and Port Isaac (720 lb).[70] In 1697, however, only two overland entries, both merchanted by Smith, were recorded.

In 1695, 1696 and 1697 the tobacco trade was heavy. In contrast, trade was much reduced in 1698 and 1699. No overland entries were recorded in these years and it is likely that the south-coast ports were importing tobacco directly from overseas or from other coastal suppliers: Exeter, which was

Table 2.6

Domestic trade in tobacco (lb) from Bideford, 1695–1704

	Coastal			Overland				Overall total
	Extra–regional	Region	Total	Exeter	Plymouth	Other	Total	
1695	17,057	250	17,307	25,570	19,578	–	45,148	62,455
1696	–	3,098	3,098	22,962	–	4,310	27,272	30,370
1697	–	29,267	29,267	2,225	–		2,225	31,492
1698		*2,050*	*2,050*	–	–	–	–	*2,050*
1699	1,717	10,361	12,078	–	–	–	–	12,078
1700	1,628	16,216	17,844	16,476		3,000	19,476	37,320
1701		*2,189*	*2,189*					*2,189*
1702	–	8,280	8,280	–	–	–	–	8,280
1703	–	–	–	–	–	–	–	–
1704		*5,922*	*5,922*	–	–	–	–	*5,922*

Note: No data available for 1703; italic indicates incomplete (half-yearly) data.
Source: PRO E190 coastal port books.

effectively cut off from Bristol in 1695 and 1696, received 21,020 lb from Bristol via its outlier, Topsham, in 1698 and 53,094 lb in 1699. This would seem to confirm Hoon's assertion that tobacco, because of its high unit value, was dispatched overland 'in times of war because of the danger to goods carried by water', and that in more stable years the regional centre of tobacco importation, Bristol, assumed a much more extensive 'metropolitan' role.[71] None the less, the Bideford data show that in 1700 land carriage accounted for the bulk of tobacco traded (19,476 lb from a total 37,320 lb). In this case it was likely that the tobacco was destined for re-export and the elaborate record of carriage was required for the securing of drawbacks and debentures.[72] For the remainder of the sample, it appears that tobacco was a largely incidental trade and wholly coastal in operation. This again may have proceeded from Bristol re-asserting a wider hegemony in the trade, or it may have been that Bideford supplies were either re-exported or did not filter into the coastal trade. Data from the 1720s suggest that Bideford retained little more than 146,000 lb of tobacco per year, less than 18 per cent of the total quantity of legal imports.[73]

However, the distinct if variable influences imposed by war were underpinned by two constants: the Bristol trade and the link with the south Wales coal ports. These trades formed the economic heartbeats of the region. Figure 2.5 presents the number of coastal voyages from Bristol for five full years between 1695 and 1704 by month of shipment. The principal feature of the graph is the general stability of trade throughout the year. Even in the winter months when climatic conditions were likely to have been adverse, and when the break between port books may have had a deleterious effect upon recording practices, around 20 voyages per month were listed. Undoubtedly, occasional bad weather imposed temporary seasonal stoppage: in January and February 1695, for example, severe frost and intermittent heavy snow impeded trade from clearing Gloucester.[74] Similarly, in the winter of 1716–7, ice prevented the movement of Severn trows above Bewdley, whilst in the following summer low water levels were blamed for delays. In both cases, however, the Bristol iron merchant Graffin Prankard dismissed such reports as an excuse to explain away dilatory procedures on the part of his Shropshire correspondents.[75]

Despite these factors, figure 2.5 reveals distinct peaks in February and August: over 30 per cent of all voyages cleared Bristol in these months. These peaks were closely related to the great marketing high points of the regional calendar, the St Paul's and St James's fairs held on 25 January and 25 July respectively. The fairs were of crucial importance in governing the association between Bristol and its regional hinterland, not only in relation to coasting, but also in the settling of accounts, procuring credit, the securing of future business, and the cementing of commercial

Figure 2.5

Voyages clearing Bristol, by month of shipment, 1695–1701

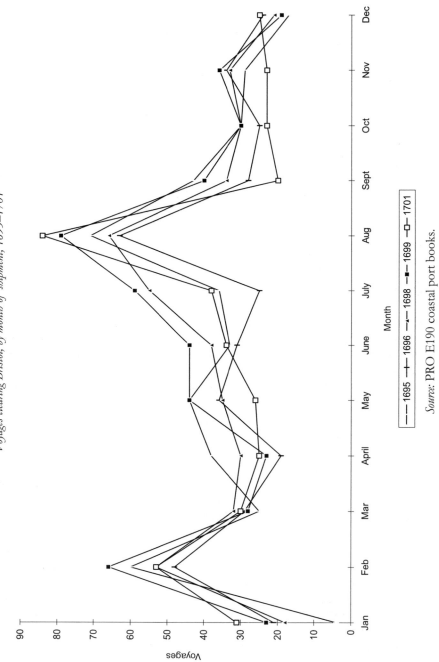

Source: PRO E190 coastal port books.

Figure 2.6

Voyages bound for Bristol, by month of shipment, sample year

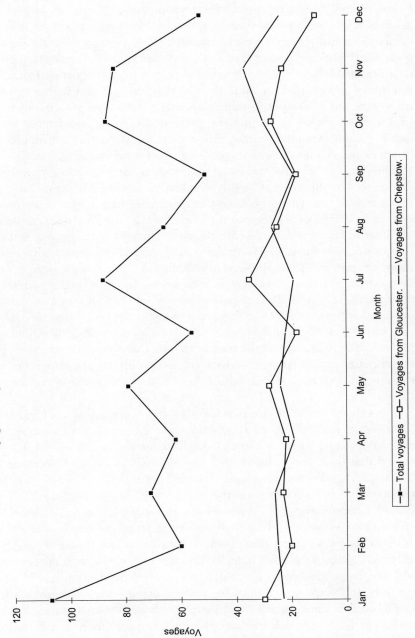

Month

Voyages

■— Total voyages □— Voyages from Gloucester. —— Voyages from Chepstow.

Source: PRO E190 coastal port books.

relationships.[76] It therefore appears that the increased commercial activity of February and August represents the ferrying back of cargoes acquired or assembled at the fairs. In reverse, inwards shipments appear to follow a similar, if slightly lagged pattern. In figure 2.6, voyages clearing regional ports for Bristol in the sample year are displayed by month. Even though the data depict the date when each vessel departed from its port of lading and not arrival at Bristol, they none the less demonstrate that higher levels of trade were recorded in both July and January, consonant with the demands of the fairs. This was despite the presumed effect of inclement winter weather upon extended journey times: even the short-haul traffic between Swansea and Bridgwater could take 'six or seaven weeks' in winter.[77]

The timing of this increased commercial activity closely followed commercial organisation at Bristol. Prankard's letters to Abraham Darby and the agents of the Coalbrookdale Company ring with urgent and frenetic appeals to deliver goods 'before the hurry of the faire'.[78] However, the pull of Bristol's fairs was felt most keenly at the Bristol Channel ports. Data for Bridgwater, Minehead, Bideford, Barnstaple and Milford suggest that coastal exports were synchronised to mesh with the fairs. In contrast, voyages from Gloucester and Chepstow were characterised by a far higher degree of uniformity, and it is likely that the supply of Bristol's weekly markets remained a more consistent commercial stimulus for both ports throughout the period. Indeed, an analysis of Severn vessels undertaking the Gloucester to Bristol run indicates that the conduct of trade depended rather more upon the impetus of the spring tide to allow navigation of the dangerous and circuitous lower Severn and Bristol Avon than the marketing concerns of Bristol.[79]

The other main cycle of trade involved the shipment of coal and culm. Most recent research, based largely upon the east-coast coal trade and the distinct seasonal patterns associated with coasting in the North Sea, has argued that trade was reduced 'to a virtual cessation . . . in December and January, and a mere trickle in November and February'.[80] However, very little attention has been focused on the Welsh coalfield and the supply of the Bristol Channel region.[81] With this in mind, tables 2.7–2.10 show the numbers of voyages trading coals and culm from the major south Wales ports in the period. The data reveal that strong seasonal and geographical influences defined the coal trade. As Hatcher has emphasised, the seasale of coal and culm was not so much dependent upon production levels, which, contrary to Nef's assertion, were neither erratic nor liable to seasonal suspension, as upon transport to the port and access to shipping.[82] Thus, trade was likely to peak in the optimum transport months of summer. Indeed, the tables demonstrate that the summer months were most prolific, with half of all recorded voyages undertaken between May and August.

Table 2.7

Voyages carrying coal and culm from Neath, 1701–1704

	1701	1702	1703	1704	Total	% Total
Jan	21	16	22	16	75	5
Feb	35	12	3	39	89	6
Mar	42	36	44	37	159	10
Apr	31	38	39	28	136	9
May	42	16	41	55	154	10
Jun	50	37	45	34	166	10
Jul	42	59	46	42	189	12
Aug	43	49	42	44	178	11
Sep	43	36	31	31	141	9
Oct	27	38	38	41	144	9
Nov	11	18	15	23	67	4
Dec	35	20	15	30	100	6
	422	375	381	420	1,598	

Table 2.8

Voyages carrying coal and culm from Swansea, 1701–1705

	1701	1702	1703	1704	Total	% Total
Jan	25	21	25	33	104	6
Feb	26	6	35	61	128	7
Mar	41	33	37	42	153	8
Apr	41	22	33	24	120	6
May	62	62	60	26	210	11
Jun	49	36	16	77	178	9
Jul	61	25	23	30	139	7
Aug	57	32	76	28	193	10
Sep	39	47	47	38	171	9
Oct	45	87	39	60	231	12
Nov	29	19	17	47	112	6
Dec	40	35	33	34	142	8
	515	425	441	500	1,881	

Note: Full years only.
Source: PRO E190 coastal port books.

However, this overall picture varied dramatically between ports. The number of coastal voyages at Swansea and Neath, close to the most developed regional coalfields, was remarkably stable throughout the year, with no significant or sustained fall-off in shipments during the traditionally slack months between November and February.[83] Voyages peaked between May

Table 2.9

Voyages carrying coal and culm from Tenby, 1695–1704

	1695	1696	1697	1698	1699	1700	1701	1702	1704	Total	% Total
Jan	0	0	1	1	2	1	1	3	2	11	1
Feb	3	3	3	0	1	6	7	2	5	30	2
Mar	7	13	18	5	7	11	16	20	18	115	6
Apr	27	24	21	6	16	25	38	49	31	237	12
May	42	67	65	57	30	35	53	14	56	419	22
Jun	52	13	58	39	45	51	55	45	36	394	20
Jul	52	52	28	33	28	51	52	44	34	374	19
Aug	28	20	12	14	14	28	18	26	19	179	9
Sep	10	13	9	14	14	21	9	3	6	99	5
Oct	6	0	5	0	4	4	1	8	6	34	2
Nov	2	3	0	2	7	2	2	4	2	24	1
Dec	1	0	0	0	1	1	2	1	2	8	0
	230	208	220	171	169	236	254	219	217	1,924	

Table 2.10

Voyages carrying coal and culm from Milford, 1696–1704

	1696	1697	1698	1699	1700	1702	1703	1704	Total	% Total
Jan	6	13	6	6	8	6	7	1	53	3
Feb	0	17	10	8	24	4	2	4	69	3
Mar	7	11	27	7	49	10	8	16	135	7
Apr	16	35	57	31	49	42	27	25	282	14
May	11	25	28	67	62	12	36	11	252	12
Jun	16	30	59	61	66	23	15	20	290	14
Jul	17	26	66	58	41	13	21	18	260	13
Aug	17	21	54	40	51	45	9	41	278	14
Sep	32	9	30	39	44	11	7	10	182	9
Oct	9	18	6	31	23	21	23	18	149	7
Nov	2	6	7	10	4	13	4	9	55	3
Dec	5	6	7	6	5	4	6	5	44	2
	138	217	357	364	426	204	165	178	2,049	

Note: Full years only.

Source: PRO E190 coastal port books.

and October, but this period only accounted for around two-thirds of mineral shipments at both ports. The evidence of the Glamorganshire ports thus indicates that coal shipments operated on a more consistent level than in the east-coast trade. This probably reflects the enclosed nature of the Bristol Channel, the effectiveness of short-haul coasting, and the development of both Swansea and Neath as efficient supply depots and harbours. It is also clear that the industrial concerns of the south-west, notably salt-boiling, demanded constant levels of fuel throughout the year and, moreover, the south Wales ports were in a more strategic position to meet these requirements.[84] In early 1697, for example, Hoare and Company was supplying the lucrative 'town trade'—coal for domestic and industrial use in Bridgwater and Taunton—as well as preparing to lay up 'a great stock' of Swansea coals, which were preferred by the Company's chapmen, slightly inferior Abbey (Neath) coals, and hard-to-acquire Pembrokeshire culm for wider trading and industrial purposes.[85]

In contrast, a different seasonal pattern governed the trade of the mainly culm-exporting ports of south-west Wales. Both Milford and Tenby were effectively closed as coal ports during the winter months, with the vast majority of colliers dispatched between April and October. The seasonal constriction of trade stemmed from the comparatively poor facilities of both ports and the relatively limited development of the Pembrokeshire hinterland.[86] Despite the natural advantages of its site as an area of protected anchorage, Milford did not develop an extensive harbour infrastructure until the later eighteenth century. What is more, its staple trade, long-distance, open sea coasting around Land's End to the south coast of Cornwall and Devon, suffered in adverse winter weather conditions: between 1695 and 1704 all such voyages were compressed into the spring and summer months. At Tenby, the exposed strand site at Saundersfoot offered very little shelter to coasters in even optimum conditions. Moreover, both ports suffered from the poorly capitalised, rural nature of Pembrokeshire mining. This factor, together with the problems of a poorly maintained system of inland transport, may have also restricted the output of culm and the movement of accumulated stocks in winter months.[87]

We began the chapter in the company of Alexander Pope, whose 'thin body' could not bear the dubious charms of the Bristol Hotwell and whose effete sensibilities were equally affronted by the ascendancy of Bristol's commercial class over polite culture.[88] Yet if Bristol was a commercial Gomorrah, Pope, like many visitors, found the quays, backs and business quarter, indeed the whole milieu of trading, compelling. This chapter has sought to reassess Bristol's trade by affirming the central importance of coasting to the economic articulation of the city and its domestic hinterland. As the analysis of the port book data has demonstrated, Bristol was the focal point of an extensive coastal and river network. The city's fairs imposed distinct seasonal patterns on trade, and its industrial and commercial contacts and growing population encouraged a regular and consistent trade with the region and beyond. Far from being an *ad hoc* aside to Bristol's main overseas and transoceanic commerce, coasting formed a highly organised system of trade that interlocked a fluid hierarchy of ports and localities into a cohesive whole. However, whilst the main patterns underpinning the seemingly erratic mass of voyages has been mapped out, apart from the most general of discussions, vessels' holds have not been filled. To comprehend the ramifications of regional trade, the full range of commodities from, quite literally, actors' goods to young fustic must be unpacked and examined with a critical eye.

Three

Cargoes, consignments and commodities

The regional trade in goods

Recent analysis has suggested that the comparative lack of development in Bristol's domestic hinterland effectively retarded the growth of the port in the later eighteenth century. To Morgan, the hinterland was the 'true Achilles' heel' in the comparative under-performance of the city.[1] In contrast, contemporary observers struck a more up-beat tone: even by the 1780s Bristol was still seen to exert an imperious, quasi-tributary control over the goods and trades of its region. In explaining this point, William Barrett, the Bristol antiquarian and one-time associate of Chatterton, was moved to as grandiose rhetoric as his ponderous style would allow. Bristol's merchants, he claimed, 'engross in a manner to themselves the whole trade of South Wales, and a great part of North Wales, as well as of the English counties bordering on those rivers [the Severn and the Wye]; and they have all the heavy goods from Birmingham and the North of England by trows, a very singular advantage to the foreign or home trade of the place'.[2] Certainly, this somewhat colourful commercial hagiography conveniently disregarded the fact that by the late eighteenth century Bristol's erstwhile prominence was very much on the wane and that much of the 'heavy goods' of the Midland hardware regions were finding markets through Liverpool.[3] Yet, Barrett was simply adding a further gloss, a more up-to-date, industrial slant to a century and more of favourable assessment. Writing in 1724, Defoe was equally emphatic in his praise: 'the Bristol merchants as they have a very great trade abroad, so they have always buyers at home, for their returns, and that such buyers that no cargo is too big for them'.[4]

However, describing these 'big' cargoes, let alone analysing them in any detail, has proved an arduous task for historians. Willan, for instance, regarded the coastal trade of Bristol as constituting a formless collection of miscellaneous goods which 'scarcely lends itself to statistical treatment'.[5] To Minchinton, 'the cargoes of goods sent coastwise . . . were so various to defy description', although he added with no little sense of frustration that merely listing the main trades 'does little to convey the immense range of articles sent out'.[6] Much of the problem has resided in an inability to deal effectively with the multiplicity of commodity descriptions. The 'hundreds of goods and diverse weights and measures' that Morgan identified in the overseas records translated directly into the domestic market.[7] With these factors in mind, it is hardly surprising that much work has limited itself to reconstructing impressionistic surveys of trade from simply sifting through the holds of randomly selected, yet supposedly 'typical' coasters. Whilst this has some illustrative worth, it scarcely conveys the range and extent of goods traded regionally. Moreover, such an approach has tended to fall into the more obvious trap of describing what might be termed as Bristol's classic commercial staples, the redistribution of nominally 'luxury' or 'consumerist' overseas wares and groceries, rather than presenting the totality of the city's trade.[8]

If the study of Bristol has been hampered by the profusion and complexity of data, analyses of the region, indeed internal trade in general, have suffered from a more one-dimensional approach. Here, there is a somewhat contradictory assumption that coastal and river trade, as opposed to overland carriage, was almost wholly concerned with the sort of high-bulk, low-value goods to which water transport conferred distinct, though variable, cost advantages. Such an impression, derived from Willan's overview of coasting and supported by the great metahistories of the mineral and agricultural trades,[9] has been augmented by recent work on transport networks and a range of commodities.[10] Certainly, a cursory examination of Bristol's hinterland would seem to suggest that for the more peripheralised economies, north Cornwall and south-west Wales for example, the trade in single, bulk staples, such as coal, copper ore, stone, and agricultural surpluses, formed the predominant commercial activity.[11] However, focusing on these shipments distorts the wider perspective. As historians of material culture have indicated, so-called 'lesser' items of goods—consumer semi-durables like small haberdashery wares, linen and table goods, pottery, tea equipage, and bedding—were traded and traded widely, percolating into the lives and households of relatively humble and culturally marginalised consumers.[12] Similarly, work on retail and distribution systems has stressed the multiform nature of trade:[13] many high-value commodities, the 'cloths, wools and manufactures' typically carried overland, found their way into the shops of mercers and grocers through long-distance water transport.[14]

This chapter seeks to combine the study of recognised bulk staples with the full range of goods traded within Bristol's hinterland. This is not without certain methodological problems. Computer analysis, for all its utility in liberating data for analysis, exposes further layers of complexity. For example, over 2,800 individual commodities and commodity terms are recorded in the regional datasets. In a tangential way it may follow from this that the carriage of bulk staples must be tempered with a realisation of the diversity of trade. Yet, it is simply not possible to indicate in hard-copy form the full variety of these goods. Similarly, it would take rather more than a lifetime, to paraphrase Morgan, and rather more than a book, to describe the traffic of each and every commodity and to untangle and convert the mass of regionally variant measures to recognised standards.[15] None the less, if the trade of the Bristol Channel is to be put into any coherent perspective, the range, importance and sophistication of the array of traded goods must be assessed. The following sections examine trade not only through easily categorised generic examples, but also with regard to the many overlooked goods that collectively gave form and substance to the coastal trade of the region.

Disaggregating diverse cargoes: the range of traded goods

Despite problems inherent in dealing with large datasets and the profusion of commodity descriptions, it is possible to provide a quantitative impression of the extent of trade if a careful critique is applied to the number of commodities and commodity terms recorded.[16] In table 3.1, all cargoes recorded clearing and entering ports between 1695 and 1704 have been analysed according to the number and frequency of discrete commodities traded. This forms a numerical representation of the precise way in which trade was recorded at each port. In the first column, data have been ordered according to the number of commodities recorded per year. All obvious synonyms have been excluded. Undoubtedly, ontological problems exist in formally combining or omitting data on these grounds and for this reason every care has been taken to avoid misinterpretation through hindsight or the desire to be semantically over-precise. Thus, 'coal', 'smiths coal', 'stone coal', 'Tenby coals' and 'culm' have all been treated as distinct commodities as there is no clear way of distinguishing between different grades of the mineral and different forms of clerical procedure. However, where reasonably equivalent descriptions occur, as, for instance, in the terms 'Newfoundland cod fish', 'Newland cod fish', and 'Newfoundland cod English taken and made', the commodity list has been duly amended. Although this concern may appear excessively fastidious, it is designed to avoid the problems of aggregating commodities where seemingly insignificant descriptors—between 'chairs'

Table 3.1

The trade in goods, annual averages, 1695–1704

Coastal exports

	Discrete Commodities	Commodities recorded > once	Commodity terms	Average Cargo Consignment per voyage
Bristol	445	240	5,367	10.89
Gloucester	218	135	2,475	7.38
Cardiff	51	24	234	7.09
Carmarthen	61	20	147	5.14
Bridgwater	125	51	428	4.79
Minehead	91	51	366	3.01
Bideford	64	21	150	2.86
Barnstaple	58	14	129	2.79
Milford	89	50	895	2.04
St Ives	16	10	85	1.99
Padstow	15	5	47	1.71
Ilfracombe	28	6	72	1.66
Tenby	33	15	302	1.62
Swansea	70	24	765	1.55
Mount's Bay	11	3	5	1.26
Neath	29	12	467	1.16
Chepstow	23	17	376	1.16
South Burry	4	1	15	1.15
Llanelli	6	1	81	1.05
Cardigan	12	9	110	1.19
Aberdovey	2	1	5	1
Liverpool	191	89	1,181	3.86

Coastal imports

	Discrete Commodities	Commodities recorded > once	Commodity terms	Average Cargo Consignment per voyage
Milford	128	69	417	7.87
Gloucester	226	124	1,985	6.51
Tenby	54	23	89	6.14
Carmarthen	86	51	280	5.89
Bridgwater	191	110	1,172	3.54
St Ives	65	35	166	3.33
Minehead	166	101	1,023	2.98
Padstow	70	40	258	2.11
Bideford	82	43	405	1.84
Ilfracombe	90	38	241	1.82
Barnstaple	81	35	458	1.75
Mount's Bay	10	5	25	1.69
Chepstow	24	11	87	1.34
Cardigan	5	4	24	1.5
Aberdovey	15	7	22	1.67
Liverpool	218	108	1,112	5.57

Source: PRO E190 coastal port books.

and 'green chairs', for example—may have conferred subtle yet perceptibly different meanings. A further revision has been to exclude commodities that occurred only once in any given year, thus eliminating goods which may have assumed a numerical importance far greater than their commercial status. The final two columns list the total number of commodity terms and the average size of each consignment of goods per voyage.

These methodologies have enabled an effective assessment of trading levels to be abstracted from the sprawl of commodities recorded in the port books. Firstly, the diversity of trade is emphasised: not only were many goods recorded frequently, but they were also listed for a surprisingly large number of ports. The most important regional centre in terms of the number of both discrete commodities and regularly traded goods was Bristol. Given the city's role in distributing regional and overseas goods, this observation is perhaps unremarkable. Yet, the variety of traded goods was not wholly limited to Bristol: Minehead dispatched such items as books, brandy, dowlas, dunsters, kelp, ox bows, red herrings, Spanish wine, serges and tobacco, whilst Milford was plying ale, beeswax, cheese, flannel, honey, leather, rabbit skins, oysters and stockings. This was in addition to the bulk staples, agricultural goods and culm, traditionally associated with these ports.

In contrast, the smaller creeks had rather more limited trades. For example, the Cornish ports recorded low numbers of discrete commodities and, more obviously, commodity terms occurring more than once. However, at Carmarthen and Cardiff, the extent of both ports' agricultural locale overrode the paucity of recorded coastal exports. Data for these ports reveal a wider range of commodities than at the much larger and more developed Glamorganshire coal ports, although the manufacturing and industrial infrastructure of Swansea was also reflected in the relatively high number of commodities recorded. At Bridgwater, Minehead and Milford, access to large local and extra-regional hinterlands and an intermittent overseas trade bolstered the overall representation of each port. Milford, in particular, benefited from its favourable location and safe natural harbour. A surprisingly consistent entrepôt trade in foreign wares dumped at Milford prior to reshipping to Bristol, Exeter, Plymouth and London ensured that commerce remained more diverse than the coal-dominated exports of nearby Tenby. At Barnstaple, Bideford and Chepstow, deficiencies in recording practices account for the low number of commodities listed.

The pronounced hierarchy of regional centres found in coastal exports is less pronounced in terms of the number of goods traded inwards, although crucially, data for Bristol are lacking. Gloucester was the most prominent port, certainly with regard to frequently-occurring commodities and the total number of commodity terms recorded. Milford, Bridgwater and Minehead were also well represented, largely due to cargoes dispatched from Bristol and, for the Somerset ports, Gloucester. For the same reason, the trade of the other ports of south-west England appears relatively extensive. Apart from the creeks at the greatest distance from Bristol—Mount's Bay, Cardigan and Aberdovey—only Chepstow appears to have had a significantly low level of coastal imports. This again may demonstrate erratic recording, rather than depressed trade: Andrews affirms from other sources that the port was commercially buoyant at this time.[17]

The data also reveal the importance of Bristol and Gloucester as the major regional entrepôts. In terms of traded commodities, no other centre in the region can be seen to match the size or diversity of Bristol's trade. The inwards trade of all regional ports relied heavily upon extensive, multi-value cargoes emanating from Bristol. A comparison with the coastal trade of Liverpool emphasises these points. Whilst both Bristol and Liverpool recorded high numbers of voyages clearing outwards, Liverpool does not appear to match the 'metropolitan' role of Bristol within its coastal region of the north-west of England and north Wales. In spite of Liverpool's growing importance in the overseas trades and the development of its immediate hinterland in the period, the number of goods it distributed coastally was markedly low, inferior not only to Bristol, but also to Gloucester.[18] This position is somewhat corrected when goods imported coastwise are examined. Here, Liverpool absorbed raw materials, producer goods and agricultural staples from its littoral hinterland for both local and overseas consumption. None the less, in terms of the number of commodities recorded, trade was still secondary to Gloucester and roughly comparable to Bridgwater and Minehead. Given the more humble trading parameters of the Somerset ports, this may indicate that, in contrast to Bristol, Liverpool was more successfully challenged in the control of the trade of its domestic hinterland.[19] Although dwarfed by Liverpool's later expansion, both Lancaster and the old head port, Chester, remained considerable maritime centres throughout the period.[20]

The final column of table 3.1 provides an index of the average size of coastal cargoes shipped per voyage. The most striking aspect of the data is the importance of Bristol cargoes. Between 1695 and 1704, each shipment clearing Bristol carried an average of just under eleven commodities, a figure that obscures the occasional single-commodity shipment of coal or wool in returning Severn trows or pot clay and ochre dispatched to Chepstow. It is also apparent that Gloucester dealt with multifarious cargoes with between six and seven goods per voyage recorded at the port. However, the data also emphasise that large and complex cargoes were widespread. Although the figures for Cardiff and Tenby (inwards) are erratic, Milford, Carmarthen, Bridgwater and St Ives were also involved in relatively extensive cargoes. Undoubtedly, the dominance of a single trade or trades, such as earthenware, tobacco pipe clay and copper ore at Bideford and Barnstaple, fish at Ilfracombe, and coal and culm throughout the region, has depressed the representation of goods traded per shipment at many of the smaller ports. Similarly, the low representation of Llanelli, Cardigan and Aberdovey reveal a combination of single commodity voyages with, in the case of Llanelli especially, lax administrative procedures. In spite of this, the figures for the major Bristol Channel centres reveal that cargoes were not defined by single bulk shipments. Even at centres strongly identified with coal, coasting was often characterised by more diverse, if small-scale commodity trades.

Goods and ports: regional commodities and trades in profile

The summary examination of cargoes presented in table 3.1 represents a form of quantitative semantics. It provides sample pathways through data that have been dismissed in the past as either too plural to permit analysis or too uniform to warrant detailed investigation. However, these figures can only indicate the most general of patterns. If the nature and species of goods are to be uncovered, a more sophisticated analysis is required. To facilitate this, a classification system has been devised to group commodities according to eight generic categories. The 2,793 identifiable commodities and commodity terms recorded in the 255 port books used have been assigned to the following classes: agricultural goods; crafts and manufactures; extractive goods (including minerals and unworked stone); food and drink (including apothecary ware); metals and metalwares; fisheries; textiles; and wood. A further 24 commodity terms were excluded for taxonomic reasons such as ambivalent meaning or cross-class generality. This is outlined in more detail in appendix 3. Naturally, the classification system is not without certain methodological problems. It would be supremely crass to suppose that a simple division of commodities can reflect the nuances of all traded goods: by definition, any compression of analysis must impose a somewhat rigid editorial structure upon research and one that invokes other commodity-based metaphors involving sledgehammers and nuts. However, the system provides a flexible means to analyse trade in accordance with broadly defined modes of production and exchange without distorting the subtle matrix of regional trade.[21] In more vernacular terms, classification allows us to separate the wood from the trees, without losing sight of the walnut and the lignum vitae.[22]

Tables 3.2 and 3.3 indicate the number of voyages and the percentage of each class of commodity recorded per shipment at each port. The tables reveal a substantial degree of commercial reciprocity: the Bristol Channel was an integral commercial enclave and one port's coastal exports were often another's imports. To obviate potential areas of repetition, the following

Table 3.2a

Voyages clearing Bristol Channel ports by commodity class, sample year

	Voyages	Agric.	Crafts	Extract.	Food	Metals	Fisheries	Textiles	Wood
Bristol	491	271	394	184	413	313	116	259	150
Gloucester	332	226	260	199	237	153	8	200	200
Bridgwater	95	84	39	11	45	17	10	19	9
Minehead	127	58	29	16	34	8	48	42	2
Ilfracombe	43	0	3	7	1	0	37	0	1
Barnstaple	54	6	23	26	14	3	7	9	4
Bideford	72	16	35	24	16	6	19	7	2
Padstow	28	0	2	26	0	13	1	2	0
St Ives	43	2	8	39	1	14	8	0	0
Mount's Bay	4	1	1	2	0	3	2	0	0
Milford	452	101	25	364	63	15	22	16	3
Carmarthen	29	25	7	2	10	5	1	2	2
Tenby	176	39	7	171	12	2	6	11	0
Llanelli	81	0	0	79	1	1	0	0	0
South Burry	13	1	0	13	0	0	0	0	0
Swansea	531	102	36	516	7	20	3	14	14
Neath	437	16	7	422	2	9	0	0	3
Cardiff	31	31	28	8	6	6	4	7	1
Chepstow	345	270	6	19	0	94	0	0	1
Liverpool	306	111	82	197	93	45	11	37	26

Table 3.2b

Percentage of voyages clearing Bristol Channel ports by commodity class, sample year

	Voyages	Agric.	Crafts	Extract.	Food	Metals	Fisheries	Textiles	Wood
Bristol	491	55	80	38	84	64	24	53	31
Gloucester	332	68	78	60	71	46	2	60	60
Bridgwater	95	88	41	12	47	18	11	20	10
Minehead	127	46	23	13	27	6	38	33	2
Ilfracombe	43	0	7	16	2	0	86	0	2
Barnstaple	54	11	43	48	26	6	13	17	7
Bideford	72	22	49	33	22	8	26	10	3
Padstow	28	0	7	93	0	46	4	7	0
St Ives	43	5	19	91	2	33	19	0	0
Mount's Bay	4	25	25	50	0	75	50	0	0
Milford	452	22	6	81	14	3	5	4	1
Carmarthen	29	86	24	7	35	17	3	7	7
Tenby	176	22	4	97	7	1	3	6	0
Llanelli	81	0	0	98	1	1	0	0	0
South Burry	13	8	0	100	0	0	0	0	0
Swansea	531	19	7	97	1	4	1	3	3
Neath	437	4	2	97	1	2	0	0	1
Cardiff	31	100	90	26	19	19	13	23	3
Chepstow	345	78	2	6	0	27	0	0	0
Liverpool	306	36	27	64	30	15	4	12	9

Source: PRO E190 coastal port books.

Table 3.3a

Voyages entering Bristol Channel ports by commodity class, sample year

	Voyages	Agric.	Crafts	Extract.	Food	Metals	Fisheries	Textiles	Wood
Gloucester	294	148	183	105	186	152	70	99	68
Bridgwater	331	118	74	282	47	57	19	46	45
Minehead	349	82	91	260	59	48	7	38	56
Ilfracombe	132	19	17	93	14	3	10	5	19
Barnstaple	266	45	29	233	30	15	1	10	7
Bideford	225	31	24	185	22	11	0	10	9
Padstow	129	16	11	121	8	8	2	6	3
St Ives	51	7	15	45	5	5	1	2	9
Mount's Bay	13	1	1	7	0	0	0	0	8
Milford	54	22	27	17	17	18	5	21	22
Carmarthen	44	8	25	24	16	16	9	13	9
Tenby	10	5	6	2	7	6	0	6	4
Chepstow	65	6	4	39	13	10	0	0	0
Liverpool	203	135	46	36	86	45	22	27	31

Table 3.3b

Percentage of voyages entering Bristol Channel ports by commodity class, sample year

	Voyages	Agric.	Crafts	Extract.	Food	Metals	Fisheries	Textiles	Wood
Gloucester	294	50	62	36	63	52	24	34	23
Bridgwater	331	36	22	85	14	17	6	14	14
Minehead	349	23	26	74	17	14	2	11	16
Ilfracombe	132	14	13	71	11	2	8	4	14
Barnstaple	266	17	11	88	11	6	0	4	3
Bideford	225	14	11	82	10	5	0	4	4
Padstow	129	12	9	94	6	6	2	5	2
St Ives	51	14	29	88	10	10	2	4	18
Mount's Bay	13	8	8	54	0	0	0	0	62
Milford	54	41	50	32	32	33	9	39	41
Carmarthen	44	18	57	55	36	36	21	30	21
Tenby	10	50	60	20	70	60	0	60	40
Chepstow	65	10	6	60	20	15	0	0	0
Liverpool	203	67	23	18	42	22	11	13	15

Source: PRO E190 coastal port books.

discussion focuses upon the analysis of coastal exports in preference to the more imperfect sample of inwards shipments. Such an approach has sought to construct a composite of trade which remains faithful to the literal record of the port books, without stitching together disparate fragments of data.

A number of broad patterns can be deduced from the tables. Firstly, it is clear that agricultural and extractive goods were key factors in the overall profile of trade. The importance of south Wales coal, discussed in the following sections, ensured that the profile of extractive goods was consistently high at regional ports. In addition, a variety of ores, quarried and partially worked stone, and salt remained important items of trade throughout the period. Similarly, agricultural goods were represented in over half of all shipments clearing Bristol, Gloucester, Bridgwater, Carmarthen, Cardiff and Chepstow. These ports were linked to major agrarian areas, orcharding and good pasturage, or, as in the case of Bristol and Gloucester, provided a commercial interface between differing zones of production. At Bristol, the figures are supplemented by quantities of overseas goods, such as cotton wool, Irish wool and hides, and Spanish merino wool.[23] Such items also formed a rather smaller share of goods traded at Bideford, Minehead, Milford and Bridgwater, the minor overseas ports of the region. The principal constituent of this class, grain, cereals and farinaceous goods, is analysed in table 3.4. The table represents total quantities of grain and malt traded in the sample year converted to the standard Winchester bushel.[24] Grain played a singularly important role in trade, appearing in over half the shipments clearing Gloucester, Chepstow, Bridgwater, Carmarthen, Cardiff and Cardigan, and forming a significant part of the total quantity of goods dispatched from Milford, Minehead and Bideford. At Cardiff, where recorded trade was dominated by the market demands of Bristol, grain featured in every shipment. Similarly, barley and wheat, destined mainly for north-west Wales and the north-west of England, were the principal cargo items shipped from Cardigan, Milford and Carmarthen. However, exports of agricultural goods were virtually absent from the ports serving the littoral strip of north Cornwall, an area largely dominated by industrial activity and subsistence farming. Mount's Bay, Padstow and St Ives, and even Barnstaple and Ilfracombe, were net importers of agricultural goods in this period. Only Bideford maintained a significant and continuous outwards trade, exporting supplies of wheat and barley from the improved arable grounds south and west of the Torridge.[25]

The main feature of table 3.4 is the centrality of Bristol. The city took over half the cereal crops traded regionally in the sample year—82 per cent if shipments beyond the region are discounted. Much of this came via Chepstow, Cardiff and Gloucester. These ports gave access to the corn-livestock economies of the Monmouthshire borders and the central Herefordshire plain; the mixed arable and pasturage grounds of the Vale of Glamorgan and the Severnside lowlands; the market garden areas of the Vale of Evesham; and the wheat and barley grounds of the Midland plain. To this extent, Bristol acted as a classic metropolitan centre, 'parasitic' almost upon

Table 3.4a

Coastal exports of grain and cereal crops (bushels) by destination, sample year

From	Bristol	Severn	Somerset	N. Devon	Cornwall	Pemb./Carm.	Swansea/Neath	Cardiff	Wye	Extra-regional	Unknown	Total
Gloucester	67,396	–	1,762	560	–	480	–	2,340	24	–	209	72,771
Chepstow	70,418	678	160	400	–	–	–	–	–	–	–	71,656
Milford	3,036	1,602	–	3,036	–	1,100	350	–	–	48,290	200	57,614
Bridgwater	7,561	3,130	2,114	2,847	–	420	427	–	745	18,185	–	35,429
Carmarthen	918	–	–	–	–	420	–	–	300	17,507	580	19,305
Minehead	8,793	6,456	330	200	–	46	114	–	13	900	500	17,352
Cardiff	14,137	–	–	–	–	–	–	–	–	–	–	14,137
Bideford	2,243	–	–	–	–	180	–	–	–	9,493	–	11,916
Bristol	–	4,353	–	–	–	10	20	104	60	1,905	–	6,452
Tenby	673	–	–	144	–	–	450	–	–	2,320	380	3,967
St Ives	–	–	–	970	–	–	–	–	–	–	–	970
Barnstaple	235	300	–	–	–	–	–	–	–	–	–	535
Swansea	150	–	–	10	10	–	–	–	–	32	10	212
Neath	30	–	–	–	30	–	–	–	–	–	–	60
Total	175,589	16,519	4,366	8,167	40	2,236	1,361	2,444	1,142	98,632	1,879	312,374

Table 3.4b

Shipments of grain and cereal crops by destination, sample year

From	Bristol	Severn	Somerset	N. Devon	Cornwall	Pemb./Carm.	Swansea/Neath	Cardiff	Wye	Extra-regional	Unknown	Total
Gloucester	189	–	6	1	–	1	–	3	1	–	2	203
Chepstow	232	2	1	1	–	–	–	–	–	–	–	236
Milford	11	1	–	16	–	1	1	–	–	63	1	94
Bridgwater	27	14	2	3	–	2	7	–	2	18	–	75
Carmarthen	5	–	–	–	–	–	–	–	1	14	2	22
Minehead	36	8	1	1	–	2	2	–	1	1	1	53
Cardiff	31	–	–	–	–	–	–	–	–	–	–	31
Bideford	5	–	–	–	–	1	–	–	–	8	–	14
Bristol	–	30	–	–	–	1	1	2	2	6	–	42
Tenby	3	–	–	3	–	–	1	–	–	2	1	10
St Ives	–	–	–	1	–	–	–	–	–	–	–	1
Barnstaple	1	1	–	–	–	–	–	–	–	–	–	2
Swansea	1	–	–	1	1	–	–	–	–	1	1	5
Neath	1	–	–	–	1	–	–	–	–	–	–	2
Total	542	56	10	27	2	8	12	5	7	113	8	790

Source: PRO E190 coastal port books.

its rural hinterland.[26] None the less, the general centripetal effect that Bristol exerted upon regional trade masked a more specialised demand for grain and cereals. Figure 3.1 indicates the level of coastal exports from Gloucester to Bristol between 1680 and 1728, distinguishing between malt and field grains. The data demonstrate that the most important commodity was malt: only in 1713 and the later years of the period, where under-recording may have been an issue, did the trade in other cereals, notably wheat, overreach the total exports of malt. Indeed, the heavy trade in the war years of 1691–2, when Bristol may have availed itself of its unique position in relation to the control of Severn grain, was largely due to increased malt shipments.[27] It is likely that malt production in these years was diverted into Bristol's distilling and brewery interests bolstered by the impositions of coastal embargo and the requirements of Bristol-based shipping convoys.[28] In general, boats of Worcester, Bewdley and Shrewsbury dominated the carrying trade. As the most important urban centres on the river and the main ports undertaking the through-trade to Bristol, they served as collection points for the agrarian economies of the Severn valley. However, from around 1713, trade in Worcester boats declined dramatically, with the shortfall taken up by operators from Tewkesbury and Gloucester, ports which tended to specialise in tran-shipment of up-river goods.

Secondly, both the classes of food and drink and crafts and manufactures were concentrated on the main centres of population and production. Unsurprisingly, Bristol also dominated these trades. By the late seventeenth century the city's range of industrial and manufacturing functions was unsurpassed in the region: Bristol possessed important processing, distilling, refining and distributive industries that fed directly into coastal trade. Similarly, its control over imported foodstuffs was represented in the large percentage share of the class in all measures of regional trade. Over 84 per cent of voyages clearing the port in 1699 carried something from a very extensive range of victuals: tobacco, wine, sugar, brandy, rum, spirits, spices, drugs and apothecary wares were only the most conspicuous of these goods. Yet Bristol did not wholly monopolise trade. Bideford and Barnstaple were important local entrepôts for tobacco, and Bridgwater and Minehead maintained a minor trade in wine and grocery wares. In comparison, the dominance of salt and cheese as primary staples at Liverpool imposed rather different commercial patterns. Whilst the port was undoubtedly a major centre for overseas trade in the north-west, and thus performed a similar redistributive function within its hinterland, it dealt with a significantly lesser share of these commodities than Bristol. Items of food and drink were present in less than a third of all coastal shipments clearing Liverpool in 1699, being significantly outweighed by the high representation of the class among coastal imports.

Figure 3.1

Grain (bushels) exported coastally from Gloucester to Bristol, 1680–1728

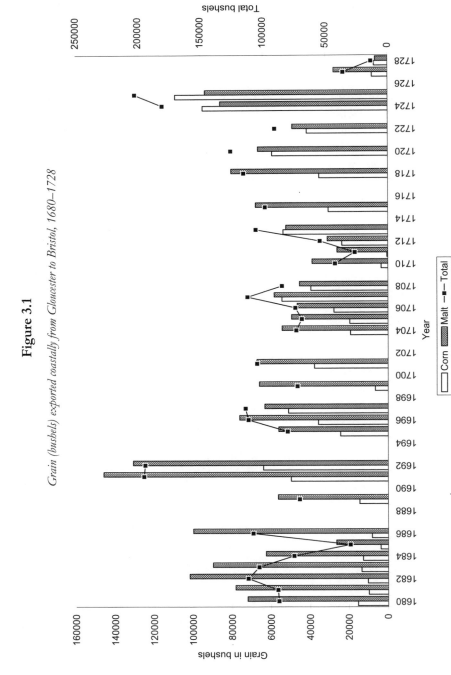

Source: Cox, Hussey and Milne, eds, *Gloucester port books database.*

The trade in metals again reveals the importance of the axis between Bristol and Gloucester. At Gloucester, 152 inwards shipments carried the class, much of which was derived from Bristol's metallurgical industries and overseas links, although the importance of Chepstow in shipping brass and latten ware from Redbrook as well as iron from Brockweir and Dean should not be underestimated.[29] In turn, a rather similar number of shipments, 153, carried metalwares via Gloucester with Bristol the main, although not the exclusive focus. Nevertheless, the Bristol–Gloucester nexus hides complex cross-regional associations involving diverse and interlinked patterns of metal production, use and working. Thus, the Cornish ports were heavily involved in the shipment of copper and tin; lead, copper and litharge were beginning to be worked in the Swansea valley and the Vale of Neath; and Newport and Caerleon handled much of the output of the Pontypool forges.

Much the same situation is revealed in the movement of textiles and crafts and manufactures, with Bristol and Gloucester forming the main commercial nodes. At Gloucester over three-quarters of coastal clearances carried manufactured goods. Bewdley, the port serving Birmingham and the adjacent hardware areas, and Worcester and Shrewsbury, the most developed corporate towns and commercial and cultural entrepôts on the river, figured strongly in this trade.[30] In addition, the larger ports of the south-west were also prominent. Earthenware constituted the bulk of the coastal exports of both Bideford and Barnstaple,[31] and at Cardiff the local specialism of stocking-knitting and a rather more sporadic trade in apparel and 'recycled' craft wares remained a locally important component of coastal shipments.[32]

Because of the diversity of the Severn valley hinterland, Gloucester also traded a variety of fine and rough cloths and upholstery fabrics, as well as textile products such as yarn. Shrewsbury boats dominated the trade in linen, woollen, mercery, drapery and haberdashery goods from the north-west of England and north and mid-Wales, whilst Bewdley and Worcester craft picked up a range of local cloths, particularly Kidderminster goods and stuffs and, with less frequency, Worcester broad cloth.[33] Bristol's importance lay largely in its entrepôt functions and in the distribution of overseas textiles, such as French canvas and German oznabriggs. Bridgwater and Minehead were the only other centres of note. Both traded regional cloths—bays, dunsters, blues, serge and penistones—which did not pass south through Totnes and Exeter, the principal finishing and distribution centres of the peninsula.[34] Elsewhere, apart from the odd cargo of Welsh frieze, the trade in textiles was minimal and largely dominated by composite shipments clearing from Bristol.

The extent and direction of trade in these classes of good are discussed more fully in the following section. However, the trade in wood and fishery goods, though far less extensive, poses greater questions. Firstly, whilst the region contained much commercially exploitable forest, the Wyre, Dean, Exmoor and west Glamorgan for example, the trade in timber and bulk wood was surprisingly limited. Wood was only recorded at any significant level at Gloucester, where it generally formed a part of larger coquet-bearing cargoes, or at Bristol, where overseas imports of Baltic softwoods and specialist dyewoods originating in the Americas formed the major items of trade. Domestic wood, it appears, was traded either as a non-customable good at most ports, or was regarded as simply ballast. Either way, it was habitually not recorded, an absence with severe implications for the trade in high-quality walnut and elm timber through Chepstow.[35]

Similarly, given the region's close association with herring and pilchard fishing and with the Irish and Newfoundland fisheries, the level of fishery goods recorded is low. In part, this again reflects customs practice rather than levels of trade.[36] Data relating to Mount's Bay, St Ives and Padstow, where only coquets were recorded, contrasts with contemporary evidence stressing both the importance of the inshore fisheries to maritime development and, more specifically, the 'prodigious shoals' of herrings 'caught in great quantities' by regionally based fishing fleets.[37] The trade in herrings is summarised in table 3.5: importing centres have been grouped according to head port, and all measures converted to the standard herring barrel.[38] The table reveals that the principal letpass-recording ports, Ilfracombe, Minehead, Milford and to a lesser extent Bideford, undertook over 90 per cent of coastal exports.[39] Overall, Bristol took in just under half the quantity of herrings traded, with extra-regional centres, notably the ports of south Devon and Cornwall, accounting for a further quarter of trade by quantity.[40] Bristol also acted as a minor centre of re-export, a result of herring being repackaged in much smaller unit quantities within large coquet-bearing shipments. In the sample year, Bristol traded an average of only 15 barrels per shipment compared to the 171 that cleared Ilfracombe or the 152 exported from Bideford.

These low figures may also have been caused by another factor. It has been suggested that the inshore fishery was geared to the overseas market and therefore did not impinge significantly upon the coastal trade.[41] Indeed, much of the regional catch appears to have been either exported[42] or consumed by local landsale.[43] Similarly, although Barnstaple, Bideford and Bristol were leading centres in exploiting the Newfoundland Banks, the recorded trade in cod and other fish was also limited.[44] This may have been due to the fact that many Newfoundland cargoes were destined for the Iberian peninsula and the Straits, and direct imports were either re-exported or did not enter the coastal trade.[45] The correspondence of local merchants confirms the importance of the triangular trade that carried miscellaneous goods, ironware, salt and consumables to Newfoundland; dry and wet fish

Table 3.5a

Herrings (barrels) traded from regional ports by destination, sample year

	Bristol	Severn	Somerset	N. Devon	N. Corn.	Milford	Cardiff	Wye	Extra-regional	Unknown	Total
Ilfracombe	1,993	–	1,530	284	608	–	–	–	1,814	80	6,309
Minehead	3,230	320	402	410	–	101	0.45	10	–	–	4,473
Milford	762	–	–	–	–	–	–	–	285	8	1,054
Bideford	–	–	–	–	–	–	–	–	759	–	759
Bristol	–	410	–	–	–	–	30	35	2	–	477
Mount's Bay	–	–	–	–	–	–	–	–	250	–	250
Cardigan	–	–	–	–	–	–	–	–	–	225	225
Bridgwater	–	30	–	–	–	–	–	–	–	–	30
Swansea	–	2	–	–	–	–	–	–	–	21	23
Gloucester	9	–	–	–	–	–	–	–	–	–	9
Padstow	6	–	–	–	–	–	–	–	–	–	6
Tenby	4	–	–	–	–	–	–	–	–	–	4
Barnstaple	–	3	–	–	–	–	–	–	–	–	3
Total	6,004	765	1,932	694	608	101	30	45	3,110	334	13,621

Table 3.5b

Shipments of herrings traded from regional ports by destination, sample year

	Bristol	Severn	Somerset	N. Devon	N. Corn.	Milford	Cardiff	Wye	Extra-regional	Unknown	Total
Ilfracombe	16	–	6	3	3	–	–	–	8	1	37
Minehead	33	4	2	1	–	2	1	1	–	–	44
Milford	6	–	–	–	–	–	–	–	9	1	16
Bideford	–	–	–	–	–	–	–	–	5	–	5
Bristol	–	23	–	–	–	–	4	2	1	–	30
Mount's Bay	–	–	–	–	–	–	–	–	1	–	1
Cardigan	–	–	–	–	–	–	–	–	1	–	1
Bridgwater	–	1	–	–	–	–	–	–	–	–	1
Swansea	–	1	–	–	–	–	–	–	–	1	2
Gloucester	2	–	–	–	–	–	–	–	–	–	2
Padstow	1	–	–	–	–	–	–	–	–	–	1
Barnstaple	–	1	–	–	–	–	–	–	–	–	1
Tenby	1	–	–	–	–	–	–	–	–	–	1
Total	59	30	8	4	3	2	5	3	25	3	142

Source: PRO E190 coastal port books.

and associated fishery products to Iberia; and finally wine, spices and smaller quantities of wool, hops, iron and salt back to the domestic market.[46] Thus, although some cod shipments were retained, very little was recorded in the coastal port books: Bideford, the regional centre, shipped a mere 52 barrels of cod and other fish in 4 consignments in 1699, whilst Bristol traded 282 barrels of generic 'fish' in 25 shipments in the same year.[47] Undoubtedly, much of this represented the re-exportation of goods sent coastwise.

The coastal trade of Bristol

In terms of the range and value of goods, Bristol occupied a central position in regional trade. Attention has already been drawn to the city's dominance of the domestic redistribution of overseas goods, at least within the limited spatial boundaries of the region. Similarly, many studies, taking their cue from Minchinton's applied model of metropolitan influence, have expressed how regional economies were dependent upon Bristol in the acquisition of both the necessaries and luxuries of foreign commerce and a wide range of domestic goods. Such analyses have seen regional economies locked into a fundamentally one-sided cycle of trade, defined, if not physically governed, by Bristol.[48] In this model, the city acted as the main focus of consumption, sucking in agrarian surpluses, raw materials and the products of rural industry, and dispensing high-cost manufactured and processed goods and overseas wares. Certainly, many goods sent up to Bristol conformed to this pattern.[49] Thus, throughout the period, kelp, soap and wood ashes, pot clay, tobacco pipe clay, timberstuff, agricultural goods and by-products such as cider and perry, unworked and partially finished manufactures, copper and lead ore, and salt were all major items shipped in large quantities to the city.

However, this very broad assessment of trade is challenged when the full profile of Bristol's coastal exports is examined. In table 3.6, coastal voyages from Bristol are expressed according to the destination and species of cargo. An indication is also given of the percentage number of voyages carrying each commodity class, and the relative importance of each destination in terms of the type of commodity traded. From these data, the apparent commercial polarisation between centre and periphery is blurred. By the early eighteenth century, Bristol was redistributing the very agricultural staples normally associated with regional supply. For example, domestic, Irish and Spanish wool for the cloth industry of the south-west and Midlands; pot clay and various metal ores, such as magnis and callamy; cheese; skins; hemp; flax; and clover and garden seeds were all regularly transported from Bristol. Of course, much of this consisted of goods transhipped from regional ports, although a proportion of agricultural goods came overland from Bristol's immediate rural environs.[50] Of the 271 voyages carrying agricultural goods

Table 3.6

Voyages clearing Bristol, by commodity class, by destination, sample year

To	Agricultural			Craft			Extractive			Food			Metal			Fishery			Textile			Wood			Voyages
	V	%V	%C	V	%V	%C	V	%V	%C	V	%V	%C	V	%V	%C	V	%V	%C	V	%V	%C	V	%V	%C	
Severn	116	50	43	162	70	41	87	38	47	184	80	45	112	48	36	66	29	57	98	42	38	51	22	34	231
Somerset	22	44	8	48	96	12	14	28	8	48	96	12	47	94	15	8	16	7	36	72	14	32	64	21	50
North Devon	22	88	8	24	96	6	12	48	7	24	96	6	22	88	7	0	0	0	22	88	9	10	40	7	25
North Cornwall	6	40	2	15	100	4	5	33	3	15	100	4	15	100	5	0	0	0	8	53	3	7	47	5	15
Pemb./Carm.	14	48	5	29	100	7	6	21	3	27	93	7	24	83	8	10	34	9	25	86	10	12	41	8	29
Swansea/Neath	8	42	3	19	100	5	7	37	4	18	95	4	11	58	4	2	11	2	18	95	7	7	37	5	19
Cardiff	14	48	5	26	90	7	12	41	7	26	90	6	20	69	6	8	28	7	22	76	9	5	17	3	29
Wye	16	64	6	15	60	4	11	44	6	18	72	4	11	44	4	7	28	6	12	48	5	5	20	3	25
Extra regional	46	78	17	50	85	13	25	42	14	47	80	11	46	78	15	14	24	12	14	24	5	20	34	13	59
Unknown	7	78	3	6	67	2	5	56	3	6	67	1	5	56	2	1	11	1	1	11	0	1	11	1	9
Total	271			394			184			413			313			116			256			150			491

Notes:

V = Voyages.

%V = Percentage number of voyages clearing Bristol by commodity class by destination.

%C = Voyages clearing Bristol by commodity class by destination, as % of all voyages with each class.

Source: PRO E190 coastal port books.

from Bristol in 1699, 43 per cent were dispatched to Gloucester, and thence to the major urban markets and dispersal centres of Worcester, Bewdley and Shrewsbury. The category represented over half the total number of shipments imported coastally by these river ports. Even shipments to Tewkesbury and Evesham, the ports through which much of the output of Midland agriculture was exported coastwise, were not inconsiderable. Agricultural goods also occupied an equally important role in Bristol's trade with the wider region. The class was a central component of most cargoes traded to north Devon, Chepstow, the south-coast ports and, in particular, London. In 1699 alone, Bristol shipped over 1,200 hogsheads of casked and bottled cider to London, as well as 4,900 bushels of apples and substantial consignments of butter, cheese, beeswax, hides and pelts.

A similar relationship is revealed in the trade in extractive goods. Apart from a small-scale and wholly local coal industry at Kingswood, Bristol had no direct access to mineral deposits.[51] Some coal percolated through to the coastal trade, although only around an average of 600 tons was shipped each year, some of which no doubt represented supplies received from south Wales. Most other extractive goods were domestic items such as pot clay, pipe clay, lead ore, stone, and quarried tile sourced from other areas. Thus, of the 253 tons of tobacco pipe clay imported from north Devon in 1699, Bristol re-shipped 17 tons mostly in the form of small consignments in mixed cargoes.[52] Similarly, whilst Bristol received some 581.25 tons of pot clay via Gloucester in 1699, principally for its glass, soap, sugar and metal industries, it exported 227 tons in 16 coastal shipments, the bulk of which (174 tons) was carried in 10 shipments to London. By the end of the period, Bristol was receiving over 2,000 tons of pot clay via Gloucester, around a fifth of which was re-exported coastally to ports including the major glass-producing centres of London and Newcastle.[53]

Bristol also combined the trade in large-scale indigenous manufacture with the output of more petty, semi-urban crafts such as joinery wares, pottery and tobacco pipes.[54] In addition, Bristol supplied the type of product largely only available through the metropolis: luxury goods, consumer novelties and overseas commodities like looking glasses; foreign wares; bespoke, crafted furniture; glass vials; and fine ceramics all filtered into the city's coastal trade. Over 70 per cent of shipments to Severn ports contained an element of Bristol-crafted or assembled manufactures, whilst the class appeared in virtually all cargoes discharging for ports below the Holms and to extra-regional locations. Two commodities, soap and glass, were central to Bristol's manufacturing and commercial base. Soap-boiling was a long-established industry protected by incorporation and borough legislation.[55] Small, regular consignments of Bristol soap and candles, supplemented by Spanish Castile and Irish hard white soap, fed into the coastal trade, although in terms of weight, soap was not a bulk commodity. Between 1695 and 1701, less than 50 tons were traded each year, a factor which speaks volumes of contemporary demand and indeed hygiene.[56] In comparison, Bristol's expanding glass industry occupied a major role in the gearing of the economy of both the city and the region.[57] As well as receiving large quantities of pot clay via Gloucester, Bristol imported raw material in the form of soap ashes and kelp from the Somerset ports. In 1699, Bridgwater shipped over 300 tons of soapers' ashes for Bristol, whereas in 1699–1700 Minehead dispatched 57.25 tons.[58] This was supplemented by growing imports of overseas pearl ash and domestic sand. Humphrey Perrot's ailing Bristol glassworks, for example, was supplied with pot clay via Gloucester and sand from both the immediate locality and from more distant sources such as Newnham and the Isle of Wight. However, as sand was generally regarded as ballast, the large quantities of even these very specialist grades which required long-distance coastal shipment were not entered in the official port book record.[59]

None the less, an analysis of the glass trade indicates a distinct separation in the direction and type of glass traded coastwise. Bristol was largely concerned with glasswares, and, in particular, bottles, glasses, drinking vessels and vials. In 1699, for example, Bristol shipped over 15,300 dozen glass bottles, 40 per cent of which cleared to extra-regional centres.[60] Yet, as glass bottles were a widely available, low-cost commodity, they were often used as an *ad hoc* filler carried under letpass in coasters returning from Bristol. As a result, the officially recorded quantities of bottles are likely to underestimate seriously the full extent of trade.

In contrast, despite contemporary assessments of the utility of Bristol broad and window glass, very little was dispatched coastally. In 1699, only 40 shipments cleared Bristol. These were very small part-cargoes sent mainly to the south-coast ports, south-west Wales and north Devon. The marginal nature of this trade appears to be linked to the development of Stourbridge, the other major regional centre of production.[61] Stourbridge broad and window glass was generally traded through Bewdley and thence Gloucester. The commodity was carried in fairly large consignments on 51 voyages passing through Gloucester in 1699, 42 of which were bound for Bristol. Clearly, the Severn market, the key to Bristol's regional hegemony, was effectively closed to this commodity, although supply through overland routes cannot be entirely discounted. These patterns suggest complex commercial alignments, and, although it may be rather overstating the case to suggest a nascent 'cartellisation' of regional marketing,[62] the trade in glass and glass products emphasises two important considerations. Firstly, it is evident that, contrary to received historical wisdom, highly fragile commodities such as glass were transported and transported large distances by turbulent water carriage.[63] Secondly, the market penetration of Stourbridge glass demonstrates that the organisation and conduct of regional trade was not always wholly subject to the demands and capacity of Bristol.

Shipments from Bristol carrying metalwares were also less focused upon the Severn. In 1699, less than half the voyages clearing for Gloucester carried the commodity, and only 36 per cent of all shipments with metals were directed to the Severn ports. In terms of quantity, though, the reciprocal link between Bristol and Gloucester still formed the principal axis of regional trade. As Johnson and Hammersley have indicated, the integration of the iron industry ensured that trade between the centres was both substantial and diverse.[64] In table 3.7, the old assumption that the 'Severn was the principal highway of the iron industry' in the eighteenth century is subjected to fresh quantitative analysis.[65] Because customs officials freely combined types of the basic good, it has not been possible to separate the various grades of iron (pig, cast, rod, sow and bar iron, for example) from large-scale worked ironware (ironmongers' wares, furnaces, pots, kettles, pans, and iron guns) and the very small amounts of steel traded coastally.[66] Even so, the data present an important overview of this central trade for a period of almost 50 years.

Table 3.7 outlines the consistently high levels of iron and ironware exported coastally through Gloucester. Bristol was undoubtedly the major market: 85 per cent of all trade by quantity was destined for the city. The great majority of this (80 per cent) was carried in boats of Bewdley, the entrepôt for the Midland hardware regions. However, the increased output of Darby's works at Coalbrookdale from *c.*1708 steadily increased the activity of Shropshire and Ironbridge Gorge boats undertaking through-shipments to Bristol.[67] The early eighteenth century also witnessed the development of a steady trade with ports other than Bristol. In particular the metal-working districts around Redbrook and Brockweir, served by Chepstow and the river Wye, were important recipients of Midland iron. Similarly, large consignments of pig iron, often up to 40 tons per shipment, were dispatched to Newport and Caerleon. It is likely, although unfortunately speculative, that Hanbury's development of Pontypool accounted for the relatively brief expansion of this trade.[68] In contrast, iron remained an important, but subsidiary cargo item at Bridgwater, where trade throughout the period was dictated by demand for Droitwich white salt.[69]

In comparison, coastal imports of iron and ironware at Gloucester lagged behind exports for much of the period. Trade from Bristol, the main entrepôt of the region's supplies of both domestic and foreign iron and steel (mostly from Sweden and Spain), was prominent in the 1680s and early 1690s. Thereafter, trade slumped. Less than 36 tons cleared Bristol for Gloucester in 1695, and although coastal imports quickly recovered, trade

Table 3.7

Iron and ironwares (tons) traded to and from Gloucester, 1680–1728

	Coastal imports to Gloucester			Coastal exports from Gloucester		
	From Bristol	From other ports	Total	To Bristol	To other ports	Total
1680	253.18	81.13	334.31	570.45	206.57	777.02
1681	188.80	107.00	295.80	788.66	80.00	868.66
1682	333.71	136.64	470.35	805.61	44.00	849.61
1683	341.80	174.46	516.27	753.52	40.87	794.39
1684	566.02	244.00	810.02	675.79	33.00	708.79
1685	349.00	167.00	516.00	378.87	31.03	409.89
1686	482.35	226.06	708.41	627.84	79.11	706.95
1689	267.14	242.00	509.14	673.83	42.50	716.33
1691	211.27	352.00	563.27	743.29	27.25	770.54
1692	377.43	291.03	668.46	938.58	64.00	1,002.58
1695	35.18	89.90	125.08	425.40	72.58	497.97
1696	179.50	160.00	339.50	628.41	52.05	680.46
1697	128.23	202.98	331.20	647.06	141.73	788.78
1699	425.24	472.65	897.89	755.72	75.00	830.72
1701	237.85	371.48	609.32	663.80	69.35	733.15
1704	158.85	509.06	667.91	711.31	85.85	797.16
1705	210.41	647.40	857.81	843.00	394.60	1,237.60
1706	300.55	707.28	1,007.83	826.12	286.70	1,112.82
1707	237.25	541.93	779.18	760.41	354.58	1,114.98
1708	370.45	418.95	789.40	897.40	425.43	1,322.83
1710	263.45	425.43	688.88	788.60	152.73	941.33
1711	132.25	520.43	652.68	802.63	96.15	898.78
1712	180.75	489.65	670.40	768.69	267.65	1,036.33
1713	446.83	718.88	1,165.70	890.70	298.48	1,189.18
1715	568.20	754.20	1,322.40	1053.59	226.00	1,279.59
1718	559.53	625.95	1,185.48	1205.68	192.36	1,398.04
1720	906.56	854.95	1,761.51	1075.19	150.05	1,225.24
1722	639.38	890.92	1,530.29	1403.30	126.10	1,529.40
1724	987.29	883.10	1,870.39	1369.67	157.40	1,527.07
1725	556.26	712.60	1,268.86	1420.96	154.95	1,575.91
1727	1,240.34	696.60	1,936.94	1260.88	272.75	1,533.63
1728	1,496.88	450.00	1,946.88	1284.02	159.23	1,443.24

Source: Cox, Hussey and Milne, eds, *Gloucester port books database.*

remained fairly stagnant until *c.*1715. The reasons for the relative decline in Bristol-sourced iron and ironwares are difficult to fathom. It may have been that the prolonged conflicts of the 1690s and 1700s disrupted Bristol's northern routes and that any shortfall was supplemented by shipments from Chepstow and Newport and, by the end of the period, the occasional large cargo of pig iron from Swansea, Neath and Carmarthen. However, the substantial, but unrecorded coastal trade from Dean probably assumed a greater importance than the records permit us to quantify.[70] In the more stable years of the 1720s, Bristol supplies grew markedly. In 1728, the final year for which reasonably reliable data can be obtained, coastal imports from Bristol represented over three-quarters of the total quantity of iron and ironwares passing through Gloucester, and over eight times the amount traded from Bristol in 1712. It appears that a substantial increase in foreign iron underpinned the rise in trade. From 1725, Swedish iron and steel were noted for the first time in the Gloucester port books. By 1728, the Bristol merchant Graffin Prankard was undercutting domestic supplies with directly imported, high-quality Scandinavian iron and steel. Prankard was able to 'to render this at Birmingham or Bewdley market' at a handsome profit using John Beale's extensive fleet of Bewdley-based trows. Although Prankard cannot be connected to all the iron cargoes shipped by Beale, it is interesting to note that Beale and his regular trowmen, Thomas Brown, Peter Tyler, Charles Corker and William Coldrick, were responsible for transporting over 718 tons of iron, almost half the quantity imported coastally from Bristol in 1728. Swedish iron accounted for 178 tons traded through Beale and his operatives.[71]

Bristol also maintained an important entrepôt trade in iron and ironwares with the wider region: over two-thirds of all shipments to below-Holms ports carried mixed cargoes of metalwares. These shipments rarely failed to include significant consignments of copper and, from 1701, brass.[72] Similarly, Bristol remained a major source of lead, shot and litharge. Supplies of lead and lead ore were drawn from Cardiff, Cornwall, Chester, Montgomeryshire and west Wales; by 1700 very little came from the once-rich mines of Mendip.[73] Compared to Hull and Chester, Bristol was not a principal shipper of raw or worked lead,[74] yet its shot industry became an increasingly important factor in the development of the city's economy in the later eighteenth century. The amount of lead and lead shot shipped coastally between 1695 and 1701 is presented in table 3.8. The data indicate that shipments were small at around a ton per voyage, and although the Severn hinterland remained the single most important centre of consumption within the region, trade was not wholly defined by the axis with Gloucester. In 1698 and 1699, the amount shipped to Severn ports was far outstripped by that traded to ports beyond the Bristol Channel. In these years, extra-regional ports accounted for 40 per cent and 46 per cent respectively of lead and lead shot traded coastally. Exeter, its deep-water outport Topsham, and London were the main centres of importation.

The results re-affirm that long-distance coastal trade was seriously affected by war and privateering. Substantial quantities of lead and shot were only traded beyond the Bristol Channel during the peacetime 'window' of

Table 3.8

Lead and shot (cwt) exported coastally from Bristol, 1695–1701

		Severn	Somerset	N. Devon	N. Cornwall	Pemb./Carm.	Swansea/Neath	Cardiff	Wye	Extra-regional	Unknown	Total
1695	cwt	1,570	701	576	282	195	61	169	30	420	–	4,004
	shipments	60	26	16	14	20	7	14	8	4	–	169
	mean	26	27	36	20	10	9	12	4	105	–	24
1696	cwt	986	251	920	260	43	20	78	30	80	–	2,667
	shipments	52	19	10	11	15	5	12	5	3	–	132
	mean	19	13	92	24	3	5	6	6	27	–	20
1698	cwt	1,063	581	309	228	152	88	30	309	1,899	40	4,699
	shipments	53	18	17	13	19	9	7	12	21	1	170
	mean	20	32	18	18	8	10	4	26	90	40	28
1699	cwt	1,103	225	435	146	79	16	15	128	1,840	10	3,997
	shipments	59	13	18	10	11	7	4	7	20	1	150
	mean	19	17	24	15	7	2	4	18	92	10	27
1701	cwt	946	621	412	174	217	5	31	143	779	–	3,327
	shipments	39	20	13	9	11	4	7	14	16	–	133
	mean	24	31	32	19	20	1	4	10	49	–	25

Source: PRO E190 coastal port books.

1698–1701. In addition, the peaking of trade, although not the number of shipments, at Gloucester in 1695 may also be related to the effects of the Anglo-French war. In this year, Gloucester boats were much more active than those of Worcester or Bewdley, despite the fact that Gloucester itself was unlikely to have been a major consumer. Of course, it is feasible that transhipment to up-river craft may have taken place at Gloucester, although it would have been an irregular practice on this scale. Alternatively, the extra quantities of lead and shot may have been diverted via Gloucester and Lechlade, the river port for the upper Thames.[75] Through such means Bristol lead may well have made its way to the south-east but avoided the disruption of privateering in the Channel. In the same way, the large quantity of lead and shot shipped in a much smaller number of voyages to Bideford, Barnstaple and Ilfracombe in 1696 may also be explained by the curtailing of long-distance routes to south Cornwall and Devon.

Entrepôt functions dominated the trade in the categories of textiles, fisheries and wood. Bristol did not possess a strong cloth-manufacturing base, although Somerset and Stroudwater were important local cloth areas.[76] The city was also neither a major centre for fishing (the lack of merchantable fish regularly troubled the Common Council[77]) nor overly endowed with exploitable woodland. None the less, trade was reasonably well represented through the dispatch of overseas and regionally produced goods. Textiles included linen and woollen goods shipped to Bristol through Shrewsbury, Bewdley and Worcester, and south-western serges sent up-Severn. These trades were supplemented by the coastal dispersal of imported goods, silkwares, East India textiles, Irish cloth and bay yarn. As table 3.6 demonstrated, Bristol tended to occupy a similar role in the trade in fish, whilst maintaining a firm hold over the more profitable, overseas products. For example, in 1699 Bristol received 189 hogsheads of train oil in seven shipments from Bideford. In the same year, 62 voyages carrying 283 hogsheads were dispatched coastally, three-quarters of which were bound for the Severn ports. Much of this was redirected to the Cotswold cloth industry, as train oil was widely used in the initial processing of raw fleeces in some of the cheaper cloths.[78] Again, wood and timberstuff was mostly represented by transhipped Severn goods such as laths, jumps, canes and hoops, and overseas timber, principally Scandinavian deals and deal boards. In the five full years between 1695 and 1701, for example, Bristol shipped 35,073 deals and deal boards, of which 18,276 were traded up-Severn with a further 8,825 distributed to the Somerset ports of Bridgwater, Minehead and Watchet.[79]

However, the centrality of Bristol was most apparent in the trade in foodstuffs, groceries and drink: at no port grouping did less than 70 per cent of shipments from Bristol include the class. Trade was grounded on traditional, well-established Bristol staples, such as Spanish, Portuguese and

Canary wines.[80] In addition, domestic ale, beer and the increasingly modish Hotwell and Bath spa waters filled the bottles of Bristol's glass producers and the holds of coasters clearing the city.[81] The growth of the trade in domestic waters is a remarkable example of the flexibility and opportunism of Bristol's coastal operation in response to escalating consumer demand. By the seventeenth century, the efficacy of often highly carbonated spring waters in the treatment of a variety of real and imagined complaints was widely acknowledged. Both Bath and Bristol water gained a certain medical cachet both at source—literally 'hot from the pump'—and when administered at some distance from the spring. In 1662, Fuller recounted how Dr Samuel Ward of Sidney College was prescribed liberal draughts of Bristol water for his chronic spleen condition, 'though it was costly to bring it through the Severn and narrow seas to Lynn, and thence by river to Cambridge'.[82]

For such reasons, spa waters remained a luxury—an apothecarial drug reserved exclusively for the elite. It is not until the last decade of the seventeenth century that evidence of wider trade is forthcoming. Aided by a largely phoney medical war, the kudos of Bath and the growth of 'resort culture' in general, and above all the commercialisation of water extraction and marketing, Bristol developed into a major centre for the bottling and dissemination of Hotwell and Bath spa water. Yet, despite the fact that coasting provided an efficient transport network, sea-borne trade remained incidental compared to overland carriage. In 1699, for example, a single voyage carried 8 baskets of Bath waters to Barnstaple. In 1701, the *George* of Bridgnorth and the *Joseph and Benjamin* of Bewdley shipped an equivalent of 21 baskets of Bath waters to Gloucester, whilst Nicholas Jones transported 3 casks of bottled Hotwell water to Chester in the *Griffin* of Chester. In contrast, as late as 1715, Graffin Prankard preferred to supply his London clients with Hotwell water by the regular Bristol carrier William Sertaine.[83] Thus, although Dr Oliver was moved to robustly defend the long-standing practice of 'the *Trade* of sending these Waters to *Ireland, Scotland,* and all parts of *England*' in 1704, coasting did not effectively develop until the growth of the London market in the 1720s.[84] In 1718, for example, Bristol dispatched just under 500 baskets, mostly of Hotwell waters, 311 baskets of which were traded to London. By 1720, the capital imported 1,944 baskets of water from a total of 2,213 baskets traded coastally. Five years later, the figure had risen to 5,075 baskets: London's share was 3,305 baskets.[85]

The Gloucester data provide a useful context to these very dispersed samples. In table 3.9, the trade in Bath and Hotwell waters clearing Bristol for the Severn ports is presented according to quantity and shipment of both types of good. The sixth column indicates the number of voyages carrying spa waters expressed as a percentage of total voyages from Bristol.[86] The data demonstrate the very minor nature of the trade from its first recording

Table 3.9

Bath and Hotwell waters (baskets) exported coastally from Bristol to Gloucester, 1701–1728

		Bath waters (baskets)	Hotwell waters (baskets)	Total	No. of shipments	% total shipments from Bristol
1701		21.00	–	21.00	2	1
1703	*	40.00	–	40.00	1	1
1704		–	–	–	–	–
1705		–	–	–	–	–
1706		1.00	6.00	7.00	4	2
1707		9.00	2.00	11.00	3	1
1708		18.00	–	18.00	4	2
1709	*	42.00	–	42.00	7	5
1710		50.00	1.00	51.00	8	4
1711		2.00	2.00	4.00	2	1
1712		16.00	4.00	20.00	5	4
1713		23.00	–	23.00	4	3
1714	*	8.00	–	8.00	3	4
1715		39.00	3.00	42.00	9	6
1716	*	–	8.00	8.00	2	2
1717	*	16.00	44.00	60.00	11	10
1718		53.00	93.00	146.00	21	10
1719	*	9.25	40.00	49.25	10	9
1720		73.00	165.50	238.50	35	17
1722		72.00	405.50	477.50	60	32
1723	*	55.50	246.50	302.00	42	43
1724		82.50	714.50	797.00	86	44
1725		52.00	520.00	572.00	78	44
1726	*	27.00	359.75	386.75	43	44
1727		61.00	629.25	690.25	96	45
1728		38.00	625.00	663.00	69	36

Note: * Data for half-year only.
Source: Cox, Hussey and Milne, eds, *Gloucester port books database.*

in 1701 to *c.*1717. The occasional trow returning from Bristol may have ventured a few baskets of Bath and Hotwell waters but the infrequency of shipment remained the characteristic feature of trade. However, from the late 1710s trade expanded dramatically. By 1724 almost 19 times as much Hotwell and Bath water was being traded by Bristol to Gloucester than in 1715. Over the same period, spa waters rose from being traded in barely 6 per cent of all voyages clearing Bristol to over 44 per cent of shipments. The increase was almost wholly linked to the production and marketing of bottled Hotwell waters. In 1715, Hotwell or Bristol waters represented only 7 per cent of the 42 baskets recorded. In 1724, over 90 per cent of the 797 baskets recorded at Gloucester contained Hotwell water. At its height, therefore, Bristol dispatched around 5,000 gallons of domestic spa water to Gloucester in 1724, mostly via Bewdley boats.[87] This figure is not extensive. Dosages of several quarts per day were required to achieve the full diuretic and thence curative effects of domestic mineral water, and it is clear that coasting suffered from the competition of faster overland routes in a commodity where delay caused putrefaction. Yet despite these factors, Hotwell and Bath waters had become integral components of Bristol's coastal trade.

Whereas domestic waters were mainly geared to London demand, the spin-offs of transoceanic trade, in particular the 'new mass consumed groceries', were central to Bristol's relation to its immediate hinterland.[88] By the late seventeenth century, Bristol was arguably the most important provincial centre for the marketing of sugar and molasses: sugar boiling flourished on the back of the West Indies trade, as did the rather later trade in rum.[89] Charting the trade in sugar, however, is problematic. In the coastal records, the output of Bristol's many refineries tended to be subsumed under the generic customs term of grocery. William Sealey of Bridgwater, for example, received parcels of sugar from Bristol 'with the chalk marke of WS on the hhd [hogshead]' contained in much larger consignments of grocery via the Bridgwater coasters the *Betty and Jane* and the *Hopewell* in 1703.[90] As a result of these types of procedure, a mere 165 tons of sugar, molasses and candy were recorded in 1699, most of which passed to ports beyond the normal regional parameters of Bristol's trade.[91]

Although grocery came in very mixed consignments and was occasionally combined with a diversity of goods including saltery, spices, tea and even chandlery, an examination of its trade is instructive. In figure 3.2, quantities and shipments of grocery and sugar products (brown, muscovado, refined, powder and loaf sugar, candy, and molasses) clearing Bristol for Gloucester are analysed for the period between 1680 and 1728. The data highlight some important indicators to the nature of trade. Firstly, in certain periods, 1691–7 and 1727–8 for example, sugar was separated out from grocery. This may indicate the size of these shipments (when sugar was recorded discretely it tended to form large individual consignments of up to 20 tons) or changes in customs procedures.[92] Secondly, grocery was traded in the vast majority of shipments clearing coastally from Bristol. Even in the slack years of the early 1690s, grocery was a major constituent of Bristol cargoes. Indeed, given the representation of single commodity shipments in the data, it could be said that it was unusual for Severn trows not to contain a consignment of grocery or grocery wares. Moreover, grocery was not a simple part-cargo, a subsidiary item, like soap, for example, loaded as a commercial makeweight alongside more extensively traded goods. Grocery was a major traded commodity that

Figure 3.2

Grocery and sugar (tons) exported coastally from Bristol to Gloucester, 1680–1728

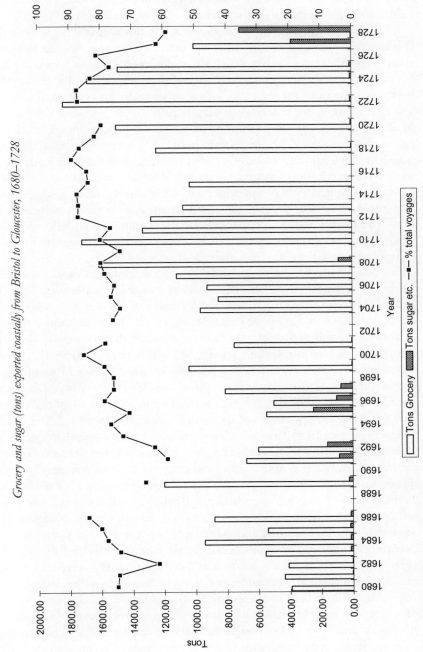

outstripped in terms of voyages and tonnage even such bulk goods as iron and ironwares, the traditional high-quantity building blocks for studies of industrialisation, transport growth, market diversity and urbanisation.

The trade in grocery demonstrates that the home market was central to Bristol's wider trading profile. Indeed, Bristol was locked into its region far more than other major ports. Much of its commerce was import-led, and as a result stood and fell upon the elasticity of consumption within its domestic hinterland. Bristol's involvement in the other main grocery trade, tobacco, was characteristic of this relationship. Between 1680 and 1730, the coastal trade redistributed around a third of all tobacco legally imported into Bristol from overseas. In 1722, when independent statistics are available, well over half the legal tobacco imports officially retained by the city's merchants were fed directly into the coastal trade.[93] Despite the inherent problems of smuggling and evasion, in which Bristol customs officials were heavily implicated, it is clear from table 3.10 that tobacco customs-certificated at Bristol accounted for over 97 per cent of the commodity traded regionally.[94] Trade with the Severn was vital: over 60 per cent of tobacco that cleared coastally from Bristol in 1699 passed to or through the customs port of Gloucester. Worcester, with its prosperous local hinterland and large urban market, was quantitatively and proportionally dominant. Between 1680 and 1724, Worcester never took less than a third of all tobacco shipped via Gloucester, and in the rather exceptional year of 1701 accounted for over two-thirds of tobacco by weight passing through the head port. None the less, the Somerset ports, Carmarthen, Milford, Cardiff and its creeks, and Chepstow imported considerable quantities of tobacco from Bristol. Extra-regional trade was also significant: Exeter, Bristol's southern rival, accounted for 53,094 lb in 1699 alone. Unexpectedly, centres more usually associated with the overseas importation of tobacco, London, Liverpool and Whitehaven, received cargoes from Bristol.[95] This may have represented the equalisation of trade: with many transoceanic cargoes, it was common practice to ship to the most convenient domestic port and then redistribute coastally.[96] In part, this explains the 7,838 lb of tobacco Bristol imported coastally from regional centres in 1699, although the bulk of Bristol's small inwards trade represented damaged or unmerchantable tobacco, for which drawbacks on duty were liable. Only Bideford and Barnstaple among regional ports were net exporters of tobacco coastwise, carving out a small hinterland for overseas-supplied tobacco in north Devon and Cornwall.[97] Elsewhere, trade was *ad hoc*. At Bridgwater, for example, the figures were buoyed by a single large shipment of 20,000 lb compiled by William Alloway via Thomas Johnson of Liverpool and dispatched to Gloucester on a returning salt vessel, the *William* of Bridgnorth.[98] In comparison, the tobacco merchants of Liverpool were far more concerned with the re-export trade. Coasting was a limited

Table 3.10a

Tobacco (lb) exported coastally from regional ports, sample year

From	Severn	Bristol	Somerset	N. Devon	N. Cornwall	Pemb./Camb.	Swansea/Neath	Cardiff	Wye	Extra-regional	Total
Bristol	962,646	–	268,621	32,544	8,173	64,778	52,091	77,067	61,391	180,445	1,707,756
Bridgwater	20,000	2,350	–	–	–	–	674	–	–	4320	27,344
Bideford	–	3,434	–	3,150	3,899	–	2,244	–	–	1,717	14,444
Barnstaple	–	1,574	9,900	–	–	248	612	–	–	–	12,334
Minehead	–	30	–	261	–	772	1,388	210	–	–	2,661
Tenby	–	–	740	–	–	–	–	–	–	–	740
Milford	–	450	–	–	–	–	–	–	–	44	494
Liverpool	–	–	11,000	400	1,805	7,200	–	–	–	259,494	279,899
Total	982,646	7,838	290,261	36,355	13,877	72,998	57,009	77,277	61391	446,020	2,045,672

Table 3.10b

Shipments of tobacco from regional ports, sample year

	Severn	Bristol	Somerset	N. Devon	N. Cornwall	Pemb./Camb.	Swansea/Neath	Cardiff	Wye	Extra-regional	Total
Bristol	145	–	45	14	7	25	16	26	17	24	319
Bridgwater	1	5	–	–	–	–	2	–	–	1	9
Bideford	–	2	–	1	2	–	6	–	–	1	12
Barnstaple	–	2	2	–	–	1	2	–	–	–	7
Minehead	–	1	–	1	–	1	1	1	–	–	5
Tenby	–	–	1	–	–	–	–	–	–	–	1
Milford	–	1	–	–	–	–	–	–	–	1	2
Liverpool	–	–	1	1	1	3	–	–	–	46	52
Total	146	11	49	17	10	30	27	27	17	73	407

Source: PRO E190 coastal port books.

operation and almost wholly confined to an abbreviated local hinterland. Of the 2.14 million lb of tobacco imported directly into Liverpool in 1699, a mere 13 per cent was traded coastally.[99]

The general trends in the domestic consumption of tobacco are confirmed by the wider sample of data relating to Gloucester. Figure 3.3 demonstrates that coastal imports of tobacco from Bristol experienced a strong rise in the 1680s before peaking in the mid-1690s. Thereafter, both internal and external factors—market saturation, erratic production in the Chesapeake, war, and the growth of the re-export trade—caused a long, slow stagnation. The recovery of tobacco consumption in the late 1720s and the uptake of other forms of popular, mass-consumed intoxication, such as gin and snuff, are unfortunately beyond the competencies of this survey.[100] Even so, the figures demonstrate the symbiotic linkage between Bristol and its hinterland: Bristol's dominance in the early tobacco trade depended upon a strong cluster of regional consumption centres. Whilst its northern rivals, Liverpool, Whitehaven and Glasgow, ports with much smaller domestic hinterlands, concentrated upon the more remunerative re-export trades, Bristol relied on high-grade, almost bespoke tobacco leaf, sold on a consignment basis and targeted at a highly inflexible home market.[101] Although this established the city as the premier outport in the years of expansion, the failure to adapt to changing patterns of consumption and supply, itself reflective of a wider business conservatism, limited Bristol's development in the eighteenth century. In the 1720s and 1730s, therefore, Bristol remained a centre of conspicuous consumption and domestic redistribution, but failed to build on its early lead in this and indeed other important commodities.[102]

The coastal trade of the region

It is possible to use the trade of Bristol as an overarching template through which regional forms of coasting are seen as merely the reflection of the market demands and commercial prominence of the western metropolis. Certainly, many studies have transposed the hegemony Bristol exerted over certain high-profile goods onto the wider picture of provincial trade. Indeed, in the case studies sketched above, the role of Bristol as the interface between overseas and domestic goods is subtly merged with the economic articulation of the region. With the 'mass-consumed' grocery goods, such as tobacco and sugar, Bristol was at once the primary agent of importation, reprocessing, marketing and distribution.[103] In this light, it is perhaps less of a cultural shift to regard the rebranding of sherry as 'Bristol-milk' as merely an oblique semantic extension of Bristol's wider control of the trade of goods.[104] Yet, it must be remembered that the extent and development of

Figure 3.3

Tobacco (lb) exported coastally from Bristol to Gloucester, 1680–1728

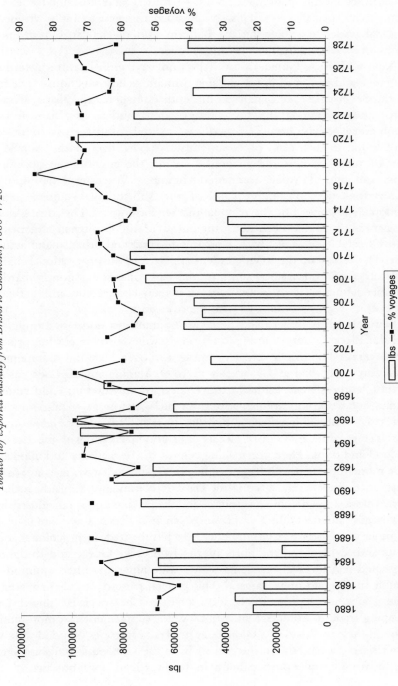

Source: Cox, Hussey and Milne, eds, *Gloucester port books database.*

Bristol's economic hinterland both permitted and sustained the city's commercial specialisation. This should warn us against simply writing out regional trade, or subjecting the patterns and mechanisms of domestic commerce to a blandly metrocentric formula.

Next to Bristol, Gloucester was the primary regional centre in terms of the range and extent of goods passing through its customs house. The trade of the Severn has been analysed in depth elsewhere, and, for reasons of space and coherence, it is only proposed to outline the main areas of commercial activity here.[105] Bristol was central to all sectors of trade at Gloucester: in each class of commodity bar extractive goods, over 86 per cent of recorded clearances were bound for the city. Of the river ports, Worcester and Bewdley dominated shipping. Worcester had important connections with the arable vales of the Midland plain and an almost monopolistic control of the regional market for hops.[106] The town was also the natural distribution centre for the output of the Droitwich brineries and enjoyed established links with a proximate rural and urban manufacturing base. The variety of the town's trade is apparent in the proportional share of each class of commodity. Only in the case of fishery goods, hardly a commercial mainstay of inland centres, did any class feature in less than 55 per cent of voyages associated with the river port.

Bewdley, on the other hand, acted as the transport node for Birmingham and the Black Country hardware region. Bewdley boats were the principal metal carriers on the river, accounting for over half the shipments of metalwares recorded at Gloucester in 1699. Manufactured goods, such as scythes, lanthorns and leather; extractive goods, mostly salt; Kidderminster textiles; and wood and wooden ware from the Wyre forest were also important sectors of trade undertaken by Bewdley carriers.[107] Bewdley and Worcester vessels shipped the majority of all classes of good recorded with the exception of food and drink. Here, the malting centres of Tewkesbury and Gloucester were more important with 84 per cent and 98 per cent of voyages in boats of these ports respectively carrying the class of commodity. Similarly, malt was carried alongside agricultural surpluses and the products of rural industry in all 15 voyages undertaken by Evesham boats in 1699. Trade was more diverse at the other river ports. Shrewsbury pursued a healthy trade in agricultural goods, crafts and textiles, and the ports of the Ironbridge Gorge and Bridgnorth combined regular coal shipments with a wide range of other commodities, notably metals and metalwares.[108] This general pattern was also apparent at Tewkesbury and Upton, where the growth of the specialist long-distance tramping trade to Somerset and south Wales supplemented a more limited through-trade to Bristol. At Gloucester itself all categories of good were well emphasised—a pattern which resulted from the small-scale transhipment of cargoes from up-river ports rather than the diversity of local produce.[109]

A similar qualitative if not quantitative breadth of goods is apparent in the trade of Bridgwater and Minehead. Coastal exports were dominated by agricultural goods traded to Bristol, and also to extra-regional ports, principally Liverpool. Bridgwater, Minehead and, in particular, its creek, Watchet, were also ideally situated to exploit the output of the productive, 'highly professional' mixed arable and market garden areas of Taunton Deane.[110] Cereals, fodder crops and garden produce formed the main coastal exports of the ports. In the sample year, 128 shipments clearing Bridgwater and Minehead carried in total 52,781 bushels of grain and cereal crops. This was dispatched to Bristol, Liverpool and Gloucester. In the same year 8,000 cabbage plants were shipped to Milford from Bridgwater alone.[111] In addition, Bridgwater was a major centre in the trade in garden seeds and nitrogen-fixing sainfoin and clover seed.[112] Similarly, flax and hemp, important for rope-making, the fishing industry, and also the regional linen industries, formed a principal component of both ports' exports.

Moreover, the Somerset harbours were equally well placed for shipping the produce of the Somerset Levels, and the less well developed upland pastures of the Brendon Hills and Exmoor.[113] These were important areas for the rearing and fattening of cattle and pigs and the grazing of sheep. Indigenous beasts were supplemented by a considerable trade in Welsh cattle and swine brought coastwise, prior to being sold at local markets and fairs, or alternatively driven westwards to Bristol and thence to the Home Counties.[114] The prevalence of the pastoral economy and the limited importance of dairying in north Somerset is demonstrated in the region's coastal exports: Bridgwater exported only small quantities of butter and cheese: 197 cwt of cheese was shipped coastwise in 1699, 60 per cent of which went to Bristol. This compares to the 249 tons of cheese traded from Gloucester and the 7,807 tons that cleared Liverpool mostly for London in 1699.[115] Hides, skins and wool, sheared locally and imported from the north-west and Ireland, were also consistent features of the outwards trade.

In other sectors commercial activity was sporadic. The Somerset ports shipped small consignments of tobacco and wine, either imported directly, or transhipped from Bristol and tramped around the coast. Similarly, rural crafts figured in local cargoes. Bridgwater supplied such goods as tanned wares, turned wood products, knitted stockings,[116] and soapers' and wood ashes as return cargoes for its principal trades with Bristol and the Severn ports: 85 per cent of all shipments carrying manufactures were traded to these centres. As Minehead and its satellite creeks, Porlock and Watchet, were directly accessible to open sea, they tended to take more of the passing trade in fishery goods than estuarine Bridgwater. Minehead had a sizeable share of the shipment, if not the amount, of white and red herring traded region-ally.[117] Similarly, textiles, especially serge and perpetuanas, other domestic cloths and also overseas goods, like canvas, appear to have been traded more through Minehead than Bridgwater.[118] Evidence suggests that much of the serge originated in south Devon and was traded overland by packhorse and wagon.[119] The total trade in textiles was also less closely associated with Bristol: 21 per cent of shipments carrying textiles were destined for Swansea and Neath largely as return cargoes in coal boats. In comparison, the Somerset ports were insignificant in the coastal export of extractive goods, metals and wood. What was traded tended to comprise small quantities of salt that was either transhipped coastally, locally reprocessed or traded in the form of prize goods. Pewter and old iron and brass, collectively known as shruff, were also shipped back to Bristol, and the occasional consignment of elm, walnut, deals, spars and poles was translocated to regional ports.[120]

At the north Devon ports, a distinct separation existed between the exposed and isolated haven of Ilfracombe, and the economically buoyant, relatively populous, corporate towns of Barnstaple and Bideford.[121] The latter centres were linked to a hinterland of established inland markets, rural crafts, and an increasingly progressive and productive agrarian regime. This area was dominated by livestock rearing and sheep grazing but also supported a growing acreage devoted to commercial as opposed to subsistence arable.[122] Agricultural goods occupied just under a quarter of Bideford's exports in 1699, half of which were to extra-regional ports, principally Liverpool. Of the 11,916 bushels of grain, mostly oats, that cleared the port in 1699, over four-fifths were destined for Liverpool. In comparison, Barnstaple conducted a limited trade in domestic and Irish hides, skins, local textiles, notably bays, and wool to Bristol and Gloucester.[123] By the end of the seventeenth century, moreover, both ports supported a flourishing overseas trade with Ireland, the Newfoundland Banks, the American seaboard, the West Indies and the Mediterranean. As a result, Bideford in particular rose to be an important entrepôt in the fitting out of overseas cargoes and the dispersal of overseas goods. Coastal shipments of tobacco, wine, fruit, spices, soap, groceries, generic 'Londoners' goods' and fish to south Wales and Bristol reflected the extent of international and domestic commerce. In contrast, Ilfracombe's commercial horizons were defined by its coastal situation and the poverty of its immediate hinterland. Michael Currant, master and part-owner of the *Michael* of Bridgwater, found it 'a poor place' when his vessel was forced to shelter there for urgent repairs in 1697. Unable to off-load his cargo of peas and malt originally destined for Liverpool, he strongly advised his merchant partners that the goods should be returned to Bridgwater 'for to leave it [at Ilfracombe] . . . will be more loss than the sending back'.[124] The port, and indeed the economy of the town, was dominated by the inshore fishery: 86 per cent of Ilfracombe's coastal exports were in fishery goods, almost wholly herrings traded under letpass.[125]

Agricultural goods, crafts, metals, textiles and wood were of minimal significance or non-existent, utterly dwarfed by the inwards trades from Bristol.
Coastal exports of extractive goods were similarly limited to small parcels of
coal or salt transhipped from south Wales and, very occasionally, Gloucester
and Liverpool.

Both Barnstaple and Bideford traded a far more comprehensive range of
commodities. Crafts and manufactures were particularly important, being
represented in over 40 per cent of all coastal clearances. This category
comprised such widely produced goods as tallow, tar and pitch and
occasional overseas items like oil and sumach from the Straits. Yet by far the
most important single traded commodity, the only commodity of note
according to Watkins, was earthenware: coarse slipware pieces, earthen ovens
and occasionally tobacco pipes.[126] Table 3.11 gives an indication of the
quantities of earthenware traded from the major regional centres.[127] With
regard to the data, two factors must be considered. Firstly, the figures are
inclusive of both domestic and imported earthenware, although identifiably
overseas products, the infrequent shipments of 'Dutch mugs' and 'Holland
earthenware' from Bristol, were comparatively insignificant.[128] Secondly, all
volumetric measures have been given notional 'piece' conversions following
Weatherill's admittedly conjectural suggestions.[129] Certainly, Weatherill's
caveats concerning the extent overland trade, erratic measurement, and the
likelihood that the Bristol industry was geared for the overseas and not the
internal market must also be borne in mind.[130] However, table 3.11 indicates
the importance of the north Devon centres, particularly in supplying the
more peripheral coastal regions such as south-west Wales. Here, earthenware
formed the only regularly available, merchantable cargo traded by returning
coal vessels and it is interesting to note that supplies from Barnstaple and
Bideford seem to have displaced the overall market share enjoyed by
manufactured goods from Bristol.

Barnstaple and Bideford also drove a moderate trade in most other classes
of commodity, although metals were poorly represented: Bristol was relied
upon for the supply of iron, ironware and steel. Bristol was also the main
destination for the shipment of extractive goods: the class accounted for 65
per cent and 58 per cent of total shipments from Barnstaple and Bideford
and was represented on all shipments clearing Barnstaple for Bristol and on
93 per cent of those from Bideford. Tobacco pipe clay and ball clay dug near
Great Torrington and shipped from Bideford were the principal commodities.
This was in great demand at Bristol and at the Severn ports not only for the
production of commercial earthenware but also for making receptacles for
the sugar, soap and glass industries.[131] Copper ore also was shipped in large
quantities, especially after the greater exploitation of the North Molton
reserves in 1696.[132] The Swedish engineer Cletscher reported on its shipment

Table 3.11a

Pieces of earthenware traded from regional ports, sample year

	Bristol	Severn	Somerset	N. Devon	N. Cornwall	Pemb./ Carm.	Swansea/ Neath	Cardiff	Wye	Extra-regional	Cross-regional	Unknown	Total
Bristol	–	13,708	9,337	7,148	–	1,319	2,989	2,310	170	6,100	–	–	43,081
Gloucester	154,843	–	2,100	–	–	800	–	–	200	–	–	35	157,978
Bideford	7,608	–	2,040	–	–	600	16,320	2,400	–	5,760	–	780	35,508
Barnstaple	2,400	2,640	600	–	–	4,200	2,160	1,200	1,440	2,160	1,200	–	18,000
Bridgwater	200	–	–	–	–	–	–	–	–	–	–	–	200
Milford	–	–	–	–	–	–	–	–	–	–	–	84	84
Liverpool	180	–	–	–	148	194	–	–	1,200	14,507	–	–	16,229
Total	165,231	16,348	14,077	7148	148	7,113	21,469	5,910	3,010	28,527	1,200	899	271,080

Table 3.11b

Shipments of earthenware from regional ports, sample year

	Bristol	Severn	Somerset	N. Devon	N. Cornwall	Pemb./ Carm.	Swansea/ Neath	Cardiff	Wye	Extra-regional	Cross-regional	Unknown	Total
Bristol	–	36	19	12	–	8	7	10	2	5	–	–	99
Gloucester	42	–	3	–	–	1	–	–	1	–	–	1	48
Bideford	8	–	3	–	–	1	13	1	–	3	–	1	30
Barnstaple	2	3	1	–	–	2	2	1	1	2	1	–	15
Bridgwater	1	–	–	–	–	–	–	–	–	–	–	–	1
Milford	–	–	–	–	–	–	–	–	–	2	–	1	3
Liverpool	1	–	–	–	2	2	–	–	1	18	–	–	24
Total	54	39	26	12	2	14	22	12	5	30	1	3	220

Source: PRO E190 coastal port books.

as 'ballast . . . taken into vessels loaded with corn and other goods of equal kinds' and emphasised the comparative importance of Bideford for long-distance coasting. From Barnstaple, he commented, 'it is generally carried by boat or pram to Bediford [*sic*] . . . for it is not possible to call [at] Barnstaple by vessels large enough for the ore's carrying direct to London or Bristol, excepting by the small coal boats from Wales. The latter however cannot carry very much'.[133] Whilst this explains the inter-port trade between Barnstaple and Bideford in extractive goods, it is does not account for the dominance of Barnstaple as the centre of the copper ore trade as recorded in the port books between 1695 and 1704. In 1699, for example, Barnstaple exported 557 tons coastally in 17 shipments, whereas only 4 voyages carrying 91 tons cleared Bideford. However, if ore was carried as ballast, as Cletscher suggested, it may have escaped customs notification altogether.

The port books of Padstow and St Ives reveal an even greater reliance on the trade in extractive goods, together with a lesser representation of metals and manufactures. Some 93 per cent of shipments clearing Padstow and 91 per cent from St Ives carried extractive goods, 46 per cent and 33 per cent carried metals, and 7 per cent and 19 per cent included manufactures respectively, almost wholly destined for Bristol and Chepstow. Trade revolved around the shipment of three vital commodities: copper ore and mundic; tin and bar tin; and pewter and pewter crafts.[134] Much of the output of the copper and tin mines, reckoned to be 'the richest and most productive in Britain, and possibly the world', passed through south-coast ports, in particular Truro and Penryn.[135] However, in the sample year 39 shipments cleared St Ives with 1,382 tons of copper ore, mostly to Chepstow, and 606 tons was traded from Padstow in 23 voyages, the bulk of which discharged at Bristol.[136] Lesser quantities of tin were also sent coastwise: in 1697, over 40 tons cleared St Ives and 33 tons were shipped from Padstow.[137]

To an extent this analysis reveals the polarisation of the Cornish economy. The north-coast ports were situated in areas of poor, subsistence arable, dominated by conservative agrarian practice and pastoralism. Here industrial pursuits had assumed far greater importance than mere by-employment.[138] Consequently, virtually all the trade in grain and agricultural goods, wood, most crafts, and textiles was inwards. Yet, the lack of diversity is misleading. The data overemphasise the commercially 'peripheral' nature of the locality. Copper ore, tin and pewter were the only goods that were required to be recorded under official customs regulations.[139] All other commodities recorded were shipped only as part-consignments of these voyages, literally what was crammed into the ship's hold after the principal dutiable goods had been enumerated. Some of the area's more common products have therefore escaped full record. For instance, hilling stones were traded as ballast or by sufferance in open boats, and fish tended to be shipped by letpasses.[140]

Similarly, the limited range of destinations fails to reveal the full commercial horizons of both ports: Bridgwater and Minehead, for example, were important importers of Padstow tile and stone throughout the period.

In contrast, more analytical weight can be placed on the figures for Milford, Carmarthen and Tenby. Letpass cargoes were habitually recorded at these ports and, although the record of Llanelli is erratic, a coherent picture of the trade of south-west Wales can be reconstructed. Culm and coal, mostly high-quality anthracite, governed coastal exports: extractive goods were represented in 81 per cent of all shipments from Milford, 97 per cent from Tenby, and 98 per cent from Llanelli.[141] As tables 3.12 and 3.13 indicate, trade was conducted along very specific lines.[142] Milford's main area of operation was divided between north Devon, principally Barnstaple, and a series of ports from beyond the region. These two areas accounted for over 97 per cent of trade by quantity between 1696 and 1704. Even so, there was a marked fluctuation in the levels of trade recorded each year. In particular, the return of more stable maritime conditions in 1698 appears to have encouraged trade with extra-regional centres, possibly a result of stock-piling. By 1700, the 'external' domestic market assumed comparatively large proportions: the 12,202.4 tons shipped beyond the Bristol Channel represented some 71 per cent of Milford's total mineral trade. Exeter, Plymouth and Dartmouth were in order of importance the major centres of coal consumption and distribution in south Devon, and in the case of Exeter, it is clear that Milford had effectively displaced Newcastle and Sunderland as the major source of coal supply in 1700.[143] In addition, Milford dispatched large regular consignments to London: on average London-bound vessels carried over 77 tons of culm and coal per voyage, compared to the 47 tons shipped by coasters discharging at Exeter, 39 tons traded in Plymouth and Dartmouth

Table 3.12

Coal and culm (tons) exported coastally from Milford, 1696–1704

	Somerset	N. Devon	N. Cornwall	Regional	Extra-regional	Unknown	Total
1696	–	2,692.20	39.20	49.00	2,009.00	–	4,789.40
1697	186.20	4,145.40	22.40	–	2,612.50	–	6,966.50
1698	84.00	3,642.80	165.20	4.20	8,855.70	–	12,751.90
1699	603.40	3,866.80	25.20	36.40	7,605.02	79.10	12,215.92
1700	742.00	4,016.60	105.00	79.80	12,202.40	–	17,145.80
1702	114.80	2,219.00	–	37.10	4,309.90	–	6,680.80
1703	42.00	2,544.50	16.80	55.30	2,350.60	–	5,009.20
1704	1.40	2,791.60	101.50	23.80	2,044.00	–	4,962.30
Total	1,773.80	25,918.90	475.30	285.60	41,989.12	79.10	70,521.82

Table 3.13

Coal and culm (tons) exported coastally from Tenby, 1695–1704

	Somerset	N. Devon	N. Cornwall	Regional	Extra-regional	Unknown	Total
1695	3,340.40	2,821.00	–	365.40	106.40	18.20	6,651.40
1696	2,724.40	2,741.20	22.40	211.40	284.20	182.00	6,165.60
1697	4,406.50	1,463.00	7.00	191.80	131.60	16.80	6,216.70
1698	2,515.80	1,007.30	36.40	259.70	698.60	36.40	4,554.20
1699	2,773.40	726.80	–	218.40	343.00	135.80	4,197.40
1700	2,965.90	1,087.80	60.20	277.20	709.80	393.40	5,494.30
1701	3,407.60	1,386.00	–	198.80	1,147.30	455.00	6,594.70
1702	2,434.60	1,783.60	–	186.20	387.80	89.60	4,881.80
1704	2,409.40	1,421.00	16.80	197.40	81.20	105.00	4,230.80
	26,978.00	14,437.70	142.80	2,106.30	3,889.90	1,432.20	48,986.90

Source: PRO E190 coastal port books.

craft, and only 29 tons shipped on the short-haul but more frequent run to Barnstaple and Bideford. However, by the end of the period, the extra-regional market had dwindled to the more modest levels obtained in 1696 and 1697. Shipments to London were hardest hit. Whilst the capital took 1,724.8 tons of culm and coal in 1698, 628.6 tons in 1699, and 1,159 tons in 1700, a mere 190 tons were dispatched in the entire three-year period from 1702 to 1704.[144]

At Tenby trade was more confined to the Bristol Channel region. Somerset remained the main focus of trade throughout the period, although Bridgwater's prominence as the major regional importer of Tenby culm was, by 1702, challenged by the growing level of imports at Watchet, the outlier port of Minehead. Again, the data show a slight increase in recorded trade with extra-regional centres between 1698 and 1701. However, as this was never a major market for Tenby and Saundersfoot supplies, the data are somewhat skewed by the odd very large shipment. Elsewhere, trade was relatively stable. Some decline in culm shipments was experienced at the north Devon centres, especially Northam and Bideford, although supplies from Milford appear to have lessened this shortfall. Ilfracombe, which ran a fleet of small 12–16 ton colliers, consistently imported around 700 tons per year throughout the period.

Milford, Carmarthen and Tenby also maintained close overland links with areas of productive arable, especially the developed coastal strip and sheltered vales of the pays, and to the immediate north and east poorer upland pasturage supported substantial livestock rearing.[145] Agricultural goods formed important traded commodities, occurring in 86 per cent of shipments from Carmarthen and 22 per cent from Milford and Tenby. The three ports shipped 80,886 bushels of cereal crops, over a quarter of the total quantity traded coastways in the region, whilst Cardigan exported a further 17,989 bushels coastally in the sample year.[146] However, unlike Chepstow and Gloucester, the major grain entrepôts above the Holms, the ports of south-west Wales were not tied to the market demands of Bristol. A mere 6 per cent of grain was traded to the south-western metropolis as opposed to the 84 per cent shipped to extra-regional ports, mostly to Liverpool.

As Osborne has emphasised, the agrarian economy of south and south-west Wales centred upon the 'ubiquity' of pastoralism.[147] In particular, rearing and dairying in the upland interior were important activities that filtered into coastal trade. Milford, Carmarthen and Tenby thus traded the by-products of animal husbandry such as hides, skins, wool, butter and cheese, and even eggs, the most friable of commodities and, as Chartres has intimated, not regularly associated with long-distance coasting.[148] With access to inland stock-rearing grounds, Tenby was the unrivalled centre for the cross-channel trade in livestock. Lean cattle, sheep and swine were traded to south-west fattening pastures, especially the Somerset Levels, via Bridgwater, Minehead and Watchet and, on occasion, Ilfracombe, Barnstaple and Bideford. This trade supplemented herds driven overland through Hereford and Gloucester.[149] In 1699 alone, 2,759 swine were shipped in 24 voyages from Tenby almost wholly to the Somerset ports,[150] whilst in the same year 67 other beasts were traded to Minehead and Watchet.[151] Other classes of commodity were less well represented. Milford and Carmarthen shipped some food goods, mostly malt, beer, small amounts of grocery and casked and bottled ale. In 1699, the equivalent of 286 barrels of ale was shipped out of Milford in 25 consignments,[152] mainly to Bristol and London.[153] In addition, there was a largely unremarkable trade in indigenous low-quality cloths like flannel, the produce of rural industries, such as stockings, leather and gloves, and some fishery goods, mostly pressed and pickled oysters traded from Milford to Bristol and Gloucester. Yet, despite the presence of an established if localised iron industry, very little in the way of metals was traded. All three ports remained net importers of both metals and wood and timberstuff.

By the late seventeenth century, the coastal port books for Swansea and Neath were little more than tabular accounts of coal exports. This is reflected in the overwhelming position of extractive goods.[154] Both ports had well-developed connections to outcropping seams of bituminous coal and, as with the ports of south-west Wales, trade was characterised by distinct regional specialisms.[155] Although the data for Swansea, Neath and indeed the very scrappily recorded exports of South Burry and Newton are limited and in general discontinuous, an impression of the directional aspect of trade can be gained for the years from 1701 to 1705. For Swansea, extra-regional ports formed the most important market. As table 3.14 shows, ports beyond the region took around 44 per cent of coal clearing Swansea. This represented somewhat of a decline from the peak level of shipment recorded in 1701. Plymouth accounted for the bulk of extra-regional shipments importing well over 2,000 tons each year.[156] At Neath, the coal trade, illustrated in table 3.15, was geared towards supplying the Bristol Channel ports, particularly Bridgwater. Throughout the four years for which continuous data are available, Bridgwater accounted for 51 per cent of all coal shipped coastally from Neath. Indeed, Bridgwater data emphasise that by the early eighteenth century, Neath had displaced Swansea as the principal supplier of coals. In addition, Neath also provided a consistent source of supply for Minehead, the ports of north Devon, principally Bideford, and the lesser centres of both Padstow and St Ives.[157] In comparison, extra-regional ports, the mainstay of the Swansea trade, took barely 7 per cent of trade clearing Neath.

The rise of Neath as a significant coal exporter was undoubtedly linked to the development of the port and its industrial base by Sir Humphrey Mackworth and the Company of Mine Adventurers. In 1695, Mackworth, discovering the town poor 'for want of trade', allegedly 'began to adventure great sums of money in finding and recovering the coal ... since which time

Table 3.14

Coal (tons) exported coastally from Swansea, 1701–1705

	Somerset	N. Devon	N. Cornwall	Regional	Extra-regional	Unknown	Total
1701	1,939.00	1,471.40	1,890.00	268.80	6,455.40	1,349.60	13,374.20
1703	1,747.20	2,297.40	1,281.00	102.20	4,463.20	–	9,891.00
1704	1,692.60	3,326.40	1,372.00	166.60	4,428.20	47.60	11,033.40
1705	1,435.00	3,183.60	1,596.00	134.40	4,951.80	981.40	12,282.20
Total	6,813.80	10,278.80	6,139.00	672.00	20,298.60	2,378.60	46,580.80

Table 3.15

Coal (tons) exported coastally from Neath, 1701–1704

	Somerset	N. Devon	N. Cornwall	Regional	Extra-regional	Unknown	Total
1701	5,577.60	2,149.00	603.40	323.40	1,275.40	117.60	10,046.40
1702	5,685.40	2,105.60	456.40	81.20	406.00	148.40	8,883.00
1703	5,418.70	2,007.60	793.80	95.20	606.20	26.60	8,948.10
1704	6,748.00	1,891.40	996.80	322.00	445.20	33.60	10,437.00
Total	23,429.70	8,153.60	2,850.40	821.80	2,732.80	326.20	38,314.50

Source: PRO E190 coastal port books.

. . . Neath . . . is now become one of the best towns of trade in south Wales'.[158] Mackworth was a consummate self-publicist and his glowing testimonials to the activity, beneficence and care bestowed by the Mine Adventurers upon Neath reflect more on his efforts to manipulate opinion than concrete achievements.[159] Even so, it appears that Mackworth's successes ruffled some important establishment feathers. He continuously and energetically claimed that he was beset by unscrupulous competition from rival coal proprietors, vandalism of his collieries and works, physical intimidation of his workforce, and a sustained campaign of disinformation regarding the quality and availability of Neath coal. The feud came to a head in 1705, when Mackworth marshalled a flotilla of Bridgwater masters and boat owners to substantiate his assertions regarding the dubious practices of his neighbours, who, rather unfortunately for him, held positions of legal jurisdiction. This episode throws an interesting light upon the operation of the port of Neath and its growing importance in the supply of coal and, as Mackworth grandly stated, 'the conveniency thereby of vending several other commodities' of Glamorganshire.[160] John Williams, master of the *Two Sisters* of Bridgwater, deposed that he was 'threatened by persons whose names were unknown to him, promoters of a trade to the coal-works of Thomas Mansell of Brittonferry, Esq., that in case . . . [he] . . . went over the Bar to load coal with Sir Humphrey Mackworth, his men should be all pressed to Sea; but in case he would load coal at Swanzy he should fare better'.[161] Despite the transparent hyperbole of this and other depositions, the concern of Swansea factors at the success of Neath coal in capturing the important Somerset market would appear to confirm the port book evidence.[162]

Other commodities recorded at Swansea and Neath were in general only allied to coal shipments. The exceptions to this were wool, which was legally required to be noted separately; the occasional shipment of glass from Swansea; pig iron, mostly carried to the Pontypool forges via Cardiff;[163] and copper, lead, red lead and litharge from the area's nascent metallurgical industries.[164] The importance of Mackworth's vertical integration of plant and supply at Neath played an important role in this. Coals were sent to Cardigan and Aberdovey, the shipment centres for lead ore mined under the aegis of the Mine Adventurers, whilst the Melin Cryddan works dispatched processed lead, lead ores and small amounts of refined silver to London and Bristol. By 1704, the control of both commodities had extended into a highly organised bilateral trade shipped in Company-owned boats. This was designed to discipline 'coasters to more moderate terms, when they see the Company [of Mine Adventurers] are resolved to provide ships for themselves, if they refuse the trade'.[165]

In addition, both Swansea and Neath were surrounded by good agricultural land. In the Gower peninsula and the coastal strip, mixed arable and extensive husbandry regimes prevailed, whilst a vast swathe of rather barren upland pasturage existed to the north of both ports where marginal grazing and livestock rearing were practised.[166] This distinction was reflected in the coastal trade.[167] Although grain was not a substantial item of trade, butter was prominent alongside coal consignments. In 1701, Swansea exported almost 446 cwt of butter in 92 shipments, the majority going to Plymouth, Bridgwater and north Devon; Neath exported a mere 22.5 cwt.[168] The ports also traded small quantities of timber goods such as barrel staves and tree nails, textiles such as flannel, a few craft goods like stockings, and tallow and other rendered animal products.

The final two customs ports, Cardiff and Chepstow, were dominated by the shipment of agricultural goods. Cardiff and its creeks were the natural centres through which the agricultural surpluses of the mixed arable and pasturage grounds of the Vale of Glamorgan and Severnside lowlands were translocated.[169] Similarly, Chepstow handled the output of the productive corn-livestock economies of the Monmouthshire borders and the central Herefordshire plain.[170] Orcharding in this area was a major agrarian specialism and cider and perry figured strongly in the coastal exports of Chepstow.[171] Secondly, although Chepstow was developing a significant overseas trade at this time, especially with Ireland, the domestic trade of both ports was almost exclusively dependent upon the Bristol market. This trend was most apparent in the trade in cereals: in the sample year, 70,418 bushels were shipped from Chepstow to Bristol and 14,137 from Cardiff.[172] Dairying and livestock rearing were also important in the Vale of Glamorgan. In the sample year, Cardiff shipped small quantities of butter (21 cwt), wool, and live sheep (224 beasts) to Bristol. Some of this trade was destined for the surrounding counties: in 1693, Edward Martindale of Bristol was buying large quantities of butter from south Wales for transportation to his clients inland.[173]

However, the data have over-emphasised the comparative significance of agricultural goods. Cardiff and Chepstow were 'coquet' ports: recorded cargoes were reduced to their most customs-worthy constituents, and smaller items of trade, such as wood and millstones, were omitted. At Chepstow, only agricultural produce or metals, largely copper from Redbrook and bar and pig iron from Dean and Brockweir traded to Bristol or up-Severn, were recorded with any degree of consistency.[174] The Cardiff records are yet more problematic. For the later seventeenth and eighteenth centuries, no account was made of the creeks under Cardiff's immediate superintendence. Thus, Aberthaw, which pursued a considerable trade in livestock, butter, flannel and stockings with Minehead, is omitted, and no record is given of the exports from the metal-working centres of Newport and Caerleon.[175] What remains is a curtailed account of goods clearing Cardiff town quay and bound solely to Bristol. If port book evidence is to be used to study this area, corrective allowances must be made.[176]

This analysis has attempted to tease out the most important features of the regional coastal trade in goods. To an extent, it has been a work of contraction and 'informed omission'. Even with the aid of computerised techniques, no work can ever do complete justice to the complexity and diversity of the total sum of commodities traded. None the less, the data have enlarged and refined initial and very tentative forays into the subject, emphasising both the general sectors of trade and the most heavily shipped goods. This has stressed the cohesion of the Bristol Channel region. Whilst long-distance, extra-regional coasting was profitable for certain trades—Cheshire salt, return cargoes of agricultural goods, and Pembrokeshire culm and Swansea coals, for example—the vast majority of trade took place within the confines of an essentially limited littoral area bounded by Milford and Penzance. For many ports, and particularly those at the periphery of the region, the single shipment of coal, salt or ore remained the definitive feature of coastal trade. Yet, even at the most marginal of centres, trade embraced a panoply of goods. High-value, miscellaneous cargoes emanated not just from the acknowledged entrepôts of the region, Bristol and Gloucester, but also from ports such as Bridgwater, Minehead and Milford, traditionally regarded as supply centres within the hegemony of the commercial 'metropolis' of Bristol.

Coasting in the Bristol Channel operated around two basic and contrasting trades. On one hand, coal was an imperative for much of the region, and the frequency and quantity of its shipment marks out the Bristol Channel as a distinctive and self-contained zone of energy use. Bristol and the links it maintained throughout the region formed the second dynamic to trade. This was felt most keenly in the sheltered 'above-Holms' area where the centripetal influence of the Bristol market was demonstrably greatest. Bristol sucked in the goods and raw materials of Cardiff, Chepstow and the Severn ports, dispensing in return large cargoes assembled from the city's extensive domestic and transoceanic trades. In the Bristol Channel proper, the 'metropolitan' impact of Bristol was rather more diffuse. In terms of shipments, Bristol played only a minor role in the trade of Cornwall and Pembrokeshire. Even so, it was still the principal centre for the coastal redistribution of high-value manufactured goods, worked metals and groceries even in areas where other centres had a proportionally larger share of total trade.

In this context, it is interesting to note that whilst the demand for Cheshire salt sparked a vigorous trade with Liverpool in this period, vessels from Liverpool rarely ventured more in addition than the odd Irish frieze when trading to the Bristol Channel. This suggests that Bristol so dominated the regional trade in goods as to exclude other avenues of supply: Liverpool was sending out large multiform cargoes to north-western centres at this time, but rarely beyond north Wales.[177] Thus, the commercial metropolitanisation of trade, reflected in the impact of Bristol cargoes, and gauged by the virtually monopoly enjoyed by the port in the tobacco and grocery trades, for example, formed the cornerstone of coasting and the economic cement to the region in the early eighteenth century. Indeed, as Morgan has emphasised, Bristol's control of these key trades was not to be seriously challenged until the very end of the period.[178]

Four

The organisation of trade
Owners, operators, merchants and boats

To Daniel Defoe, the English tradesman was the unsung hero of British commerce. Whether in his shop, or engaged in a variety of business transactions, the tradesman was a ubiquitous and omnicompetent agent who moved easily between retail and wholesale trading, factoring goods and brokering deals in an unassuming, sober manner. The tradesman oiled the wheels of domestic trade. 'Almost all the shopkeepers and inland traders in seaport towns', Defoe asserted, 'are necessarily brought in to be owners of ships, and concerned at least in the vessel, if not in the voyage'.[1] This proficiency extended somewhat further at Bristol. In the late seventeenth century, Roger North, the civic recorder, commented that 'all men that are dealers, even in shop trades, launch into adventures by sea, chiefly to the West India plantations and Spain. A poor shopkeeper, that sells candles, will have a bale of stockings, or a piece of stuff for Nevis or Virginia etc.'[2] However, the role of such traders in the organisation of Bristol's domestic trade remains largely unwritten. Firstly, the inland trader appears to be a far more shadowy and elusive figure than Bristol's incorporated mercantile oligarchy. Despite the recent and long-overdue interest in the seventeenth- and eighteenth-century business community,[3] little has been added to the traditional assumption that the complex layers of mercantile agency, capital and financial gearing required to maintain the overseas trades were not apparent or were simply not necessary for the great mass of coastal voyages.

This returns us to the nature and extent of coasting. The pre-industrial coastal trade was not, in the words of Freeman, locked into some un-sophisticated 'pseudo-primeval' form of organisation.[4] Just as canal and wagon transport responded to subtle market fluctuations, the decisions of merchants to opt for coasting in preference to competing systems were the products of convoluted and individualistic stimuli.[5] Coasting offered a highly developed form of transport and the framework through which trade in a variety of goods was undertaken was no less complex. However, analysis has been limited. Willan's seminal study pivoted upon the highly capitalised east-coast coal trade to London.[6] Elsewhere, he found coasting to be comparatively 'casual and haphazard', and its organisation 'largely a misnomer'. This assessment, he admitted, sprang from a lack of 'more intensive research [and] more detailed studies of the trade of particular ports and even of particular merchants'.[7] It is fair to say that whilst subsequent work has begun to piece together local merchant networks for a number of ports, these studies have tended either to focus on earlier periods, where data are far more manipulable, or to extend analysis to the more prominent overseas operators.[8]

At Bristol, the formal, collective action of the city's merchants in organising the economic and political response of the city to increased commercial opportunity in the seventeenth and eighteenth centuries has been examined in depth.[9] Similarly, the challenge posed by the expanding Atlantic economy to Bristol's mercantile elite has received exhaustive study. However, apart from the partial reconstruction of the role Bristol's hinterland played in the compilation of overseas cargoes, very little discussion has been spent describing how the internal linkages of Bristol were constructed. Most work has been content to reiterate Minchinton's metropolitan paradigm in order to flesh out the domestic perspective of the city's growth.[10] The lack of criticism concerning the organisation of Bristol's home trade is reflected in studies of the wider region. Here, descriptions of trade are related to Bristol's perceived centrality. Although some work has addressed how goods, in particular agricultural staples, were marketed regionally and how this was affected by greater capitalisation, urbanisation and demand during this period, little has been written about the local middlemen, the wholesale factors, and especially the merchant-shippers who controlled and dispersed such goods.[11] Willan's call for more attention to be paid to how local merchants operating in the coastal trade organised their businesses has thus been very largely ignored.[12]

Undoubtedly, the careers of some individual merchants, albeit with tenuous connections to coasting, have been briefly examined.[13] However, the potential of coastal port books to aid research into operators and traders has perhaps only been explored in any depth by studies of the river Severn. Even here it has proved difficult to separate merchant-carriers—the sort of hired trowmen and boat operatives that formed the backbone to many commercial transactions—from a discrete body of merchant-dealers who owned and organised shipments.[14] We are at a loss to determine how coastal ships and river trows were chartered, who freighted the boats, and what direct interest boat masters had in the cargo. Where independent evidence exists, clear similarities are apparent between domestic and overseas merchant houses. In 1669, for example, the established Bristol merchant William Browne, himself involved in the nascent tobacco and sugar trades of the city, was acting on behalf of Charles Marescoe of London to sell pitch and tar 'up Severne as at Gloucester, Worcester, Tuexbury, Upton, Bewdley, Shrowsbury etc.'.[15] Similarly, much of Abraham Darby I's iron and castware was traded via the Severn to Bristol in the holds of selected river trows. These returned with coal, iron, callamy and an assortment of high-value groceries and comestibles. Although the trow owners appeared in the port books as merchants, it is clear that commercial control rested with Darby and his Bristol correspondents, Richard and Nehemiah Champion, Thomas Goldney and Graffin Prankard, all of whom dealt extensively in the overseas trade.[16]

The trade in iron castware was considerable and involved sophisticated organisational arrangements. By 1718 Coalbrookdale goods accounted for around 17 per cent of the 1,398 tons of iron and ironwares traded through Gloucester to Bristol.[17] Darby used trowmen from the immediate vicinity of the Coalbrookdale works, principally Edward Owen of Madeley, George Bradley of Benthall and Thomas Williams of Broseley, all of whom were prepared to undertake the through journey to Bristol. These were supplemented by owners based at Bewdley, Worcester and Gloucester chosen largely on the basis of extended kinship ties to Darby's regular local carriers. Such forms of trade and delivery were not 'casual and haphazard': Prankard demanded speedy delivery with the minimum amount of water damage, not an easy request given the open nature of most Severn trows. To achieve these ends Prankard sent a stream of increasingly desperate and occasionally vitriolic letters to Darby complaining about the consistency and quality of the product (mostly iron pots and kettles) and advising on the necessity of building proper warehouses, of loading and covering his goods correctly, and of disciplining unreliable or truculent trowmen. In 1715, for example, Prankard informed Darby that:

> [Trow owner] Bradley shifts his potts into Perks' wett salty trow that is moist & most times dropping under the decks (as it was now for I saw it myself). I would desire you to send what comes to me by Beele's or some other good trow which hath good decks & if any extraordinary charge I will allow 18d. p[er] tun out of my own pockett rather than have them rusty.[18]

The activities of Darby and Prankard serve as an important case study and reminder of some of the potential pitfalls of using data uncritically. We have to ask whether the example of these traders as the hidden organisers and merchants behind Bradley, Perkes and Beale was typical of other industrialists and factors. Unfortunately, the historian is not readily able to decode the web of capital and familial linkages that underpinned the bald description of 'master and merchant' that accompanies so many port book records from the late seventeenth century. Such commercial relationships can only be deciphered by accessing other sources that may open up chinks of light into hitherto largely impenetrable areas. As Sacks has stressed, 'economic history demands attention to literary documents and cultural artefacts as well as statistical sources, and an ability to read and observe as well as to count'.[19] This chapter seeks to integrate such an approach with a quantitative analysis of coastal port books. The discursive sources used in this section are more scattered, survival is erratic and the evidence they contain is more impressionistic and much less comprehensive in geographical and chronological terms than port book data. For these reasons, it has not been possible to reconstruct every merchant community for Bristol and its region. However, it is hoped that through such sources, a more perceptive analysis of the systems that underpinned regional trade can be pursued.

Merchants, masters, and coasting in the Bristol Channel

In his survey of Elizabethan Chester, Woodward concluded that the port books provided an almost untapped 'index of merchants and an account of their trading activities'.[20] This most basic form of analysis is presented in tables 4.1 and 4.2. The tables summarise the total numbers of merchants and masters trading between the main coastal ports in the sample year. Before commenting upon the data, however, a number of methodological issues must be addressed. As with many large prosopographical datasets, differentiating between individuals poses specific challenges. In the data presented here, a flexible procedure of separating traders according to standardised surnames has been adopted. This has compressed an explosion of information caused by variant practices and phonetic transcriptions, whilst preserving the integrity of the original data structure.[21] Undoubtedly, there are in-built difficulties with this approach. Dynasties of merchants and boatmen often operated concurrently and the distinction between senior and junior operatives is not always preserved in the records. Where explicit reference is made, as in the case of James Harrison senior and junior, who traded on Tewkesbury and occasionally Evesham boats, the figures have been amended accordingly. Where such potential areas of confusion have arisen, the trading patterns of individual operators have been compared in order to establish valid distinctions.

The data describe commercial activity and not the operational base of traders. Clearly, a master or merchant recorded shipping goods between coastal ports could be associated with both, one, or neither of the centres. For example, between 1695 and 1697, Henry Herle of Truro, a merchant 'in tyn and tyn affaires', maintained 'a constant trade to Leverpoole, wth his own

Table 4.1a

Merchants recorded exporting goods coastally, sample year

	Total voyages	Merchants	Unknown	Merchants >3 voyages	% regular merchants	Voyages per merchant
St Ives	43	6	–	2	33	7.17
Gloucester	332	52	1	29	56	6.38
Cardiff	31	6	–	3	50	5.17
Bristol	491	196	30	38	20	2.51
Ilfracombe	46	22	–	5	23	2.09
Milford	452	256	14	43	17	1.77
Minehead	127	73	–	12	16	1.74
Bridgwater	95	55	1	8	15	1.73
Padstow	28	17	2	3	18	1.65
Carmarthen	29	20	1	3	10	1.45
Bideford	72	50	4	4	8	1.44
Mount's Bay	4	4	–	–	–	1.00
Barnstaple	54	20	26	1	–	–
Tenby	176	–	176	–	–	–
Llanelli	81	–	81	–	–	–
Swansea	531	2	529	–	–	–
Neath	437	–	437	–	–	–
South Burry	13	–	13	–	–	–
Chepstow	345	8	337	–	–	–
Cardigan	96	65	1	7	11	1.48
Liverpool	306	151	2	21	14	2.03

Table 4.1b

Masters recorded exporting goods coastally, sample year

	Total voyages	Masters	Unknown	Masters >3 voyages	% regular masters	Voyages per master
Chepstow	345	54	1	22	41	6.39
Gloucester	332	59	1	32	54	5.63
Cardiff	31	6	–	3	50	5.17
Bristol	491	194	–	40	21	2.53
Tenby	176	76	2	27	36	2.32
Neath	437	210	1	43	20	2.08
Minehead	127	63	8	13	21	2.02
Bridgwater	95	50	1	10	20	1.90
St Ives	43	24	1	4	17	1.79
Milford	452	252	14	41	16	1.79
Swansea	531	312	2	54	17	1.70
Barnstaple	54	33	–	6	18	1.64
Ilfracombe	46	29	–	3	10	1.59
Padstow	29	19	–	3	16	1.53
Llanelli	81	56	1	7	13	1.45
Bideford	72	51	3	4	4	1.41
Carmarthen	29	21	–	2	7	1.38
South Burry	13	13	–	0	–	1.00
Mount's Bay	4	4	–	–	–	1.00
Cardigan	96	70	2	3	4	1.37
Liverpool	306	207	2	18	9	1.48

Source: PRO E190 coastal port books.

Table 4.2a

Merchants recorded importing goods coastally, sample year

	Total voyages	Merchants	Unknown	Merchants >3 voyages	% regular merchants	Voyages per merchant
Minehead	349	96	–	38	40	3.64
Bridgwater	331	92	–	33	36	3.60
Gloucester	294	84	–	25	32	3.50
Barnstaple	266	81	119	18	22	3.28
Ilfracombe	129	56	1	14	25	2.30
Bideford	225	108	13	26	24	2.08
Padstow	129	80	–	15	19	1.61
St Ives	51	33	7	3	9	1.55
Carmarthen	44	32	3	2	6	1.38
Milford	54	43	2	1	2	1.26
Mount's Bay	13	12	–	–	–	1.08
Tenby	10	–	–	–	–	–
Chepstow	65	–	–	–	–	–
Cardigan	14	12	2	–	–	1.17
Liverpool	203	150	1	13	9	1.35

Table 4.2b

Masters recorded importing goods coastally, sample year

	Total voyages	Masters	Unknown	Masters >3 voyages	% regular masters	Voyages per master
Gloucester	294	68	1	25	37	4.32
Bridgwater	331	83	–	32	39	3.99
Minehead	349	90	–	36	40	3.88
Barnstaple	266	112	5	31	28	2.38
Ilfracombe	129	61	1	13	21	2.11
Bideford	225	108	13	24	22	2.08
Padstow	129	77	–	17	22	1.68
Tenby	10	6	1	1	17	1.67
St Ives	51	32	6	4	13	1.59
Chepstow	65	42	–	3	7	1.55
Carmarthen	44	33	2	2	6	1.33
Milford	54	45	2	1	2	1.20
Mount's Bay	13	12	–	0	–	1.08
Cardigan	14	12	2	0	–	1.17
Liverpool	203	140	17	9	6	1.45

Source: PRO E190 coastal port books.

vessell', the *John* of Truro, under Edward Parsons delivering tin and occasionally copper ore from Padstow and receiving white and rock salt from the north-west.[22] Similarly, the Bridgwater merchant William Alloway traded through Watchet, Minehead and Ilfracombe, being recorded not only in the port books of the Somerset and north Devon centres, but also in the records of the ports with which he traded regularly: Gloucester, Bristol and Liverpool.[23] This multiple presence is registered in the figures for all six ports. Although Alloway remained consistently associated with the trade of Bridgwater, no comparative weight has been attached in the data to an implied 'home' base.

Two further devices have been employed to categorise the role of regional merchants and masters. Firstly, the number of traders is expressed in terms of the total number of voyages clearing or entering regional ports. Secondly, the tables provide a functional index of regular operatives by listing the numbers of merchants and masters associated with each port recorded on three or more separate voyages. This allows the core patterns of coasting distinctive to each port to be assessed. The highly atypical merchant, for example Sir Edward Mansell who shipped a single cargo of household goods and lumber from London to Milford in 1699 and never apparently ventured near a coastal vessel again, is, therefore, numerically separated from the more regular traders from Liverpool, Bristol and the south-west.[24] Obviously, merchants could and did charter numerous vessels, as well as occasionally freighting goods as part of mixed consignments under the commercial hegemony of other merchants. The index of 'regular' merchants may therefore be an underestimate of mercantile activity. None the less, these figures represent participation every four months in the coastal trade and imply a fairly substantial interest in the trade of the locality.

In contrast to merchants, boat masters were generally attached to one vessel. In such cases, it is clear that being recorded on a regular basis, either clearing or entering a port, usually meant that a reciprocal voyage had been made. Thus, a 'regular' master was often involved in many more than three discrete voyages. The number of 'regular' traders, presented as a percentage of the total recorded number of operatives per port, also gives an insight into how commerce was organised. From these data, it is possible to assess whether trade was focused upon a core body of shippers, or, as Willan has suggested, was spread thin amongst a large number of merchants and masters who operated an *ad hoc* trade involving a multitude of boats which made few journeys per year.[25]

The roles of master and merchant represented quite different facets of the coasting trade. However, the port books reveal a remarkably high relation of masters acting, at least on paper, as merchants to their vessels. This was especially true in the coal trade of south Wales. Here capital outlay was small and likely to represent appreciably less of a financial risk for a ship's master than a cargo of high-value goods from Bristol or a large quantity of excisable goods such as copper ore, tin, or salt. The Barnstaple coal warden's accounts reveal cargoes purchased directly from ship's masters. However, master-merchants also carried coal for large mercantile concerns.[26] Mackworth's legal run-in with the Mansells of Swansea and Briton Ferry in 1705 makes it clear that Neath coal was carried by masters under their own account as well as under the directives of more distant merchants. Some Bridgwater masters, Thomas Boon of the *Turtle*, William Vaughan of the *Lion*, and John Williams of the *Two Sisters*, independently deposed that they were forcibly turned away from Neath, and had to look elsewhere for their cargoes, a factor which suggests a high degree of control over the direction and trade of their vessels.[27] In contrast, Mackworth's own 80 ton-vessel, the *Mine Adventurer* mastered and to all intents and purposes merchanted by Thomas Turner, regularly plied the coal route from Neath to Aberdovey, returning with lead and lead ore to south Wales and occasionally London.

Likewise, coal was one item which Shropshire boat operators purchased in large amounts on credit from colliery owners or landowners.[28] Such trowmen invariably appeared in the Gloucester port books as master-merchants. In these cases it is fair to assume that operation of boat and ownership of cargo were effectively combined: the trowmen were both masters and merchants in a very real sense. Similarly, it has been implied that where only a single commodity was shipped, the recorded merchant, even if he mastered the vessel, must have had a considerable stake in the cargo. Indeed, for much of the small-scale letpass trades of the south-west—hilling stones and earthenware, for example—this may have been the case. However, with high-value single item cargoes—salt is the best example—the nature of the good ruled against simple master-merchant ownership. From a slightly different perspective, high-value goods were often traded in multiple cargoes mastered by traders acting ostensibly as the merchant to the entire shipment. In such cases, it is highly unlikely that such masters owned anything more than a very small share of the consignment.

The position is further complicated by the omission of merchants from many port books. This was common practice for the ports under the control of Swansea and Neath and by the early eighteenth century had been adopted at Chepstow, Tenby, Llanelli, and, depending on the customs clerk, Barnstaple and Bideford. Such procedural laxity implies that the master invariably acted as merchant in the kind of petty relationship described by Westerfield, Willan and Evans.[29] Yet, however much this dual function is borne out in the entries of other port books, it does reveal a creeping vacillation in the process of record. The tables have maintained this distinction with high numbers recorded as 'unknown' for the ports mentioned above. No calculations as to the number of voyages per merchant or the regularity of mercantile activity have been made in these cases and the reader is directed to the figures for masters to gain an impression of the organisation of trade. In other cases, Bristol and Bideford for instance, the relatively high proportion of 'unknown' merchants, 6 per cent and 19 per cent of recorded merchants respectively, is due less to this kind of slack compilation than to data rendered illegible or simply obliterated by the ravages of time and poor preservation.

A further refinement to these figures has been adopted in table 4.3. A distinction has been drawn between those merchants who accompanied their vessels as masters ('merchant seamen' to use Willan's rather misleading phrase) and 'men who were purely merchants and left the actual transport of goods to others'.[30] These 'pure' or 'independent' merchants have been expressed as a percentage of the total number of merchants isolated in the outwards and inwards sections of each port's respective coastal records. Despite the uneven coverage and the omission of key data for certain ports, a comprehensive account of independent merchant activity is provided for roughly two-thirds of the sample. This index is based solely upon the port: a 'pure' merchant at one centre could quite feasibly be a master-merchant elsewhere, although examination of the figures for the wider period has failed to provide positive evidence of such occurrences.[31] Most importantly, the table includes additional merchants normally associated with supplementary wool coquets, or very occasionally with goods moved by ancillary customs documentation, in addition to the main coquet cargo.[32]

In order to assess the importance of 'pure' merchants in regional commerce, and to analyse whether either distance or specialist trade affected the record, the seventh column of table 4.3 expresses the number of such traders who were involved in long-distance coastal trade. For the ports of the Bristol Channel, this has been defined by trade conducted with centres beyond the parameters of the region. Trade would thus be less 'long-distance' to peripheral centres like Milford and Mount's Bay than, for example, Bristol or Swansea. In the case of Gloucester, trade was dominated by the physical restrictions to commerce imposed by both the navigational capacities of river craft and the dominance of the link with Bristol. Here a distinction has been made between local, above-Holms trade (trade within the Severn estuary comprising dealings with Bristol, Chepstow and Cardiff and its creeks) and 'long-distance' trade to and from the ports of the wider Bristol Channel.[33] In the case of Liverpool, all trade beyond the port's immediate hinterland of the north-west and north Wales (comprising the coastline from Whitehaven to Aberdovey) has been deemed 'long-distance'.

The three tables reveal much about merchant activity in the region. At a basic level, the numbers of merchants and masters are shown to be fairly consistent, with high numbers of traders being recorded at each port. This is

Table 4.3a

'Independent' merchants exporting goods coastally, sample year

	Total voyages	Total merchants	Total masters	Independent merchants	Wool merchants	Long-distance merchants	% independent merchants
St Ives	43	6	24	6	0	2	100
Ilfracombe	46	22	29	15	0	4	68
Minehead	127	73	63	34	2	1	47
Mount's Bay	4	4	4	1	0	1	25
Bridgwater	95	55	50	10	0	4	18
Bideford	72	50	51	6	0	4	12
Gloucester	332	52	59	6	3	1	12
Padstow	28	17	19	1	0	1	6
Carmarthen	29	20	21	1	0	0	5
Bristol	491	196	194	6	2	0	3
Milford	452	256	252	6	0	4	2
Cardiff	31	6	6	0	0	0	0
Liverpool	306	151	207	126	0	68	83

Table 4.3b

'Independent' merchants importing goods coastally, sample year

	Total voyages	Total merchants	Total masters	Independent merchants	Wool merchants	Long-distance merchants	% independent merchants
Gloucester	294	84	68	24	5	6	29
Bridgwater	331	92	83	23	3	9	25
Carmarthen	44	32	33	8	0	6	25
Ilfracombe	129	56	61	12	0	8	21
Milford	54	43	45	9	0	5	21
Minehead	349	96	90	18	5	6	19
St Ives	51	33	32	5	0	4	15
Bideford	225	108	108	12	0	9	11
Padstow	129	80	77	7	0	3	9
Mount's Bay	13	12	12	1	0	1	8
Liverpool	203	150	140	98	0	67	65

Source: PRO E190 coastal port books.

largely due to the prevalence of 'merchant-master' combinations, the dispersal of trade amongst a wide sector of traders, many of whom made only one or two voyages in a single year, and, conversely, the fact that at some ports trade was concentrated in the hands of a distinctive merchant class. In the case of coastal exports, only Gloucester, St Ives and Cardiff show evidence of concentrated mercantile activity, with an average of over five voyages per merchant recorded. At St Ives this resulted from the control exerted by Edward Crofts.[34] Crofts, an owner of copper and tin mines, was involved in 34 of the 43 voyages that cleared St Ives in 1697, acting as merchant on boats nominally 'of' Bristol, Bridgwater, Briton Ferry, Dartmouth, Oystermouth, Neath, St Ives, and Swansea. These boats carried mainly copper, copper ore, and tin to Chepstow and Liverpool. Crofts was evidently freighting a wide range of boat masters: each master clearing St Ives was involved on average in only 1.79 voyages, a figure which suggests a large number of small independent boatmen. In contrast, Crofts was not involved in a single inwards shipment in 1697. Here the numbers of merchants and masters reverts to the pattern of dual function associated with the staple coal, salt, and Bristol trades.[35] Clearly, the masters Crofts freighted outwards returned either in ballast, with goods for other merchants, or on their own account. This pattern is further stressed in table 4.3. Every merchant involved in coastal clearances from St Ives can be classed as an 'independent' or 'pure' merchant in that they were not involved in the physical shipment of goods. In the case of coastal imports, less than a seventh of all merchants recorded acted independently, a pattern more generally common to the trade throughout the south-west.

The concentration of trade at Cardiff under six merchants reveals both the poverty of the record and the importance of one trader, William Williams, senior. Williams acted as master and merchant for 18 voyages and 5 wool coquets. The Cardiff trade, aimed entirely at supplying Bristol, was operated solely by merchant-masters. In comparison, although merchant-masters dominated shipments passing through Gloucester, trade was conducted on a much wider scale. Using the criteria of three voyages a year as an index of regularity, only Gloucester demonstrated high numbers of established and recurrent traders, with over half of all masters and merchants involved in trading on a regular basis. Clearly, this pattern resulted from the diversity of the Severn hinterland and, unlike the wider region, the number of centres trading through the head port. Thus, at Shrewsbury trade was dominated by John Jones (18 voyages in 1699); at Bewdley by Francis and George Perkes (30 voyages) and John Beale (18 voyages); at Worcester by William Perkes (33 voyages), John Chance (24 voyages) and Peter Noxon (21 voyages); at Tewkesbury by William Fisher (18 voyages); and at Gloucester by William Bailey (21 voyages) and Richard Lewis (18 voyages). These port book merchants generally acted as masters, although a minority, like Francis Perkes, freighted others in addition to mastering their own trows. Only six 'independent' merchants were recorded on shipments clearing Gloucester, three of whom were wool merchants associated with separate coquets.

Generally, the activity of merchants in the outwards trade of the region was limited. Only at Bristol and Ilfracombe were the number of 'regular' merchants greater than a fifth of the total number of traders recorded. However, the figures are slightly more demonstrative with regard to masters. Masters were intimately associated with particular vessels, a correlation which suggests strongly that many traders either owned the craft outright, or, perhaps more commonly, possessed a fractional share.[36] Boat masters also appear to have been employed by owners as the senior operative on a long-term basis. Table 4.4 illustrates the fluidity of these relationships through the career of John Tyler, a Severn trow master trading through Gloucester between 1704 and 1724. Tyler came from a dynasty of trowmen who were associated with Perkes and Beale, the principal Bewdley trow owners.[37] At the beginning of the period, Tyler was very much a jobbing operative, picking up freights as and when they occurred. Between 1704 and 1713, he was master to 16 vessels undertaking 30 voyages and was noted as merchant on 9. From 1715, however, Tyler was linked more solidly with certain vessels. In 1715, he undertook four voyages in John Beale's aptly named *Marlborough* of Bewdley, and, after returning to largely opportunistic or one-off freights in a variety of Severn trows, he mastered 27 consecutive voyages in the *Society* of Bewdley from 1722 to 1724. Twenty-three of these voyages were undertaken in the name of Benjamin Beale; in the other three Tyler appeared as supercargo.

The experience of Tyler indicates how Severn trowmen and indeed owners could move about between craft and yet be very closely associated with one or two specific boats. At the other end of the scale, an almost total

Table 4.4

Merchants recorded on boats mastered by John Tyler, 1704–1724

Name	Home port of vessel	No. of voyages
Benjamin Beale*	Bewdley	26
John Beale	Bewdley	14
John Tyler	Bewdley	13
Francis Perkes	Bewdley	6
George Perkes	Bewdley	4
Thomas Detheridge	Tewkesbury	2
Nicholas Harrison	Tewkesbury	2
Samuel Price	Bewdley	2
William Smith	Bewdley	2
William Johnson	Bewdley	1
Joseph Penn	Bewdley	1
John Rebbells	Bewdley	1
Total		74

Note: *Includes John Sextie and John Beale, merchants on separate wool coquets.
Source: Cox, Hussey and Milne, eds, *Gloucester port books database.*

separation between the role of merchant and hired master is evidenced in the shipping patterns of the *Pen Trow* of Bewdley on which Tyler was freighted on one occasion. Table 4.5 depicts the brief activity of the vessel between 1709 and 1715. The 13 voyages indicate three stages of use. The earlier period is wholly concerned with shipping small amounts of coal from Bristol, whilst the last, and somewhat dubious attribution reveals the boat returning up-Severn with a typically miscellaneous cargo from Bristol. Between 1712 and 1714, however, the trow was freighted by Joseph Penn and, apart from the single wool coquet, was mainly concerned in the trade in iron and ironwares. The loads involved were relatively light, and the vessel was irregularly employed on the through trades to Bristol and Chepstow. Ballasting or trade in non-customable goods remained a consistent feature of back-voyages. Whilst it may be reasonably conjectured that Penn maintained a controlling interest in the craft, whilst also acting as its occasional master, the other masters were a motley collection of recognised trowmen and lesser operatives, whose main employment was to be found elsewhere.[38] From the 1690s onwards, John Hoskins, for example, was mostly associated with the *John and Ann* of Bewdley, under John Beale; Samuel Milner was a river Wye specialist being freighted on a variety of vessels out of Brockweir, Redbrook and Chepstow; and Stephen Perkes, the slovenly carrier of Prankard's iron, appeared on many of the Perkes-owned flotilla of trows operating out of Bewdley.

No merchants are recorded in the Chepstow books, which itself suggests that the master exercised an effective mercantile role for customs purposes. However, the number of masters gives an insight into the operation of the Wye trades. Like Gloucester, trade was concentrated in the hands of a smaller number of traders, a high proportion of whom carried goods on a regular basis. On average every master recorded shipping goods from Chepstow skippered over six voyages in 1699. In the same period, over two-fifths of these masters operated a regular service, trading on three or more separate occasions. As with Gloucester, Chepstow served a number of prominent up-river nodes. Dynasties of master-owners, like the Lewises of Brockweir responsible for 56 voyages in 1699, and the Cutts of Redbrook and Brockweir (30 voyages), were pivotal in coastal exports. Similarly, George Mann and John Wheeler, who mastered 31 and 35 voyages on Chepstow boats respectively, and John Gosling of Chepstow, who mastered 49 shipments, figured strongly in the outward trades in 1699. However, it would be a mistake to attribute dual status to all such traders. The longer series of data for Gloucester reveals that boats were on occasion chartered by independent merchants and industrialists. For example, between 1691 and 1717, John Coster, the copper producer of Redbrook and Bristol, was responsible for 166 voyages mostly from Chepstow to Gloucester.[39] Table 4.6 indicates the

Table 4.5

Voyages of the Pen *Trow of* Bewdley, *1709–1715*

Date	Merchant	Master	From	To	Cargo
16/07/1709	John Benbow	Thomas Tyler	Bristol	Gloucester	8 chaldron London measure coals*
08/08/1709	Thomas Tyler	Thomas Tyler	Bristol	Gloucester	8 chaldron London measure coals*
28/01/1712	Joseph Penn	John Tyler	Gloucester	Bristol	15 ton stone coal
01/10/1712	Joseph Penn	John Hoskins	Gloucester	Bristol	30 ton lead
16/02/1713	James Read	John Hoskins	Bristol	Gloucester	245 tod of 28 lb wool
02/04/1713	Joseph Penn	John Hoskins	Bristol	Gloucester	10 ton pig iron
06/04/1713	Joseph Penn	Samuel Milner	Chepstow	Gloucester	5 ton pig iron
08/07/1713	Joseph Penn	Stephen Perkes	Gloucester	Bristol	15 cwt rod iron; 15 ton timberstuff
31/07/1713	Joseph Penn	Stephen Perkes	Bristol	Gloucester	10 ton iron; 20 ton old broken guns + bushel iron
04/01/1714	Joseph Penn	John Hoskins	Gloucester	Bristol	15 ton stone coal; 4 ton ironware; 1 ton timberstuff
16/01/1714	Joseph Penn	Joseph Penn	Bristol	Gloucester	2 ton English iron; 0.5 ton grocery; 5 basket Spanish wine
22/03/1714	Samuel Milner	John Hoskins	Chepstow	Gloucester	20 ton pig iron*
08/08/1715	John Beale	Thomas Browne	Bristol	Gloucester	0.5 ironware; 8 ton logwood; 20 barrel pitch + tar; 4 pack girth web; 16 ton kelp

Note: There are no data extant for the periods 26 December 1708–25 June 1709 and 26 June 1714–25 December 1714.

Boat specified as the Pen *of Bewdley.

Source: Cox, Hussey and Milne, eds, *Gloucester port books database.*

Table 4.6

Masters and boats freighted by John Coster, all voyages, 1691–1717

Master	Boat name	Home port	Dates operative	Voyages
John Syner	*Jane*	Redbrook	1703–1709	30
John Cutt	*Welcome*	Redbrook	1693–1701	28
John Syner	*Betty*	Redbrook	1706–1712	25
John Cutt	*James*	Redbrook	1691–1701	16
John Cutt	*Betty*	Redbrook	1708–1712	9
John Cutt	*Jane*	Redbrook	1701	8
John Syner	*Welcome*	Redbrook	1700–1705	7
John Cutt	*John*	Redbrook	1696–1710	6
John Lewis	*Betty*	Redbrook	1710–1711	6
John Syner	*John*	Redbrook	1701–1710	3
Thomas Jackson	*Providence*	Brockweir	1715–1716	3
John Syner	*Teacy*	Redbrook	1705–1710	2
John Syner	*Elizabeth*	Redbrook	1706	2
William Tyler	*William*	Bridgnorth	1693	1
John Hickes	*James*	Redbrook	1697	1
John Hooper	*Thomas*	Worcester	1698	1
William Tyler	*Royal Oak*	Bridgnorth	1699	1
Richard Whittington	*William*	Redbrook	1699	1
Richard Whittington	*James*	Redbrook	1700	1
Henry Bailey	*Francis*	Benthall	1701	1
John Cutt	*William*	Redbrook	1703	1
John Coster	*Jane*	Redbrook	1703	1
John Lewis	*Jane*	Redbrook	1704	1
John Syner	*William*	Redbrook	1704	1
John Syner	*James*	Redbrook	1704	1
James White	*Jane*	Redbrook	1705	1
James Willett	*Elizabeth*	Redbrook	1706	1
John Cutt	*Elizabeth*	Redbrook	1707	1
John Hancox	*Michael + Margaret*	Worcester	1707	1
John Pitt	*Betty*	Redbrook	1712	1
John Syner	*Confederate*	Hereford	1712	1
John Syner	*Richard*	Gloucester	1713	1
Richard Syner	*Confederate*	Redbrook	1715	1
Thomas Jackson	*Thomas*	Brockweir	1717	1
Total voyages				166

Source: Cox, Hussey and Milne, eds, *Gloucester port books database.*

masters and vessels used by Coster between 1691 and 1717, and table 4.7 quantifies the principal cargoes of metals shipped from Chepstow to the Severn. The remarkable feature of the data is Coster's reliance on the maritime expertise of a relatively small group of Wye-based masters. The bulk of trade was undertaken in a fleet of Redbrook vessels, the *James*, the *Jane*, the *John* and the *Welcome* (replaced by the *Betty* in 1706), mastered initially

Table 4.7

*Voyages merchanted by John Coster, and quantities of metals shipped (tons),
Chepstow to Gloucester, 1691–1717*

		Voyages	Copper	Iron	Bell metal	Wire	Ironwares	Total
1691		1	3.00	–	4.00	–	–	7.00
1692		1	5.00	–	0.08	–	0.08	5.15
1693	*	3	21.50	16.00	11.50	1.40	0.40	50.80
1694	*	3	34.00	4.00	–	–	0.25	38.25
1695		4	50.00	0.50	5.00	–	2.00	57.50
1696		6	33.50	20.00	6.50	0.60	–	60.60
1697		8	70.00	32.00	–	2.43	3.40	107.83
1698	*	3	22.00	4.00	3.50	1.05	–	30.55
1699		9	63.00	6.00	–	8.05	1.68	78.73
1700	*	8	52.00	43.00	–	7.75	1.00	103.75
1701		19	148.50	101.00	21.50	7.80	2.48	281.28
1703	*	5	52.00	8.15	–	1.58	5.50	67.23
1704		15	113.50	40.00	13.50	4.70	2.20	173.90
1705		12	115.00	64.00	0.03	4.25	1.10	184.38
1706		11	125.30	50.00	10.20	2.80	0.50	188.80
1707		8	68.00	40.50	5.00	1.90	0.50	115.90
1708		6	39.13	23.00	5.28	0.60	0.75	68.75
1709	*	4	34.50	–	9.15	0.55	0.15	44.35
1710		12	93.00	2.00	11.00	2.65	1.00	109.65
1711		7	62.00	6.00	13.50	0.85	0.50	82.85
1712		10	70.00	–	–	11.10	1.00	82.10
1713		1	7.00	8.00	–	–	–	15.00
1715		3	23.00	28.50	8.00	1.30	0.45	61.25
1716	*	1	15.00	33.50	0.10	1.05	–	49.65
1717	*	1	18.00	11.00	-	2.05	–	31.05
Total		161	1,337.93	541.15	127.83	64.45	24.93	2,096.28

Note: *Data for half-year only.
Source: Cox, Hussey and Milne, eds, *Gloucester port books database.*

by John Cutt, and from *c.*1703 by John Syner. Trade, mostly in copper and bar iron, peaked in the early 1700s before tailing off by 1713 as Coster shifted his business interests from Redbrook to Bristol. Coster's control of the principal items of trade is undoubted, but the minor consignments, ranging from apples to rabbit skins and even a shipment of plumbers' tools and dross, may well have been carried under the account of Cutt, Syner or other unnamed and unrecognised Wye and Severn merchants.

In a wider context, the organisation of trade at Cardiff, Chepstow and Gloucester shared a common feature: shipments were conducted through a central group of masters who operated regular packet services to the regional metropolis. These coastal traders were not, in the words of Kaukiainen, the operatives of 'peasant shipping' (the means by which petty agrarian and proto-industrial surpluses were conveyed to market), they formed a highly specialised and developed transport system in their own right.[40] In contrast, only masters operating out of Bristol, Tenby, Neath and Minehead were involved in more than two voyages each, whilst regular masters occupied over a fifth of recorded traders only at these ports and Bridgwater. Significantly, trade at the south Wales ports from Neath westwards was widely dispersed amongst a large section of merchant-masters. Milford recorded the highest number of traders, most of whom figured in only one shipment, a result of the activity of boats and traders from extra-regional coastal centres. A similar pattern occurred at Swansea, although trade at Tenby and Neath was more in the hands of 'regular' Bristol Channel operatives.

These representations of merchant and master activity emphasise that the common experience for most coastal centres was that trade remained geographically widespread yet distributed amongst a fairly large class of essentially small operators. This can be partly explained by the prominence of dual functions, with the shipper invariably acting as merchant. However, a more distinctive picture can be gained if table 4.1 is compared with table 4.3. The complete separation of merchant and master at St Ives has already been stressed, which may imply that recording practice at the port was especially stringent or that the recorded cargoes, mostly of high-grade copper ore and tin, were too important and too expensive to be handled by petty master-merchant operations. Similarly, at Ilfracombe the imbalance between merchant and master is revealed both in the frequency of traders and the number of independent merchants recorded. Here trade consisted almost wholly of herrings exported by letpass, a practice which seems to have encouraged the existence, or rather the recording, of a distinct bloc of merchants. Almost a quarter of all merchants exporting goods from Ilfracombe were 'regular' traders, whilst only 10 per cent of masters satisfied this criterion. What is more, only 7 out of the 22 merchants identified in the records also doubled as masters of vessels: the trade was firmly in the hands of established domestic and overseas merchants like William Alloway of Bridgwater and Minehead and Anthony Juliot of Bideford.[41]

Of the major ports, only Minehead had a significant proportion of independent merchants. Most were either well-known local merchants with a network of regional interests, like John Baston or Joseph Alloway,[42] or specifically wool merchants, such as Charles Hayman and John Cleaveland. By the late seventeenth century, Cleaveland ran an impressive trade, importing combing wool direct from Ireland and Midlands wool via Gloucester for dispersal inland.[43] More peripheral merchants, like Andrew Hare and Edward Rogers, combined coastal trade with the overland distribution of goods initially imported from overseas.

In contrast, the figures for Bristol demonstrate that coastal trade was dominated by merchant-masters based in the regional ports, whilst regular traders and individual merchants were rare. In 1699, the Bristol port books recorded only six 'independent' merchants, two of whom (John Hudson and Richard Jefferies) were associated with wool coquets. From these data, it would appear hard to refute the late Professor McGrath's assertion that from 'the impression of the Port Books [the coastal trade] was to a considerable extent in the hands of men who were not, strictly speaking, merchants'.[44] By his own admission, the classification of who was and who was not a merchant may be too prescriptive: underneath an 'official' merchant class ('those who became free as merchants or who were classified as merchants by contemporaries') existed an ambiguous collection of traders who were involved in both overseas and internal trade.[45] Even so, despite the existence of a strong, autonomous and expanding trading community in the city, only Edward Hackett can be firmly identified in the Bristol records as a Bristol merchant.[46] The absence of Bristol men may be a peculiarity of the chronological sample or the fact that the Bristol port books register outwards voyages only. We know from other records that substantial Bristol merchants—Sir William Hayman, Sir Abraham Elton and Nehemiah Champion, for example—were associated with coastal cargoes shipped to and from the city.[47]

However, if Bristol can be seen to dominate regional trade in terms of volume and value, why was a vigorous base of Bristol merchants not as central to the coastal trade as it was in overseas commerce? Firstly, the implied notion that Bristol merchants were solely concerned with the status and wealth of overseas trade, leaving the unseemly business of internal distribution to grubby shopkeepers and wholesale tradesmen, whilst persuasive and somewhat entertaining, must be discounted.[48] In effect, the true level of commercial organisation is obscured by a veneer of practical operation. The similarity between the numbers of merchants and masters recorded at Bristol indicates that the local 'shuttle' dominated trade. The regular comings and goings of the Severn and Wye river trows and the cyclical monthly or quarterly shipments from the wider region formed the basis of the coastal trade of Bristol. The diversity of trade undertaken by these craft tended to discourage any concentration of formal mercantile activity: the sheer number of regional merchants owning individual consignments in the highly miscellaneous cargoes clearing the city encouraged customs officials to record the supervising master or trow owner as a convenient *locum mercatoris*. By 1680, this simple procedure had been adopted for all voyages save large, irregular or single shipments of certain customable goods.

The situation was markedly different at Liverpool. Here, the independent merchant predominated and master-merchants, whether operating from the

Mersey estuary or elsewhere, accounted for less than 17 per cent of the total number of traders recorded clearing the port in 1699. Even though the records for inwards trade reveal more master-merchant combinations, the independent 'land-based' merchant represented almost two-thirds of merchants listed in the Liverpool records. The significance of independent shippers was due to two main factors. Firstly, the importance of the trade in cheese shipped to London in large single consignments promoted the direct involvement of large-scale cheesemongers and wholesale merchants, such as George Harvey. In 1699, for example, Harvey and Company shipped 720 tons of cheese in 15 voyages from Liverpool.[49] Secondly, Liverpool's trade was dominated by a caucus of 'super merchants', men like the colourful Thomas Johnson of Liverpool and Nantwich, or John Cleveland, 'merchant and proprietor of Liverpool' who combined substantial coastal and overseas interests with the active physical and political development of the town and port.[50] The majority of these 'fixed' merchants were also those engaged in long-distance coasting. Some 54 per cent of independent merchants shipping goods from Liverpool and 68 per cent of those organising inwards shipments dealt with ports considerably removed from the north-west of England.

The attenuated communication lines and completion times of long-distance coasting, both in terms of cargo delivery and customs validation, appear to have encouraged the extra security provided by the independent, 'fixed' merchant. With salt, the principal Liverpool cargo, fiscal considerations underpinned the recording of trade. The securing of excise duties was the responsibility of the producer in the first instance. Failing that, the agent or merchant-shipper identified at Liverpool customs house would be pressed into standing surety for the cargo. In consequence, these traders were routinely recorded as merchants in the port books. This position is clarified by Thomas Warburton, owner of rock salt refineries at Frodsham. Writing from Chester in 1696, Warburton roundly attacked the assumption held by Bridgwater importers that 'the King's duty lyes on the buyer to pay. I wish I found it so, I could sell 5 ton for one that I do now, but being obliged to secure or pay the duty to the King has made me very cautious who I deale with.'[51] Warburton appeared as merchant on two voyages carrying salt to Bridgwater in 1696: in both instances, the cargo was almost certainly owned and freighted by other merchants.[52]

The distinction between different forms of mercantile activity at Bristol and Liverpool emphasises the importance of chartering and the flexible response of regional coasters. Most shipments from Bristol were of a very mixed nature. High-cost and high-value assemblages of overseas and domestic produce were bundled into the holds of coastal craft alongside such goods as grain, metal ores and salt. In part, these cargoes were constructed at the behest of provincial merchants who would venture goods that would meet a ready local market. Naturally, this depended upon the availability of goods, the prospects of selling them, the ability to obtain advance credit in Bristol, and whether the master or merchant of a vessel had the financial wherewithal or the orders to trade on his own account. Surviving account books suggest that the more substantial coastal masters, particularly those who had a direct stake in their craft, often engaged in opportunistic forms of trade. For example, in April 1697, whilst waiting for Hoare and Company's salt to be unloaded at Plymouth, John Neale, master and part-owner of the *Providence* of Bridgwater, was approached by a local merchant to take a cargo of serge to London. This he was willing to do only if the Company would 'consider a freight back againe or elce it will not be worth our going there'. Failure of the Company to respond in time cost Neale his freight, and the *Providence* completed the final home leg of her hazardous and bitterly unprofitable trip in ballast.[53]

Such commercial decisions were dependent upon individual traders and coasting concerns. At Bristol the regularity of return voyages and the rather confined port site may have militated against this kind of activity. Waiting around for cargoes, however potentially profitable they might be, was an expensive business and many a vessel cleared empty rather than incur additional port charges.[54] In 1701, for example, customs officials at Aberystwyth briefly noted the *Success* of London, merchant Daniel Peck and master Nicholas Cook, with 'nothing butt Ballast from Bristoll for Aberdovey' to load a return cargo of lead.[55] Merchanting also depended upon more contingent factors. A master unloading goods at Bristol might procure a return freight or part-freight from Bristol merchants if this was available and the commission was attractive. Alternatively, a master may have been contracted to deliver a specific cargo on behalf of regional concerns. In May 1697, for example, Richard Tuthill of Bristol was contracted by Hoare and Company of Bridgwater to arrange the shipment of a load of hemp and pitch from Bristol received overland from London.[56] Tuthill was only able to transport 6 of the 17 bundles of hemp in his charge on board the regular Bridgwater coaster, the *Satisfaction* of Bridgwater, mastered by Edward Davis. This was because Davis could not be persuaded 'to carry any more nor take in any of the pitch alledging that he was forced to take in goods for Exon & Wellington fair'. None the less, Tuthill hoped to charter Davis for the remainder of the cargo after the *Satisfaction* returned from Bridgwater or failing that to dispatch the remainder by the next available coaster.[57] The coastal records show that on 10 May, the *Satisfaction* cleared Bristol, discharging its cargo of overseas and domestic goods, including Hoare's hemp, at Bridgwater on 22 May. However, neither Tuthill nor Hoare and Company are identified as merchants in the record, the cargo progressing under Davis as master and merchant. Although the *Satisfaction* cleared Bridgwater on 26 May with a freight of agricultural goods and wood for Bristol, the vessel did not reoccur until 1698. It may have cleared in ballast or for another port, in which case the remaining hemp and pitch was probably conveyed in either the *Prosperity* of Bewdley or the *Olive Branch* of Bridgwater.[58] Davis meanwhile spent the summer and autumn months of 1697 shipping culm and wool from Tenby on the *Two Sisters* of Bridgwater.

The experience of Tuthill indicates the presence of an amorphous body of traders omitted from the port books. Tuthill was by no means a major merchant, and without the testimony of Hoare and Company's letters his role as factor would not have been recognised. This raises important interpretational questions: was Tuthill representative of a wider section of 'latent' Bristol-based coastal merchants and agents? Perhaps more tellingly, if Tuthill was involved in coasting, to what extent did the high-profile merchants of the city control his actions? Were the 'real merchants', the elite of Bristol society, effectively behind the coastal trade of the city?

Like McGrath, we have to lament the absence of the kind of business papers and accounts which may have confirmed the involvement of such merchants in internal trade of this period.[59] None the less, the port books throw an important though oblique light upon some of their activities. In particular, major Bristol merchants were mentioned in relation to items of overseas cargo imported at Bristol for which they were initially responsible for securing customs duties. When these commodities were subsequently moved coastwise, certificates verifying legal import (and the names of the importers) were recorded in some coastal books. For example, the Minehead port books record 49 additional merchants associated with goods shipped from Bristol between Midsummer 1699 and Midsummer 1700. These merchants were associated with 87 cargo consignments, with tobacco and Iberian wine the most frequently specified commodities. The extent and character of this activity is summarised in table 4.8. Merchants are organised by the number of voyages on which commodities bearing specific details of overseas importation are recorded. Further columns indicate whether and when freedom of the Society of Merchant Venturers of Bristol was attained,[60] and the amount of tobacco, wine and other commodities listed in the port books.[61] Because merchants were concerned jointly with individual consignments, no attempt has been made to provide cumulative totals of commodities traded.

The table provides a snapshot of the most important merchants involved in the trade of Bristol in the late seventeenth and early eighteenth centuries. These merchants, unlike Tuthill, were men of the highest rank maintaining powerful connections with the civic and mercantile hierarchy of Bristol. Nineteen had firm links with the Society of Merchant Venturers, often, as in

Table 4.8

Additional Bristol merchants recorded at Minehead, sample year

Merchant	Frequency	SMV member	Tobacco (lb)	Wine (gal.)	Other goods
Thomas Richardson	7	1672	–	1228	–
Sir William Daines	5	1690	21,662	8	–
Cornelius Serjeant	5	–	18,791	–	–
John Blackwell	4	1697	–	273	–
Edward Lloyd	4	–	–	122	–
Nicholas Lott	4	–	7,952	–	–
Arthur Hart	3	1668	–	252	–
Edward Martindale	3	–	11,219	–	–
George Mason	3	1690	13,307	–	–
Richard Bayley	2	–	–	–	70 gallon oil
Robert Bodenham	2	–	–	–	87 cwt tallow
Aubery Buckler	2	–	3,240	–	–
John Day	2	1695/1698	–	–	15 cwt Spanish iron
Jospeh Earle	2	1697	–	1020	–
James Hollidge	2	1690	600	–	6 cwt tallow
Charles Jones	2	1688	2,442	–	–
James Peters	2	–	2,228	–	–
Christopher Scandrett	2	–	1,543	–	–
John Anthony	1	–	2,750	–	–
Thomas Anthony	1	–	450	–	–
Stephen Baker	1	–	–	–	57 cwt tallow
Joseph Baugh	1	–	–	–	405 bushel Spanish salt
Henry Bradley	1	–	97	–	–
Alexander Doleman	1	–	–	–	200 ell canvas
John Donning	1	1695	–	–	55 bushel white salt
Sir John Duddleston	1	1691	2,252	–	–
Abraham Elton	1	1690/1700	–	–	68.75 cwt tallow
Richard Franklyn	1	1692	3,778	–	–
Edward Hackett	1	?1691	2,146	–	–
Charles Harford	1	refused 1711	539	–	–
Charles Haydon	1	–	2,128	–	–
Henry Hayman	1	–	5,043	–	–
Abraham Hooke	1	1691	1,050	–	–
Joseph Jefferies	1	?warden 1745	–	–	20 cwt tallow
John Jones	1	–	2,252	–	–
Thomas Lewis	1	–	–	–	1 pack paper
Edmund Mountjoy	1	–	200	–	–
John Mylam	1	–	1,543	–	–
John Plaister	1	–	2,750	–	–
John Prevoe	1	–	–	2268	–
Francis Rogers	1	1695	–	–	1 ton lignum vitae
Thomas Scrope	1	1663	–	24	–
James Stevens	1	–	1,690	–	–
Samuel Stokes	1	–	240	–	–
Bryan Tandy	1	–	264	–	–
Henry Watts	1	1695	1,000	–	–
Thomas Whittuck	1	–	3,112	–	–
Aaron Williams	1	–	450	–	–
Peter Young	1	–	597	–	–

Source: PRO E190 coastal port books.

the case of William Daines, John Day and Abraham Elton, rising to high office. In addition, Daines, Hart, Day, Elton, Jeffries, James Hollidge and Edmund Mountjoy served as mayors of the city, with Daines, Joseph Earle and Elton becoming MPs for the borough later in the eighteenth century. Others, like Charles Harford, James Peters and Edward Lloyd, were important Quaker merchants. In 1700, Harford and Lloyd were associated with Hollidge, Jones and others in a prospective brass-making enterprise; Lloyd bankrolled Darby's brass works at Baptist Mills in Bristol; and Peters was to enter into partnership with Darby at Coalbrookdale in 1709.[62] Martindale and Edward Hackett were also clearly significant traders in their own right, even though they appear to have remained formally unconnected with the Merchant Venturers.[63] Lesser merchants who operated mainly in the coastal trade, like Stephen Baker of Bristol, are also represented,[64] as are a rather smaller number of other trades: Doleman, for example, was a mercer.[65]

The Minehead records, although not unique, provide far more detail than the records for other ports. The inclusion of such data appears to be a device to ratify that overseas goods imported elsewhere and thence shipped coastally had paid the requisite customs dues. It is, however, questionable whether these traders functioned as coastal merchants. On paper there remains only a tenuous link between the Bristol merchants of table 4.8 and the coastal cargoes discharging at Minehead. We know that they were responsible for customs duties, and we can infer from this that they owned a substantial part of these cargoes when initially imported, but without explicit corroborative evidence one cannot imply full mercantile control over coastal consignments. None the less, the fragmentary survivals of merchant accounts for this period suggest that the 'real' merchants of Bristol, to use McGrath's distinction, were often involved in trading coastwise goods imported from abroad. For example, Charles Jones junior of Bristol was responsible for trading 40 barrels of pitch and tar on his own account to William Alloway of Bridgwater on board the *Satisfaction* of Bridgwater in 1696. The vessel was directed by its regular master, Edward Davis, who appeared in both the Bristol and Bridgwater records as merchant for a large cargo including Jones's goods.[66] A similar pattern is also apparent in the activities of Graffin Prankard in the early eighteenth century. Prankard traded overseas and domestic goods to local customers via a network of regular trows and vessels, and, although he was not generally recorded as merchant for customs purposes, he was central to the shipment and distribution of goods. In February 1715, for instance, he informed Thomas Harvey that '8 hhds [hogsheads] of tobacco' were 'put on board the May Flower belonging to owner Bradley the 6th Instant'. Duly enough, the *Mayflower* of Worcester, merchanted by George Bradley and mastered by Samuel Pitt, cleared Bristol for Gloucester on a coquet dated 6 February.

Amongst a general cargo of textiles, grocery, earthenwares, Bath waters and wood was Prankard's tobacco, albeit subsumed within a consignment of nine hogsheads weighing 4,960 lb.[67]

The absence of a complete series of data for inwards shipments prevents the construction of a full regional sample. Although data gleaned from other port books affords a measure of comparison, the process is unwieldy and cannot tackle the problems of erratic compilation or poor extancy. Even so, the data reveal two principal characteristics of coastal organisation. Firstly, the concentration of the coal trade in the hands of a small body of local shippers is reflected in the high ranking of the ports of the south-west. This ascendancy is stratified: the market and distribution centres of Somerset (Bridgwater and Minehead) display a conspicuously higher position in terms of voyages per trader and number of regular traders than do those of north Devon (Bideford, Barnstaple and Ilfracombe), which in turn rank higher than the Cornish ports. In addition, the ports that depended most upon Bristol—Chepstow and Gloucester, in particular—display lower ratios of voyages per merchant inwards than that obtained in the outwards trade. None the less, the primacy of Severn masters in the hierarchy of coastal importers cannot be doubted. Masters recorded trading through Gloucester were responsible for over 4 shipments on average, compared to the 3.5 voyages undertaken by each separate merchant. At Chepstow, the large ratio of masters to voyages suggests that single voyages remained the operational standard, and that many boats must have returned empty or in ballast.

In order to provide a level of comparison, the exercises tabulated above have been applied to a wider chronological sample for seven major regional ports. The results, presented in tables 4.9 and 4.10, represent a cross-section of the principal geographical and administrative divisions of the region combined with maximum record extancy and data capture. Although the data are influenced by local contingencies, the general pattern established in the findings for the sample year is confirmed. Thus, merchants exporting goods coastwise at Bristol were consistently involved in around 2 to 3 voyages, and at Padstow between 1.25 (the highly aberrant record for 1703) and 1.65 shipments. At Bridgwater, despite peaks at the beginning and end of the ten-year sample, an average of around 1.75 voyages per trader was recorded. In comparison, the proportion of voyages to traders involved in the inwards trade at the main coal-importing ports, Bridgwater, Bideford and Padstow, reveals a rather different trend. Here, whilst the close association of merchant and master is emphasised, there is some fluctuation in the numbers of traders recorded from year to year. Of these ports, the data for Bideford are the most consistent, with 1699 representing a peak in the activity of masters consonant with an overall increase in trade.[68] At Bridgwater and Padstow (with the slight exception of 1703), the number of traders remained generally constant throughout the period. The increase in both merchants and masters importing goods coastally at Bridgwater in 1697 correlates directly with the proportional expansion in the level of recorded trade in the year.

At Gloucester, the more settled conditions that existed between 1698 and 1701 encouraged a greater concentration of trade. Although voyages clearing the port remained more or less stable, with a slight peak in 1697, rather fewer merchants were recorded in 1699, 1701 and even 1704. In contrast, the numbers of masters recorded per outwards voyage continued at a relatively high level. This situation appears to reflect a greater number of freighted shipments, with major trow-owners, like John Beale senior and junior of Bewdley, who combined mastering vessels with more fixed mercantile roles. In 1701, for example, the Beales merchanted 30 shipments clearing Gloucester, of which 20 were undertaken by such lesser operatives as John Coldrake,

Table 4.9a

Merchants per voyages outwards, 1695–1704

		1695	1696	1697	1698	1699	1700	1701	1702	1703	1704
Bristol	Voyage	430	383	–	445	491	–	412	–	–	–
	Merchant	162	169	–	175	196	–	196	–	–	–
	Unknown	0	1	–	21	30	–	5	–	–	–
	Voyages per merchant	2.65	2.27	–	2.54	2.51	–	2.10	–	–	–
Gloucester	Voyage	289	334	357	–	332	–	335	–	–	331
	Merchant.	61	83	79	–	52	–	51	–	–	47
	Unknown	21	0	0	–	1	–	1	–	–	1
	Voyages per merchant	4.74	4.02	4.52	–	6.38	–	6.57	–	–	7.04
Bridgwater	Voyage	55	56	55	55	95	–	73	–	70	–
	Merchant	23	30	31	38	55	–	44	–	33	–
	Unknown	0	1	0	0	1	–	0	–	0	–
	Voyages per merchant	2.39	1.87	1.77	1.45	1.73	–	1.66	–	2.12	–
Bideford	Voyage	70	70	57	–	72	83	–	72	–	–
	Merchant	29	4	1	–	50	2	–	9	–	–
	Unknown	17	58	56	–	4	76	–	60	–	–
	Voyages per merchant	–	–	–	–	–	–	–	–	–	–
Padstow	Voyage	19	29	28	–	–	–	–	–	5	–
	Merchant	14	20	17	–	–	–	–	–	4	–
	Unknown	0	0	2	–	–	–	–	–	0	–
	Voyages per merchant	1.36	1.45	1.65	–	–	–	–	–	1.25	–

Table 4.9b

Masters per voyage outwards, 1695–1704

		1695	1696	1697	1698	1699	1700	1701	1702	1703	1704
Bristol	Voyage	430	383	–	445	491	–	412	–	–	–
	Master	153	160	–	173	194	–	184	–	–	–
	Unknown	0	2	–	2	0	–	3	–	–	–
	Voyages per master	2.81	2.39	–	2.57	2.53	–	2.24	–	–	–
Gloucester	Voyage	289	334	357	–	332	–	335	–	–	331
	Master	63	82	79	–	59	–	76	–	–	80
	Unknown	25	0	0	–	1	–	2	–	–	1
	Voyages per master	4.59	4.07	4.52	–	5.63	–	4.41	–	–	4.14
Bridgwater	Voyage	55	56	55	55	95	–	73	–	70	–
	Master	25	33	28	36	50	–	41	–	31	–
	Unknown	0	1	0	0	1	–	0	–	0	–
	Voyages per master	2.20	1.70	1.96	1.53	1.90	–	1.78	–	2.26	–
Bideford	Voyage	70	70	57	–	72	83	–	72	–	–
	Master	32	38	39	–	51	48	–	51	–	–
	Unknown	17	14	10	–	3	12	–	0	–	–
	Voyages per master	2.19	1.84	1.46	–	1.41	1.73	–	1.41	–	–
Padstow	Voyage.	19	29	28	–	–	–	–	–	5	–
	Master	14	19	19	–	–	–	–	–	4	–
	Unknown	0	0	2	–	–	–	–	–	0	–
	Voyages per master	1.36	1.53	1.47	–	–	–	–	–	1.25	–
Tenby	Voyage	232	209	221	181	176	244	259	224	–	221
	Master	95	99	81	82	76	97	115	115	–	107
	Unknown	1	3	1	1	2	21	6	0	–	1
	Voyages per master	2.44	2.11	2.73	2.21	2.32	2.52	2.25	1.95	–	2.07
Neath	Voyage	–	–	–	–	–	–	437	401	440	440
	Master	–	–	–	–	–	–	210	192	176	150
	Unknown	–	–	–	–	–	–	1	0	0	0
	Voyages per master	–	–	–	–	–	–	2.08	2.09	2.50	2.93

Source: PRO E190 coastal port books.

Henry Malpas, Humphrey Tyler and Francis Huxley. With up-river voyages, the profile of traders remained far more constant between years, although, significantly, the pronounced increase in voyages recorded in 1699 was not linked to a rise in the number of masters. Unlike the experience of Bridgwater in 1697, it appears that in response to higher levels of trade

Table 4.10a

Merchants per voyage inwards, 1695–1704

		1695	1696	1697	1698	1699	1700	1701	1702	1703	1704
Gloucester	Voyage	235	190	235	–	294	–	216	–	–	252
	Merchant	76	69	67	–	84	–	67	–	–	72
	Unknown	10	0	2	–	0	–	0	–	–	1
	Voyages per merchant	3.09	2.75	3.51	–	3.50	–	3.22	–	–	3.50
Bridgwater	Voyage	382	282	442	321	331	–	345	–	360	–
	Merchant	86	90	125	78	92	–	97	–	88	–
	Unknown	6	2	1	0	0	–	1	–	0	–
	Voyages per merchant	4.44	3.13	3.54	4.12	3.60	–	3.56	–	4.09	–
Bideford	Voyage	186	170	166	–	225	245	–	207	–	–
	Merchant	92	0	5	–	108	56	–	18	–	–
	Unknown	13	170	166	–	13	177	–	190	–	–
	Voyages per merchant	–	–	–	–	–	–	–	–	–	–
Padstow	Voyage	95	117	129	–	–	–	–	–	129	–
	Merchant	60	60	80	–	–	–	–	–	56	–
	Unknown	4	2	0	–	–	–	–	–	3	–
	Voyages per merchant	1.58	1.95	1.61	–	–	–	–	–	2.30	–

Table 4.10b

Masters per voyage inwards, 1695–1704

		1695	1696	1697	1698	1699	1700	1701	1702	1703	1704
Gloucester	Voyage	235	190	235	–	294	–	216	–	–	252
	Master	63	65	67	–	68	–	59	–	–	73
	Unknown	8	0	3	–	1	–	0	–	–	1
	Voyages per master	3.73	2.92	3.51	–	4.32	–	3.66	–	–	3.45
Bridgwater	Voyage.	382	282	442	321	331	–	345	–	360	–
	Master	84	81	119	74	83	–	95	–	95	–
	Unknown	5	1	1	0	0	–	1	–	0	–
	Voyages per master	4.55	3.48	3.71	4.34	3.99	–	3.63	–	3.79	–
Bideford	Voyage	186	170	166	–	225	245	–	207	–	–
	Master	94	96	96	–	108	125	–	112	–	–
	Unknown	0	0	0	–	13	3	–	0	–	–
	Voyages per master	1.98	1.77	1.73	–	2.08	1.96	–	1.84	–	–
Padstow	Voyage	95	117	129	–	–	–	–	–	129	–
	Master	58	60	77	–	–	–	–	–	54	–
	Unknown	0	0	2	–	–	–	–	–	0	–
	Voyages per master	1.64	1.95	1.68	–	–	–	–	–	2.39	–
Tenby	Voyage	25	17	14	17	10	10	26	12	–	23
	Master	11	10	12	17	6	6	10	9	–	10
	Unknown	0	0	0	0	1	1	3	0	–	0
	Voyages per master	2.27	1.70	1.17	1.00	1.67	1.67	2.60	1.33	–	2.30

Source: PRO E190 coastal port books.

Severn masters merely made more through-journeys. This probably reflected the relatively small number of vessels on the river capable of navigating the longer routes beyond the upper Severn estuary and the existence of a central group of trowmen proficient enough to engage in through-trade.

At the coal ports of Tenby and Neath, numbers of masters involved in coastal exports were linked directly to the very different operational conditions at both ports. At Neath trade was concentrated upon an established body of key traders, based in the main south-western ports. Whilst voyages remained fairly constant across the four full years of the sample, the numbers of masters recorded at Neath declined significantly. This reflected the overall tailing-off in the level of long-distance shipments to the more remote centres of the south coast of England, coupled with an increase in the frequency and indeed efficiency of the trade to Bridgwater and Minehead. In contrast, the steady ratio of voyages to masters in the coastal exports of Tenby was indicative of the more abbreviated commercial horizons of the port. The culm trade was effectively partitioned between a nucleus of Somerset and north Devon boats and masters, who plied the route with monotonous regularity. Imports were a different matter. Inwards shipments were erratic and limited to returning Bristol packets, the odd cargo discharging from the colliers of the south-western ports, and an *ad hoc* trade with nearby centres in petty items such as timber.

Deviations from the sample year can be explained in part by such factors as warfare and embargo and the transference of coastal operations to overland routes. Whilst the general reduction of trade in 1695–6 may have constricted the numbers of voyages undertaken by traders, it did not excluded them altogether from coasting. On the other hand, greater economic opportunity involved both increased activity by existing traders as at Gloucester and expansion in the base of operatives. Thus, merchants and masters who were otherwise employed in purely local or intra-port activities were more involved in regional and especially extra-regional forms of trade in times of economic stability. For example, on the Severn and the Wye, short-haul carriage to and from river centres remained as important as the long-distance trade through the administrative head port. Tramping and transhipment within the boundaries of Gloucester were always profitable commercial activities involving a large body of traders and trow owners that only very occasionally ventured out into the estuary.[69] Such traders, probably the bulk of Severn trowmen, were more likely to be freighted when conditions were at their optimum. Similarly, short-haul river trade, like overland trade, increased during periods when coastal traffic was impeded by privateering or was prohibitively uneconomic.

However, it must not be forgotten that underpinning these data is the question of opportunity. Masters and especially those not tied to the relative security of fixed routes or linked to larger mercantile concerns operated on low margins: they and their craft usually went where the most competitive freight could be gained. Long-distance coastal enterprises and even overseas ventures could absorb their activities for months, even years. For example, Sebastian Llewellyn, a typical Bridgwater master-merchant, was regularly involved in shipping coal and culm from south Wales to Somerset on board the *Comfort* of Bridgwater. On occasion he picked up a freight in other vessels, notably the *True Love* of Bridgwater, on the Bristol and Liverpool routes. Between 1695 and 1704, Llewellyn was associated with around 16 coastal shipments a year. During most of 1698, however, he was absent mastering the *Willing Mind* of Bridgwater for William Alloway and partners to the West Indies, returning only in September.[70] His role as master of the *Comfort* was taken by John Parsons and Nathaniel Vosper.[71] It is clear, therefore, that the regional staples, the coal trade and the links with Bristol, operated as a useful standby from which a large available pool of tonnage and labour could be diverted to other coastal runs or to overseas ventures as the need arose.[72] In such circumstances, regular traders could effectively disappear from the official record of coasting, their trade distributed to either existing or new operatives.

Traders and vessels: the means of coasting in the Bristol Channel

As we have seen, port book data have been used widely to study the mechanisms by which goods were moved from port to port, the vessels employed in regional coasting and their association with particular masters, merchants, regional ports and specific trades.[73] Even so, any analysis of coastal craft must be undertaken with caution. The principal methodological stumbling block concerns the status of the 'home' port attached to boats. In some quarters it has been assumed that a boat nominally 'of Padstow', for example, was firmly, even unequivocally, associated with that port: a kind of practical, if informal recognition of ship registry predating the Act of 1786.[74] Other scholars have implied that the home port indicated the residence or port of operation of the boat's principal merchant or master. In effect, the home port could refer to all, some, or none of these explanations. Traders were often based in the port described, although quite equally many were either professional masters chartered from elsewhere, or remote merchants paying freightage.[75] Similarly, boats were often located at the specified named home port. However, examples exist of the recorded home port changing within the same port establishment or at either end of a single recorded shipment. Thus, the *Blessing* 'of' Brockweir was usually defined by its Wye home port when trading between Chepstow and Bristol. Clearing Liverpool in 1699, it was described as 'of' Chepstow and yet 'of' Brockweir when it arrived later in

Chepstow. To the Liverpool customs officials, it was sufficient to note the superintending customs port, whilst at Chepstow, because of the existence of a *Blessing* of Chepstow, officials were required to be more precise.

The convention adopted by this work has been to interpret home ports as indicating the port from which shipment commenced.[76] In most cases this indicated the centre from which the vessel habitually traded, particularly in cases where cyclical shipments (characteristic of the coal and salt trade), or regular packet services (to and from Gloucester and Bristol, for example), formed the main coastal routes. This is not to say that port designations were always used in a consistent way. In 1699, for example, Chepstow recorded 15 voyages of the *Richard and Mary*, 13 of which were mastered by Richard Ellis. In 12 shipments the vessel was described as of Brockweir, two voyages were specified as of Tintern (or of Abbey), and one of Chepstow. It is possible that three separate vessels were involved, although the association of Ellis with each port makes this unlikely. Yet, as all home ports were under the administration of the same customs house, such changes have less serious implications than if two discrete jurisdictions were involved. To the customs system, the most important factor remained the identification of the customs house responsible for noting the shipment and holding bond money or promissory notes as surety. At Liverpool in the same year, the *Diamond*, skippered by Thomas Moneley, was variously 'of' Chester, Frodsham and Liverpool, all technically subject to Chester customs house. A problem does occur, however, when common boat names occur with imperfect or erratic port designations. In such cases it becomes difficult for the historian to disentangle the voyages of quite separate vessels which may have shared a common name and operated out of identical ports and home ports simultaneously. In such highly infrequent instances, association with regular masters generally provides a workable discriminator.[77] Indeed, these potential areas of confusion were not unknown to contemporary traders. For instance, when William Perkes was indicted for an excise fraud in 1700, he argued disingenuously, but successfully, that an overload of salt found in his trow, the *Providence* of Worcester, was the result of porters inadvertently substituting a consignment rightly intended for the *Prosperous* of Worcester.[78]

For these reasons, a simple numeric schedule of vessels sorted by recorded home port provides a limited means of analysing both boat operation and the comparative importance of regional ports in the carrying trade. Certainly, numbers of vessels cannot exhibit the range of trade undertaken at each port or the types and trading patterns of coasters that either 'belonged' to or traded most regularly with a given centre. What is more, many outports blatantly ignored the express instructions of the Board of Trade and failed to record consistently the home ports of vessels.[79] Nevertheless, an impression of the frequency with which individual vessels were utilised can be gained from tables 4.11 and 4.12. In the tables, boats have been systematically isolated and data of uncertain provenance excluded. As such, the figures err on the side of conservatism: where there has been any possible doubt as to the designation of a boat, whether by name or home port, its voyage has been discounted. At Barnstaple, Tenby, Milford and Carmarthen, where home ports were not habitually recorded, the overwhelming amount of blank data has prevented any form of comparative analysis. These ports are flagged and have been included only to contextualise the regional sample.

Table 4.11 separates the number of individual boats trading to and from regional ports from unknown, blank or illegible data. In the case of Minehead and Bideford, entries describing overland trade have also been excluded. The data are expressed in terms of the total number of voyages recorded at each port establishment ordered by the frequency with which each boat appeared in the respective coastal books. The above-Holms centres, Gloucester, Cardiff and Chepstow, which were most intimately associated with Bristol, display the highest ratio of boats to voyages. This concentration of trade was most apparent at Gloucester, where each trow accounted for an average of almost

Table 4.11

Boats trading at Bristol Channel ports, sample year

		Total voyages	Total boats	Unknown	Voyages per boat
Gloucester		626	74	1	8.46
Cardiff		31	5	0	6.20
Bridgwater		426	75	1	5.68
Chepstow		410	75	0	5.47
Minehead		476	88	8	5.41
Barnstaple	*	320	89	10	3.60
Tenby	*	186	55	2	3.38
Milford	*	506	157	10	3.22
Bristol		491	172	1	2.85
Neath		437	160	0	2.73
Bideford		297	111	12	2.68
St Ives		93	35	1	2.66
Ilfracombe		175	69	1	2.54
Padstow		157	65	0	2.42
Carmarthen	*	73	36	2	2.03
Swansea		531	268	1	1.98
Llanelli		81	53	0	1.53
Mount's Bay		17	15	1	1.13
South Burry		13	13	0	1.00
Liverpool		509	224	3	2.27

Note: *Data incomplete.

Source: PRO E190 coastal port books.

8.5 voyages in the sample year, and at Cardiff where coasters undertook just over 6 shipments. At Gloucester, the nature of long-distance river trade encouraged a core number of boats. As most trading was confined to the Severn itself, the traders and vessels recorded in the port books represented an acknowledged elite, able, willing and experienced enough to venture into the more turbulent waters of the Bristol Channel. In addition, a small collection of vessels mainly associated with Tewkesbury, Upton, Bewdley and, to a lesser extent, Worcester specialised in the wider routes to Somerset, Devon and south Wales. By the later seventeenth century, Tewkesbury and Upton masters in particular had carved out a very profitable niche by exploiting these longer, more speculative and more hazardous coastal voyages. Trading beyond the normal horizons of Severn craft had its own particular difficulties. In 1708, for example, Thomas Claroe, trow owner and acting merchant of four Upton trows, was arrested for evading payment of *ad valorem* duties levied on salt imported at Cardiff.[80] Such minor setbacks did not deter the small but energetic band of Upton traders from undertaking the more irregular freights. Between 1680 and 1724, over 60 per cent of voyages undertaken in Upton boats were to ports other than Bristol.[81]

At Chepstow, a similar group of boats and traders formed the basis of trade. For example, in 1699 the *Blessing* of Brockweir was mastered on 27 voyages by John Phillips and on 7 by William Marsh, whereas Thomas Hughes, Thomas Richards and an unspecified master supervised one voyage apiece. In the same year, the *Blessing* of Chepstow was mastered on all 59 voyages by John Gosling. Even so, the ratio of boats to voyages at Chepstow was appreciably lower than at Gloucester. This was directly the result of the omission of letpass cargoes and a comparatively stunted inwards trade: boats returning with customable goods to port represented only 16 per cent of Chepstow's total trade. Again, most Chepstow boats were tied to the supply of Bristol, although a small proportion of long-distance craft were recorded. These more robust, 'open-sea' vessels undertook the trade to and from Liverpool, Cornwall and the south Wales coal ports. However, with the exception of the notably seaworthy *Blessing* of Brockweir, these voyages tended to be one-off shipments undertaken by specialist craft and traders who, by tramping cargoes elsewhere, appeared only once in the Chepstow sample.

In contrast, the absence of a comparative series of inwards data at Bristol has adversely affected the representation of trading at the port. It is clear from the regional sample that many of the 172 individual vessels isolated in table 4.11 returned to Bristol, and, for that matter, undertook rather more voyages with customable cargo on the inward leg. As there is no acceptable way of fully reconstructing this trade without severely compromising the records, the much more limited data relating to coastal exports offer only a highly partial view. None the less, the figures indicate that the steady procession of regular packet-like craft to Gloucester, Chepstow and the region was offset by single long-haul voyages to the more distant ports of the north-west and south coast of England. This greatly increased the number of vessels recorded at Bristol—voyages to London and Liverpool were undertaken by specialist craft employed on an *ad hoc* basis—whilst conversely serving to limit the frequency of annual voyages undertaken by coastal craft.

At Bridgwater and Minehead boats were involved in between five and six voyages. This resulted from a high degree of flexibility in the employment of coastal vessels. Boats in the coal and salt trades were frequently redeployed in the trade with Bristol or in tramping goods to local centres both within the boundaries of the customs port itself and to proximate ports, predominantly north Devon.[82] A related practice can also be seen in the activity of Severn trows shipping salt and other goods through Gloucester to the Somerset centres. These vessels were often involved in transporting local letpass cargoes and in the seasonal freighting of coal from south Wales whilst waiting for return freights to Bristol or Gloucester.

The case of Thomas Hooper, master of the *Samuel* of Upton, illustrates this point. In February 1699, Hooper cleared Gloucester with a cargo of salt, flax seed, cloth, and flax and hurds bound for Bridgwater, arriving on 3 March. A week later he shipped a letpass consignment of herrings from Ilfracombe to Minehead on behalf of William Alloway, picking up another small cargo of tallow, fish and Irish paper for Joseph Holland *en route* to Bridgwater. He eventually discharged both cargoes at Bridgwater on 17 March bearing dual documentation. The *Samuel* was next encountered carrying two further herring cargoes for Alloway from Ilfracombe to Minehead in April. After this Hooper proceeded to Bristol, most probably in ballast, and was chartered to carry a small letpass cargo of glass bottles to Bridgwater, arriving in Somerset on 15 May. From here he returned to Bristol with another letpass cargo of cider, wood ashes, cheese and hair on 22 May. By 5 June, the *Samuel* was shipping a load of rock salt from Bristol by coquet probably to Neath; no destination is specified in the Bristol port book. From Neath, the *Samuel* then took coals to Bridgwater, arriving in late June, before taking a cargo of wood and soapers' ashes and peas under coquet to Bristol on 3 July. Fourteen days later Hooper was back at Neath again shipping coals to Bridgwater. There is then a hiatus of over a month before the *Samuel* reappears entering Bridgwater on 4 September carrying coals from Neath on a coquet dated 19 August. From Bridgwater the boat most probably returned to Neath in ballast, picking up a coal freight on 2 September bound for Gloucester. By the following month, the *Samuel* was shipping white salt and brine to Ilfracombe, arriving back in the Severn at sometime before 30

October to freight another salt and brine cargo to Minehead. On 24 November, Hooper cleared Minehead for Gloucester (the Gloucester records specify the head port, Bridgwater) carrying oats, peas and white herrings.

Thus, in 1699 the *Samuel* of Upton completed 16 recorded shipments of goods, a remarkable rate of productivity given the wider assessments of coasting efficiency.[83] This involved not only the staple long-distance trade in salt, but also the odd opportunistic local letpass cargo, a couple of freights from Bristol, four voyages as a collier, and three return cargoes with Somerset goods to Bristol and Gloucester. On most of these shipments, Hooper nominally acted on his own account but was on occasion explicitly freighted by Alloway and Holland. The range of the *Samuel's* activity was exceptional even by the standards of the more adventurous extra-regional coasters. However, Hooper's travels indicate that the classic bilateral relationship between exporting and importing centres in the coastal trade, especially that which existed between Severn ports and Bristol, was not universal. Boats, even open trows, went where the goods were and where the most profitable terms could be gained.

At Neath, Bideford, St Ives, Ilfracombe and Padstow, the prominence and regularity of the coal trade accounts for the degree of consistency between centres of markedly differing size. Below this stratum come ports at which trade was spread thinly, or where large numbers of vessels were involved. At Swansea, for example, the healthy demand for coal from relatively far-flung markets resulted in a large number of more distant traders using a wider selection of boats. In 1701, 268 craft were recorded in the Swansea port book, many of which were from the smaller centres and creeks of the south coast of England. In comparison, the more confined parameters of Neath's trade in essentially the same commodity meant that rather fewer numbers of craft were used. These vessels were mainly based in the region and thus made proportionally more voyages of a much shorter distance in the sample year. Elsewhere, the single voyage dominated the smaller centres such as Llanelli. At Mount's Bay and South Burry the level of recorded trade was too small to draw firm conclusions.

The general assessment of coastal vessels indicates that important concentrations of trading activity existed in the region. In table 4.12 vessels 'local' to the regional port establishment are assessed in order to analyse the patterns and direction of trade. In this context, the term 'local' has been defined to include all craft which were explicitly deemed to be 'of' the port in question, or 'of' a creek or inlet under its immediate jurisdiction. Thus, local boats for Minehead include all vessels nominally of Watchet and Porlock as well as those of the main customs port. Of course, such criteria are dependent upon the integral nature of customs administrations. Where the

Table 4.12

Local boats trading at Bristol Channel ports, sample year

	Total voyages	Local boats	Other boats	Unattributed boats	% local boats	Voyages by local boats	% trade in local boats
Cardiff	31	5	0	0	100	31	100
Gloucester	626	65	9	0	88	601	96
Chepstow	410	35	39	1	47	355	87
Bideford	297	80	31	0	72	237	80
Bridgwater	426	37	38	0	49	317	74
Minehead	476	34	48	6	39	294	62
St Ives	93	10	25	0	29	55	59
Ilfracombe	175	18	50	1	26	100	57
Padstow	157	33	32	0	51	79	50
Carmarthen	* 73	6	13	17	17	28	38
Swansea	531	39	227	2	15	142	27
Mount's Bay	17	2	13	0	13	2	12
Milford	* 506	20	28	109	13	51	10
Neath	437	5	142	13	3	26	6
Llanelli	81	2	51	0	4	4	5
Bristol	491	5	151	16	3	8	2
South Burry	13	0	13	0	0	0	0
Barnstaple	* 320	0	2	87	–	–	–
Tenby	* 186	0	0	55	–	–	–
Liverpool	509	31	156	37	14	93	18

Note: *Data incomplete.

Source: PRO E190 coastal port books.

'extents, bounds and limits' of certain ports were disputed, some confusion exists in the attribution of minor ports to immediate member and head ports. The prime example of this occurs in the relationship of the small ports and inlets of the Taw–Torridge estuary with the head port, Barnstaple, and its more important satellite, Bideford.[84] For the purposes of the table, all creeks within the bounds of Barnstaple and Bideford have been deemed 'local' to both ports.

Table 4.12 reveals three broad categories relating to trade conducted in local craft. Firstly, at Cardiff, Gloucester and Chepstow, the vast majority of trade was confined to vessels nominally of the head port or subject creeks. The limitations of the Cardiff sample have already been stressed, although even if missing data for inwards traffic and for the inferior creeks gleaned from other port books are included, the exclusive nature of the boats operating from the port jurisdiction is confirmed. Only four boats from other designations can be identified as trading to Cardiff or its creeks in the sample year, and such shipments were far outweighed by voyages from Bristol undertaken entirely in local craft.[85] At Gloucester, only nine craft were not associated with the navigation proper or with the immediate estuary under the control of the head port. These vessels, mostly from the Wye or the south Wales ports, were involved in 25 voyages, 4 per cent of total shipments. The concentration of trade upon local craft is also demonstrated at Chepstow. Here, boats with home ports outside the immediate jurisdiction of the port were numerically greater, yet they were involved in less than 1.5 voyages per annum. Local craft carried 87 per cent of coastal trade by shipment and almost wholly controlled the regular routes. Only the inwards trades in salt from Gloucester and copper ore from St Ives were branches of commerce undertaken in non-Wye vessels that were not opportunistic in nature.

A second tier of importance revealed by table 4.12 comprises the ports at which between roughly a half and three-quarters of all trade was conducted in local boats. This sector is dominated by the major south-western ports, although given the uncertain status of Bideford vessels, the results may over-represent commercial activity: almost 72 per cent of craft carrying 80 per cent of trade at Bideford were nominally local. Many of these vessels were 'shared' with Barnstaple. At the other south-western ports non-local craft predominated. However, the proportion of trade engrossed by these vessels was much smaller: around a quarter of shipments at Bridgwater and two-fifths at Minehead. Padstow was the exception to this pattern. A majority of boats frequenting the port were either of the main centre or its creek, Port Isaac. Yet these local craft accounted for only half the recorded coastal shipments, with tramping boats of and from St Ives and Clovelly under-taking a relatively large slice of trade.

The final grouping incorporates ports where local craft were both less numerous and cumulatively less active than vessels from more distant ports. This was a particular characteristic of the south Wales coal ports at which numbers of local craft were far exceeded by boats operating out of the main importing centres of the south-west of England. None the less, there was much differentiation between these centres. At Swansea, for example, 39 vessels were associated with local home ports. These vessels undertook 142 voyages, an average of 3.64 shipments per craft per year.[86] At Neath, trade was almost entirely the province of boats of remote ports: only five local boats were active in the sample, representing 3 per cent of total vessels recorded and 6 per cent of shipments. A similar situation existed at Llanelli, with only two local vessels, the *John* and the *Joanna*, both mastered by Abraham King, appearing amidst a fleet of coasters from Northam, Bideford and other south-western ports. North Devon boats also dominated the trade of South Burry entirely. At Milford, Tenby and, to a lesser extent, Carmarthen, the erratic record of home ports has obscured effective analysis. However, data from the ports of the south-west confirms that non-local coasters effectively controlled the trade of south-west Wales. At these ports only the occasional vessel carrying culm or agricultural staples and Bristol packet boats—the *Amity* of Milford, the *Providence* of Tenby, or the *Assistance* of Laugharne, for example—can be identified as local craft.

The lowly position of Bristol in the table reveals a telling assessment of its largely vicarious role in regional coasting. Only five vessels undertaking six voyages were recorded as 'of Bristol' in the total sample of 156 boats recorded in 1699. These boats were essentially independent, occasional craft, only marginally involved in the main business of coasting. Some of these vessels, like the *Duke Humphrey* of Bristol, mastered by William Davis and bound for Swansea, were overseas craft pressed into coastal service. Such ships appear to have resumed overseas trading without figuring in the coastal records of the period again. The two boats that appear consistently across the wider sample, the *Mary and Martha*, skippered by Henry Keating, and Henry Roe's *Roe Sloop*, were linked to the long-distance routes to Liverpool, the south coast of England, London, and beyond. In June 1700, for instance, the *Roe Sloop* cleared Bristol for Yarmouth with a cargo of cider and bacon. Other vessels, like the *True Love* of Bristol, skippered by Francis Cockhill and clearing for Liverpool, appear to be errors caused by the casual slip of the customs officer's pen rather than genuine attributions.[87]

In the same vein, Bristol did not operate regular trows or river barges. Although Bristol craft undoubtedly plied the lower reaches of the Severn estuary, only two vessels were involved in more than three voyages in the entire series of Gloucester port books from 1680 to 1730. In 1691, a boom year in the number of shipments to Bristol, the *William and Mary* of Bristol undertook six voyages from Gloucester under John Brookes and Joseph Powell carrying mostly meal and agricultural surpluses. A further three voyages were recorded between 1709 and 1713, although it is probable that an entirely different vessel was involved.[88] In addition, the *John* (occasionally *John Trow*) of Bristol was chartered on 12 customs-worthy voyages from Bristol to Gloucester from 1703 to 1707, returning with cargo on only one occasion. The intermittent frequency of this trade and the very limited nature of the goods involved, mostly small consignments of coal and glass bottles, indicate that petty letpass trades may well have formed the bulk of the vessel's activity. Compared to the fleets of trows based at the Severn ports, the involvement of Bristol craft was meagre: throughout the period, the staple trades of the port, the products and markets of the Severn, Wye and Welsh borderland, were conducted almost wholly in the holds, or rather on the decks of regional boats.

The coastal craft of the Bristol Channel

The data discussed above emphasise the need to provide an assessment of
the number of boats attached to each port. Table 4.13 presents broad indices
of the shipping and tonnage involved in the coastal trade in the sample year,
comparing these to the Musgrave figures for 1709.[89] In addition, the figures
extracted by Andrews from letters dispatched from the customs commissioners to the Admiralty in 1701/2 are included, although, as they relate to
both overseas vessels and coasters, their utility is more comparative.[90]
Undoubtedly, the figures are somewhat problematic and, as Jarvis once
stressed, there is a very real danger of 'comparing the non-comparables'.[91] In
particular, severe doubts underpin the accuracy and consistency of the
Musgrave series: at some ports the early figures appear little more than
hopeful back-projections of mid-century enumerations. Overall, the coastal
trade seems suspiciously small, especially in relation to the east-coast coal
trade, and the implications of war may have also imposed delimiting effects
on the 1709 material, although this should not render the data less reliable
for coastal assessments at least.[92] What is more, as the Musgrave figures
deal solely with tonnage, any conversion from carrying capacity or burden
weight to actual ships lying at anchor is necessarily speculative. The metrological differences between registered, measured and burden tonnages await
the unwary historian, although for both the period under study and the
comparative purposes used here such concerns pose less intrinsic difficulty.[93]

Rather different considerations underpinned the compilation of the two
'official' central lists and the procedures governing coastal port books. It is
clear that the Musgrave figures and the Admiralty list deal to a large extent
with head ports, reducing vessels 'belonging' to certain subject creeks to
an unrecognised, constituent status. Thus, whilst the port book data for
Gloucester represent 'open sea' or through-trade vessels based mainly at
Severn and Warwickshire Avon ports, it is possible that a proportion of boats
that were confined to the navigation in 1699, and thus did not figure in the
coastal records, were included in the enumerations of 1701 and 1709. This
may also explain the erratic record of Chepstow, Carmarthen, Llanelli, Tenby,
Cardigan and Aberdovey. Boats of these ports may well have inflated the
figures of Cardiff and Milford, the respective head ports and sites of
customs administration. However, the most important subject members and
creeks of the region, Minehead, Bideford, Ilfracombe and the Cornish ports,
appear to be recorded consistently and independently.

Mindful of the somewhat tortuous statistical gymnastics that have
surrounded the interpretation of these data, it has been necessary to adopt
a simple tonnage:ship conversion for the data presented in table 4.13. As
there is no sufficiently extensive contemporary assessment readily available,

Table 4.13

'Home' boats recorded in the coastal port books (sample year),
Musgrave figures (coastal and overseas, 1709) and Admiralty figures (1701)

(a) Coastal port books (sample year)   (b) Musgrave figures (coastal: 1709)

Port	Local vessels	Tonnage (conv. B)	Tonnage (conv. A)	Port	Vessels (conv. B)	Vessels (conv. A)	Tonnage
Gloucester	65	2,600	1,755	Gloucester	71	106	2,850
Bideford	80	2,240	2,240	Swansea	77	77	2,148
Swansea	39	1,092	1,092	Barnstaple	58	58	1,620
Bridgwater	37	1,036	1,036	Bideford	39	39	1,080
Chepstow	35	980	945	St Ives	32	33	900
Minehead	34	952	952	Minehead	30	30	850
Padstow	33	924	726	Padstow	24	30	670
Milford	20	560	560	Bridgwater	20	20	550
Ilfracombe	18	504	432	Milford	19	19	532
St Ives	10	280	270	Ilfracombe	14	17	400
Carmarthen	6	168	168	Mount's Bay	13	13	350
Cardiff	5	140	100	Bristol	6	6	180
Neath	5	140	140	Neath	3	3	82
Bristol	5	140	140	Cardiff	3	4	79
Mount's Bay	2	56	56	Llanelli	1	1	20
Llanelli	2	56	56	Chepstow	–	–	–
South Burry	0	0	0	Carmarthen	–	–	–
Barnstaple	–	–	–	Tenby	–	–	–
Tenby	–	–	–	South Burry	–	–	–
Total	396	11,868	10,668	Total	409	456	12,311
Liverpool	31	868	868	Liverpool	21	21	592

(c) Musgrave Figures (overseas: 1709)   (d) Admiralty figures (coastal and overseas: 1701)

Port	Vessels (60 ton)	Vessels (80 ton)	Tonnage	Port	Vessels	Tonnage	Mean
Bristol	256	192	15,365	Bristol	165	17,338	105.08
Bideford	32	24	1,930	Bideford	84	6,299	74.99
Barnstaple	24	18	1,430	Barnstaple	78	3,489	44.73
Milford	7	5	426	Swansea	37	1,468	39.68
Penzance	7	5	420	Gloucester	48	1,289	26.85
Minehead	5	4	300	Bridgwater	33	1,287	39.00
Gloucester	3	2	170	Minehead	30	1,094	36.47
Bridgwater	3	2	150	Milford	32	995	31.09
Swansea	3	2	150	Chepstow	28	744	26.57
Chepstow	1	1	60	Padstow	23	509	22.13
St Ives	0	1	24	St Ives	15	404	26.93
Padstow	0	0	0	Ilfracombe	15	358	23.87
Ilfracombe	0	0	0	Penzance	8	236	29.50
Cardiff	–	–	–	Cardiff	11	218	19.82
Neath	–	–	–	Neath	–	–	–
Llanelli	–	–	–	Llanelli	–	–	–
Carmarthen	–	–	–	Carmarthen	–	–	–
Tenby	–	–	–	Tenby	–	–	–
South Burry	–	–	–	South Burry	–	–	–
Total	340	256	20,425	Total	607	35,728	58.86
				Liverpool	102	8,619	84.50

William Barrett's summary figures of coastal vessels trading to and from Bristol in 1787 have been used. Barrett indicated that Bristol handled a total of 128,339 tons of coastal shipping comprising 3,493 ships with an average tonnage of 36.74 tons per vessel.[94] However, these calculations are not without difficulties. For a start, the figures are anachronistic to the port book, Musgrave and Admiralty assessments and it is likely that, given the relatively low overall assessment, Barrett's sketchy enumerations may have included small market craft, barges, open boats and vessels in ballast omitted from the official lists.[95] Moreover, Barrett's figures were almost certainly compiled according to registered or measured tons and as such provide a somewhat skewed comparison to the burden tonnage figures of the earlier data. None the less, if the conventions suggested by Davis and McCusker are applied, the 1787 figures can be used to obtain a working burden tonnage conversion of *c.*28 tons per vessel.[96]

Of course, many regional craft were far in excess of 28 tons burden. The *Hope* of Bridgwater, for example, was reckoned to be 'about 50 ton, a strong ship but [a] dull sailer' when assessed in 1699; Mackworth's *Mine Adventurer* was rated at 80 tons burden at Aberdovey in 1704 and was able to carry loads of up to 120 tons of lead and lead ore; and John Scott of Fowey, recommending a coaster for the salt trade, proposed 'a new ship of about fifty tunns, two decks ready for launching'.[97] Whilst these were long-distance coasters quite able to make overseas runs, they should not be confused with specialist ocean-going vessels of upwards of 100 tons which dominated the Admiralty figures for Bristol and Liverpool, and which featured strongly in the assessments of Bideford, Barnstaple and other centres involved in overseas enterprises. Despite the problems associated with war—the inevitable laying up of vessels by cautious owners, the refitting of craft for government service, and the simple delays caused by disruption of international trade routes and the inefficiency of convoy protection—the Musgrave figures for overseas vessels emphasise the activity of large ocean-going vessels at all these ports.[98] Even at the lesser regional ports, overseas craft could be comparatively large. For example, in 1696 Hoare and Company invested over £300 in the *Fortune*, a Swedish-built barque of about '200 tons deadweight' before refitting it for the Newfoundland and Iberian trades.[99] Even so, many vessels engaged in foreign trade were sometimes of a very meagre tonnage, especially those involved in the shorter round trips to Ireland or France.[100]

Despite these individual examples, the mean tonnage figures derived from the Admiralty list also reveal that the average of coastal *and* overseas craft fell below 28 tons burden at many ports. Two prominent Cardiff coasters, the *Speedwell* and the *Lyon,* were assessed for probate purposes at 24 tons and 20 tons in 1685 and 1694 respectively.[101] Similarly, the erratic record of burden tonnages in the Cardiff port books indicates that local coasters ranged from very small craft (the *Two Brothers* was rated at a paltry 11–12 tons in 1695) to relatively large vessels (the *Speedwell* weighed in at 27 tons in 1704).[102] To account for these instances, in cases where the tonnage per craft assessment is lower than the standard 28-ton conversion, a second calculation has been included alongside the figure derived from Barrett in table 4.13. This has been flagged as A (Admiralty) as distinct from B (Barrett).

Whilst these conversions suffice for purely coastal vessels, the tonnage of trows, (the flat-bottomed, river craft operating on the Severn and probably the lower reaches of the Wye), remains a problem. Trows were capable of carrying much larger loads than the more seaworthy and sturdily constructed sea coasters, although this was balanced by their lack of manoeuvrability outside the confined waters of the upper Bristol Channel. In terms of tonnage, however, assessments are somewhat confusing. In 1692, John Chance senior and junior, trow owners of Worcester, deposed that they had mastered or crewed boats of 'a burthen of twenty tons or thereabouts' between 16 and 18 times in the previous year. Data from the port books confirm that the Chances' main trows, the *John*, the *Thomas and Mary* and the *Thomas,* were carrying between 17.15 and 29.78 tons cargo weight in 1691 and 1692. However, these vessels were mostly engaged in up-river voyages shipping cargoes like cotton wool and tobacco that had a high stowage to weight factor.[103] By the early eighteenth century, open trows carrying salt and agricultural goods to Bridgwater and Minehead, the furthest regular destination for Severn craft, were quite capable of transporting 40–50 ton loadings.[104]

Two near-contemporary estimations also deserve consideration. In 1756, George Perry reckoned that Severn trows were 'generally from 16 to 20 ft. wide and 60 ft. in length' and 'from 40 to 80 tons burden'. These he distinguished from 'barges and frigates from 40 to 60 ft. in length . . . [which] carry from 20 to 40 tons'.[105] Undoubtedly, Perry's figures were broad simplifications of a more complex commercial situation. It remains unclear, for example, whether the barges and frigates described by Perry and indeed the much smaller 5–6 ton wherries were confined to the limits of the river or entered into the kind of long-distance trade recorded by the port books. In comparison, Barrett, writing some 13 years later than Perry, argued that '103 trows from 50 to 130 tons [37.5 to 97.5 tons burden] . . . [were] employed in carrying goods upon the Severn to and from Bristol'.[106]

Trows in 1699 were certainly large vessels, although perhaps not as large as the upper figures proposed by Perry and Barrett. For the purposes of the table, therefore, a compromise figure of 40 tons, more in line with port book evidence, has been adopted as a general rule for craft from the Severn and Warwickshire Avon.[107] Nevertheless, the mean tonnage per vessel 'belonging' to Gloucester and Chepstow revealed by the Admiralty figures suggests two additional factors at work. Firstly, it is clear that not all trows were as large as has been suggested and that a proportion of trade was conducted in smaller vessels. This may well have been the case with the fairly specialist coal trows that ventured beyond Gloucester. In 1699, these vessels carried an average of just over 11 tons per shipment to and from Bristol.[108] Secondly, the very low Admiralty assessment cannot be attributed to the inclusion of smaller overseas boats in the figures. At Gloucester, overseas trade was sporadic and mostly confined to the small-scale Newnham–Ireland routes.[109] In contrast, Chepstow's overseas trade was an important and growing facet in the expansion of the port and must have represented a significant tranche of the Admiralty figures. For these reasons, it would appear that the coastal and river craft of the Wye, especially those based above Brockweir, were much smaller than their Severn counterparts.[110]

However, underpinning the question of tonnage lie important issues concerning the operational efficiency and flexibility of shipping. Ralph Davis has argued strongly that the seventeenth and eighteenth centuries witnessed marked improvements in the carrying capacity, ton per man ratios, and turn-around times of sea-going vessels.[111] If Davis's assertions can be applied to coastal shipping, and both Willan and Davis suggest that 'the non-coal coasting trade was growing in volume at a faster rate than foreign trade', bald burden tonnage assessments are likely to err on the side of conservatism.[112] Similarly, the flexible uses of shipping are not wholly reflected in the figures. For example, the Musgrave lists detailed (at least on paper) ships involved either in coasting or overseas trade, 'accounting each vessel but once'. One has to assume naively that coasters never ventured beyond home shores and that ships designated for the overseas trade never entered into coasting. This was not an immutable iron law and, as such, the data must be seen as stylised snapshots of trade.[113] In the same way, the coastal port books noted all vessels which at some time in the year became involved in coastal shipping, whether these were nominally 'coasters' or 'foreign traders'. Thus, the aforementioned *Hope* of Bridgwater, which was normally employed on the Liverpool run, appeared only once in the Bridgwater records for 1699 discharging salt on 14 January. In February, the boat was chartered to Jamaica under the Huguenot John Grislier, returning to Bridgwater late in December. In 1700 it was back plying between Bridgwater, Milford, Liverpool and occasionally Dublin.[114]

The chequered career of the *Hannah* of Bridgwater demonstrates the blurring of overseas and coastal operations. In 1696, Hoare and Company, owning a five-twelfths share in the vessel, deployed the *Hannah* in the then booming salt trade. The disposal of the Company's interest to John Palmer in October was followed by four years' fairly continuous trading to and from

Liverpool.[115] By 1701, however, these freights had ceased, and the *Hannah* was employed on mostly local routes: in October 1701 the vessel mastered by Hezekiah Stocker shipped a letpass cargo of tallow from Minehead to Bridgwater for Joseph Holland. Thereafter, the *Hannah* with Stocker as master appears to have been used in the France and Holland trades. Stocker was evidently nobody's fool, and, according to the report of William Sealey of Bridgwater, one of the vessel's owners, was guilty of a catalogue of gross mismanagement. Firstly, Stocker missed the convoy at Torbay, and then flatly refused to sail without sufficient protection. In Holland, goods were dumped at Rotterdam, causing the owners and their Dutch factors considerable expense in transhipping the cargo to Amsterdam. Against express orders, Stocker declined to return for Newcastle and thence Topsham unless in convoy and then only if his wages were paid immediately and in full. To compound matters, Stocker was already held in some suspicion for the allegedly heinous crime of illegally landing a Jew at Falmouth without the consent of the owners, for which he pocketed seven pistoles, probably the greater crime in the eyes of his Bridgwater employers. To top it all, Stocker with five of his men, George Drake, Thomas Harris, Amos Webber, William Williams and Thomas Buckenham, managed to get the *Hannah* condemned for their wages, the ship being 'sold at abt. halfe value' of her market price. When Sealey's account ends in April 1703, Stocker was still abroad and Amos Webber, an old and now poor Watchet mariner and erstwhile master of coasting vessels, was skulking about in Exeter.[116]

These anecdotes emphasise that the means of enumeration was not bound by hard and fast rules. It is likely, therefore, that double-counting is present in the figures extrapolated from the three sources, especially if the home port was erratically recorded. However, as the tables are intended to examine usage rather than to analyse deficiencies between the provision of coasting as opposed to overseas craft, this is not vitally important. Bearing these caveats in mind, table 4.13 highlights the principal features of shipping in the Bristol Channel and its environs. Firstly, the outstanding importance of boats trading through Gloucester is confirmed, especially as craft restricted to the navigation were excluded from the port book figures and probably, although not definitely, from the Musgrave and Admiralty figures also. There is, however, a marked dissimilarity between the tonnage derived from the port book data and the Admiralty figures. If a trow's average burden is less generously assessed at 28 tons, the conversion would be reduced to a more credible 1,820 tons, broadly similar to the data presented by the Musgrave and Admiralty lists.

In the regional sample, Barnstaple and Bideford vessels featured strongly in both coastal and overseas trade. This was despite the fact that Bideford boats were probably overemphasised in the port book assessment and that figures for Barnstaple are fragmentary and hence rather difficult to reconstruct. The prominence of the Taw–Torridge ports in these lists again suggests that Bristol was subject to direct competition in a number of overseas trades.[117] In comparison, the data indicate that Minehead and Bridgwater were mainly coastal ports. Both centres were prominent in the coastal port book and Admiralty lists, but less so in both the Musgrave lists. Certainly, the number of vessels converted from the Musgrave overseas tonnage (between four and five boats at Minehead, two and three at Bridgwater) appears very low, although double-counting, confusion with coastal vessels, or simple omission cannot be discounted. In the Musgrave coastal series the ports of north Cornwall, St Ives and Padstow enjoyed relative parity with Bridgwater and Minehead in boats and tonnages recorded. Indeed, the number of boats recorded for Padstow in the coastal port books was on a level similar to that of the more commercially active Somerset centres. However, both Padstow and St Ives were decidedly inferior to their Somerset counterparts in both the Musgrave overseas list and the Admiralty figures. The latter series of figures also shows that the Cornish ports possessed comparable numbers of vessels and tonnages to Ilfracombe, the small outlier of Barnstaple. It is possible that the Musgrave overseas list is unrepresentative in this case or that Ilfracombe's inshore fishing fleet, supposedly enumerated separately, was partially included within the assessment. In comparison, Mount's Bay (Penzance) recorded only two local vessels in the coastal port book sample, whereas the Admiralty assessment noted eight serviceable coastal and overseas craft, and the Musgrave lists indicated that 770 tons of shipping, both overseas and coastal, were linked to the port. This represented between 18 and 20 individual craft, an assessment that reflected the importance of the pilchard trade to southern Europe rather than the residual coastal trade of the port.[118]

Two other features emerge from the table. Despite the amount of trade carried in boats based in the south-west of England, Swansea maintained a large fleet of colliers and regular coasters. Both the port book data and the Musgrave coastal figures confirm that the provision of shipping at Swansea was not only larger than the port's main trading partners, Bridgwater and Minehead, but also more extensive in tonnage and probably number than the combined total for the rest of south Wales, excluding Chepstow. In terms of overseas trade, however, Swansea was not overly endowed with vessels. The 150 tons of overseas shipping recorded in 1709 represents an insignificant level of provision for a port with an increasing overseas trade in coal.[119] Indeed, the largely underdeveloped port of Milford possessed a greater recorded tonnage of overseas craft.[120]

Lastly, the lowly position of Bristol in terms of coastal craft is again stressed. Both the port books and the Musgrave coastal figures indicate that Bristol operated a meagre body of coasters. This contrasted to the extensive combined tonnage of the vessels employed in the overseas arm of the port's trade. The gross imbalance towards overseas craft at Bristol remains the most significant factor in defining the extent to which 'metropolitan' influences can be deduced in regional shipping. Clearly the coastal trade of Bristol was conducted in vessels owned or berthed almost exclusively in the provinces. In comparison, the experience of Liverpool throws a rather different light upon the operation of an important provincial port within its hinterland. In common with Bristol, Liverpool shipping was dominated by overseas craft, as the tonnages and vessels recorded in the Admiralty assessment and tonnage figures outlined in the Musgrave overseas list reveal. This is unsurprising given the expansion witnessed in the trans-oceanic commerce of the port in the late seventeenth century.[121] Liverpool also relied on its coastal hinterland to supply the bulk of coastal vessels. In 1699, Chester, Lancaster, Poolton, Grange-over-sands and Pielfowdrey[122] were the most prominent suppliers of coastal shipping at Liverpool, operating in a similar manner to the relation between Bristol and the Bristol Channel ports. Even so, Liverpool operated a substantial number of coasters directly, 31 according to the port book record of 1699, 21 if the 1709 coastal figures are stressed. The relative concentration of coastal shipping at Liverpool reflected the high capital outlays involved in the long-distance routes common to the salt and cheese trades. These types of large, one-commodity trades were not a central feature of coasting at Bristol, and although the peacetime years of 1698– 1701 saw a rise in the bulk trade of such goods as cider, callamy, magnis, ochre and pot clay to London and the south coast, this was conducted in large boats of and from such centres as Topsham, Brighton and London.

Whilst Bristol and Liverpool can be compared directly, data for London are more difficult to reconstruct. No figures are available in the Musgrave series until 1751 and even these appear defective. Even so, the importance of supplying the capital with coals from the north-east encouraged the wide-spread distribution of colliers and coastal hoys throughout many east-coast ports.[123] Although London factors do not appear to have been especially prominent in the ownership of such colliers, a significant number of vessels were associated with the capital, perhaps as much as a sixth of the total tonnage employed in the Newcastle trade in 1702–4, if Brand's admittedly sketchy estimates are to be trusted.[124] Carriage and boat ownership were therefore rather more centrally focused upon London than was the case at Bristol. In this, the difference between the two metropolitan centres was conspicuous.[125] Whereas a locally maintained coal fleet was both desirable and commonplace for the ports of the east coast, the south-west and indeed London, it remained much less an economic and commercial imperative at Bristol, which had ready access to proximate supplies of coal.

In this context, it is worth emphasising that other factors underpinning the supply of coastal shipping may explain the lack of a Bristol-based coasting fleet. Perry's figures for the numbers of owners and boats located in the Severn ports stress that the Ironbridge Gorge ports and Bridgnorth had by far the greatest concentrations of operatives. As Trinder and Wanklyn have argued, this may have proceeded from the more open nature of the riverside community, the very *ad hoc* commercial arrangements common to the staple coal trade, and the vagaries of eking a living through an unreliable navigation. In comparison, Bristol did not exist within this uncertain and fluctuating economy or for that matter engender this type of petty boatman. To this extent it was likely to be more profitable for Bristol merchants to leave the physical business of coastal shipping to outsiders and concentrate their capital upon the more profitable if more risky overseas trades.[126]

This chapter has emphasised that coherent quantitative assessments can be made of the organisation of regional trade from the 'soft data' of merchants, boat masters and their vessels. It has firmly established that the master-merchant combination seen by Willan as the definitive form of coastal operation does not fully describe the extent of trade. Although coal shipments and the regular Bristol services were dominated by single operators frequently associated with one or two boats, certain high-value commodities, often liable to excise scrutiny and transported over longer distances than was generally the case, demanded a more precise definition of the roles of the financially responsible 'independent' merchant and the 'sea-faring' master. Ports associated with these types of good—St Ives and non-ferrous metals; Ilfracombe and consignments of herrings; Bridgwater, Minehead, Liverpool and to a lesser extent Gloucester and the shipping of salt; and Minehead and the trade in wool—all show a more complex form of mercantile organisation than ports dominated by coal or more miscellaneous shipments. Even so, the relationship between the named merchant and the ownership of the cargo is not explicit: in some, perhaps a majority of transactions, a hidden mercantile hand lay behind the generalised port book description. Where corroborative records exist, both recognised Bristol-based merchants, like Graffin Prankard and Charles Jones, and their regional counterparts underpinned, if not directly supervised, the shipment of goods.

In the mid-sixteenth century, the commonwealth propagandist Robert Crowley directed his righteous anger against those merchants who sought to forestall the market. He roundly complained that:

> The fryses of Walis
> to Bristowe are brought;
> But before thei were wouen,
> in Walis they are bought.[127]

Crowley was not concerned with how Welsh frieze was traded to Bristol, merely that the traditional, open market had been subverted by the invidious and surreptitious agency of an obscure class of Bristol merchant. As the trade of Bristol and indeed Bristol itself was subjected increasingly to the forces of capitalism as the seventeenth century progressed, such activities became standard.[128] However, if we are to unpick Crowley's diatribe and understand more fully how the different elements that facilitated coasting interacted, it is necessary to get behind the generic descriptions of trade and examine the activity of specific traders in detail. The following chapter dissects the coasting operations of Hoare and Company and William Alloway, merchants of Bridgwater, in order to demonstrate how port book data can be used in conjunction with ancillary sources to begin to piece together the tangled network of local shipments and commercial associations that formed the basis to the coastal trade of Bristol and its region.

Five

The coastal trade in operation

In the ports and on the quays of Bristol and the major regional centres high-profile overseas merchants and large-scale industrialists rubbed shoulders with factors, shipping agents, masters and an unruly proletariat of hired boatmen and lesser traders. A vast social and commercial gulf existed between, for example, Sir Abraham Elton, the high-profile and high-living merchant and industrialist of Bristol,[1] and the peripatetic trow owner, like John Beale of Bewdley, or, at the very bottom of this hierarchy, the sort of uppity jobbing boatman, personified by Hezekiah Stocker of Bridgwater. Yet even such very different cultural and commercial archetypes as these mixed freely and directly: diversity and flexibility characterised coasting. Clearly, many of Bristol's mercantile bourgeois regarded the coastal trade and its more robust operatives as a wholly benighted profession: Graffin Prankard, for example, oversaw his coastal transactions with almost fanatical zeal, constantly berating the negligence of the crew he chartered, checking up on correct loadings, and warning fellow correspondents and merchants of both 'the roaguery of the saylers' and the alleged sharp and dilatory practice to be found in various branches of the trade.[2] Prankard's caution probably reflects more the rigidity of the man than endemic delinquency in the coastal and river trades, although Prankard's Quaker contemporaries, Richard Ford and Thomas Goldney, showed a similar lack of forbearance towards such oversights.[3] Elsewhere, the odd grievance arose concerning the confusion or misplacement of cargoes, and port officials were not always enamoured with the brusque and occasionally obstructive action of certain boatmen, but in general most merchants and shippers recognised the regularity and efficiency of coasting.

The use of quantitative and structured data has enabled historians to tease out many of the principal relationships that linked the various branches of the coastal trade into a coherent whole. In this sense, the discussion has provided a contextualising aggregate, the key upon which further layers of

151

interpretation can be fixed. Yet in some ways statistical data can produce an arid, depersonalised history. To understand fully the subtleties of trade, we need to uncover the motives as well as the mechanisms that lay behind the bald customs descriptions of merchants, masters and cargoes. In effect, this reiterates the perennial call for intensive 'biographical narrative' or the ambivalently termed 'thick description' to be applied to economic and commercial history. Of course, biographical discourse is not a simple heuristic solution: without a 'statistical' template, it can and often does descend into mere reportage and an antiquarian obsession with anecdotal minutiae.[4] With these issues in mind, this chapter seeks to reconstruct the activity of two major Bridgwater merchant houses, Roger Hoare and Company and William Alloway and partners. By integrating quantitative port book data with an especially large body of business records, the following sections examine the coastal trade in salt and in other commodities and suggest how the study of regional merchants' accounts and commercial papers can throw light upon the operation of Bristol and its domestic hinterland.

Hoare and Company, 1696–1700

Like many pre-industrial joint-stock partnerships, Hoare and Company represented a fluid assemblage of merchants and lesser traders.[5] In March 1696, when the surviving record begins,[6] the Company comprised twelve prominent, mostly Presbyterian, Bridgwater merchants and citizens: Roger Hoare, John Harvey, Valentine Smith, John Franklin, Richard Drake, George Balch, Isaac Heard, John Syms, George Thomas, John Roberts, Joseph Greenway and Nathaniel Galpine.[7] As MP for Bridgwater, Hoare served to protect the interests of both the Company and the port's commercial-maritime lobby in London. In practice, this amounted to very much the same thing: Hoare was prominent for town and self in the debates concerning the Salt Act of 1699;[8] in petitioning the Board of Excise 'against the oppressive coal duty';[9] and in the passing of the private Bill for rebuilding Bridgwater quay in 1699.[10] On a more prosaic level, Hoare acted as the financial fulcrum of the Company, discounting all bills drawn on himself and the Company's unofficial bankers in London, John and Thomas Fisher, and Obadiah Grevill; chasing up recalcitrant private and official debtors; and procuring additional financial gearing as and when the Company's occasionally overstretched excise commitments required.[11]

The other partners managed the Company's interests in the south-west. Nathaniel Galpine oversaw the day-to-day administration of Company business at Bridgwater, acting as agent to both the 'factory' of coals, salt and general merchandise at Ham Mills, the inland depot at the head of the Parrett navigation,[12] and the 'fishery' at Lynmouth, operated in conjunction with

William Alloway.[13] Isaac Heard was a salt merchant in his own right before the formalisation of the Company,[14] and Richard Drake appears to have acted as the 'principall manager' and intermediary with the Company's Bristol partners and associates, notably Abraham Hooke, during the prolonged absences of Hoare in London.[15] The remaining members were less active, although they were closely associated with the political and mercantile hierarchy of Bridgwater.[16]

In September 1696 the Company was reconstructed with an initial capitalisation of £7,500 divided into 25 shares of £300.[17] When Roberts and Greenway left the following year, a further seven partners—Joseph Denham, William Symons, John Gilbert, William Methwen, Samuel White, Thomas Ledgingham and Alexander Wallis—joined the original compliment.[18] Methwen appears to have become joint manager with Galpine of the Company's affairs in Bridgwater, and also brought to the Company important commercial links with Bristol,[19] whilst Ledgingham was an overseas merchant of some importance.[20] As business dictated and trade expanded, other merchants were co-opted. Richard Lowbridge, for example, was admitted in March 1697 largely due to his heavy involvement in Company salt contracts, and Samuel Codrington, merchant of Bridgwater, joined in September 1697.[21]

However, the partnership was relatively short-lived. In February 1699 the Company resolved to limit its enterprises especially in overseas markets by cutting back on its fleet of vessels.[22] By the end of the month, financial uncertainties, competing interests and personal animosity had alienated six prominent members. As Galpine starkly informed Hoare, 'the persons that will continue on a new establishment are Mr Syms, the two Mr Balches, Mr Lowbridg, Mr Codrington, myselfe, Mr Gilbert, Mr Denham, William Methwen &, we suppose, yourselfe'. In addition, the reformed Company would be joined by new mercantile blood in the shape of Manassee Whitehead of Bridgwater, Richard Oliver of Bristol, and Anthony Juliot of Bideford.[23]

The sudden death of Roger Hoare in London in May 1699 severely rocked an already over-extended Company.[24] In response, the Company agreed to continue trading under the title of 'George Balch, Esquire and Company', and, optimistically, 'to unite farther . . . [and] . . . if possible to gett one member in every noted port we may have occation to have advise from'. None the less, most of the main assets in ships and fixtures were sold off to individual partners and their associates, probably to meet Hoare's other financial liabilities.[25] Galpine acquired the ocean-going, two-decked *Mary and Elizabeth* for £440; Robert Balch the *Speedwell* for £240; Drake the three-quarter share in the *Michael* for £268 10s, the other quarter share retained by the vessel's operator Michael Currant; John Gilbert the *Hope* for £186;

Robert Harvey the *Fly* for £160; and Ambrose Hozee of Exeter, a regular correspondent of the Company, Hoare's own ship, the *Mary*, for £153. In addition, Syms bought out the half share in the fishery at Lynmouth for £434 and Hozee acquired the 'Butts' for an additional £97.[26] Despite the apparent alienation of much of its fixed capital, the Company did not collapse but stuttered on until April 1700 at which time substantial salt contracts were still undischarged.[27] Although a Balch and Company was active in 1701 and may have been trading as late as 1703, the Company was probably reduced to only a rump of the initial compliment.[28] By August 1700, Galpine and Heard, two of the most prominent founding members, were heading separate companies.[29]

This somewhat potted history serves to outline the basis of Hoare and Company. Although a fitful but occasionally remunerative overseas trade was maintained with Ireland, Barbados, France, Newfoundland, Sweden, Spain and Portugal, the Company's main area of operation was the domestic market. However, the Company was important far beyond its immediate locality. It encompassed in both formal and informal association not only a large body of Bridgwater merchants, but also many important traders from throughout the Bristol Channel region and further afield. Linked by a complex association of extended kinship and more depersonalised commercial and credit ties, the Company engaged in regular commercial contact with the main coastal towns of the region, the smaller ports of south Cornwall and Devon, the salt-producing centres of Worcestershire, Cheshire, Flint and Liverpool, and, most importantly, the principal commercial and financial centres of Bristol and Exeter. Underpinning these connections was the trade in salt.

Liverpool, Gloucester and Bridgwater: mapping the coastal trade in salt

Salt was a vital primary commodity in the pre-industrial economy of England. Apart from its far from negligible domestic uses, salt had important industrial applications, not least in soap and glass manufacture. But in an age before refrigeration, its primary use as a bulk preservative could not be matched. In the late seventeenth century, the region's highly developed inshore and Newfoundland fisheries demanded large quantities of strong 'searching' salt.[30] The ports of south-west England naturally dominated these trades, and although Bridgwater boats were not as prominent in the catching or curing of fish compared to the inshore fleets of Devon and Cornwall or the larger Newfoundland vessels operating mainly out of Barnstaple, Bideford and Plymouth, the port served to supply the many salt pans, factories and fisheries that had developed along the coasts of Somerset and north

Devon.[31] The expansion of the salt trade coincided with the enforced disruption of foreign supplies which had hitherto sufficed for the needs of the Bristol Channel region. In particular, the embargo imposed upon directly imported French bay salt during the Anglo-French conflict of 1689–97 and the subsequent general dislocation of overseas trade badly affected traditional sources of supply. Although port book evidence suggests that Iberian salt and French prize salt were traded coastally, they remained marginal items of trade.[32] Even in the short peacetime period between 1698 and 1701, proscriptive duties prevented a full-scale recovery of the import trade and only a very small amount of foreign salt filtered into coasting.[33]

Under such conditions, the domestic salt industry gained an increasing share of the home market. The principal beneficiaries were the salt fields of Cheshire and Droitwich in Warwickshire. A small amount of salt was also produced locally by evaporating brine or sea water and a similarly minor quantity found its way into the region from Tyneside and Shropshire.[34] In Cheshire, white salt was made by boiling salt brine at three principal centres: Northwich, Middlewich and Nantwich.[35] By the late seventeenth century, accessibility to coastal waters ensured that Northwich salt found ready markets via Frodsham in the Mersey estuary, appearing in coastwise cargoes clearing Liverpool and, with less frequency, Chester. Supplies from the two other, less developed Cheshire brineries were comparatively limited, although white salt from Middlewich and Nantwich was occasionally traded through Liverpool and, more especially, via Shrewsbury and the river Severn. Cheshire white salt, and often a fair amount of rock salt, thus formed a small but regular proportion of salt passing through Gloucester.[36]

By the late seventeenth century, the Cheshire brinemen were under increasingly fierce competition from the rock salt interest. Rock salt was cheap, potent, and moreover exempt from the full strictures of excise payment by way of generous adjustments in the weight of the official bushel and drawbacks of duty available on rock used in the fisheries.[37] Although the advantages rock salt enjoyed over wich salt were quickly if not entirely redressed by the Acts of 1696, 1699 and 1702, the impetus given to the trade was significant.[38] According to William Stout, by 1689 'rock [was] carryed . . . by sea to all parts of England and Ireland, and melted . . . with sea water and boiled . . . up into a strong salt, as good [as] French [or] Spanish salt'.[39] During the 1690s, a glut of rock salt refineries was established along the Mersey and Dee seaboard and the coastline of the south-west of England and south Wales, where access to cheap supplies of coal encouraged investment.[40]

Stout's comments are reflected in the coastal exports of salt from Liverpool. In 1690, Liverpool shipped 95,400 bushels of unspecified Cheshire salt, the equivalent of 2,385 tons, if the lower 56 lb bushel of white salt (likely to have formed the vast majority of trade at this time) was used. The bulk of this trade, 2,042 tons, was destined for the ports of the Bristol Channel.[41] By 1699, the combined quantities of rock and white salt clearing Liverpool amounted to 7,509 tons. By this stage quantities traded to Bristol Channel ports had almost doubled to 4,025 tons. However, this now represented only 54 per cent of Liverpool's coastal trade in salt, with the smaller ports of Lancashire, Cheshire and north Wales accounting for substantial quantities of the commodity.

In contrast, for most of the seventeenth century, the output of the Droitwich salteries had been strictly and prescriptively controlled by local salt proprietors in order to maintain price levels. However, this cartel was challenged by Robert Steynor who between 1693 and 1695 sank new brine pits explicitly contesting the rights and privileges of the old monopoly. Steynor's actions, reinforced by a vigorous defence in Chancery and a rare aptitude in self-promotion, succeeded in blowing open the monopoly in 1695, encouraging further speculative enterprises. In consequence, the wholesale price of Worcestershire salt fell dramatically both at Droitwich and at Bristol.[42]

As table 5.1 and figure 5.1 indicate, the upsurge in activity at Droitwich was reflected in the coastal trade of Gloucester.[43] Between 1680 and 1686, Gloucester was a net importer of salt, mostly in the form of French and Iberian salt traded through Bristol.[44] However, with the advent of war and embargo in 1689 and the development of consistent domestic supply, trade in foreign salt all but vanished.[45] In comparison, coastal exports rocketed. Between 1695 and 1704, the number of shipments more than doubled and the quantity of salt traded multiplied by a factor of over nine. The size of consignments also rose from an average of 5.33 tons per voyage in 1695 to just under 22 tons in 1703 and 1704. In ten years, Droitwich salt developed from a small part-cargo in miscellaneous down-river shipments to the central item of trade, included in up to 45 per cent of all voyages clearing Gloucester. This pattern is emphasised across the longer sample.[46] Salt exports from Gloucester grew steadily until experiencing something of a slump in the early 1720s. However, the data for 1727 and 1728 indicate that trade was prosecuted with renewed vigour. Moreover, discounting these two slightly aberrant years, it is clear that the ports of Somerset, Devon and south Wales collectively dominated trade: Bristol, the regional entrepôt for most Severn goods, barely accounted for half the quantity of salt shipped through Gloucester.

The development of the Cheshire and Droitwich salt fields and brineries ran parallel to the growth in the salt trade at Bridgwater. Table 5.2 shows the quantities of white and rock salt imported coastally at Bridgwater between 1695 and 1703, recording the number of voyages and the mean quantity

Table 5.1a

Salt (tons) exported coastally from Gloucester, 1680–1704

Year		Quantity	Shipments	Mean	Total shipments	% shipment with salt
1680		0.58	2	0.29	304	1
1681		0.00	0	0.00	322	0
1682		0.16	1	0.16	313	0
1683		0.61	2	0.31	310	1
1684		0.15	2	0.08	252	1
1685		0.00	0	0.00	138	0
1686		0.03	1	0.03	296	0
1689		172.45	39	4.42	270	14
1691		145.38	55	2.64	451	12
1692		108.85	27	4.03	375	7
1693	*	69.03	24	2.88	171	14
1694	*	57.64	22	2.62	161	14
1695		308.90	58	5.33	289	20
1696		852.48	135	6.31	334	40
1697		1,131.30	126	8.98	357	35
1698	*	882.48	60	14.71	141	43
1699		1,806.54	123	14.69	332	37
1700	*	1,262.75	71	17.79	158	45
1701		1,926.50	126	15.29	335	38
1703	*	1,479.55	68	21.76	159	43
1704		2,861.05	132	21.67	331	40

Table 5.1b

Salt (tons) imported coastally to Gloucester, 1680–1704

Year		Quantity	Shipments	Mean	Total shipments	% shipment with salt
1680		26.90	6	4.48	199	3
1681		10.00	3	3.33	219	1
1682		50.25	8	6.28	232	3
1683		24.95	8	3.12	273	3
1684		34.93	10	3.49	263	4
1685		26.00	5	5.20	195	3
1686		57.38	12	4.78	213	6
1689		15.13	9	1.68	270	3
1691		0.08	1	0.08	262	0
1692		0.05	1	0.05	250	0
1693	*	0.00	0	0.00	138	0
1694	*	0.00	0	0.00	110	0
1695		0.10	1	0.10	235	0
1696		0.08	1	0.08	190	1
1697		0.00	0	0.00	235	0
1698	*	0.28	2	0.14	101	2
1699		2.90	4	0.73	294	1
1700	*	0.00	0	0.00	124	0
1701		0.00	0	0.00	216	0
1703	*	0.00	0	0.00	121	0
1704		0.00	0	0.00	252	0

Note: *Data for half-year only.
Source: Cox, Hussey and Milne, eds, *Gloucester port books database.*

Figure 5.1

Salt (tons) exported coastally from Gloucester, 1680–1728

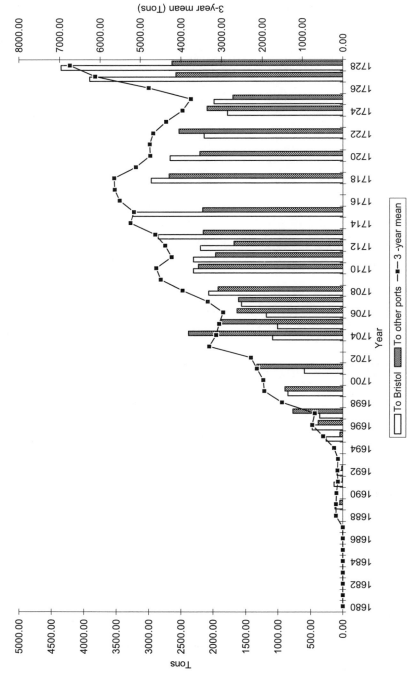

Source: Cox, Hussey and Milne, eds, *Gloucester coastal port books database.*

Table 5.2

Coastal imports of salt (tons) to Bridgwater, 1695–1703

		Salt and white salt						Rock salt			
		Gloucester	Liverpool	Bristol	Chester	Others	Total	Gloucester	Liverpool	Bristol	Total
1695	quantity	2.50	787.62	0.50	-	0.25	790.87	–	55.85	–	55.85
	voyage	2	18	1	–	2	23	–	7	–	7
	mean	1.25	43.76	0.50	–	0.13	34.39	–	7.98	–	7.98
1696	quantity	182.36	973.74	2.29	37.50	35.00	1,230.89	24.00	556.34	–	580.34
	voyage	14	27	1	1	1	44	2	20	–	22
	mean	13.03	36.06	2.29	37.50	35.00	27.97	12.00	27.82	–	26.38
1697	quantity	401.31	304.96	–	–	7.00	713.27	–	279.41	–	279.41
	voyage	20	10	–	–	1	31	–	6	–	6
	mean	20.07	30.50	–	–	7.00	23.01	–	46.57	–	46.57
1698	quantity	704.51	46.26	19.78	35.00	–	805.54	–	361.76	–	361.76
	voyage	23	5	1	1	–	30	–	8	–	8
	mean	30.63	9.25	19.78	35.00	–	26.85	–	45.22	–	45.22
1699	quantity	393.50	19.20	–	37.50	27.00	477.20	–	689.05	33.00	722.05
	voyage	14	6	–	1	1	22	–	18	3	21
	mean	28.11	3.20	–	37.50	27.00	21.69	–	38.28	11.00	34.38
1701	quantity	407.91	–	2.30		3.00	413.21	7.06	638.17	–	645.24
	voyage	16	–	1		1	18	2	13	–	15
	mean	25.49	–	2.30		3.00	22.96	3.53	49.09	–	43.02
1703	quantity	724.77	–	–	–	12.75	737.52	5.69	523.10	–	528.79
	voyage	33	–	–	–	1	34	1	11	–	12
	mean	21.96	–	–	–	12.75	21.69	5.69	47.55	–	44.07

Source: PRO E190 coastal port books.

carried per shipment. The distinction between the two main grades of salt has been preserved for, although the goods were used in similar ways, they continued to be regarded as distinct commodities for commercial, administrative and fiscal purposes throughout the period. Very generous measuring standards were applied to rock salt, reflecting its separate excise status: an anomaly that greatly favoured the voluble rock interest and was only partially ameliorated by the remedial statutes of 1699 and 1702. Changes in the rock salt bushel enforced by these Acts impacted strongly upon local merchants. News, or even rumour, of the impending revision of 1699 prompted a flurry of activity to buy up rock at 'old duty' rates. Hoare and Company, who had more than a little insider warning of Parliament's action and also found themselves in the uneasy position of having nearly depleted their existing stocks, scoured their sources with increasing desperation. The Company wrote to Edward Hackett, their agent in Bristol, entreating him to purchase (at the rather hopeful price of £6 per ton) any rock salt that had been sent to Bristol from Liverpool. The need to acquire additional supplies was such that Hackett was required to 'imploy some trusty freind to look out at their coming in either at Hung Road or elce where' and to buy as much as possible and dispatch it directly to Bridgwater unless further news abating the proposed legislation should reach him.[47] Similarly, Robert Hyde, the salt proprietor of Liverpool and Sutton, was also petitioned to 'procure one hundred ton [of rock salt] . . . purchased and removed from off the pitts if it may be done before the double duty commenceth'.[48] Further agreements with Hyde and Thomas Warburton were proposed to get as much rock salt of the old duty as possible bought and warehoused before the provisions of the Act were in place. The Company, having secured the duty, could then let the salt 'ly to our account afterwards a month or two untill we get opportunity to ship it home if no opportunity falls out sooner'.[49]

This reaction to what amounted to a covert, but major tax hike was understandable. However, Hoare's frenetic actions in 1699 highlight a central problem in assessing the levels of rock salt traded. In 1699 and 1702, the years of greatest change, it is difficult to distinguish between shipments of rock salt traded under different official bushels. Merchants wanted to accumulate as much 'old duty' rock as possible, providing certificates thereafter that contracts for the commodity had been secured (and bonds for the requisite duties taken) before the provisos of the new statute came into force. The chronological 'cut-off' points established by statute did not, therefore, translate automatically into trading practice. Writing to Hyde in May 1699, Galpine, Hoare and Company's Bridgwater manager, detailed specific orders on how to load the *Fly* of Bridgwater with rock salt. The boat's master, Charles Hyman, was physically to separate cargoes of old and new duty salt, thus preserving the different official ratings and the Company's old duty

'Drawback on Refining'.[50] In this light, it is probable that the ton conversions derived for 1699 are underestimates as an unspecified amount of trade was conducted under the old bushel.[51]

Although confusion over the official standard may have posed problems for excise collectors and historians alike, it is clear that the statutory imposed bushel was not merely a fiscal construct of the excise, but entered the commercial language of customs accounts, and directly affected the coastal trade. Merchants, and indeed customs clerks, operated under the strictures of the sporadically revised bushel and did not use, for example, the Winchester bushel as the means of *trade* whilst deferring to the 'Parliamentary' bushel in dealings with the Board of Excise and its myriad local agents, or, tellingly, adopt local, variant and highly irregular measures in official dealings. This is unsurprising, for excise officials hounded coastal and river vessels unremittingly at both the ports of clearance and destination to prevent fraud by concealed underweighing or unstandard measures, and were equally tenacious in prosecuting alleged abuses. In all such cases, the excise bushel was the enforced mercantile measure.[52] This is not to say that irregular measures disappeared, but that, despite the almost universal 'fragmentation of measuring standards' that existed in pre-industrial trade, the data obtained for salt appear remarkably consistent.[53]

The results of table 5.2 are summarised in tables 5.3 and 5.4. These data reveal important patterns in the distribution of salt imports. Firstly, Gloucester and Liverpool dominated the coastal shipment of salt. Bristol regularly transhipped small consignments of white salt and in 1699 it dispatched rather more Cheshire rock salt, largely the result of the rush on trade caused by the manipulation of the official bushel. The occasional large cargo of white salt also emanated directly from Chester, probably from the salt works on the Flintshire coast which came under the customs jurisdiction of the port. The other centres recorded dealing in white salt were of minor importance and trade prosecuted with them was of a singular, *ad hoc* nature. In 1699, for example, a letpass cargo of 27 tons of white salt was brought from Minehead after being discharged there on the account of William Alloway, and in 1703, 12.75 tons (510 bushels) of locally refined or transhipped white salt was traded from Newnham. Small parcels of salt were also imported coastally on letpasses from Swansea in 1695, including the only occurrence of French salt (presumably traded as prize goods given the stipulation of the embargo then in force); from Cardiff in 1697; and from London in 1701.

Yet, the steady expansion of the salt trade implied by the data for Gloucester and Liverpool was not directly replicated at Bridgwater. In this period, the quantity of salt traded and the consequent number of shipments peaked early. In 1695, 23 voyages, a mere 6 per cent of total inwards voyages,

Table 5.3

*Total quantities of rock and white salt (tons) imported coastally to Bridgwater,
from ports of clearance, 1695–1703*

	Total	Liverpool	Gloucester	Other ports	% quantity Liverpool	% quantity Gloucester
1695	846.72	843.47	2.50	0.75	100	0
1696	1,811.23	1,530.08	206.36	74.79	84	11
1697	992.68	584.37	401.31	7.00	59	40
1698	1,167.30	408.02	704.51	54.78	35	60
1699	1,199.25	708.25	393.50	97.50	59	33
1701	1,058.45	638.17	414.97	5.30	60	39
1703	1,301.44	523.10	730.46	12.75	40	56
Total	8,377.07	5,235.46	2,853.61	252.87	62	34

Table 5.4

*Total quantities of rock and white salt (tons) imported coastally to Bridgwater, 1695–1703,
expressed in terms of total inwards shipments*

	Total	Shipments	Mean	Total shipments	% carrying salt
1695	846.72	23	36.81	382	6
1696	1,811.23	48	37.73	282	17
1697	992.68	31	32.02	442	7
1698	1,167.30	34	34.33	315	11
1699	1,199.25	38	31.56	331	11
1701	1,058.45	31	34.14	344	9
1703	1,301.44	45	28.92	360	13

Source: PRO E190 coastal port books.

carried just 846.72 tons of salt into Bridgwater. However, by 1696 over 1,811 tons of white and rock was shipped in 48 voyages. This represented the highest mean shipment, over 37 tons per voyage, recorded in the sample. In terms of the percentage share of total inwards voyages, 1696 was also the most important year: over 17 per cent of all voyages entering the port carried salt, although this was the result of lower levels of trade in other sectors. In comparison, 1697 was relatively slack. Less than 1,000 tons of salt were imported coastally in this year and it is possible that domestic supplies may have come under competition from disembargoed French salt and increased imports of Iberian salt. In the early months of 1697, Hoare and Company encountered much difficulty shifting two cargoes of white salt brought coastways from Liverpool to the south coast of Cornwall. The long and dangerous voyage, poor brokerage, bad advice, and the availability of even highly priced French salt ensured that the Company's salt sold at a loss.[54] By 1698, the quantity of salt had recovered somewhat, with almost 1,200 tons discharged. Thereafter, levels appear to have balanced out, with signs of a modest increase in both quantities and shipments apparent in 1703, at which time warfare may have diminished overseas supply. Even so, the amount of salt traded to Bridgwater in 1703 represented less than three-quarters of the levels obtained in 1696.

This broad quantitative outline masks a dramatic shift in the directional basis of the salt trade at Bridgwater. In 1695, Bridgwater obtained the vast majority of its coastal supply from Liverpool. This consisted mostly of Cheshire white salt: rock salt was carried only as a part-cargo, as witnessed by the low mean shipment size per voyage. In comparison, trade via Gloucester had yet to make an impression upon coastal imports. In 1696, the peak year for total trade, Liverpool was still the most significant provider of domestic salt: some 84 per cent of salt unloaded at Bridgwater was either Cheshire white or rock salt or salt refined in the Mersey estuary. By this time, rock salt accounted for a proportionally larger share of the trade, occupying over a third of the tonnage shipped via Liverpool. Although Droitwich salt was beginning to be traded in small quantities, its share of the Bridgwater trade (11 per cent) was still limited. In 1697, salt derived from Liverpool constituted under 60 per cent of trade, with rock salt far more prominent than in earlier years. Whilst more ships carried white salt from the Mersey, the increased mean shipment size of rock salt cargoes was indicative of its changed importance. In addition, imports of Droitwich salt had more than doubled to supplement the decline in white salt from Cheshire.

The tendency for trade to become polarised between Droitwich white salt and Cheshire rock salt was more pronounced in 1698. Overall, the reliance upon the north-west declined: only around a third of all salt shipped coastally to Bridgwater passed through Liverpool customs house. Almost all of this was rock salt. Cheshire white salt and white salt refined from rock had dwindled to minor levels and was mainly traded as a cargo makeweight. Both Bristol and Chester, essentially small transhippers or producers throughout the period, were now dealing in more white and refined salt than Liverpool. The demise of Cheshire white salt was more than compensated by the rise in Droitwich supplies. In 1698, 704.51 tons of Worcestershire salt, some 60 per cent of the total trade, were shipped to Bridgwater in 23 voyages.

To an extent, the pronounced geographical specialisation of trade at Bridgwater was linked to the aggressive marketing of Droitwich salt. For example, in August 1698, Hoare and Company wrote to Partington and Massey, owners of salt works in Cheshire and Flint, requiring the firm to load the *Speedwell* of Bridgwater with white salt for Ireland or Bridgwater. In this, the Company expressed the hope that their hitherto profitable trade would 'not be ruined by Droitwich men'.[55] However, Massey's failure to supply cheap and ready white salt forced the Company to insist on 'good rock salt' instead.[56] In the following month, the Company informed Massey that 'if your loading of white [salt] will soon be ready & can be so shipt as to turn to any account . . . you may keep her [the *Speedwell*] for white, but here you are to take notice that we do buy Droitwich salt, delivered at this port, for 8s per ton/ and if yours, allowing the vessell a convenient freight, will not come so cheap, she was better [to] come away direct with her Rock, iff she tarrys for white at Fraudsham'.[57] The implication of this veiled threat was clear: neither Cheshire white salt, nor salt refined from rock on site, staple items of trade in 1695 and 1696, could now compete with the lower production and transport costs enjoyed by Droitwich salt. With rock salt, however, low initial costs, supplementary excise drawbacks and other financial incentives were enough for the more arduous and costly journey from the north-west to remain profitable. Refining, however, gravitated towards the Company's own salt works in the south-west.

The pattern was repeated in 1699 and 1701. Cheshire white salt declined to negligible levels, and eventually ceased to be traded at all. For a time rock salt from Liverpool assumed a much greater proportion of inwards trade, accounting for around three-fifths of all salt traded. This may have been the result of more stable international conditions which encouraged the prosecution of long-distance coasting. In 1703, however, when war had recommenced and statutory limits had contained the rock salt interest, Droitwich salt once again assumed a pre-eminent position. In this year Severn trows undertook substantially more voyages (33) than vessels clearing Liverpool (11), although Severn vessels carried far less salt per shipment, accounting for only 56 per cent of salt discharged coastally at Bridgwater. The presence of additional bulk items of trade, predominantly grain and ironwares, that were carried alongside salt in most Severn trows tended to limit the amount of salt traded. In comparison, Liverpool boats tended to specialise in salt to the exclusion of other commodities bar the odd consignment of wool and cheese and the occasional piece of linen or Irish flannel.

The organisation of the salt trade: Hoare and Company and William Alloway

The Bridgwater figures give a broad narrative of the local trade in salt. However, understanding how trade was organised imposes rather more stringent requirements upon the analysis of these data. As the previous chapter stressed, coastal port books provide much detail on the merchants, masters and the means by which trade was conducted. Yet such evidence is often highly equivocal. In particular, the relationship between the named merchant or cargo indenturer and the 'true' merchant who financed, compiled and ultimately disposed of each shipment remains only partially resolved by the coastal records.

Table 5.5 gives an insight into the activity of five main groups of salt merchants as listed in the Bridgwater port books between 1695 and 1703. In terms of the size of operation, the most prominent class of trader was the salt proprietor, refiner, or large dealer from Liverpool and Cheshire. These men organised shipments on their own account and risk and acted as surety for Bridgwater-based merchants. The latter formed a second group of traders characterised by their involvement in a variety of other commodities and by the fact that they were not associated with the physical business of coasting. This was undertaken by the combined master and merchant, owners and carriers who operated vessels out of the Severn ports, Liverpool or Bridgwater, being paid a set freightage by Cheshire and Droitwich producers or Bridgwater merchants.

This simple classification does little to emphasise the fluidity of commercial relations. Bridgwater merchants, for example, often acted in concert or as supercargo for other local traders and merchant houses. As far as the legal requirements of the Exchequer were concerned, officials were more interested in establishing fiscal liability should the cargo be adulterated or traded overseas illicitly than in determining ownership. This is demonstrated by the number of salt proprietors and refiners from Cheshire and Liverpool noted as merchants or indenturers in the Bridgwater Books. Men such as Thomas Johnson of Liverpool, the renowned MP, overseas merchant, joint 'proprietor of rock salt near Nor[th]wich', and the Dungeon works at Liverpool, Robert Hyde of Sutton, Henry Parr of Liverpool, or Sir Thomas Warburton of Liverpool were often obliged to extend credit to more distant merchants by securing customs bonds at Liverpool or Frodsham and paying excise duties liable on salt shipped coastally themselves.[58] This arrangement was fairly typical. Asked to account for the loss of 101 bushels of rock salt amongst a cargo of 1,065 bushels shipped from Liverpool to Bristol in 1703, Richard Says, master of the *Griffin* 'of and belonging to Brockweir', and his boatswain, Thomas Hodges, revealed a similar system by which salt was traded and recorded by customs clerks. Says swore that the discrepancy between the full coquet and excise documentation and the amount discharged at Bristol was due to inundation of the cargo during a 30-hour storm off St David's Head. Duty (and apparently the customs bond) had been secured by 'Mr Cleeveland of Leverpoole . . . proprietor of rock salt', but the cargo was shipped 'on the proper account and risque' of Stephen Baker, merchant of Bristol.[59]

Table 5.5

Port book merchants importing salt coastally to Bridgwater, 1695–1703

Salt and white salt

	1695 ton	1695 voy.	1696 ton	1696 voy.	1697 ton	1697 voy.	1698 ton	1698 voy.	1699 ton	1699 voy.	1701 ton	1701 voy.	1703 ton	1703 voy.
Liverpool salt proprietors and merchants	105.22	2	101.79	7	4.28	1	11.08	2	1.48	3	–	–	–	–
Bridgwater merchants	291.04	7	241.27	6	47.81	1	20.89	2	1.10	1	–	–	–	–
Bridgwater merchant–masters	326.13	9	523.17	12	195.64	6	49.29	2	37.50	1	2.30	1	–	–
Liverpool merchant–masters	65.88	2	147.30	4	57.23	2	–	–	16.62	2	–	–	–	–
Severn merchant–masters	2.50	2	182.36	14	401.32	20	724.28	25	393.50	14	407.91	16	737.52	34
Others	0.10	1	35.00	1	7.00	1	–	–	27.00	1	3.00	1	–	–
	790.87	23	1,230.89	44	713.28	31	805.54	31	477.20	22	413.21	18	737.52	34

Rock salt

	1695 ton	1695 voy.	1696 ton	1696 voy.	1697 ton	1697 voy.	1698 ton	1698 voy.	1699 ton	1699 voy.	1701 ton	1701 voy.	1703 ton	1703 voy.
Liverpool salt proprietors and merchants	–	–	369.12	8	69.05	1	121.21	3	369.66	9	551.36	11	449.04	9
Bridgwater merchants	17.15	2	56.40	5	54.10	1	150.40	3	131.13	3	–	–	–	–
Bridgwater merchant–masters	27.70	4	130.32	6	156.26	4	37.49	1	98.82	5	55.11	1	–	–
Liverpool merchant–masters	11	1	0.50	1	–	–	52.65	1	122.44	4	31.70	1	74.06	2
Severn merchant–masters	–	–	24.00	2	–	–	–	–	–	–	7.06	2	5.69	1
Others	–	–	–	–	–	–	–	–	–	–	–	–	–	–
	55.85	7	580.34	22	279.41	6	361.75	8	722.05	21	645.23	15	528.79	12

Source: PRO E190 coastal port books..

Many salt proprietors were of course merchants in their own right. This accounts for the presence of Jonathan Blackburn, a 'gentleman refiner of Flintshire' who had salt works at Liverpool and salt mines and pans at Northwich by the early eighteenth century. In 1699, Blackburn shipped over 150 tons of rock salt and rather less than a ton of white salt to Bridgwater in four shipments undertaken by Liverpool boats.[60] Similarly, Jeffrey Houghton, later of Nantwich and lessee of the New Witton salt works, acted as merchant on two voyages carrying over 128 tons of rock, whereas Robert Haydock of Liverpool was also responsible for a single cargo of 25.6 tons of rock salt in 1699.[61] In 1701, four salt proprietors and merchants, Thomas Nixon, Thomas Edgar, Thomas Johnson and Thomas Slyford, accounted for over three-quarters of all rock shipped into Bridgwater.[62] Shipments of rock salt merchanted by Cleaveland, Edgar, Samuel Brockenbrough[63] and Johnson comprised 86 per cent of the quantity imported coastally in 1703.

Bridgwater merchants were more apparent in the port book record in the earlier years of the sample. These included William Alloway and his associate Alexander Holmes, active between 1695 and 1699, and Isaac Heard, Michael Currant, William Methwen and Samuel Burnall, all of whom were associated with Hoare and Company, itself explicitly noted as an importer of rock and white salt in 1698 and 1699. Other merchants were mainly involved in one-off voyages: Thomas Holwell for example occurred as merchant on a single letpass voyage from Minehead in 1699. These merchants were far outweighed by the combined master-merchant: regular traders such as Charles Corker of Bewdley, Giles Vinecott and Philip Cockrem of Bridgwater, and James McMullen of Liverpool. In addition, the odd small shipment of salt was carried by the regular Bridgwater packets that traded with Bristol, although, as with the activity of merchant-masters, establishing the ownership of goods carried remains conjectural without additional evidence.

These types of relationship are more fully understood when the accounts of Hoare and Company are examined in detail. Salt formed the commercial backbone of the Company's business. Its primary interest in the coastal trade stemmed from the need to convey Cheshire and Droitwich salt as cheaply as possible from source to both the Company's own factory and fishery and also its many agents and clients throughout the south-west. Salt dwarfed all other commercial interests, forcing the Company into forms of vertical integration, including ship-owning and managing.[64] Indeed, the highly lucrative and occasionally profitable transatlantic voyages undertaken by the Company were speculative concerns financed by the continued profitability of the domestic salt trade.

The Company's accounts do not effectively begin until May 1696, at which time three vessels had already been freighted to Liverpool for rock and white salt.[65] In April the *Providence* of Bridgwater, mastered by John Neale, and the

Mary and Elizabeth of Liverpool under John Higginson, 'master and one quarter owner', discharged salt at Bridgwater, closely followed by the *Blessing* of Bridgwater, under John Pettitt, 'master and half owner', with Samuel Burnall acting as supercargo.[66] In addition, Philip Jefferies was contracted to ship 2,410 bushels and 5 lb of white salt (60.25 tons) and 3 tons, 13 cwt rock 'att 7d per bushell on our account as per Mr Hyde's charge' in his vessel the *True Love* of Bideford. The vessel arrived in Bridgwater in June, with Isaac Heard recorded as merchant.[67] It is also probable that the Company freighted its regular vessels, the *Blessing, Exchange* and *Hannah*, to Liverpool in the early months of 1696, although no direct evidence exists to determine whether the Company was explicitly involved.[68]

The activities of the Company become more apparent from May 1696 when shipments are reported in more detail in the Letter Book. By the end of the month, Michael Currant's ship the *Hannah* of Bridgwater, five-twelfths owned by the Company, had proceeded to Frodsham and been loaded with white salt procured from Thomas Hyde of Middlewich and Thomas Minshall of Erdswick. Despite problems connected with excise payments and scarcity of supplies (occasioned by lack of coal and labour), Currant returned to Bridgwater on 12 June.[69] During this month, the Company also freighted the *Exchange* and the *Providence*, mastered by Philip Cockrem and John Neale respectively. The vessels were loaded with salt at Frodsham, with Thomas Webb supplying Cockrem, and Hyde supplying Neale. Their cargoes discharged at Bridgwater in mid-July.[70] Between June and August, two further Company ships, the *Blessing* and the *Mary and Elizabeth*, under Pettitt and Higginson, were delayed at Liverpool by lack of salt, a glut of coasters awaiting loading, contrary winds and the threat of privateers. Pettitt and Higginson eventually managed to load white salt from Hyde and Webb respectively, discharging in Bridgwater in September and October.[71]

A further six voyages to the Mersey estuary were undertaken in boats owned or chartered by the Company in 1696. The *Mary* of Bridgwater, mastered by John Page, and the *Hannah*, again under Currant, loaded over 95 tons of rock salt from Warburton at Frodsham.[72] Currant intended to seek a market for his quarter share in south Wales, yet, beset by inclement weather, discharged the whole cargo at Bridgwater, selling his share directly to the Company. The *Hannah* was promptly offloaded to John Palmer.[73] In September, Robert Hyde shipped on board the *True Love* of Bridgwater, mastered by Hugh Baldwin, just under 2,143 bushels of white salt at Frodsham Bridge. A further loading of rock salt was supplied by Warburton when the vessel cleared from Liverpool on 8 October.[74] At the same time, the *Betty* of Watchet, mastered by Robert Dashwood, was dispatched by Warburton. The vessel arrived at Bridgwater in late November with 55 tons of rock and smaller amounts of white: Warburton acted as the named merchant.[75] In addition, after a notably unsuccessful voyage with coals and glass to Dublin in the *Providence*, John Neale procured a loading of white salt from Webb, the vessel clearing Liverpool on 20 October.[76] Following a lucky escape when the vessel was grounded and holed off Beaumaris, Neale limped home with more brine than salt in December.[77] The last voyage undertaken by the Company and completed in 1696, involved John Higginson, once more merchanting the *Mary and Elizabeth*. Higginson loaded 2,585 bushels of Middlewich white salt from Webb at Frodsham and also shipped another 20 cwt from 'Mr Ludlow . . . a projector, who said he had an order to put it on board . . . for the Company's use and risque'.[78] Beset with similar difficulties to Neale, Higginson eventually reached Bridgwater on 14 December.[79]

In 1696, the Company also sought to develop its trade in Droitwich salt. From September to October, five shipments of salt were freighted through Gloucester, using George Perkes's trow, the *Prosperity* of Bewdley, under Charles Corker, and Thomas Claroe's trow, the *Thomas* of Upton, mastered on a regular basis by William Jefferies. The shipments were organised by John Padmore of Broadwater near Kidderminster and brokered by the Company's agent, Richard Lowbridge.[80] Initial supplies of salt 'made in leaden pans' met a decidedly lukewarm reception from the Company's local customers, more accustomed to the 'small, heavy salt' of Cheshire.[81] According to Padmore, Droitwich salt was 'as keen and dry a white salt as any is made in Cheshire, and such as I have formerly sold from Namptwich and Middlewich to Bridgwater'. Although salt of a greater grain was 'made at severall places at the sea side on salt rock and sea water', this salt, Padmore assured the Company, was manufactured from 'the strongest brine' making 'bigger grain salt than ever was made in this Country before' and would more than suffice the needs of their agents and chapmen. Consequently, Padmore proposed to supplement Lowbridge's initial agreement by taking 'all [the salt] that the iron pans make' if the Company so desired. The new contract would provide salt 'as well dryed and as big graine as the brine will make', amounting to around '30 or 40 ton each spring [tide]' consigned in '2 or 3 vessells'.[82]

The efficacy of coal-fired Droitwich salt appears to be borne out by the increasing frequency of trade between Gloucester and Bridgwater. From November 1696, Hoare and Company received regular cargoes from Padmore and Lowbridge often directed through Perkes and Corker. Thus, the *Prosperity* with Corker on board entered Bridgwater on 18 November carrying 25 tons of white salt which was sold ten days later.[83] The boat returned with another consignment of 20 tons on 8 December, the Company dispatching moneys to cover Padmore's excise payment (via George Perkes) when the trow, with Corker as the recorded master and merchant, finally cleared Bridgwater on 15 December.[84]

Hoare and Company also bought up supplies of salt brought coastwise by other merchants. In July 1696, Richard Chinn of Newnham was paid £125 4s in not altogether good bills for 20 tons and 14 cwt of Cheshire white salt 'received of him out of the *Endeavour* [of Newnham], William Williams, master'.[85] In October, salt was purchased from William Methwen and Thomas Musgrave, who had earlier freighted the *Speedwell* of Bridgwater under John Vinecott to load white salt from Thomas Partington's works at Flint.[86] The *Speedwell* and her fittings were later purchased outright from Methwen on his admittance to the partnership.[87]

The Company's voracious appetite for salt brought coastally continued in 1697, although the reliance upon supplies from Liverpool was not as pronounced. This was due in part to the greater uptake of Droitwich salt and in part to the Company's notably unsuccessful decision to exploit the reported deficiency of salt along the south coast of Cornwall and Devon. Cockrem, on board the *Exchange* loaded with over 1,748 bushels (43.76 tons), was fairly unenthusiastic about making the dangerous and costly trip around Land's End in winter, even though the decline of Lymington sea-salt—the wet summer having 'prejudissed their pickle'—suggested lucrative returns.[88] Cockrem was followed by Samuel Burnall, captain of the *Blessing*,[89] John Higginson, master and acting supercargo of the *Mary and Elizabeth*,[90] and John Neale aboard the *Providence*.[91] All four shippers found extreme difficulty in off-loading the Company's salt. Cockrem bargained at a loss at Truro, Falmouth and eventually St Ives,[92] whilst Burnall, Higginson and Neale, despite actively seeking buyers in the ports and inland market towns around Falmouth, Fowey, Plymouth and Dartmouth, were undermined in their efforts by local sharp practice and the 'constant rumour of a peace [with France]'. The Company eventually cut its losses and settled at rates far below what was initially expected.[93]

The employment of four of the Company's regular traders on these long-distance coasting enterprises meant that only five voyages from Liverpool were completed in 1697. Robert Dashwood in the *Betty* entered Bridgwater on 16 April with rock and white salt loaded from Thomas Warburton's works,[94] and in the following month, Michael Currant's new vessel, the *Michael* of Bridgwater, discharged over 52 tons of salt.[95] In September, the *Hope* of Bridgwater with Nicholas Griffiths on board arrived at Bridgwater with almost 55 tons of white salt for the Company, and the *Michael*, with Currant as merchant and Sebastian Llewellyn as master, entered with over 29 tons of white and 33 tons of rock salt in October.[96] The final voyage saw Cockrem's *Exchange* carrying white salt break bulk in Bridgwater on 2 December.[97]

Any shortfall of supplies from Cheshire was more than compensated by the expansion of the trade in Droitwich salt. In 1697, Hoare and Company freighted 12 of the 20 shipments recorded entering Bridgwater from Gloucester. Much of this salt was contracted from Lowbridge and Padmore at £5 5s per ton and shipped on board Corker's trows, the *Prosperity* and the *Success* of Bewdley. Corker completed roughly a voyage each month for the Company between January and August delivering in all over 183 tons of salt, being paid £8 freight for every 20 tons delivered.[98] The Company also chartered Thomas Claroe and the *Thomas* of Upton on three separate voyages, Claroe shipping small consignments of salt alongside much larger cargoes of corn and wool.[99] The final shipment of Droitwich salt in 1697 represented a commercial departure. On 16 December, Edward Jackson on board the *Charles* of Bridgnorth entered Bridgwater carrying 20 tons of salt, which was sold at 1.5 cwt overweight to the Company's regular agents.[100] This salt was received directly from Robert Steynor, the proprietor responsible for the breaking of the old Droitwich monopoly, and by 1697 among the most prominent of Worcestershire salters.[101] The use of a Bridgnorth vessel, hardly proximate to the Worcestershire salt field, demonstrates the strong familial association between individual trow owners and the salt trade that was to characterise river trade in the eighteenth century. Jackson's business was to be defined by the long-distance carriage of salt and was the principal motivation for his permanent relocation to Worcester, the main market and entrepôt for Droitwich salt, by 1714.[102]

Steynor and Jackson were to supply a further 94 tons and 18 cwt of white salt in three successive voyages of the *Charles* of Bridgnorth between January and April 1698, Jackson shipping Cheshire cheese and other sundries on his own account.[103] Steynor was also involved in a shipment of 39.5 tons of white salt delivered at £5 15s per ton in March, conveyed in the *Thomas* of Worcester, with John Chance recorded as the master and merchant.[104] Steynor's activities, however, were outweighed by the quantities Padmore and, from November, his associate Robert Hall consigned to the Company via Charles Corker. Corker's trows, the *Prosperity* and the *Success* of Bewdley, were freighted from Gloucester on every convenient spring tide and took whatever salt Padmore had ready. In total 137.78 tons were delivered in 1698.[105]

However, Padmore's salt was increasingly undercut by salt delivered 'at very low rates' from Sir Robert Throgmorton's works at Droitwich. The Company's response was to persuade Padmore to renegotiate his contract by emphasising the relative cheapness of other forms of supply and by dangling the financial carrot of not only renewing the agreement to supply 50 tons, but also doubling it if required.[106] A further two consignments were dispatched by Padmore in 1698 and a single shipment of 10 tons of clod salt, a concentrated salt held in high repute for bacon and cheese making, was delivered by Corker from Thomas Herbert in November.[107]

In response to Hoare's order to engross as much salt as possible, the Company sought to acquire salt directly from other merchants.[108] In May 1698, just over 20 tons were bought from a loading of 38 tons shipped by 'owner' Thomas Claroe on the *Thomas* of Upton.[109] Another shipment of 37 tons 14 cwt was obtained in July via William Smith, the Company's correspondent in wool and grain in the *Elizabeth* of Tewkesbury.[110] More enterprisingly, the Company contracted with Throgmorton and Norris, salt producers in Worcestershire, to buy 95 tons of salt.[111] In September, 40 tons carried on the *William* of Bridgnorth were purchased from 'Mr Robert Bobbet and received out of William Oakes' trow, it being a parcel of salt Mr Bobbett bought of Sir Francis Throgmorton's steward'.[112] This was followed by further shipments in the *William*, mastered by John Clarke, with Oakes acting as supercargo for salt delivered to him by William Norris. On 19 October, the Company took delivery of 16 tons 3 cwt of salt from the 33 tons shipped by Oakes and Clarke and a further 15 tons 5 cwt that entered the port by this means on 2 December.[113] This, however, represented a poor return: the Company was 'streightened for the rest' of the salt. Galpine found the consignments very 'short on weight' and was forced to warn Norris that, if freight could not be arranged as cheap as that afforded by Perkes and Corker at 9s per ton, the deal was off. None the less, a further 40 tons was ordered for the next spring tide the following year.[114]

The absence of the Company's main fleet abroad in 1698 curtailed its long-distance coasting activities.[115] None the less, five voyages were completed, three of which were undertaken by the *Speedwell*, mastered by Giles Vinecott. In April, Vinecott landed a cargo of white and rock salt loaded by William Hyde, and returned to Liverpool as 'purser' to load 1,008 bushels (54 tons) of rock and a small quantity of white for Hoare.[116] Thereafter the vessel was dispatched to Chester to load white salt with Partington and Massey at Flint in August. After several delays and an abortive trip to Frodsham, the *Speedwell* cleared Chester in October.[117] In addition, the Company received rock salt from William Hyde on board the *Mary*, which discharged at Bridgwater in September. Also the *Friendship* of Bridgwater under Joseph Cross brought back almost 53 tons of rock salt from Hyde's works after freighting Tenby coals to Dublin and yarn to Liverpool.[118]

The reconstruction of the Company's salt business in 1699 is more problematic. Although the contracts with Padmore and Norris for Droitwich salt were upheld, the records only provide a sketchy outline of how salt purchased in this way was brought to Bridgwater. Two consignments totalling 68 tons carried in William Oakes's trow, the *William* of Bridgnorth, in January and February almost certainly were undertaken in completion of the bargain struck with Norris.[119] Oakes also delivered a further 37 tons of white salt from Norris on the *Francis* of Bridgnorth, mastered by John Clarke, which entered Bridgwater on 22 May.[120] A one-off shipment of 22 tons of white salt was procured from John Hooper, master of the *Samuel* of Upton, in March,[121] and in April, Corker on the *Prosperity* delivered 20 tons from Padmore and Hall.[122] In addition, the Company contracted with Hall and Penrice of Droitwich to supply a further 100 tons of 'merchantable white salt, large grayn, made in iron pans' from Michaelmas 1699, 'that is to say 20 tons unto 25, the beginning of every month untill the bargaine is compleated'.[123] Corker completed three voyages in the *Success* of Bewdley before the new contract was enforced, shipping 80 tons of white salt.[124] Thereafter, Corker mastered the *John and Mary* of Bewdley, which discharged a cargo of 20 tons on 18 October, and oversaw a final shipment of 12 tons on the *Success* which broke bulk on 21 November.[125]

Because of the deficiencies in the extant record, evidence of Hoare and Company's interests in Cheshire salt in 1699 is limited. For much of the year, the fleet was abroad and it is only possible to firmly identify six voyages freighted for the company from Liverpool and Chester. On 2 February, Michael Currant brought home the *Hope* with rock and white salt loaded by Robert Hyde.[126] Two days later the *Elizabeth* of Bideford, freighted by Isaac Heard, entered Bridgwater with a cargo of rock salt, presumably for the Company.[127] At this time the *Speedwell* under John Vinecott was dispatched to Partington and Massey. Despite much confusion over whether to ship or warehouse old duty rock salt, the vessel returned to Bridgwater in May with 1,500 bushels (37.5 tons) of white salt from Chester.[128] Also in May the *Mary and Elizabeth* reached Bridgwater after loading rock with Robert Hyde.[129] The Company's final two return shipments to Liverpool in 1699 were in the *Michael* skippered by Michael Currant, and the *Exchange* mastered and merchanted by Philip Cockrem. In June, the vessels discharged over 90 tons of rock salt which had been acquired by the Company before the imposition of the new duty.[130] Two more Company ships, the *Fly* and the *Mary*, also collected salt at Liverpool in 1699, although they were ordered to discharge at Ilfracombe and in Ireland respectively. In addition, the Company's need to secure supplies of rock salt before the proposed Salt Act 'be brought into the hous', prompted Galpine to raid the Bristol market.[131] As a result, 15 tons were consigned by Edward Hackett on board 'Offield's bark', the *Isaac and John* of Bridgwater, on 6 April The vessel arrived at Bridgwater two days later with Robert Nurton acting as master and merchant. A further 6 tons purchased by Hackett were also sent on the *Isaac and John* in June, before the Company's temporary shortage of rock salt was met by cargoes discharging from Liverpool.[132]

The activity of Hoare and Company is not recorded after 1700. However, very similar patterns of organisation were in place in both 1701 and 1703. The fact that traders such as Corker and Perkes continued to be prominent in the shipment of Droitwich salt suggests that the contractual arrangements hammered out with Worcestershire salters like Penrice, Norris and Hall were still in force, although they were almost certainly not organised under the aegis of the Company. In 1701, Corker accounted for 82.01 tons in three shipments and 311.2 tons in 12 voyages in 1703. In addition, Perkes acted as merchant on seven voyages undertaken by Corker in the *Success* of Bewdley and the *Joseph and Benjamin* of Bewdley in 1703. The vessels transported over 137 tons of white salt to Bridgwater.

In the four years in which an impression of the Company's interests can be reconstructed, salt was without doubt the principal traded commodity. Table 5.6 summarises the control Hoare and Company exerted over supplies of white and rock salt brought coastally to Bridgwater in this period. Only in 1699, when the record is incomplete, did the Company fail to control a majority of the total amount of salt entering the port in any given year. This ascendancy was founded squarely on white salt: the Company consistently took over half the quantity of the commodity shipped coastally to Bridgwater. In 1696, almost 800 tons of white salt were traded on behalf of the Company, over 80 per cent of which was Cheshire salt emanating from Frodsham and Liverpool. Thereafter, the Company, like most Bridgwater traders, concentrated upon Droitwich for its supplies of white salt. Between 1696 and 1699, the Company accounted for the lion's share of salt transported to Bridgwater via the Severn. Although doubts existed concerning the comparative strength of the commodity, it could be freighted more cheaply and far more safely than supplies of Cheshire salt, which faced the lengthy and often perilous sea journey from the north-west. The Company also became less reliant upon Cheshire rock salt over the period, even though a steady running order of around 200 tons per year was maintained with proprietors such as Robert Hyde and Thomas Warburton. Much of this was directed to the Company's own salt works and pans at Ham Mills and Lynmouth. However, as the Company diversified its regional interests, the trade in rock salt became less focused on Bridgwater. Instead, rock salt was transported on a much larger scale to other areas, notably the fishery centres of the south coast of Cornwall and Devon and also Ireland. Here potential gains were higher, but the voyages were more speculative and the disadvantages involved in long-distance trade, even in optimum, peacetime conditions, rose in proportion. High overhead costs, truculent factors and surly crews undermined the Company's best attempts to extract a profit from these trades.

Hoare and Company were not the only Bridgwater merchants importing salt coastally at this time. A significant proportion of Cheshire white and rock salt was also freighted by William Alloway, a substantial Quaker merchant who combined 'dealing in wool and English goods' with interests in the domestic herring fisheries and the transatlantic trade.[133] By 1695 Alloway had

Table 5.6a

Coastal imports of white and rock salt (tons) to Bridgwater, 1696–1699, organised by Hoare and Company

		White salt				Rock salt				Total salt
		Gloucester	Liverpool	Others	Total	Gloucester	Liverpool	Bristol	Total	
1696	tons	182.36	973.74	74.79	1,230.89	24.00	556.34	–	580.34	1,811.23
	Hoare	117.78	640.58	37.50	795.86	–	250.68	–	250.68	1,046.53
	% Hoare	65	66	50	65	–	45	–	43	58
1697	tons	401.31	304.96	7.00	713.27	–	279.41	–	279.41	992.68
	Hoare	211.93	190.83	–	402.76	–	95.31	–	95.31	498.07
	% Hoare	53	63		56	–	34	–	34	50
1698	tons	704.90	46.26	54.78	805.94	–	361.76	–	361.76	1,167.70
	Hoare	385.03	15.08	35.00	435.11	–	201.17	–	201.17	636.28
	% Hoare	55	33	64	54	–	56	–	56	54
1699	tons	393.50	19.20	64.50	477.20	–	689.05	33.00	722.05	1,199.25
	Hoare	261.00	1.10	37.50	299.60	–	196.95	21.00	217.95	517.55
	% Hoare	66	6	58	63	–	29	64	30	43

Table 5.6b

Coastal shipments of white and rock salt to Bridgwater, 1696–1699, organised by Hoare and Company

		White salt				Rock salt			
		Gloucester	Liverpool	Others	Total	Gloucester	Liverpool	Bristol	Total
1696	total	14	27	3	44	2	20	–	22
	Hoare	12	15	1	28	–	8	–	8
	% Hoare	86	56	33	64	–	40	–	36
1697	total	20	10	1	31	–	6	–	6
	Hoare	10	5	–	15	–	2	–	2
	% Hoare	50	50	–	48	–	33	–	33
1698	total	23	5	2	30	–	8	–	8
	Hoare	16	3	1	20	–	4	–	4
	% Hoare	70	60	50	67	–	50	–	50
1699	total	14	6	1	22	–	18	3	21
	Hoare	10	1	1	12	–	5	2	7
	% Hoare	71	17	100	55	–	28	67	33

Source: PRO E190 coastal port books; PRO C104/12.

shares in at least four independent salt works in Somerset and Cornwall, refitting his principal works at Bridgwater in 1697 with 'a salt pann, vates, and materialls'.[134] Later he enjoyed an informal but close association with the Hoare partners, jointly owning the Lynmouth fishery.[135]

Alloway's involvement in the salt trade was organised on two levels. Insofar as supply was concerned, his association with Thomas Johnson of Liverpool was vital. Johnson was the central figure in the mercantile community of Liverpool in this period and had several fingers in the white and rock salt trade. Alloway's salt consignments were invariably procured through Johnson, who in turn was supplied with large quantities of grain, pulses and other agricultural goods sent coastwise from Somerset.[136] At a local level, Alloway entered into partnerships with merchants and ship owners to freight salt. Alloway owned three-quarters of the *Willing Mind* of Bridgwater, the remainder being controlled by the boat's regular merchant, Alexander Holmes; a half-share in the *Satisfaction* of Bridgwater with John Wheddon; and a three-eighths share of the *Robert and Thomas* of Bridgwater with Thomas Musgrave, an association which appears to have been short-lived.[137] In addition, Alloway was the sole owner of the *Friendship* of Minehead, which was largely employed in the transoceanic and Irish trades. Like Hoare and Company, other vessels were freighted as and when required.

The activity of William Alloway and associates between 1695 and 1699 is shown in table 5.7. Alloway is first encountered acting as merchant on the *Satisfaction* in 1695 with John Matthews as master. The vessel made two voyages from Liverpool in the year carrying just under 95 tons of white salt and almost 17 tons of rock before being captured by a French privateer in September.[138] Alloway's other boat, the *Willing Mind*, completed two voyages from Liverpool in August and November carrying a total of just under 122 tons of white salt and a very small amount of rock. On both occasions, the vessel was navigated by John Eaves, with Alloway's partner, Alexander Holmes, appearing as merchant.[139]

In 1696, however, the picture becomes rather less clear-cut. In February, the *Willing Mind* carrying just over 44 tons of white salt in 564 barrels and a small quantity of rock salt discharged at Bridgwater. In the port book, John Goodson was noted as merchant with John Aymes the recorded master. However, from Alloway's accounts, only Goodson was contracted.[140] Two months later, the *Satisfaction* with Robert Dashwood on board delivered over 57 tons of rock salt from Thomas Johnson, who acted as merchant for customs purposes.[141] Also in April, Alloway and Musgrave freighted the *Robert and Thomas* of Bridgwater with Robert Anstice mastering the vessel. Anstice loaded 42.63 tons of rock and a minor quantity of white salt from Johnson, who again stood surety as merchant.[142] In June, two shipments of predominantly rock salt were received from Alloway's regular coasters: the

Table 5.7a

*Coastal imports of white and rock salt (tons) to Bridgwater, 1695–1699,
organised by William Alloway*

		White salt			Rock salt		
		Liverpool	Others	Total	Liverpool	Total	Total salt
1695	tons	787.62	3.25	790.87	55.85	55.85	846.72
	Alloway	178.11	–	178.11	17.15	17.15	195.26
	% Alloway	23	–	23	31	31	23
1696	tons	973.74	257.15	1,230.89	556.34	580.34	1,811.23
	Alloway	186.48	–	186.48	234.02	234.02	420.50
	% Alloway	19	–	15	45	40	23
1697	tons	304.96	408.31	713.27	279.41	279.41	992.68
	Alloway	107.56	–	107.56	60.95	60.95	168.51
	% Alloway	35	–	15	22	22	17
1698	tons	46.26	759.28	805.54	361.76	361.76	1,167.30
	Alloway	20.29	–	20.29	43.44	43.44	63.73
	% Alloway	44	–	3	12	12	5
1699	tons	19.20	458.00	477.20	689.05	689.05	1,166.25
	Alloway	–	27.00	27.00	30.47	30.47	57.47
	% Alloway	–	6	6	4	4	5

Table 5.7b

*Coastal shipments of white and rock salt to Bridgwater, 1695–1699,
organised by William Alloway*

		White salt			Rock salt	
		Liverpool	Others	Total	Liverpool	Total
1695	total	18	5	23	7	7
	Alloway	5	–	5	2	2
	% Alloway	28	–	22	29	29
1696	total	27	17	44	20	22
	Alloway	7	–	7	7	7
	% Alloway	26	–	16	40	36
1697	total	10	21	31	6	6
	Alloway	3	–	3	2	2
	% Alloway	30	–	10	33	33
1698	total	5	25	30	8	8
	Alloway	1	–	1	1	1
	% Alloway	20	–	3	13	13
1699	total	6	16	22	18	21
	Alloway	–	1	1	1	1
	% Alloway	–	6	5	6	5

Source: PRO E190 coastal port books; SRO DD/DN 463.

Satisfaction, navigated by Matthews and loaded and ostensibly merchanted by Johnson, and the *Willing Mind*, loaded by Thomas Minshall, arrived under Holmes and John Diaper respectively in convoy with Hoare and Company's ships.[143] The same combination returned to Liverpool in August to be loaded by Johnson. However, problems with excise payment, the lack of good ready money, poor supplies of salt, and severe weather seriously delayed Holmes. The *Willing Mind* finally broke bulk in Bridgwater only in October.[144] At this time Alloway had again freighted Anstice in the *Robert and Thomas* to load salt with Robert Hyde.[145] A final voyage organised by Alloway in 1696 involved the chartering of Philip Voss in the *Ann and Sarah* of Milford. Voss, again supplied by Johnson with Alloway appearing as the named merchant, discharged almost 48 tons of white salt and 11.25 tons of rock in December.[146] Alloway and his partners, therefore, accounted for some 186.46 tons of white salt and a rather larger amount, fractionally over 234 tons, of rock salt in 1696. The latter formed 40 per cent of the total traded to Bridgwater. More interestingly the combined coastal imports of Alloway and Hoare and Company reveal that in 1696 the local salt trade was effectively divided between the two groups of merchants: a minimum of 81 per cent of all salt discharging coastally at Bridgwater was organised or controlled by these merchants.

The year 1696 represented the high point of Alloway's involvement in the salt trade. Like Hoare and Company, he subsequently employed his vessels in potentially more lucrative areas: shipping salt to Ireland and the south coast of Devon; delivering Irish wool to Bridgwater and Minehead, staple ports for the Devonshire cloth industry; and engaging in the Virginian and Newfoundland trades. For much of 1697, for example, the *Willing Mind* was employed in a complex quadrilateral of trade, clearing Bridgwater in ballast for Milford; taking a cargo of culm from Milford to Dublin; thereafter transporting wool and linen to Liverpool; and finally shipping white salt from Liverpool to Topsham.[147] In 1698 and 1699, the ship was trading to the West Indies.[148] None the less, Alloway still accounted for over 35 per cent of the white salt and 22 per cent of the rock salt clearing Liverpool for Bridgwater in 1697. This was carried in three voyages: the *Willing Mind* under Holmes discharged almost 48 tons of white salt in January, and the *Ann and Sarah*, mastered by Voss, completed voyages in April and October transporting almost 61 tons of rock salt and 60 tons of white salt.[149]

By 1698, however, Alloway's interest in shipping salt directly to Bridgwater had waned: only one voyage, in which Anstice was freighted on board the *Robert and Thomas*, can be confidently ascribed to Alloway.[150] In 1699, a solitary voyage in the *Prosperous* of Liverpool freighted by Henry Parr and mastered by James Norris unloaded Cheshire rock salt for Alloway,[151] whilst a further 27 tons of white salt, landed at Minehead the previous year, were shipped on board the *John and Ann* of Minehead, mastered by William Harding.[152] Alloway continued to deal in salt throughout the period covered by his accounts, although by 1699 neither the port books nor his accounts detail the vessels through which supplies were being shipped.

Where did this salt go? Hoare and Company's Waste Book records the principal users, agents and carriers who purchased salt brought coastwise by the Company between May 1696 and December 1698. The 55 consumers who took a minimum of 1 ton of salt are presented in table 5.8 together with an account of warehoused stock, salt sold coastally to Swansea, and a cumulative total of goods sold to a further 14 smaller traders. In map 5.1, the geographical extent of the Company's trade is compared to that reported for 'coles, culm and other merchandizes' dispatched by Richard Bobbett, a Bridgwater merchant operating out of Ham Mills in 1672.[153]

The table reveals that the Company retained more rock salt than white salt. Only 66 per cent of rock salt acquired by the Company was accounted for by the end of the period, whereas almost all Cheshire and Droitwich white salt (94 per cent) was either sold, processed or warehoused. Much of the discrepancy in rock salt can be explained by the requirements of the Company's growing network of pans and works.[154] Of the 358.47 tons of rock salt traded, a fifth (73.19 tons) was either reserved for the Company at the Ham Mills factory or warehoused in Cellars B and K. Rather more was sold directly to major local users like Thomas Lockyer of Ilchester, who took over a quarter of all rock salt traded, Henry and William Hambridge of Uphill, Jeans and Burford of Martock, and Hugh Woodbury of Ham Mills. These merchants may have used rock salt to supply their own salt works, especially those like Woodbury who also had access to coal shipped up the Parrett and Tone.[155]

The Company's supplies of white salt were more widely traded. By the end of detailed accounts in December 1698, the Company had traded almost 322 tons to its factory at Ham Mills or to Alexander Wallis, its principal on-site manager. A further amount (around 13 per cent) was cellared in Bridgwater. This was designed predominantly for the domestic and Newfoundland fisheries, but a small, largely unrecorded proportion was sold for ready cash to local consumers and traders. Salt from the quayside, warehouse and factory was also sold to a highly organised army of local chapmen, agents and regular carriers who served the hinterland. Men like Thomas Kirby and Thomas Coggan, both of Langport, operated small vessels in which a ton or so of salt, along with other merchandises, was frequently ventured. Kirby and Coggan exploited the many inland trading routes radiating out from Bridgwater and Ham Mills, at the head of the navigable river Parrett.[156] The extent of this system is supported by the dealings of Robert Bobbett's father, Richard. Deponents in the Exchequer case of 1672 attested that 'time out of mind' barges and trows were employed conveying goods 'out of any shipps or

Table 5.8

Principal buyers of salt from Hoare and Company, 1696–1698

Buyer	Status	Place	Tons White	Tons Rock	Total
Factory of salt	Factory of salt	Ham Mills	261.15	36.00	297.15
Robert Bobbett	Merchant/factor	Ham Mills	244.32	–	244.32
Joan Diaper	Salter	Bridgwater	135.05	4.50	139.55
Thomas Lockyer	Salter	Ilchester	23.28	93.45	116.73
Vincent Boldy	Merchant/carrier	Langport	64.88	10.95	75.83
Hugh Woodbury	Salter	Ham Mills	40.63	30.00	70.63
Henry + William Hambridge	Merchants	Uphill	4.00	51.00	55.00
Nathaniel + Hannah Scorch	Merchant/master	Bridgwater	48.40	2.50	50.90
Sebastian Llewellyn	Merchant/master	Bridgwater	47.15	3.00	50.15
John Burford	Salter	Ilchester	25.31	23.00	48.31
James Bowles +CO	Merchants/salters		36.95		36.95
Hannah Francis	Salter	Bridgwater	36.63	–	36.63
Ambrose Hozee	Merchant/salter	Bridgwater	31.60	–	31.60
Jeans + Burford	Salters	Martock	3.50	28.00	31.50
Michael Currant	Merchant/master	Bridgwater	26.95	–	26.95
Mr Wallis	Manager, factory	Taunton	24.75	–	24.75
John Venicott	Merchant/master	Bridgwater	23.28	0.50	23.78
Edward Davies	Merchant/master	Bridgwater	21.35	0.50	21.85
Joan Porker	Salter		16.00	–	16.00
Thomas Anstice	Merchant/master	Bridgwater	15.25	–	15.25
George + Samuel Smith			15.15		15.15
John Hill			14.40	0.50	14.90
William Alloway	Merchant/fishery	Bridgwater/Lynmouth	–	14.30	14.30
Thomas Palmer			12.80	–	12.80
John Pettitt	Merchant/master	Bridgwater	12.42	–	12.42
Joan Drake		Taunton	10.40	1.25	11.65
Joseph Taylor		Ottery	9.20	1.41	10.61
Jonathan Thomas			10.30	–	10.30
Thomas Kirby	Carrier	Langport	8.78	0.45	9.23
Thomas Coggan	Carrier	Langport	8.25	–	8.25
George Glass	Carrier		7.00	1.00	8.00
Isaac Heard	Merchant/partner	Bridgwater	1.50	6.00	7.50
John Rood	Carrier	Glastonbury	6.35	0.50	6.85
Mr Roberts +CO	Merchant/factor	Ham Mills	6.60	–	6.60
Mr Capon	Carrier		5.30		5.30
John Wheddon	Merchant/shipper	Watchet	–	5.25	5.25
William Milnor			5.00	0.25	5.25
Anthony Baker			4.85	–	4.85
Charles Lyst	Carrier	Glastonbury	4.80	–	4.80
Mary Smith			3.70	–	3.70
John Turner	Carrier	Glastonbury	3.00	0.50	3.50
Ambrose Marshall			1.00	2.00	3.00
Benjamin + Richard Sully	Carriers	Stowell?	2.25	0.25	2.50
Oliver Woodward	Pilot	Bridgwater	2.10	–	2.10
Henry Ruscombe		Wells	2.05	–	2.05
John Martin			–	2.00	2.00
Jasper Porter	Carrier		1.98	–	1.98
John Adams	Carrier	Bishop's Lydeard	1.50	–	1.50
John Turner	Carrier	Langport	1.25	–	1.25
Richard Drake	Merchant/partner	Bridgwater	1.25	–	1.25
Philip Cockrem	Merchant/master		1.15	–	1.15
John Bastone	Merchant/shipper	Minehead	–	1.00	1.00
Henry Sweeting		Lydiard	1.00	–	1.00
Elizabeth Hathman		Langport	–	1.00	1.00
Henry Peddle			1.00	–	1.00
Others (14)			4.68	0.21	4.89
To Swansea + William Beaver	Merchant	Swansea	30.00	–	30.00
Cellars A,B,K + Warehouse		Bridgwater	204.34	37.19	241.53
		Total	1,535.74	358.47	1,894.21

Source: PRO C 104/12.

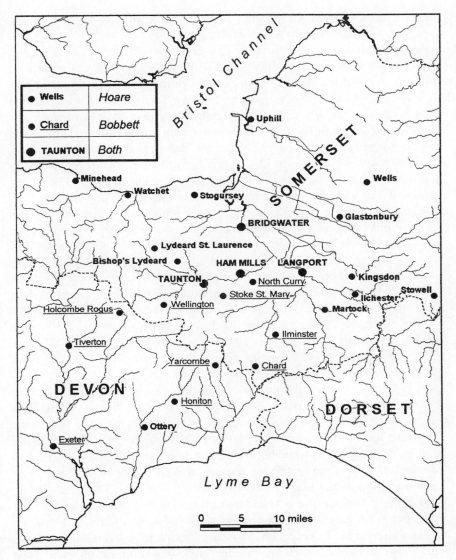

Map 5.1

Consumers of Hoare and Company salt (1696–1698) and centres of trade for coal and
general goods from Richard Bobbett (1671).

vessells rideing in the port of Bridgwater to Ham Mills, Langport or any other
place or places lying on the . . . river'. Such merchandises were then 'carryed on
horses and other carriages into the country thereabouts for the supply of the
inhabitants thereof'. Bobbett's carriers claimed to serve places as distant as

Exeter, Tiverton, Honiton, Holcombe Rogus and Yarcombe, as well as Taunton, Ilminster, North Curry, Chard, and Wellington.[157]

Many of Hoare and Company's customers operated over an equally large area. Regular contacts were maintained with carriers based in Glastonbury, Bishop's Lydeard, Taunton and Kingsdon. Company salt also found its way to Stogursey, Chard, Wellington, Ottery St Mary, Tiverton and Exeter through such traders, although these transactions were usually recorded in the Company accounts in the form of money payments or extended credit and not in tonnage dispatched. Throughout the period, Thomas Galpine, Alexander Wallis and Richard Drake were busy at all the major regional fairs and markets 'in the countrey' hunting down bad salt debts.[158] The major carrier of salt was Vincent Boldy, a Quaker of Langport and Shapwick.[159] Boldy accounted for over 75 tons of mostly white salt, traded on his own account and for local agents. This was transported in a fleet of small craft and barges which Boldy owned, and which were navigated by himself and lesser operatives like Joseph Tibbs, Edward Coombe and Richard Sillivent. At Langport, salt appears to have been distributed to land carriers.[160]

The Company also enjoyed a curiously ambivalent association with Robert Bobbett, who possessed rival large-scale warehouses and works at Ham Mills. On the one hand, Bobbett consistently bought large quantities of Cheshire and Droitwich salt from the Company, taking around 16 per cent of all white salt traded inland. This he supplemented with salt purchased directly from salt proprietors and other Bridgwater merchants, notably Alloway.[161] However, Bobbett's relationship with the Company, always competitive, quickly soured. By early 1697, Wallis and Galpine, managers of the Ham Mills enterprise, reported that Bobbett was severely undercutting the factory by supplying local carriers at reduced rates, compounding such 'underhand dealings' by refusing to settle his account.[162] Even so, Bobbett continued to be supplied until relinquishing his business in September 1698 to the more accommodating James Roberts and Company.[163]

Local dealers formed the 'bread and butter' of the Company's white salt trade. For example, Joan Diaper, widow of Nicholas, took almost 140 tons of salt and also traded heavily with Alloway.[164] In addition, the Company sold salt to a number of quasi-independent Bridgwater merchants and boat operators. In the case of Michael Currant, John Vinecott and John Pettitt, some of the salt delivered was by way of entitlement either for their share in the cargo or 'portlage' payment for duties rendered. However, the far larger amounts taken by Sebastian Llewellyn, Nathaniel Scorch and Thomas Anstice, traders who regularly mastered their own coastal vessels, reveal that the Company sold to men who were both dealing on their own account and were not formally associated with the Company. It is likely that salt sold in this way was ventured abroad. A third category of purchasers comprised the partners and associates of the Company. Drake, Heard, Methwen, Balch, Denham and Wheddon all appeared as dealers in Company salt, yet the amounts they took were insignificant. In contrast, William Alloway, as co-partner in the fishery at Lynmouth, took a substantial quantity of rock salt. Given Alloway's access to independent supplies of salt, this probably represented the contractual requirements of the Company's half-share in the enterprise.

Hoare and Company and the wider coastal trades

Unlike overseas merchants, the Company did not actively seek out return cargoes for the fleet of salt vessels it owned and chartered. Occasionally a cargo of corn, malt or peas would be traded as letpass goods to Liverpool, and returning Severn trows and the local Bristol packet would sometimes pick up a consignment of goods the Company had either imported from overseas or assembled from domestic sources. In 1698, for example, Thomas Claroe shipped Castile soap and grocery goods on behalf of the Company to Bristol, [165] whilst Charles Corker was entrusted to deliver small parcels of Newfoundland fish and train oil, Spanish iron, wine and sherry and local serge to agents and customers in Bristol, Gloucester, Kidderminster (via Bewdley) and Nantwich (via Shrewsbury).[166] Generally, Edward Hackett, the Company's factor in Bristol, was employed to handle these cargoes. In January 1699, Hackett sold on a large shipment of sumach and fruit shipped in the *Isaac and John* of Bridgwater and a consignment of red port wine of a rather variable quality and '14 Chests China Orringes, 7 ditto sowre, 12 ditto Lemons shipt on Charles Corker'.[167] Elsewhere, the Company was involved in a host of minor, one-off coastal shipments: wood was shipped from Tenby and Carmarthen in 1696; cinders came from Chepstow in 1697; and vinegar from Francis Stonard of Bristol in 1698.[168]

However, the bulk trades in coal and grain were undertaken on a more consistent basis. From 1696, the Company and its agents actively procured supplies of coal from proprietors in south Wales, notably Sir Humphrey Mackworth of Neath. Mackworth had constructed new docks and store-houses in order to exploit nearby supplies of coal and, despite strong opposition, drove a substantial trade in 'great coal', 'small coals' and 'stone coal'. The stone coal, he assured the Company in characteristically overblown fashion, was 'famous . . . for the making of malt'.[169] In addition, Company dealt with the Mansells of Briton Ferry (through Swansea) and a number of smaller pit and staithe owners in Glamorganshire and Pembrokeshire.[170] Three grades of coal were traded. Prime cost 'hearth coal', a rough, bituminous, principally domestic coal initially much preferred by the Company's carriers and customers, was shipped from Swansea.[171] A slightly smaller and lesser graded 'Abbey coal' was traded coastwise from Neath with increasing regularity from 1697, and culm, a small form of anthracite intended mainly for industrial purposes, was shipped from Tenby and Milford, and with less frequency, from Neath. Milford culm was favoured, with Saundersfoot culm, traded through Tenby, generally regarded as the least merchantable and the coal of last resort.[172] Like much of the salt discharged at Bridgwater, coal was traded to local carriers via the factory at Ham Mills.

Owing to the unstandard nature of measures, quantifying the coal trade is not easy. The port books recorded coal shipments in chaldrons, usually London measure chaldrons, whereas the Company habitually used the wey, quarter and bushel. Recent research has stressed the difficulty in accurately gauging the south Wales wey, and, by implication, the wey in use in the south-west of England at this time. According to Nef, Rees and Symons, the wey not only differed from standard measurement, but also varied between areas of production and over time, weighing anything between 2 and 5 tons.[173] Hatcher's assessment, suggesting 'good reasons for believing that the seventeenth century Glamorgan wey contained approximately 5 tons', has been adopted for the purposes of this research.[174]

The general confusion over the wey measure is compounded by two additional factors. Firstly, it is unclear whether the amounts scrappily recorded in the Company records refer to an entire cargo discharged at Bridgwater or merely a part of it. Secondly, doubts surround the size of the chaldron applied to coals and culm traded coastally. Nef and Willan were under the impression that the 'Pembrokeshire' chaldron of 2 tons, as distinct from the London measure chaldron of 1.4 tons used by Swansea and Neath, was in use at Milford and Tenby, largely on the assertion that 'if the chaldron adopted had been that of London we should have expected the customs officers to have written "Coales London" at the beginning of each book, as they did at the ports of Glamorganshire'.[175] However, the evidence of ships that carried both Pembrokeshire culm and Glamorganshire coals suggests that there was little difference in the number of chaldrons carried no matter the port of clearance or grade of mineral. Similarly, by matching port book evidence with Hoare's accounts, it appears that the London measure chaldron was universally applied. Certainly, it is clear that culm as distinct from coal did not require strict measurement by weight as required by the Act of 1694. Moreover, when coals were the sole item of trade from Milford and Tenby, the London standard was always used.[176] Although such findings suggest that Hatcher's London measure conversion of 28 cwt per chaldron should be adopted, the distinction between coal-exporting ports has been maintained in all discussions of the trade.[177]

Table 5.9 compares the tonnage and shipments of coal organised by Hoare and Company between 1696 and 1699 with total quantities imported coastally at Bridgwater. These figures are minima: the Company's recording of coal brought coastwise was erratic, and although ships owned and freighted by the Company engaged in the coal trade, there is not always an explicit connection mentioned in either the accounts or the port books. The first substantial dealings were not noted until August 1696 when Alexander Wallis delivered £186 5s 12d for 106 weys 1 quarter and 6 bushels (around 530 tons) 'bought

Table 5.9a

Coal and culm (tons) imported coastally to Bridgwater, 1696–1699, controlled by Hoare and Company

		Swansea	Neath	Tenby	Milford	Others	Total
1696	tons	3,665.20	2,107.00	1,512.00	–	28.00	7,312.20
	Hoare	1,216.60	763.00	383.60	–	–	2,363.20
	% Hoare	33	36	25	–	–	32
1697	tons	5,231.80	5,231.80	2,658.60	133.80	64.40	13,320.40
	Hoare	1,113.00	1,251.60	1,029.00	46.20	–	3,439.80
	% Hoare	21	24	39	35	–	26
1698	tons	2,536.80	4,439.40	1,082.20	–	69.06	8,127.46
	Hoare	145.60	471.80	47.60	–	–	665.00
	% Hoare	6	11	5	–	–	8
1699	tons	970.20	5,105.80	1,366.40	345.80	1.00	7,789.20
	Hoare	39.20	702.80	432.60	39.20	–	1,213.80
	% Hoare	4	14	32	11	–	16

Table 5.9b

Shipments of coal and culm recorded at Bridgwater, 1696–1699, controlled by Hoare and Company

		Swansea	Neath	Tenby	Milford	Others	Total
1696	total	87	54	32	–	1	174
	Hoare	23	18	8	–	–	49
	% Hoare	26	33	25	–	–	28
1697	total	121	139	59	4	1	324
	Hoare	24	28	22	1	–	75
	% Hoare	20	20	37	25	–	23
1698	total	76	119	29	–	3	227
	Hoare	4	11	1	–	–	16
	% Hoare	5	9	3	–	–	7
1699	total	31	148	37	10	1	227
	Hoare	1	17	10	1	–	29
	% Hoare	3	11	27	10	–	13

Source: PRO C104/12; PRO E190 coastal port books.

on the bank of Ham Mills'. Clearly, the Company's interest in coal was by this stage long-standing. Later in August, Wallis agreed to continue an earlier contract 'for the run of his trow to Wales for one whole year . . . if she shall reign so long', Wallis to effect all repairs and the Company to provide victuals and crew.[178] From this date scattered references to coal and culm bought by the Ham Mills factory reveal a consistently high proportion of colliers freighted by the Company. Until the end of 1696, the Company chartered five vessels: Wallis's elderly trow, the *William and Richard* of Bridgwater under Philip (or Lyshon) Richards; the *Diligence* of Bridgwater owned by Isaac Heard and mastered by Jerman Gibbs; the *Thomas* of Bridgwater navigated by Lawrence Bryant and employed on a more casual basis; and the Company's own vessels the *Mary*, chartered from Hoare himself and under the control of John Page, and the *Speedwell*, mastered by either John Vinecott or John Syms.[179] From internal evidence it may fairly be assumed that these vessels traded for Hoare and Company throughout 1696, carrying over 2,363 tons of coal and culm, with over half coming from Swansea. This accounted for almost a third of all coal and culm shipped coastally to Bridgwater.

In 1697, the Company responded vigorously to the competition encountered from Bobbett and others in supplying the hinterland with coal. In particular, the managers at Ham Mills were concerned to secure advance supplies of culm and Abbey coals ahead of Bobbett, whose price manipulation was threatening to take away the factory's business.[180] Consequently, the Company employed more vessels more frequently, importing 3,439.8 tons of coal and culm divided almost equally between Neath, Swansea and Tenby.[181] The *William and Richard* undertook 18 voyages from south Wales, nine of which brought back 504 tons of Tenby culm, with a further 400.4 tons of coals shipped from Swansea and Neath. The *Diligence* carried 487.2 tons of coals and culm from Neath in eleven shipments, 112 tons of culm from Tenby in three shipments, and made a solitary voyage from Swansea with 44.8 tons of coals. The *Speedwell* completed eleven voyages taking 238 tons of coal from Swansea in five consignments, 166.6 tons from Neath in four shipments, and 85.4 tons of culm from Tenby on two voyages. The *Mary* discharged 254.8 tons of coals from Swansea in five voyages, 98 tons of coals and culm from Neath in two shipments, and a further two cargoes of 105 tons of culm from Tenby.

Richard Drake also freighted his trow, the *Two Sisters* of Bridgwater, for the Company in 1697. This craft completed sixteen voyages in the year: seven shipments carried 312.2 tons of coals from Swansea; five more accounted for 228.2 tons of coals and culm from Neath; and a further four voyages were loaded with 189 tons of culm at Tenby.[182] In addition, six more vessels appear shipping coal: the *Thomas* of Bridgwater undertook at least two voyages carrying 53.2 tons from Neath and 47.6 tons from Swansea; the

Laurel of and from Swansea was freighted on one journey carrying 33.6 tons of coals; the *Exchange* of Watchet under George Priest returned to Bridgwater with 25.2 tons of culm from Tenby; the *Exchange* of and from Tenby brought 7 tons of stone coal; the *Mayflower* of Watchet under Francis Washer shipped a single load of 19.6 tons of coals from Neath; and John Neale, returning from Liverpool in the *Providence*, loaded 46.2 tons of coal at Milford for Bridgwater.

The records are less explicit for 1698 and 1699. No further reference is made to the vessels freighted by Heard, Drake or Wallis, although it is possible that the Company maintained a direct stake in the coal they carried.[183] Instead only coal from the *Mary* and the *Speedwell* that was traded via the Ham Mills factory was recorded in the Company's books.[184] Thus, in 1698, the *Mary*, variously under John Page, Richard Jones and Giles Vinecott, was freighted on nine occasions to south Wales, returning with 221.2 tons of coals from Neath, 112 tons from Swansea, and 47.6 tons from Tenby. In contrast, the *Speedwell* was detained in Chester for much of the year and undertook only seven shipments. A single voyage brought 33.6 tons of coal from Swansea, whilst the remaining shipments accounted for 250.6 tons of coals and culm from Neath. This pattern was repeated in 1699, although the decline in recording standards and the gradual dispersal of the Company's assets make reconstructing the trade highly conjectural and limited to known company ships. Hence, the *Mary*, navigated by Jones and Nathaniel Vosper, made seven shipments from Neath with 310.8 tons of coals and culm, five shipments from Tenby with 222.6 tons of culm, and a single voyage from Milford with 39.2 tons of culm. The *Speedwell* undertook a remarkable 15 round shipments as a collier: nine voyages transported 352.8 tons of coals from Neath; 210 tons of culm came from Tenby in five shipments; and a single consignment of 39.2 tons of coals was dispatched from Swansea. Charles Hyman in the *Fly* also completed one journey from Neath in July carrying 39.2 tons of coals.[185]

In contrast, the coastal trade in grain represented an important but transient interest for the Company. In 1696, it entered into an arrangement with John Smith of Exeter to bring corn and wool from Warwickshire and Oxfordshire to Bridgwater. Supplies were to be collected at Stratford and transported on barges via the Avon to the Severn. The cereals were then to be transhipped at Tewkesbury, Upton or Gloucester onto one of the regular salt trows or another convenient vessel. In October, Smith dispatched a consignment of 44 bags of malt and eight bags of wool on Thomas Claroe's trow, the *Thomas* of Upton.[186] It is also highly likely that the three other voyages completed by Claroe and the vessel's regular master, William Jefferies, in 1696 carried grain and wool for Smith and Hoare as Smith appeared as the named indenturer on the associated wool coquets.[187] At the close of the year, Smith was in Stratford putting together a cargo of 2,000 bushels of malt, barley and wheat and 53 bags of wool to be loaded by Claroe. The *Thomas* finally entered Bridgwater late in February, having missed the January spring tide and been further hampered by frost, ice and contrary winds at Gloucester.[188]

By this time Smith had entered into a formal joint venture with the Company: Smith was to oversee the buying and selling of corn and wool delivered at Stratford mostly by John Hutchings of Banbury, and the Company was to organise delivery to Bridgwater and thence overland to Exeter.[189] Claroe was chartered in May to deliver 981 bushels of wheat, malt, barley and maslin and 45 packs of wool containing 414 tods.[190] The *Thomas* completed a further three voyages in 1697 discharging 3,796 bushels of malt, wheat and mixed corn.[191] To deliver the rest of Smith's wares, much of which had been warehoused in Gloucester, the Company freighted a number of other trows. In July, Corker on one of his regular salt runs in the *Success* of Bewdley picked up 1,200 bushels of wheat and mixed corn and 139 tods of wool.[192] In the same month, James Harrison on the *John and Elizabeth* of Evesham delivered 1,216 bushels of malt, barley, peas and oats, and William Fisher, master and merchant of the *New Royal Oak* of Bridgnorth, transported 1,310 bushels of malt and wheat that was almost certainly picked up at Gloucester.[193] In August, Corker transported 920 bushels of grains and beans along with his usual salt delivery, and Henry Bailey carried 1,402 bushels of malt, barley and wheat and 242 tods of wool in the *Elizabeth* of Gloucester with John Harbor as master. A small letpass cargo of wheat and a much larger wool coquet of 56 packs and 1 fodge, 51 packs of which were consigned to the partners, was also carried by the *Elizabeth* in October, with Smith appearing as the customs merchant.[194]

The Company supplemented formal arrangements with more opportunistic trading. For example, in March 1697, 894 Winchester bushels of wheat, barley and oats were dispatched from Milford on the *Swan* of Pembroke under Michael Hopkins.[195] Most of this was procured through the Company's factor, Richard Smith of Haverfordwest, who was able to exploit the lack of ready money in south Wales following the recoinage crisis to strike favourable bargains with impecunious dealers.[196] However, activity in this sector was brief. By 1698, the Company's sole interest in the grain trade was limited to putting together cargoes of corn and root crops for coasters returning to Liverpool.[197]

None the less, in 1697, the Company, mostly in partnership with Smith, accounted for 12,973 bushels of mixed grains. This amounted to over half the quantity of all cereals imported coastally at Bridgwater in a year in which trade rose markedly.[198] The rise in coastal imports may have been linked to the run of bad or deficient harvests between 1695 and 1698 and the cumulative depletion of local supplies of seed corn. Indeed, the years of widespread dearth in 1696 and 1697 were, as Hoskins has emphasised, experienced most acutely in the south-west.[199] Certainly, scarcity in Exeter and south Devon, the areas to which most of Hoare and Company's grain was dispatched, may explain the expansion of trade at Bridgwater and the high incidental costs and freight charges involved in shipping a basic commodity such long distances.[200] However, the impact of Company policy, given its established contacts in the Severn trades, cannot be discounted. It may well be that the Company's brief association with shipping grain, initially as a cargo filler alongside its salt shipments, was in itself a primary cause of the general increase in trade recorded at Bridgwater.

Mercantile organisation and the coastal trade of the Bristol Channel

Although Hoare and Company and William Alloway were important merchants in the coastal trade of Bridgwater and the Bristol Channel in the late seventeenth century, the extensive survival of their business records creates a partial and slightly deceptive impression. Uncomfortable questions remain to be asked about how representative such fairly large-scale concerns were of general mercantile practice. Certainly both Hoare and Alloway exerted an impressive control over the coastal trade in salt. Yet, can the activities in this important but none the less specialist trade be seen as a paradigm for Bristol and the rest of the region? It is interesting to note in this context that in all but the bulk trades, Hoare and Company deferred to the western metropolis. Bristol merchants, such as Abraham Hooke, mediated much of the Company's initial and speculative forays into transatlantic trade. Foreign goods, groceries and comestibles were either supplied by Bristol, or, more generally, traded to the port as soon as ships returning from overseas discharged their cargoes at Bridgwater. Similarly, finance, credit, insurance and, more basically, domestic and international markets were procured through Bristol. The importance of Bristol in the conduct of business thus remained a constant commercial factor throughout the brief life of the partnership.

No comparable merchant papers relating to Bristol in this period exist and it is to be lamented that an important perspective on how the region's primate city functioned cannot be comprehensively reconstructed.[201] Certainly, the correspondence of Abraham Darby and Graffin Prankard gives a brief snapshot of some components of the Severn iron trade, and hints at the mechanisms by which merchants underwrote much of the coastal trade of Bristol. However, it offers more tantalising glimpses than substantial insights, and whilst Prankard's later and more extensive salt and iron dealings deserve more study, they are beyond the competencies of port book data.[202] None the less, a number of excise prosecutions for inconsistencies occurring in the delivery and loss of salt carried to Bristol do survive and shed light upon how this branch of coasting was organised. Excise officers were required by the Salt Acts of 1693, 1696 and 1699 to reweigh all cargoes discharging coastally in order to ensure that embezzlement, false loading by design or negligence, or erroneous documentation did not occur. Equally, shippers and merchants were eager to confirm to the Bristol magistrates that accidental discrepancies and losses caused by act of God or inundation did not leave them with a hefty excise payment for goods that were unmerchantable or had simply been washed away.

The recognisances reveal that trade was organised in a similar way to that of Bridgwater. In the case of rock and white salt traded from Liverpool and Frodsham, the owners of the commodity were quite distinct from the shippers and merchants appearing in the port books. For example, in 1699, Benjamin Stokes, master of the *Amity* of Milford, was charged with bringing to Bristol 7.5 bushels of rock salt over the 840 bushels registered in the salt certificate and coquet as recorded in the Liverpool port book. Stokes argued, somewhat circuitously, that the extra load was merely oversight, or failing that, the difference in recording standards, or, yet more ingeniously, the result of moisture seeping into his cargo. Even so, Stokes was adamant that he was merely the hired carrier and that the salt 'did belong to Mr Peter Wadding' to be 'delivered to Mr Abraham Elton'. To complicate matters, Thomas Leine, 'merchant owner' of the salt, gave testimony that he had initially ordered 880 bushels from Wadding in the first place.[203]

This tripartite division between owner, merchant and an independent group of factors is confirmed by the case of the *Recovery* of Liverpool. In August 1699, William Trewell, 'master and comander' of the vessel, was presented alongside James Hollidge 'of the city of Bristoll, merchant' for fraudulently shipping 65 bushels of rock salt with no certificate from a total cargo of 1,008 bushels. Trewell was indicted for repeated non-appearance, but Hollidge tellingly argued that 'he was not otherwise concerned in the vessell *Recovery* or in the salt then brought upon her', but acted 'barely as a factor and a person employed to sell and dispose of such salt as should be brought upon her . . . to Bristol'. The Liverpool port books record John Cleaveland, the salt proprietor, as merchant.[204]

Further recognisances reveal that owners of salt works in Cheshire and Liverpool featured strongly as merchants, especially after the Act of 1702 had restricted the trade in rock salt. For example, a triumvirate of salt proprietors, Dr Woodruffe, Thomas Johnson and Thomas Nixon, were responsible for an overload of rock salt on the *George and Benjamin* of Chepstow in 1705.[205] The same vessel was again indicted in 1707 with

Cleaveland apparently liable for the cargo.[206] A further case involving the
holing of the *Swan* of Liverpool on the English ground off Steep Holm in
1706 revealed Cleaveland to be acting as merchant to salt bought of Daniel
Hignett 'proprietor of rock salt near Northwich'.[207] Proprietors such as
Hignett, Henry Whitehead and Matthew Page clearly sold to Liverpool-based
merchants who freighted for the Bristol market. Thus, Thomas Bickclish,
'merchant of Liverpool', was held responsible for a cargo of rock salt wind-
driven to Youghall in 1706, and Richard Ashton appeared as the merchant of
a cargo of 3,020 bushels of rock salt, 145 bushels of which were lost in
transit.[208] In addition, Bristol merchants who did not feature in the customs
records seem to have organised salt shipments. Apart from Elton, who was
heavily involved in regional and international trade,[209] John Scandrett 'grocer
of Bristol' freighted at least four craft from Liverpool and Frodsham in
1701;[210] John Bearpacker, described as a 'salt refiner', was responsible for
1,181 bushels of rock salt on board the *Society* in 1701;[211] and in 1704, 1,065
bushels of rock salt purchased from Cleaveland were dispatched on the
Griffin of Brockweir 'on the proper account and risque of Stephen Baker',
merchant of Bristol.[212]

It is more difficult to understand who controlled Droitwich and Cheshire
salt brought via the Severn to Bristol. In the most recent study of the trade,
Wakelin did not come to any firm conclusions linking the major shippers
recorded in the port books with salt owners in Droitwich or users in Bristol.
None the less, he did note the correlation between the Cardonel list of salters
in 1732 and the port book merchants recorded at Gloucester in 1733,
suggesting that proprietors may have both merchanted vessels and chartered
the more regular carriers.[213] However, the excise presentments appear to
emphasise that the forms of regular association between producer, shipper
and owner, demonstrated by Hoare and Company, were replicated in the
trade to Bristol. For instance, William Perkes, who was earlier active on
behalf of Hoare, was indicted on three occasions between 1700 and 1702 for
carrying overloads or consignments of dubious legality on the *Providence* of
Worcester. Similarly, Francis Perkes was also found guilty of shipping salt
without proper licence on board the *Francis* of Worcester in 1702. In these
cases, the Perkeses were described merely as 'master and commander' of the
trows they accompanied or consigned to subordinate trowmen like Samuel
Jackson, Samuel Bowd or John Crumpe.[214]

Of course, the presentments can only provide impressionistic evidence:
by their very nature they relate to the more atypical of the many voyages
discharging goods at Bristol. None the less, they open up important new
vistas on how the Severn trade operated. As with the trade in Cheshire white
and rock salt, a separate sector of merchants who did not appear explicitly in
the port books appears to have had a controlling interest. This group was

divided between merchant-owners closely associated with production, and general merchants and factors organising shipments from Bristol. Hence, in January 1701, Richard Lane, the salt proprietor of Droitwich, deposed that 1,567 bushels of his white salt had been lost off Minehead the previous year when the *William* of Worcester bulged.[215] Earlier, in July 1699, the *William* was involved in another presentment, wherein John Chance, her 'master and owner', was charged with carrying 11.5 bushels of white salt in excess of the certificated quantity of 2,000 bushels (50 tons). The salt was delivered for Peter Evett, merchant of Bristol, although Chance remained the accredited merchant for customs purposes.[216] Also in August 1699, Samuel Packer, a cooper of Bristol, was accused of transporting 26 bushels of rock salt without certificate from Gloucester to Bristol on Richard Lewis's trow, the *Hester* of Gloucester. Packer successfully argued that the requisite duties had been secured at the Cheshire works and it was merely an oversight by an excise officer at Shrewsbury that a warrant had not been issued for the shipment to Gloucester.[217] The port books note Lewis as the merchant of a general cargo in which Packer's salt was included.[218]

The combination of business and legal records with the vast catalogue of port book data has emphasised the relationships that fashioned and completed the commercial cycle, from producer via shipper, factor, coastal merchant and, to a lesser extent, inland carrier and consumer. From this a typology of merchant-shipper can be ascertained. Firstly, it is apparent that much of the regular coasting trade was conducted by a large sector of masters: boatmen who were freighted on vessels owned or controlled by other merchants. These men were solely confined to navigating the craft, had very little or no interest in the vast bulk of the cargo they carried, and were generally paid a fixed rate per voyage. This form of association was typified by John Matthews, who mastered the *Satisfaction* for Alloway and Wheddon, and Thomas Fisher, who skippered the *Robert and Thomas* on behalf of Thomas Anstice, himself freighted by Alloway and Musgrave. Similarly, many of the ships chartered by Hoare and Company operated in this way. Sebastian Llewellyn mastered the *Hope* in 1697 under Michael Currant, and Thomas Claroe invariably freighted William Jefferies on his trow the *Thomas* of Upton, even though he appears to have pre-accompanied the vessel. This is not to say that on other occasions these masters did not assume more responsible positions: Llewellyn, for example, was a noted local boatman and salt trader in his own right.

The functional base of the coastal trade was the master-merchant. This type of trader maintained a close association with one or two boats, but like the simple jobbing master, was not commercially involved with the goods carried, being freighted by other dealers and paid simple remuneration per ton transported. For example, Robert Nurton and Thomas Flemon were regularly master and merchant of the Bristol–Bridgwater packet the *Isaac and John*. However, the boat was owned outright by Thomas Offield who tended to act as supercargo. A slightly more advanced relationship of this type can be seen in the activities of John and Giles Vinecott. Both men were engaged on a more or less frequent basis by Hoare and Company, being freighted on board the *Blessing* and the *Speedwell*. In the port books, the Vinecotts usually appeared as both master and merchant, although John Vinecott on occasion acted as master to accompanying factors like Samuel Burnall who oversaw the commercial side of the transaction.[219] None the less, the Vinecotts remained peripatetic traders, often acting on their own account in between contracting with the Company.

The complex arrangements behind the cargoes of salt carried by Charles Corker illustrate a similar relationship. Corker was freighted by independent salt producers and dealers like Padmore and Norris in conjunction with Hoare and Company. However, he remained merely an operative, albeit a senior one, of major Severn-based trow owners like William Perkes and John Beale. It is unclear whether Corker had any direct interest in the craft he mastered or the miscellaneous goods traded alongside the salt. Certainly, the number of Bewdley boats on which he appeared as master—the *Prosperity*, the *Success*, the *Joseph and Benjamin* and the *John and Mary* were only the most regularly freighted craft of the fourteen boats he mastered in the 1690s— suggests the flexibility of an unfixed trader. Even so, Corker was established and trusted. Money consigned to Padmore and Steynor was delivered by Corker, and he also appeared to have had a hand in organising small items of back cargo to Gloucester and Bristol.

A third set of traders can also be distinguished: men who acted as both merchants and masters, and yet maintained a conspicuous economic relationship with both the vessel and the goods carried. On occasion such traders acted solely as merchants, leaving others to deal with the business of navigating their craft. However, they usually functioned as masters to independent merchants, such as Alloway and Isaac Heard, or to salt proprietors and bond payers like Thomas Johnson, John Cleaveland and Robert Hyde. Hoare and Company's main shipmasters, Currant, Neale, Cockrem, Page and Higginson, all possessed substantial shares in their vessels and habitually ventured a stake in the cargo. Although they received orders from the Company, these quasi-merchants were independent enough to organise return shipments. Similarly, Alexander Holmes owned a quarter share of the *Willing Mind* in partnership with William Alloway. When the vessel was employed in the overseas trade, Holmes appeared as a conventional merchant-master on board the *Ann* of Bridgwater. In the Severn trade, trow owners such as Claroe, Edward Jackson and William Oakes fulfilled similar roles. These men had very little to do with the salt they carried for Hoare and

Company, being paid a standard freight. Nevertheless, they had a much freer hand in the lesser items they carried. Thus, the Company bought cheeses out of the *Charles* of Bridgnorth directly from 'owner Jackson' in 1697.[220]

The pinnacle of this hierarchy of traders was occupied by the merchants proper. High-level, high-status central traders, like Alloway, Heard and Drake of Bridgwater, or Sir Abraham Elton of Bristol, filled the traditional picture of the 'real' merchant, as defined by Defoe: they dealt in the overseas trades, and whilst they maintained considerable interests in local commerce and industry, they were distinct from the 'warehouse-keepers', 'wholesalemen', retail tradesmen, ship masters and associated commercial artisanry that were the core of the inland and coastal trades.[221] Sometimes, like Roger Hoare, MP for Bridgwater, these 'true' merchants rarely went near a vessel. However, even large-scale merchant partnerships were not adverse to acting as part-factors in the sale of goods, particularly, as in the case of Hoare and Company and its short-lived association with the grain trade, if there was spare capacity and the price was right. This system was kept ticking over by a host of lesser, largely unnoticed agents and factors, who often chartered vessels and organised cargoes, although they appear to have operated in a far move irregular way. The actions of Bristol factors such as, Scandrett, nominally a grocer, Hollidge, a merchant, and Bearpacker, a salt-refiner in the movement of goods, may thus be more characteristic of the types of merchant behind the city's coasting trade.

This was not a fixed structure. A highly fluid, sophisticated system of organisation, oiled by an integrated network of merchants, agents, factors, boatmen and credit, underpinned the operation of coasting at Bristol and its region. Adaptability—'elasticity', to borrow Willan's phrase—was the hallmark of the coastal trade.[222] Even in the case of the small boatmen, the lowest rung of the commercial hierarchy, there was much diversity in how trade was conducted. Naturally, such boatmen entered into occasional relationships with larger merchants, navigating vessels and carrying goods in which they had only a token stake. Many port book merchants initially served their trade in this way as masters and commanders of ships controlled by others. Over the period, the more successful masters and trowmen seem generally to have graduated to a more organisational and 'mercantile' role and abandoned practical, 'on board' involvement the older and presumably the more prosperous they became.

In the final analysis, the importance of Hoare and Company and William Alloway was not merely limited to the mercantile community of Bridgwater. Hoare's untimely death in 1699 left a stack of bad personal and corporate debts, a wide range of property in Bridgwater and throughout Somerset, and a strangely old-fashioned house. Yet Hoare was clearly an important merchant: despite a modest estate of little more than £1,000, his wife and son expended the considerable sum of over £103 on 'funerall expenses' alone.[223] Although the passing of Hoare removed the partners' representation in the capital and, albeit in a minor capacity, the national arenas of influence, the Company maintained its regional prominence. All its active members prospered in the early years of the eighteenth century. George Balch made it to mayor, and even John Syms, the most recumbent of sleeping partners, possessed shares in five ocean-going and coastal vessels and a large and, for the times, modishly furnished house in Bridgwater at the time of his death in 1716.[224] The Alloways fared even better. The Quaker connection with thrift, hard work and an even harder-nosed attitude to business served William Alloway well. Both through his own marriage, and that of his daughters, Sarah and Hannah, Alloway consolidated an already extensive trading network. His sons-in-law, Graffin Prankard and John Galton, were to become important Bristol merchants in their own right, largely thanks to Alloway influence and capital.[225]

Conclusion

To contemporaries and historians alike, the aggressive, almost brutish economic spirit of Bristol merchants in the late seventeenth and early eighteenth centuries was founded squarely upon overseas trade. Undoubtedly the shining 'Gateway to Empire' that Bristol presented to the commercial world masked both the unpleasant effluvia of the city's muddy and barely improved quays and the slave-driven monocultures of the Caribbean and the Chesapeake tobacco estates.[1] But somewhere in this enduring vision of 'Golden Age' Bristol, the development of the port has become entangled in an extended, deterministic narrative of English commercial expansion and colonial exploitation. Whilst the ghost of John Cabot still stalks present-day civic consciousness, it is perhaps entirely understandable that historical attention should be monopolised by the feats of overseas trade. After all, the commercial interests of the grandees of this world—the Whitsons, Eltons, Goldneys and Pinneys and their like—bore tangible and lasting fruit in the physical enhancement, beautification and educational provision of Bristol.[2] Indeed, for all their 'sharp and hard dealings', Bristol's mercantile bons bourgeois were the nearest thing to aristocracy the city possessed.[3] Yet, as this book has argued, Bristol cannot be wholly read through the comparative waxing and waning of overseas trade. The city's commerce had profound domestic dimensions which have been consistently obscured by the traditionally more 'significant' sectors of its trade.

Despite a recent and welcome reappraisal of the social and cultural impact of Bristol upon its immediate rural environs, historians have generally struggled to define and analyse the domestic arena of Bristol's trade.[4] Hamstrung by limited or intractable sources, most work has fallen back on a sketchy metropolitan model first outlined by Professor Minchinton over 40 years ago.[5] Minchinton argued that eighteenth-century Bristol imposed a form of centralised hegemony over the trade and economy of 'a large area of south-west England, south Wales and the south-western Midlands', sucking in raw materials and dispensing high-cost manufactured goods, consumables and the products of its overseas ventures.[6] Finance, credit, capital, business expertise, and, more arguably, forms of cultural experience were to follow these commercial vectors in the later eighteenth century. Yet whilst these fairly crude rehearsals of central place and periphery have neatly described some of Bristol's core trades, they have left us with an economic landscape that has elevated Bristol above its region. Moreover, it has perpetuated the received importance of overseas trade as the gear to civic and regional development.[7]

Whilst this book has acknowledged the utility of the metropolitan construct, it has attempted to redress some of the more persistent assumptions regarding Bristol and its hinterland. This is not to say that the central thesis of Minchinton's early work should be casually dismissed. As the analysis of the coastal port books has demonstrated, Bristol acted as the focal point of an extensive coastal and river network that linked and, to a limited extent, determined the economies of the hinterland. Bristol's twice-yearly fairs formed centripetal nodes and important commercial spaces in which merchants from throughout the region brokered credit deals and discharged the kind of business and social debts that distance and occasional recalcitrance encouraged. Expansion in the city's industrial and commercial base allied to the steady growth in population also imposed selective demands upon regional production. By the end of the period, the main agricultural and market gardening areas of the Midlands and Welsh borderlands, served by the Severn and Wye, were strongly associated with the Bristol market. Similarly, control over the production and redistribution of a range of key domestic, semi-industrial and manufactured commodities and the importation and processing of foreign goods ensured that Bristol's entrepôt functions were not seriously rivalled. By the late seventeenth century, Bristol was a major source of iron and ironwares, brass, lead, glass, soap, ceramics and spirits. In the same period, the city dispatched over 1,500 tons of sugar and grocery wares each year to domestic ports and around 1.7 million lb of tobacco per year, perhaps a third of the city's retained imports. Only Bideford and Barnstaple, minor players on the international stage, were net tobacco exporters amongst the other regional ports. Indeed, the sheer amount of tobacco traded from Bristol reinforces Morgan's assertion that the city, far more than its northern competitors, Liverpool, Whitehaven and Glasgow, was tied to domestic demand. Certainly it appears that Bristol merchants working on a commission basis were content to supply large quantities of quality leaf for an increasingly inelastic and conservative home market. Although the failure to develop the more lucrative, if more un-predictable re-export trade in the 1720s smacked of business conservatism and hinted at the later structural haemorrhaging of Bristol's main trans-atlantic trades, it none the less emphasised the symbiotic relation of town and hinterland.[8]

However, it would be a mistake to view the wider region as an inert penumbra, a pliant source of supply and a convenient dumping ground for Bristol commodities. The western metropolis functioned along distinct geographical and commodity-specific lines. Central to its operation was the continued viability of the Severn and Wye trades, a factor in part determined by the limited navigational capacity of river craft which ensured that transhipment at Bristol was as much a physical necessity as an economic imperative. By the later eighteenth century, the development of an integrated communications infrastructure in the north-west and Midlands certainly appears to have drawn trade away from the city.[9] In addition, the trade in coal, salt, and many other goods was dominated by regional centres. Undeniably, Bristol concerns maintained an important stake in the salt trade, yet the output of the Droitwich and Cheshire salteries, vital for the inshore and overseas fisheries, was directed by regional demand and regional merchants. Similarly, the Bristol Channel represented a distinct zone of energy use focused upon the collieries of south Wales and Shropshire. Throughout the period, the shipment of coal and culm remained the defining trade, at any one time occupying the bulk of the region's coastal tonnage. In contrast, the absence of a large collier fleet at Bristol, where supplies of the mineral were close by, provided an effective ceiling to the levels of coasting maintained at the port. Certainly, Celia Fiennes's fickle gaze may well have noted 'the harbour . . . full of shipps carrying coales and all sortes of commodityes', but Bristol's coastal imports were limited to a mere 600 tons a year, mostly it seems carried as either commercial ballast, or specialist grades to supplement indifferent local supplies.[10]

Bristol also played a very ambiguous role in the organisation of coasting. The port books imply that both the traditional mercantile elite of Bristol and the city's broad base of inland traders were not directly involved in the merchanting of goods, although it is still likely that substantial Bristol factors underwrote much of the port's coastal trade in indirect ways. Shipping was a different story. The ownership and direction of coastal craft remained firmly in the hands of regional operatives. Apart from the odd long-distance coaster and a few craft pressed from overseas voyages, Bristol's main domestic trades were carried out by trows and vessels based at the regional ports. In Pope's chimeric vision of the city's streets 'full of ships', it was coasters of and from Bristol's major domestic trading partners that thronged the quays, backs and slips of the port.[11] This partially reflected Bristol's underdeveloped and expensive port facilities. Despite piecemeal attempts to overhaul the central dock site, Bristol's Merchant Venturers signally failed to address the lack of capacity.[12] Compared to other regional ports and especially Liverpool, coasting at Bristol in the early eighteenth century was characterised by very quick turn-around times. Many coasters, especially those not concerned with the regular routes, returned home in ballast: it simply was not economic for merchants to allow coasters to lie idle at Bristol on the off-chance of an economic return cargo.

From a wider perspective, the Bristol Channel acted as the highway for not only standard, staple cargoes, but also a diversity of regional goods and products. Undoubtedly, the cost advantages conferred by water transport made coastal and river trade the only practical means of moving coal, metalwares, a variety of ores, pot clay, grain, salt and timber over long distances. Unsurprisingly, these basic commodities absorbed much of the commercial activity of regional traders. However, the old argument which reduced coasting to a medium of solely bulk carriage must be seen as untenable.[13] Goods ranged from high value-to-weight consumer-oriented items and 'semi-durables', like glasswares, ceramics and a whole variety of local 'cloths, wools and manufactures', to industrial products like soap, overseas exotica such as spices, citrus fruits, and dyewoods, and even Sir Edward Mansell's personal effects and household gear.[14] Merchant papers confirm the utility and flexibility of coasting. In 1716, for example, Graffin Prankard shipped from London to Bristol an expensive and somewhat extravagant 'tea table, teapott, dishes & all things according to the newest faision' bought as a present in the capital. The modish tea equipage was assigned to a linen draper on Bristol Bridge from whom Prankard, obviously perturbed that the righteous sensibilities of his Quaker brethren might be affronted by such ostentation, surreptitiously availed himself of the goods.[15]

Coasting also provided a fluid, regular and highly organised service. When Hoare and Company found that the *Satisfaction*, the Bridgwater packet operated by Edward Davis, was too full to take in a cargo of hemp at Bristol in 1697, the goods were consigned to the next coaster clearing for the Somerset port.[16] Clearly Hoare could exploit a number of vessels, the forerunners of the 'constant coasters' of the later eighteenth century, that plied a given route as regularly as the variables of weather and freightage allowed.[17] The Severn trade was perhaps even more responsive. In 1684, for example, Sir Robert Southwell was advised that 'the best & cheapest way of conveieinge . . . lumber forwards & backwards' from Bristol to Banbury was 'by water to Stratford uppon Avon'. At the Bristol end, Southwell was directed to 'Richard Vicres . . . a bargeman' who was to be found 'upon the key att Bristoll every springe tide'. Vickers mastered the *Richard and Sarah* of Tewkesbury on a cyclical service between Bristol and the Warwickshire Avon.[18] Both examples reveal a coherent system to be in place through which any variety of consignments could be delivered as demand required. Indeed, Chartres's pessimistic view of the output of coastal tonnage would seem to be questioned by the regular practices of the principal Bristol Channel trades, although the short-haul nature of these voyages, the shallow draught of

many of the coastal craft and the relatively swift turn around times compared
to the east-coast coal trade are important ancilliary factors to bear in mind.
None the less, it is clear that many coasters could and did 'achieve ten or
twelve voyages a year' and that those 'smaller ships making no more than one
or two voyages' were very much the exception.[19]

Far from being 'casual and haphazard', coasting represented an effective,
highly structured, yet adaptable commercial system.[20] Hoare and Company,
for example, exploited its regular salt routes to transfer money to their
Droitwich and Cheshire salt partners and more speculative cargoes of
overseas goods to Bristol agents to be sold in the city or hawked up the
Severn.[21] Although port book data reveal the prevalence of merchants who
either doubled up as masters—the ubiquitous 'merchant seaman'—or who
operated in an generally 'unspecialised' fashion,[22] mercantile accounts
indicate that the commercial organisation of cargo was far more developed.
This involved established provincial merchant houses supporting a network
of factors, agents, supercargo masters, and lesser middlemen. The Hoare
partners, for example, linked the 'super-merchants' of Liverpool with major
Bristol traders like Abraham Hooke and Edward Hackett.[23] In the organisation of supply, Hoare and Company worked through sophisticated forms
of delivery. Thus, in a single shipment of grain and wool from Banbury to
Exeter in 1697, Hoare entered into formal agreement with regional wholesale
merchants, Banbury corn factors, Stratford-based carriers, bargemen on the
river Avon, the trowman Thomas Claroe on a fixed freight from Tewkesbury
to Bridgwater, and more carriers to dispatch the goods overland to Devon.
Regional and national credit networks financed the operation. In addition,
the Company was advised of grain prices in the immediate locality, in south
Wales, the north-west, and in Ireland through a communications network
that cut through regional particularism. The cost benefits conferred by
the integration of both inter-regional and distant trade, allied to savings
produced by the greater division of labour, economies of scale, and the
rationalisation of distribution, remained important, if somewhat neglected,
factors in the development of the regional economy.

In a memorable and pithy sentence, Defoe commented that 'trade, like
Religion, is what every Body talks of, but few understand'.[24] For the master
and crew of an Ilfracombe collier who encountered a merman rising from
the Bristol Channel with 'long hayre on the face & head much like an old
gray haird-man' in 1678, commerce and the metaphysical were briefly and
bizarrely intertwined.[25] Yet behind the measured epigrams of the professional
writer and the breathless reportage of a dumbstruck coastal trader, indeed
behind the mass of voyages that plied the Bristol Channel and its waterways,
the importance of coastal and river trade to Bristol and its domestic

hinterland is clear. This system provided a flexible, consistent and highly structured transport service that conveyed an astonishing variety of regional and overseas goods quickly and regularly, and in the process bound together very dispersed local economies. The region both fed and watered Bristol as well as underpinning many of the city's overseas enterprises in terms of markets and levels of consumption. To this extent, Bristol's 'Golden Age', long associated with the dramatic, capital-intensive and more visible sectors of overseas commerce, owed far more to the low-status trades that formed the city's economic sinews. The commercial gateway that Bristol opened out onto the world swung back to reveal the importance of the domestic market. If Bristol truly commanded 'the staple of the western trade', its roots were planted firmly in home soil.

Appendix 1

Gloucester coastal port books, 1680–1730

Year	PRO Ref. (E190)	Recs	Year	PRO Ref. (E190)	Recs	Year	PRO Ref. (E190)	Recs
1680	**1250/05**	**510**	**1701A**	**1253/14**	**273**	**1715A**	**1258/04**	**328**
1681	**1250/08**	**542**	**1701B**	**1254/01**	**307**	**1715B**	**1258/05**	**330**
1682	**1250/09**	**580**	1703B	1254/05	290	1716A	1258/06	330
1683	**1251/02**	**580**	**1704A**	**1254/07**	**303**	1717B	1258/13	388
1684	**1251/01**	**515**	**1704B**	**1254/09**	**307**	**1718A**	**1258/17**	**346**
1685	**1251/04**	**332**	**1705A**	**1254/10**	**324**	**1718B**	**1259/01**	**355**
1686A	**1251/07**	**188**	**1705B**	**1255/05**	**317**	1719A	1259/02	382
1686B	**1251/12**	**321**	**1706A**	**1255/01**	**317**	**1720A**	**1259/07**	**371**
1689	**1251/14**	**539**	**1706B**	**1255/07**	**305**	**1720B**	**1259/09**	**370**
1691	**1251/15**	**747**	**1707A**	**1255/08**	**343**	**1722A**	**1259/10**	**335**
1692A	**1252/02**	**321**	**1707B**	**1255/14**	**332**	**1722B**	**1260/04**	**376**
1692B	**1252/01**	**343**	**1708A**	**1255/11**	**352**	1723B	1260/06	339
1693B	1252/03	326	**1708B**	**1256/01**	**352**	**1724A**	**1260/11**	**384**
1694B	1252/06	290	1709B	1256/05	393	**1724B**	**1260/09**	**363**
1695A	**1252/07**	**253**	**1710A**	**1256/06**	**306**	**1725A**	**1260/07**	**367**
1695B	**1252/08**	**297**	**1710B**	**1256/08**	**336**	**1725B**	**1261/01**	**377**
1696A	**1252/09**	**291**	**1711A**	**1256/11**	**297**	1726A	1261/06	332
1696B	**1252/14**	**281**	**1711B**	**1257/03**	**291**	**1727A**	**1261/07**	**339**
1697A	**1252/17**	**320**	**1712A**	**1257/05**	**282**	**1727B**	**1261/12**	**334**
1697B	**1253/03**	**314**	**1712B**	**1257/08**	**293**	**1728A**	**1261/10**	**296**
1698A	1253/05	280	**1713A**	**1257/07**	**331**	**1728B**	**1262/05**	**308**
1699A	**1253/06**	**311**	**1713B**	**1257/12**	**345**	1729A	1262/01	240
1699B	**1253/09**	**353**	1714A	1257/11	320	1730A	1262/06	235
1700B	1253/12	292						

Notes: Years run from Christmas to Christmas.
Year suffix A - Christmas to Midsummer.
Year suffix B - Midsummer to Christmas.
Full years in bold.

Appendix 2

Extant coastal port books, Bristol Channel ports, 1695–1704
(PRO class E190/piece number)

Year	Gloucester	Bristol	Bridgwater	Minehead	Ilfracombe	Barnstaple	Padstow	St Ives	Mount's Bay	Milford	Carmarthen	Swansea & Neath	Cardiff	Chepstow
1695 A	1252/07	1151/02	1095/10	1095/15	969/04	969/01	1055/17	1055/06	1055/24	–	1313/09	1284/06	1284/04	–
1695 B	1252/08	1153/03	1096/04	1096/01	970/04	970/15	1056/02	1056/19	1056/10	–	1313/10	–	1284/09	–
1696 A	1252/09	1153/02	1096/02	1096/05	970/14	970/13	1056/24	1056/18	1056/17	1313/19	1313/22	–	–	–
1696 B	1252/14	1154/03	1096/10	1096/07	971/12	971/02	1057/08	1057/34	1057/26	1313/18	1313/17	–	–	–
1697 A	1252/17	–	1096/08	1096/11	971/10	971/11	**1057/02**	**1057/06**	**1057/23**	1314/05	1314/06	–	–	–
1697 B	1253/03	–	1097/09	1097/07	972/16	972/15	**1058/22**	**1058/03**	**1058/13**	1314/12	1314/08	–	–	–
1698 A	1253/05	1155/01	1097/04	1097/01	972/17	972/06	–	–	–	1314/13	1314/11	1285/05	–	–
1698 B	–	1157/02	1098/03	1098/07	**973/15**	–	–	–	–	1314/18	1314/19	–	–	–
1699 A	**1253/06**	**1157/03**	**1098/05**	–	**973/10**	**973/16**	–	–	–	**1314/15**	**1314/20**	1285/12	–	**1285/02**
1699 B	1253/09	1158/02	1099/09	1099/01	–	**801/37**	–	–	–	**1315/01**	**1315/07**	–	**1285/08**	**1285/13**
1700 A	–	1158/03	–	**1099/07**	974/06	974/07	–	–	–	1315/10	1315/04	–	**1285/09**	–
1700 B	1253/12	–	1099/13	1099/16	975/08	975/04	–	–	–	1315/20	1315/15	1285/28	1285/24	1286/21
1701 A	1253/14	1159/01	1099/18	1099/12	975/09	–	–	–	–	1315/19	1315/18	**1286/04**	1285/22	1286/18
1701 B	1254/01	1160/01	1100/06	–	976/12	976/02	–	–	–	1316/05[1]	1316/07	**1286/01**	1286/11[2]	1286/13
1702 A	–	–	–	1100/01[3]	–	976/05	–	–	–	1316/06	1316/09	1287/01[4]	1286/10	1287/09
1702 B	–	–	–	–	977/09	977/10	–	–	–	1316/18	1316/14	1287/13	–	1287/11[5]
1703 A	1254/05	–	1100/09	–	977/03	–	1062/10	–	1062/27	1316/15	–[6]	1288/13	1287/07	–
1703 B	–	1160/04	1101/07	–	978/02	–	1063/21	1063/34	–	1317/01	1317/02	1288/05	1287/06	1288/12
1704 A	1254/07	–	–	–	978/01	980/13	1063/07	1063/20	1063/33	1317/08	1317/06	1289/04	1288/08	1289/10
1704 B	1254/09	–	1101/10	–	–	–	–	1064/03	1064/13	1317/10	1317/16	1289/03	1288/03	1289/15
TOTAL	15	12	16	13	17	15	9	9	9	18	19	12	12	10

Notes: Year suffix A – Christmas to Midsummer. Year suffix B – Midsummer to Christmas. Sample year in bold.

[1] Imperfect, not produced.
[2] Period covered in schedule: 25/12/1700–24/12/1701.
[3] Imperfect, 2 fols only.
[4] Data for Swansea is a copy of 1288/13. South Burry entries refer in part to 1706.
[5] Also 1287/10 intended for 1697 apparent duplicate of 1287/11.
[6] Schedule gives 1317/17 a searchers overseas book for Milford.

Appendix 3

A simple classification of goods recorded in the port books

The following list outlines the commodity classification employed in chapter 3. An indication is also given of the main commodities within each sector (and the number of direct, discrete references) as recorded in the Gloucester coastal port books, 1680–1730.

Sector	Criteria	Commodities
Agriculture	Primary agricultural products, including items traded in a raw state or with limited processing.	Cider (5,019); hops (3,649); wool (3,110); cheese (2,328); cotton wool (1613); wheat (1,458); bacon (825); barley (623); calf skins (597); teasels (558)
Crafts and manufactures	Products of large-scale and small-scale (proto-) industrial and craft activity	Earthenware (3,162); leather (2,398); glass and glasses (2,385); soap (1,932); paper (1,859); pitch and tar (1,519); household goods (1,380); oil (1,256); chairs (1,035); pipes (791)
Extractive	Minerals and ores, unworked stone and clay	White salt (4,238); coal (3,102); pot clay (2,007); salt (1,029); tobacco pipe clay (330); scythe stones (217)
Fishery	Raw fish and related goods from the inshore and Newfoundland fisheries	Train (1,172); herrings (779); fish (319); white herrings (215)
Food and drink	Victuals produced for consumption, including overseas grocery goods	Grocery (6,770); tobacco (5,309); malt (5,093); Spanish and Port wine (4,151); English spirits (1,726); sugar (963); tobacco stems (763); Hotwell waters (501); raisins (463); vinegar (448)
Metals	Metals and large-scale metalwares, excluding worked goods and metal crafts	Iron and ironware (4,343); lead and shot (2,377); bar iron (926); copper (831); brass (573); pig iron (538); tin (447); steel (372); old brass (331)
Textiles	All textile materials, including yarn, but excluding raw wool	Manchester ware/goods (2,713); linen (1826; Kidderminster stuff (1,091); serge (987); woollen (880); wick yarn (842); thread (577); bay yarn (485); cloth (483); woollen yarn (478)
Wood	Forestry goods, excluding finished or turned ware	Timber and timberstuff (4,161); deal boards (911); laths (545); rods (476); hoops (472); logwood (282); bark (274)

Abbreviations

Add. MSS	Additional Manuscripts
BCL	Bristol Central Library (Manuscripts and Collections).
BHA	Bristol Historical Association
BL	British Library
BM	British Museum
BRO	Bristol Record Office
BRS	Bristol Record Society
CRO	Cornwall Record Office
CSPD	*Calendar of State Papers Domestic*
CTB	Calendar of Treasury Books
CTP	Calendar of Treasury Papers
DRO	Devon Record Office
EcHR	*Economic History Review*
MGRO	Mid-Glamorgan Record Office
NDRO	North Devon Record Office
NLW	National Library of Wales
PRO	Public Record Office
PSANHS	*Proceedings of the Somerset Archaeological and Natural History Society*
RO	Record Office
TBGAS	*Transactions of the Bristol and Gloucestershire Archaeological Society*
TRHS	*Transactions of the Royal Historical Society*

Notes

Place of publication is London unless otherwise stated

Introduction

1 This section is based on a reading of P.V. McGrath, *The Merchant Venturers of Bristol: a history of the Society of Merchant Venturers of the city of Bristol from its origins to the present day* (Bristol, 1975), pp. 24–39, 90–101, 124–69; P.V. McGrath, 'The Society of Merchant Venturers and the port of Bristol in the seventeenth century', *TBGAS*, LXXII (1953), pp. 119–28; W. E. Minchinton, 'The port of Bristol in the eighteenth century', in P. V. McGrath, ed., *Bristol in the eighteenth century* (Newton Abbot, 1972), pp. 128–30, 140–7; R.H. Quilici, 'Turmoil in a city and empire: Bristol's factions, 1700–1775', unpublished Ph.D. dissertation, University of New Hampshire (1976), ch. 1; F. Walker, *The Bristol region* (1972), pp. 175–88; C.M. MacInnes and W.F. Wittard, eds, *Bristol and its adjoining counties* (1955, 2nd edn. 1973), pp. 207–42; K. Morgan, 'The economic development of Bristol, 1700–1850', in M. Dresser and P. Ollerenshaw, eds, *The making of modern Bristol* (Tiverton, 1996), pp. 48–76; P. Fleming, 'The emergence of modern Bristol', in Dresser and Ollerenshaw, eds, *The making of modern Bristol*, pp. 1–4; D. H. Sacks, *The widening gate: Bristol and the Atlantic economy, 1450–1700* (Berkeley, Los Angeles, 1991), pp. 19–127, 331–62; K. O. Morgan, *Bristol and the Atlantic trade in the eighteenth century* (Cambridge, 1993), ch. 1; and E. Baigent, 'Economy and society in eighteenth-century English towns: Bristol in the 1770s', in D. Denecke and G. Shaw, eds, *Urban historical geography. Recent progress in Britain and Germany* (Cambridge, 1988), pp. 109–16.

2 See T.H. Breen, 'An empire of goods: the anglicization of colonial America 1690–1776', *Journal of British Studies*, XXV (1986), pp. 467–99 and his '"Baubles of Britain": the American and consumer revolutions of the eighteenth century', *Past and Present*, CXIX (1988), pp. 73–104 for thoughts on this 'imperialisation' of trade. For the importance of colonial consumption to urban growth, albeit from the perspective of London, see N. Zahedieh, 'London and the colonial consumer in the late seventeenth century', *EcHR*, XLVII (1994), pp. 239–61.

3 D. Defoe, *A tour through the whole island of Great Britain* (1724–6, repr. 1974), p. 361. See also C.J. French, '"Crowded with traders and a great commerce". London's domination of English overseas trade, 1700–1775', *London Journal*, 17 (1992), pp. 27–35.

4 F.M. Eden, *The state of the poor* (1797), II, p. 183.

5 For population change, see Sacks, *Widening gate*, pp. 353–7; E. Ralph and M.E. Williams, *The inhabitants of Bristol in 1696* (BRS, XXV, 1968), introduction; P. Clark, *The English county town* (Leicester, 1982), p. 16; C. Chalklin, *The provincial towns of Georgian England*

207

(1974), pp. 18–25; E.A. Wrigley and R.S. Schofield, *The population history of England 1541–1871* (Cambridge, 1981), pp. 532–3.

6 Pope quoted in P.T. Marcy, 'Eighteenth-century views of Bristol and Bristollians', in P.V. McGrath, ed., *Bristol in the eighteenth century* (Newton Abbott, 1966), p. 20.

7 The full extent of work relating to the trade of Bristol is too large to be rehearsed here. However, useful surveys are provided by the works listed in note 1 and J. Vanes, *The port of Bristol in the sixteenth century* (Bristol, 1977); P. McGrath, ed., *Records relating to the Society of Merchant Venturers in the city of Bristol in the seventeenth century* (BRS, XVII, 1952); P.V. McGrath, ed., *Merchants and merchandise in seventeenth-century Bristol* (BRS, XIX, 1955); W.E. Minchinton, *The trade of Bristol in the eighteenth century* (BRS, XX, 1957) W. E. Minchinton, ed., *Politics and the port of Bristol in the eighteenth century: the petitions of the Society of Merchant Venturers, 1698–1803* (BRS, XXIII, 1963); W.B. Stephens, 'Trade trends at Bristol, 1600–1700', *TBGAS*, XCIII (1974), pp. 156–61; and D.P. Hussey, 'Re-investigating coastal trade: the ports of the Bristol Channel and the Severn Estuary, c.1695–c.1704', unpublished Ph.D. thesis, University of Wolverhampton (1995) pp. 9–13.

8 C.M. MacInnes, *Bristol: a gateway of empire* (Bristol, 1939, repr. Newton Abbot, 1968), chs. IX–XIII. The comparison of Bristol to the 'navel of the world' is addressed in a different context by Sacks, *Widening gate*, p. 143 and section 2.4. For mercantile wealth and investment, see W.E. Minchinton, 'The merchants of Bristol in the eighteenth century', in *Sociétés et groupes sociaux en Aquitaine et en Angleterre*, Fédérations Historiques du Sud-ouest (Bordeaux, 1979), pp. 193–9. For the belated reconstruction of Bristol in the eighteenth century, see T. Mowl, *To build the second city: architects and craftsmen of Georgian Bristol* (Bristol 1991).

9 For the comments of Pepys and North, see J. Bettey, *Bristol observed. Visitors' impressions of the city from Domesday to the Blitz* (Bristol, 1986), pp. 53–5, 58–9.

10 A choice selection of comments and anecdotes is contained in Marcy, 'Eighteenth-century views', pp. 11–40; Bettey, *Bristol observed*, pp. 61–92; and E. Martin and B. Pickard, eds, *Six hundred years of Bristol poetry* (Bristol, 1973), pp. 7–25.

11 Cox, *Magna Britannia* quoted in Minchinton, 'Port of Bristol', p. 129.

12 G. Jackson, 'The ports', in D.H. Aldcroft and M.J. Freeman, eds, *Transport in the industrial revolution* (Manchester, 1983), p. 180.

13 W.E. Minchinton, 'Bristol–metropolis of the west in the eighteenth century', *TRHS*, 5th ser. 4 (1954), pp. 69–89. For adaptations of the model see Vanes, *Port of Bristol*, pp. 12–4; McGrath, ed., *Merchants*, introduction; Sacks, *Widening gate*, pp. 52–53. Corfield has identified similar patterns in the development of Norwich in the seventeenth century: P.J. Corfield, 'A provincial capital in the late seventeenth century: the case of Norwich', in P. Clark and P. Slack, eds, *Crisis and order in English towns, 1500–1700* (1972), pp. 263–310.

14 See E. Wolf, *Europe and the people without history* (Berkeley, 1982), pp. 83–8 and discussions in J.D. Tracy, ed., *The rise of merchant empires. Long distance trade in the early modern world, 1350–1750* (Cambridge, 1990), pp. 3–7.

15 See Minchinton, 'Metropolis', pp. 82–5 and J.A. Chartres, 'The marketing of agricultural produce in metropolitan western England in the late seventeenth and eighteenth centuries', in M. Havinden, ed., *Husbandry and marketing in the south-west, 1500–1800* (Exeter Papers in Economic History, 8, Exeter, 1973), pp. 64–7. For examples of Bristol investment see R.O. Roberts, 'Industrial expansion in south Wales', in D. Moore, ed., *Wales in the eighteenth century* (Swansea, 1976), pp. 109–26; A.H. John, *The industrial development of south Wales, 1750–1850: an essay* (Cardiff, 1950), pp. 31–32; R. Jenkins, 'The

copper works at Redbrook and Bristol', *TBGAS*, LXIII (1942), pp. 145–67; J. Day, *Bristol brass: the history of the industry* (Newton Abbot, 1973), pp. 55–60; J. Day, 'The Costers: copper smelters and manufacturers', *Transactions of the Newcomen Society*, 47 (1974–6), pp. 48–58; R.O. Roberts, 'The development and decline of the copper and other non-ferrous metal industries in south Wales', *Transactions of the Honourable Society of Cymmrodorion*, 52 (1956), pp. 78–115; R.O. Roberts, 'A further note on Dr. John Lane', *Gower*, 22 (1971), pp. 22–5; N.C. Cox, 'Imagination and innovation of an industrial pioneer: the first Abraham Darby', *Industrial Archaeology Review*, XII (1990), pp. 127–44; P.K. Stembridge, 'A Bristol-Coalbrookdale connection: the Goldneys', *Bristol Industrial Archaeological Society*, 19 (1986); P.K. Stembridge, *The Goldney family: a Bristol merchant dynasty* (BRS, XLIX, 1998), pp. 10–83. Bristol's cultural role is examined by J. Barry, 'The cultural life of Bristol, 1640–1775', unpublished D.Phil. thesis, University of Oxford (1986); C.B. Estabrook, 'Urbane and rustic Bristol: social spheres and cultural ties in an English city and its hinterland: 1660–1780', unpublished Ph.D. thesis, Brown University, (1992); C.B. Estabrook, *Urbane and rustic England: cultural ties and social spheres in the provinces, 1660–1780* (Manchester, 1998), especially pp. 42–87, 128–63; E. Baigent, 'Bristol society in the later eighteenth century with special reference to the handling by computer of fragmentary historical sources', unpublished D.Phil. thesis, University of Oxford (1986); J. Barry, 'Bristol pride: civic identity in Bristol, c.1640–1775', in Dresser and Ollerenshaw, eds, *The making of modern Bristol*, pp. 25–47; and P. Borsay *The English urban renaissance: culture and society in the English provincial town, 1660–1770* (Oxford, 1989), pp. 157–60.

16 For more recent critiques of central place theory and the models projected by von Thunen and Christaller, see K.S.O. Beavon, *Central place theory: a reinterpretation* (1977), pp. 10–22. For a reinterpretation of the role of the periphery: P. O'Brien, 'European economic development: the contribution of the periphery', *EcHR*, XXXV (1982), pp. 1–18. See also the articles contained in E. Aerts and P. Clark, eds, *Metropolitan cities and their hinterlands in early modern Europe* (Tenth Economic History Conference, Leuven, 1990) and A. van der Woude, A. Hayami and J. de Vries, 'The hierarchies, provisioning, and demographic patterns of cities', in A. van der Woude, A. Hayami and J. de Vries, eds, *Urbanization in history* (Oxford, 1990), pp. 1–19.

17 See Grassby's highly conservative critiques in *The business community of seventeenth century England* (Cambridge, 1995), pp. 1–8.

18 See J.A. Chartres, *Internal trade in England* (1977), pp. 10–19, 31–6, 43–6; J. Armstrong and P.S. Bagwell, 'Coastal shipping', in Aldcroft and Freeman, eds, *Transport in the industrial revolution*, p. 152; J. Armstrong, 'The significance of coastal shipping in British domestic transport', *International Journal of Maritime History*, III (1991), pp. 71–3; T. S. Willan, *The English coasting trade 1600–1750* (Manchester, 1938, repr. new York, 1967), chs. 5–6; and Willan *River navigation in England, 1600–1750* (Manchester, 1936, repr. 1964), pp. 2–5.

19 William Goldwin, *A Poetical Description of Bristol* (1712), pp. 1, 8–9 (BCL B27023).

Chapter 1

1 Marginal note in S. and N. Buck, 'The south-east prospect of the city of Bristol, 1734', in R. Hyde, *A prospect of Britain: the panoramas of Samuel and Nathaniel Buck* (1994), plate 7.

2 See A.F. Williams, 'Bristol port plans and improvement schemes of the eighteenth century', *TBGAS*, LXXXI (1962), pp. 138–42; Minchinton, 'Port of Bristol', pp. 135–57;

S.J. Jones, 'The growth of Bristol', *Transactions of the Institute of British Geographers*, XI (1954), pp. 55–83; and Lovell, 'Bristol: a satire', in Martin and Pickard, eds, *Bristol poetry*, p. 21.

3 The persistence of cultural difference between the urban and rural mentalités of Bristol and its surrounding area is examined skilfully by Estabrook, *Urbane and rustic England*, pp. 22–36.

4 J.E. Pritchard, 'The great plan of Bristol, 1673', *TBGAS*, XLIV (1922), pp. 203–20.

5 Hyde, *Prospect of Britain*; T.S. Willan, 'Bath and the navigation of the Avon', *PSANHS, Bath and District Branch* (1936), pp. 139–40.

6 See Estabrook, *Urbane and rustic England*, pp. 44–50 for a detailed examination of residential patterns, zoning and urban/rural development.

7 For a wider discussion of these themes, see P.J. Corfield, *The impact of English towns, 1700–1800* (1982), ch. 1; P. Clark, ed., *The transformation of English provincial towns, 1600–1800* (1984), pp. 13–30; P. Large, 'Urban growth and agricultural change in the West Midlands during the seventeenth and eighteenth centuries', in Clark, *English provincial towns*, pp. 169–89; P. Borsay, ed., *The Eighteenth century town, 1688–1820* (1990), pp. 1–11; E.A. Wrigley, 'Urban growth and agricultural change: England and the Continent in the early modern period', in Borsay, ed., *Eighteenth century town*, pp. 39–82; A. Everitt, 'Country, county and town: patterns of regional evolution in England', in Borsay, ed. *Eighteenth century town*, pp. 83–115; J.A. Chartres, 'City and towns, farmers and economic change in the eighteenth century', *Historical Research*, LXIV (1991), pp. 138–55; Morgan, 'Economic development', pp. 48–75. A wider perspective is outlined in J. de Vries, *European urbanization, 1500–1800* (1984), pp. 85–120; P. Bairoch, 'Urbanization and the economy: the findings of two decades of research', *Journal of European Economic History*, 2 (1989); J. de Vries, 'Problems in the measurement, description, and analysis of historical urbanization', in van der Woude, Hayami and de Vries, eds, *Urbanization in history*, pp. 43–60; and E.A. Wrigley, 'Metropolitan cities and their hinterlands: stimulus and constraints to growth', and P. Bairoch and G. Goertz, 'A note on the impact of large cities on the surrounding cities, Europe 1500 to 1800', in Aerts and Clark, eds, *Metropolitan cities and their hinterlands*, pp. 12–21 and pp. 48–57 respectively.

8 Campbell, *Political survey of Great Britain*, quoted in W. Barrett, *The history and antiquities of the city of Bristol* (Bristol, 1789, repr. Gloucester, 1984), p. 168.

9 See Defoe, *Tour*, p. 362; Barrett, *Bristol*, pp. 167–9, 183–5; and P.T. Marcy, 'Bristol's roads and communications on the eve of the industrial revolution, 1740–1780', *TBGAS*, LXXXVII (1969), pp. 149–72.

10 Willan, *River navigation*, pp. 3–5; Willan, *Coasting trade*, pp. xiv–xvi. This view is reassessed in Chartres, *Internal trade*, pp. 42–4; Armstrong and Bagwell, 'Coastal shipping', pp. 142–3; Armstrong, 'Significance of coastal shipping', pp. 63–94; and Hussey, 'Coastal trade', pp. 14–20.

11 Willan, *River navigation*, pp. 114–30 gives an indication of transport savings occasioned by improvement. R. Davis, *The rise of the English shipping industry in the seventeenth and eighteenth centuries* (1962), pp. 60–1 argues that greater carrying capacity, savings on the number of crew, and quicker turn-around times made coasting a more efficient operation in the later seventeenth century.

12 The map was produced using software supplied by Digital Map Data © Bartholomew 1999. My thanks are to Martin Roberts for his painstaking efforts in creating and annotating this map.

13 Steep Holm and Flat Holm were islands at the mouth of the Severn belonging to the customs jurisdictions of Cardiff and Bristol respectively.

14 For the Severn trade see T.S. Willan, 'The river navigation and trade of the Severn valley, 1600–1750', *EcHR*, VIII (1937), pp. 68–79; A.P. Wakelin, 'Pre-industrial trade on the river Severn; a computer-aided study of the Gloucester port books, *c*.1640–*c*.1770', unpublished Ph.D. thesis, CNAA, Wolverhampton Polytechnic (1991), esp. ch. 3; M.D.G. Wanklyn, 'The impact of water transport facilities on English river ports, c. 1660–c. 1760', *EcHR*, XLIX (1996), pp. 1–19; A.P. Wakelin and D.P. Hussey, 'Investigating regional economies: the Gloucester port books database', in C.E. Harvey and J. Press, eds, *Database systems and historical research* (1996), pp. 14–21; D.P. Hussey, G. Milne, A.P. Wakelin and M.D.G. Wanklyn, eds, *The Gloucester coastal port books, 1575–1765: a summary* (Wolverhampton, 1995), chs. 4–9; and N.C. Cox, D.P. Hussey and G.J. Milne, eds, *The Gloucester port books database, 1575–1765, on CD-ROM* (1998) Individual river ports are discussed in P. Ripley, 'Trade and social structure of Gloucester, 1600–1700', *TBGAS*, XCIV (1976), pp. 117–23; P. Ripley, 'The economy of Gloucester 1660–1740', *TBGAS*, XCVIII (1980), pp. 135–53; S.W. Davies, 'An economic history of Bewdley before c.1700', unpublished Ph.D. thesis, University of London (1981); M.D.G. Wanklyn, 'The Severn navigation in the seventeenth century: long-distance trade of Shrewsbury boats', *Midland History*, XIII (1988), pp. 34–58; A. McInnes, 'The emergence of a leisure town: Shrewsbury 1660–1760', *Past and Present*, 120 (1978), pp. 53–87; and M.D.G. Wanklyn, 'Urban revival in early modern England: Bridgnorth and the river trade', *Midland History*, XVIII (1993), pp. 37–64.

15 For the capabilities of Severn craft, see Wanklyn, 'Shrewsbury boats', pp. 34–5; B.S. Trinder, *The industrial revolution in Shropshire* (Chichester, 1973, 2nd edn. 1981), pp. 61–72; and G. Farr, 'Severn navigation and the trow', *Mariner's Mirror*, XXXII, 2 (1946), pp. 71–6. The problems associated with the navigation of the Bristol Avon are discussed in Williams, 'Port plans', pp. 140–6 and McGrath, *Merchant Venturers of Bristol*, pp. 150–9.

16 Willan, *River navigation*, pp. 36–7, 45–6; Jenkins, 'Redbrook', pp. 145–67; Day, *Bristol brass*, pp. 49–50; J.H. Andrews, 'Chepstow: a defunct seaport of the Severn estuary', *Geography*, XL (1955), pp. 97–107.

17 See M. Hechter, *Internal colonialism: the Celtic fringe in British national development, 1536–1966* (1975); P. Payton, *The making of modern Cornwall: historical experience and the persistence of 'difference'* (Redruth, 1994), ch. 1; and N. Evans, 'Two paths to economic development: Wales and the north-east of England', in P. Hudson, ed., *Regions and industries: a perspective on the industrial revolution in Britain* (Cambridge, 1989), pp. 201–4.

18 F. Emery, 'Wales', in J. Thirsk, ed., *The agrarian history of England and Wales. Volume V: 1640–1750. I: Regional farming systems* (Cambridge, 1985), pp. 409–21; E.G. Bowen, 'The regional divisions of Wales', in E.G. Bowen, ed., *Wales. A physical, historical, and regional geography* (1957), pp. 267–9; B. Osborne, 'Glamorgan agriculture in the seventeenth and eighteenth centuries', *National Library of Wales Journal*, 20 (1977–8), pp. 387–405.

19 B.J. George, 'Pembrokeshire sea-trading before 1900', *Field Studies*, 2, 1 (1964), pp. 1–39; M.I. Williams, 'Carmarthenshire's maritime trade in the sixteenth and seventeenth centuries', *The Carmarthenshire Antiquary*, 14 (1978), pp. 61–70.

20 J.U. Nef, *The rise of the British coal industry*, 2 vols (1932, repr. 1966); J. Hatcher, *The history of the British coal industry. Volume 1: before 1700* (Oxford, 1993); T.S. Ashton, *The coal industry of the eighteenth century* (Manchester, 1929), ch. 1; and B.M. Evans, 'The Welsh coal trade during the Stuart period, 1603–1709', unpublished M.A. thesis, University of Wales (1928) are the best overviews. See also W. Rees, *Industry before the industrial revolution: incorporating a study of the Chartered Companies of the Society of Mines Royal and of Mineral and Battery Works* (Cardiff, 1968), pp. 79–115; M.V. Symons, *Coal mining in the Llanelli area*.

Volume 1: sixteenth century to 1829 (Llanelli, 1979); C. Trott, 'Coalmining in the borough of Neath in the seventeenth and eighteenth centuries', *Morgannwg*, 13 (1969), pp. 47–74; G. Edwards, 'The coal industry in Pembrokeshire', *Field Studies*, 1, 5 (1963), pp. 33–64; and E. Phillips, *Pioneers of the south Wales coalfield* (Cardiff, 1925).

21 Rees, *Industry*, pp. 302–8, 521–78; W.J. Lewis, *Lead mining in Wales* (Cardiff, 1967); W.J. Lewis, 'Some aspects of lead-mining in Cardiganshire in the sixteenth and seventeenth centuries', *Ceredigion*, I (1951), pp. 177–90; O. Beynon, 'The lead mining industry of Cardiganshire from 1700 to 1800', unpublished M.A. thesis, University of Wales (1937).

22 See Willan *Coasting trade*, pp. 167–71. The main trades of the ports are indicated in J. de L. Mann, *The cloth industry in the West of England from 1640 to 1880* (Oxford, 1971, repr. Gloucester, 1987), pp. 63–88, 255–79; W.G. Hoskins, *Industry, trade and people in Exeter, 1688–1800* (Manchester, 1935, 2nd edn. Exeter, 1968), pp. 66–86, 154–59; K.G. Ponting, *A history of the west of England cloth industry* (1957), pp. 31–3; K.G. Ponting, *The woollen industry of south west England* (Bath, 1971); J.H. Bettey, 'The livestock trade in the west country in the seventeenth century', *PSANHS*, 127 (1984), pp. 123–8; C. Skeel, 'The cattle trade between Wales and England from the fifteenth century to the eighteenth century', *TRHS*, 4th ser. IX (1926). See also D.M. Woodward, 'The Anglo-Irish livestock trade of the seventeenth century', *Irish Historical Studies*, XVIII (1972–3) and P.R. Edwards, 'The cattle trade of Shropshire in the late sixteenth and seventeenth centuries', *Midland History*, VI (1981), pp. 72–94.

23 G.V. Harrison, 'The south-west: Dorset, Somerset, Devon, and Cornwall', in Thirsk, ed., *The agrarian history of England and Wales. Volume V: 1640–1750. I: Regional farming systems*, pp. 370–3; E. Kerridge, *The agricultural revolution* (1967), pp. 115–16; M. Overton, *Agricultural revolution in England. The transformation of the agrarian economy, 1500–1850* (Cambridge, 1996), pp. 89–98; M. Williams, *The draining of the Somerset Levels* (Cambridge, 1970); and J. Thirsk, *Agricultural regions and agrarian history in England, 1500–1750* (Cambridge, 1987), p. 55.

24 Hoskins, *Industry, trade and people*, pp. 30–1; E. Kerridge, *Textile manufactures in early modern England* (Manchester, 1985), pp. 146–7.

25 See Harrison, 'South-west', pp. 376–7; R.G.F. Stanes, 'Devon agriculture in the mid-eighteenth century: the evidence of the Milles enquiries', in M.A. Havinden and C.M. King, eds, *The south-west and the land* (Exeter Papers in Economic History, 2, Exeter, 1969), pp. 50–3; J. Watkins, *An essay towards a history of Bideford* (Exeter, 1792), pp. 68–74; J.B. Gribble, *Memorials of Barnstaple*, (Barnstaple, 1830), pp. 471, 532; Hoskins, *Industry, trade and people*, p. 162; W.B. Stephens, 'The west-country ports and the struggle for the Newfoundland fisheries in the seventeenth century', *Transactions of the Devonshire Association*, LXXXVIII (1956); M. Nix, 'A maritime history of the ports of Bideford and Barnstaple, 1786–1841', unpublished Ph.D. thesis, University of Leicester (1991), introduction; D.J. Starkey, 'Devonians and the Newfoundland trade', in M. Duffy, S. Fisher, B. Greenhill, D.J. Starkey and J. Youings, eds, *The new maritime history of Devon. Volume I: from early times to the late eighteenth century* (Exeter, 1992), pp. 163–71.

26 Defoe, *Tour*, pp. 247–8.

27 A. Grant, *North Devon pottery: the seventeenth century* (Exeter, 1983); C.M. Watkins, *North Devon pottery and its export to America in the seventeenth century* (US Natural Museum Bulletin 225, Washington D.C., 1960); A. Grant and D. Jemmett, 'Pipes and pipe-making in Barnstaple, Devon', in P. Davey, ed., *The archaeology of the clay tobacco pipe. Volume IX* (British Archaeological Reports, British Series, 146, ii, 1985), pp. 439–553; L.T.C. Rolt, *The potters' field: a history of the south Devon ball clay industry* (Newton Abbot, 1974).

28 See the articles by A.J. Southward and G.T. Boalch, 'The marine resources of Devon's coastal waters'; A. Grant, 'Devon shipping, trade, and ports, 1600–1689'; and S. Fisher, 'Devon's maritime trade and shipping, 1680–1780' in M. Duffy et al., eds, *New maritime history of Devon*, pp. 51–61, 130–8 and 232–41.

29 M. Oppenheim, 'Maritime history', in W. Page, ed., *The Victoria history of the county of Cornwall. Volume I* (1906), pp. 475–6.

30 See M.I. Williams, 'The port of Aberdyfi in the eighteenth century', *National Library of Wales Journal*, XVIII, i (1973); L. Lloyd, 'The ports and shipping of Cardigan Bay', *Maritime Wales*, 4 (1979), pp. 33–42; and Rees, *Industry*, pp. 457–61.

31 E.A.G. Clark, *The ports of the Exe estuary, 1660–1860: a study in historical geography* (1960), pp. 73–88, 93–4; Oppenheim, 'Maritime history', pp. 502–3.

32 Chartres, *Internal trade*, pp. 9–13; Armstrong, 'Significance of coastal shipping', pp. 63–5. For a more in-depth, if somewhat later emphasis on the importance of coasting to the economies of small ports and their regions, see H.C. Brookfield, 'Three Sussex ports, 1850–1950', *Journal of Transport History*, II (1955), pp. 34–7.

33 For a summary of this literature, see Hussey, 'Coastal trade', pp. 26–41; Cox, Hussey and Milne, eds, *Database*, pp. 6–14.

34 Apart from Willan's overview, and recent work on Gloucester (see above), there is a large and variable body of work on local port establishments. See, for example, T. Barrow, 'Corn, carriers and coastal shipping: the shipping and trade of Berwick and the borders, 1730–1830', *Journal of Transport History*, 21 (2000), pp. 6–27; R. Davis, *The trade and shipping of Hull, 1500–1700* (1964); G. Jackson, *Hull in the eighteenth century: a study in economic and social history* (1972); G. Jackson, *The trade and shipping of eighteenth-century Hull* (York, 1975); R.W.K. Hinton, ed., *The port books of Boston, 1600–1640* (Lincoln Record Society, 50, 1956); G.A. Metters, 'The rulers and merchants of Kings Lynn in the early seventeenth century', unpublished Ph.D. thesis, University of East Anglia (1982); J. Barney, 'Shipping in the port of King's Lynn, 1702–1800', *Journal of Transport History*, 20 (1999), pp. 126–40; N.J. Williams, *The maritime trade of the East Anglian ports, 1550–1590* (Oxford, 1988); J.H. Andrews, 'The customs ports of Sussex, 1680–1730', *Sussex Notes and Queries*, XIV (1954), pp. 1–3; J.H. Andrews, 'The port of Chichester and the grain trade, 1650–1750', *Sussex Archaeological Collections*, 92 (1954), pp. 93–105; J.H. Andrews, 'The Thanet seaports, 1650–1750', *Archaeologia Cantiana*, 66 (1954), pp. 37–44; J.H. Andrews, 'The trade of the port of Faversham, 1650–1750', *Archaeologia Cantiana*, 69 (1955), pp. 125–31; J.L. Wiggs, 'The seaborne trade of Southampton in the second half of the sixteenth century', unpublished M.A. thesis, University of Southampton (1955); Hoskins, *Industry, trade and people*; Duffy et al, eds, *New maritime history of Devon*; Minchinton, 'Metropolis'; E.A. Lewis, ed., *The Welsh Port Books, 1550–1603* (Cymmrodorion Record Series, 12, 1927); M.I. Williams, 'A contribution to the commercial history of Glamorgan', *National Library of Wales Journal*, XI (1959–60), pp. 330–60; George, 'Pembrokeshire sea-trading'; and D.M. Woodward, *The trade of Elizabethan Chester* (Hull, 1970). For the trade in goods, see N.S.B. Gras, *The evolution of the English corn market, from the twelfth to the eighteenth century* (1915); L. Weatherill, *The pottery trade and north Staffordshire 1660–1760* (Manchester, 1971); Grant, *North Devon pottery*; Nef, *Coal industry*; Hatcher, *Coal industry*; R. Burt, 'Lead production in England and Wales, 1700–1770', *EcHR*, XXII (1969), pp. 249–68; Bettey, 'Livestock trade'; and D.M. Woodward, '"Swords into ploughshares": recycling in pre-industrial England', *EcHR*, XXXVIII (1985).

35 Not all administrations continued to compile books in the later eighteenth century: N.J. Williams, *Descriptive list of Exchequer, Queen's Remembrancer, Port Books, Parts 1–111: 1565–1700; 1700–1799* (1960).

36 E.E. Hoon, *The organisation of the English Customs system, 1696–1786* (1938, repr. Newton Abbot, 1968), pp. 5–25, 36–38; R.C. Jarvis, 'The appointment of ports', *EcHR*, 2nd ser. XI (1958), p. 463; H. Crouch, *A complete guide to the officers of His Majesty's Customs in the outports* (1732), pp. 1–6; and R.C. Jarvis, 'Critical historical introduction' to Hoon, *English Customs system*, pp. xii–xvii.

37 Crouch, *Complete guide*, p. 38. These directives were not always rigorously applied, especially in the recording of inward voyages.

38 MGRO B/C CH 2, pp. 134–5.

39 Willan, *Coasting trade*, pp. 1–10; Wakelin, 'Pre-industrial trade', pp. 40–2; Williams, *East Anglian ports*, pp. 13–8.

40 See Jarvis, 'Appointment of ports', pp. 457–63; R.C. Jarvis, 'Sources for the history of ports', *Journal of Transport History*, 3 (1957–8), pp. 80–1; N.S.B. Gras, *The early English customs system* (1918); N.S.B. Gras, 'Memorandum on the port books', *First Report of the Royal Commission on the Public Records*, Appendix IV (16), Parliamentary Papers 1912–13, XLIV (1913), pp. 125–7; G.N. Clark, *Guide to English commercial statistics, 1696–1782* (1938), pp. 50–4; and Hoon, *English customs system*. Crouch, *Complete guide*, pp. 1–30 and H. Crouch, *A complete view of the British Customs* (1725) provide an indispensable contemporary view.

41 Clark, *English commercial statistics*, pp. 50–4; Hoon, *English customs system*, pp. 170–3, 195–242; J.H. Andrews, 'Two problems in the interpretation of the port books', *EcHR*, 2nd ser. IX (1956), pp. 119–22; S.E. Aström, 'The reliability of the English port books', *Scandinavian Economic History Review*, XVI (1968), pp. 125–36; W.B. Stephens, 'The Exchequer port books as a source for the history of the English cloth trade', *Textile History*, 1 (1969), pp. 206–13; D.M. Woodward, 'Short guides to records 22: port books', *History*, 55 (1970), pp. 207–10; D.M. Woodward, 'The port-books of England and Wales', *Maritime History*, III (1973), pp. 147–65; and Williams, *East Anglian ports*, pp. 47–8.

42 MGRO B/C CH 2, pp. 77, 130. Record-keeping at the major ports was altogether more professional: R.C. Jarvis, ed., *Customs letter-books of the port of Liverpool, 1711–1813* (Chetham Society, 3rd ser., 6, 1954), introduction, pp. 6–28.

43 For financial perquisites, see Somerset RO DD/BR/gr 10. Corruption at Bristol was notorious: see PRO E134 13 William 3 Mich 52; Morgan, *Bristol*, pp. 155–7.

44 For smuggling, see N. Williams, *Contraband cargoes: seven centuries of smuggling* (1959), pp. 50–1; G.D. Ramsey, 'The smuggler's trade: a neglected aspect of English commercial development', *TRHS*, 5th ser. II (1952), pp. 131–57; W.A. Cole, 'Trends in eighteenth-century smuggling', in W.E. Minchinton, ed., *The growth of English overseas trade in the seventeenth and eighteenth centuries* (1969), pp. 121–43; A.G. Jamieson, 'Devon and smuggling' in Duffy et al., eds, *New maritime history of Devon*, pp. 244–50; R.C. Nash, 'The English and Scottish tobacco trades in the seventeenth and eighteenth centuries: legal and illegal trade', *EcHR*, XXXV (1982), pp. 354–72; and C. Shammas, *The pre-industrial consumer in England and America* (Oxford, 1990), pp. 70–82.

45 BL Add. MS 61611: Blenheim Papers, abuses at Bristol customs house, 1718, f. 238. See also PRO T 64/143, report on the complaints against customs officers at Bristol, 1718 and T 64/143 London and the Western ports, schedule of revenue frauds, 1723–32.

46 The system of recording coastal trade is outlined in Crouch, *Complete guide*, pp. 2–38; Hoon, *English customs system*, pp. 264–9; and Cox, Hussey and Milne, eds, *Database*, pp. 9–12.

47 See Jarvis, 'Appointment of ports', pp. 461–2; Cox, Hussey and Milne, eds, *Database*, pp. 6–18; Crouch, *Complete guide*, pp. 3–12; Crouch, *Complete view*, pp. 247–9; and Hoon,

English customs system, pp. 8–10. R.C. Jarvis, 'The head port of Chester; and Liverpool, its creek and member' *Transactions of the Historical Society of Lancashire and Cheshire*, CII (1950), pp. 69–84 and Andrews, 'Two problems', p. 119 supply useful examples of local practice.

48 Armstrong and Bagwell, 'Coastal shipping', p. 180. See also Jarvis, 'Appointment of ports', pp. 462–6.

49 Williams, *Descriptive list*, I.

50 The increase in trade was noted by 1699. New appointments of customs officials at Barnstaple, Appledore, Plymouth, Clovelly and Bideford 'all as recommended by Capt. Ward in his late survey of Bideford port because of the great increase of business in that port' were ordered by Treasury warrant. *CTB*, XV, p. 212. See also Starkey, 'Newfoundland trade', pp. 163–6; Watkins, *Bideford*, pp. 58–62; and Defoe, *Tour*, p. 246.

51 Williams, *Descriptive list*, III.

52 Some 84 entries from a total of 2,099 were recorded as being 'of' Clovelly. Some of these shipments may, of course, have been to or from Bideford itself and merely reveal that such ships were only berthed in Clovelly. Without comparative evidence, there is no way of separating such voyages satisfactorily.

53 This is evidenced in extensive quay provisions and the possession of rights and duties. See NDRO 1843 A/PR 3 and 2239 B add 5/m 1. NDRO 1843A/PF 76, 4227m/T2, and B9/18/30 (b) indicate the activities of John Quick, Philip Anderton and John King, mariners and boat owners of Northam. All appeared on Northam boats recorded at Bideford.

54 See NDRO B1 1128 and B1 1129 for disputes over the status of Appledore.

55 Andrews, 'Two problems', p. 121.

56 Jarvis, 'History of ports', pp. 81–2.

57 Somerset RO T/PH/gc 10 and T/PH/gc 11 indicate the development of Porlock; Somerset RO DD/L 2; DD/WY bx 10 E 3/1, 2; DD/WY/bx 40 and 41, Watchet. See also Somerset RO DD/L 1 54/42 legal deposition concerning wool ports, 1732.

58 Willan, *Coasting trade*, pp. 64, 169–73. See also W. Wedlake, *A history of Watchet* (Williton, 1955), pp. 83–4; R. W. Dunning, ed., *The Victoria county history of Somerset. Volume V.* (Oxford, 1988), pp. 147–8.

59 At Swansea and Neath, Carmarthen and Milford, the official customs house head port and not the actual ports of discharge were often listed in the port books.

60 For the discussion of the interpretation of the 'home' port, see Cox, Hussey and Milne, eds, *Database*, pp. 26–7.

61 Boats 'of Watchet' often traded to and from centres unconnected with the 'home' port.

62 Watchet imposed a series of *ad valorem* duties on goods and vessels in order to maintain the quay and harbour: Somerset RO DD/WY/bx 40, Harbour trust deed, 1665. The harbour was badly damaged by storms in 1697 and 1705, requiring a private Act of Parliament to levy new dues: Somerset RO DD/WY/bx 41 articles between William Row, mason, and Sir William Wyndham. These failed to remedy the faults and by 1721 the head of the pier was in 'a tottering, ruinous and dilapidated condition': Somerset RO DD/WY/bx 41 Wyndham vs. Stone, interrogatories and breviates.

63 From Michaelmas 1719 to Michaelmas 1727 duties were leased to Richard Wheddon, a prominent Watchet merchant 'att the Yearly rent of One hundred pounds clear of all outgoings'. Somerset RO DD/WY/bx 40 Account Book of Quay Duties, Watchet, 1708–65.

64 Andrews, 'Two problems', p. 120.

65 This process may have happened much earlier: Lewis, *Welsh port books*, introduction; M.I. Williams, 'Cardiff, its people and its trade, 1660–1720', *Morgannwg*, VII (1963), pp. 74–97.

66 *CTB*, XV, pp. 130, 427; Andrews, 'Chepstow', pp. 97–107.

67 MGRO B/C CH 2, p. 130.

68 Oystermouth maintained a few colliers, having 'a common port or passage into England wherein is builded a kay for that purpose'. Port Eynon was described in the 1690s as maintaining 'a common passage to England, a new kay was lately builded there by Sr Edward Mansell and the aid of the country of Gowyr': E. Lhwyd, *Parochalia, being a summary of answers to parochial queries (Volume III*, ed. R.H. Morris (1911), pp. 141–3.

69 J.W. Dawson, *Commerce and customs—a history of the ports of Newport and Caerleon* (Cardiff, 1932), pp. 6–7, 22–5.

70 MGRO B/C CH2, pp. 83, 163; G.M. Jones and E. Scourfield, *Sully: a village and parish in the Vale of Glamorgan* (1986), pp. 125–36; W. Rees, *Cardiff, a history of the city* (Cardiff, 1969), p. 124.

71 Bettey, 'Livestock trade', pp. 123–8.

72 See, for example, the activities of John Bird, customs officer at Newport: MGRO CL MS 4.266, fos 87–92.

73 Dawson, *Commerce and customs*, pp. 22–5, 39–41.

74 Crouch, *Complete guide*, pp. 3–7, 11; Hoon, *English customs system*, pp. 5–25.

75 Wakelin, 'Pre-industrial trade', pp. 35–8; 54; B.L.C. Johnson, 'The charcoal iron industry in the early eighteenth century', *Geographical Journal*, 117 (1951), pp. 167–77; B.L.C. Johnson, 'The Foley partnerships: the iron industry at the end of the charcoal era', *EcHR*, 2nd ser. IV (1952), pp. 322–40; Cox, Hussey and Milne, eds, *Database*, pp. 8–9.

76 The map was produced using software supplied by 'Digital Map Data © Bartholomew 1999'. My thanks are again to Martin Roberts for all his efforts in translating my amateur sketches into both digital and hard copy versions.

77 Minchinton, 'Port of Bristol', pp. 135–8 (corrected).

78 The development of the port of Bristol is described by McGrath, *Merchant Venturers of Bristol*, pp. 150–70; Williams, 'Port plans', pp. 139–45; and McGrath, 'Merchant Venturers and the Port of Bristol', pp. 105–28. For the role and turbulent life of Bristol's pilots, see G.E. Farr, 'Bristol Channel pilotage, historical notes on its administration and craft', *Mariner's Mirror*, XXXIX (1953), pp. 27–44 and P. Stuckey, *The sailing pilots of the Bristol Channel* (Newton Abbot, 1977).

79 For the vigorous debate concerning the status of Gloucester and its eventual separation from Bristol in 1584, see J. Vanes, *Documents illustrating the overseas trade of Bristol in the sixteenth century* (BRS, XXXI, 1979), pp. 9, 34–6

80 For later trades, see *Felix Farley's Bristol Journal*, 2 August 1752.

81 See F.A. Knight, *The sea-board of Mendip* (1902, 2nd edn 1988), pp. 263–4.

82 From 1729, letpasses sufficed for all trade conducted above Steep Holm and Flat Holm. As Uphill had only a small customs establishment boat masters were discovered specifying Uphill for voyages bound for Somerset and Devon which required coquets: MGRO B/C CH 1, p. 132.

83 Crouch, *Complete guide*, pp. 2–39, Crouch, *Complete view*, pp. 247, 255, Willan, *Coasting trade*, pp. 1–11; and Hoon, *English customs system*, pp. 264–9 outline the official regulations behind the coastal books. Williams, *East Anglian ports*, pp. 13–8; Wakelin, 'Pre-industrial trade', pp. 40–2; and Hussey, 'Coastal trade', pp. 34–40 indicate local practice. R. Score, *A guide to the customers and collectors clerks or a new index to the Book of Rates* (1699), pp. 342–7 demonstrates contemporary practice.

84 Andrews, 'Two problems', pp. 119–22; Willan, *Coasting trade*, pp. 7–8; Hoon, *English customs system*, pp. 265–8; Wakelin, 'Pre-industrial trade', pp. 41–4; and Hussey, 'Coastal trade', pp. 37–40 discuss the use of non-coquet documentation. Crouch, *Complete guide*, pp. 16–17, and p. 11 ms. note 2 in British Library copy of the text (BL 522 n.8) gives specific examples of trade by letpass and transire.

85 See Andrews, 'Customs ports of Sussex'; Andrews, 'Chichester and the grain trade'; Andrews, 'Thanet seaports'; Andrews, 'Faversham' for the results of such omissions. Failure to assess unrecorded traffic has compromised some trade statistics: Willan, *Coasting trade*, pp. 129–31.

86 Chepstow began recording letpasses in 1700, albeit highly erratically.

87 Williams, 'Commercial history of Glamorgan', pp. 330–60; M.I. Williams, 'Further contributions to the commercial history of Glamorgan', *National Library of Wales Journal*, XII (1962), pp. 354–66; M.I. Williams, 'Some aspects of the economic and social life of the southern regions of Glamorgan, 1600–1800', *Morgannwg*, III (1959), pp. 21– 40; and Bettey, 'Livestock trade', pp. 123–8.

88 The pilchard trade is discussed by J.C.A. Whetter, 'Cornish trade in the seventeenth century' *Journal of the Royal Institute of Cornwall*, new series, IV, 4 (1964), pp. 405–6; J. Scantlebury, 'The development of the export trade in pilchards from Cornwall during the sixteenth century', *Journal of the Royal Institute of Cornwall*, X (1989), pp. 330–59; and A. Southward, G. Boalch and L. Maddock, 'Climatic change and the herring and pilchard fisheries of Devon and Cornwall', in D.J. Starkey, ed., *Devon's coastline and coastal waters* (Exeter Maritime Studies, 3, Exeter, 1988), pp. 37–9. The trade connections of Robert Corker, merchant of Falmouth and Penzance, indicate that the shipping of pilchards overseas and to London was commonplace: NDRO B 69/38, pp. 1–2 and J.C.A. Whetter, 'The rise of the port of Falmouth, 1600–1800', in H.E.S. Fisher, ed., *Ports and shipping in the south-west* (Exeter Papers in Economic History, 4, Exeter, 1970), pp. 9–10, 24.

89 Willan, *Coasting trade*, pp. 76, 165, 179. Whetter has based a perceived sectoral shift in trade of hilling stones from Fowey to Padstow on the evidence of erratic port book samples: 'Cornish trade', pp. 407–8.

90 The best survey remains Wakelin, 'Pre-industrial trade', ch. 1, revised in the light of Hussey et al., *Summary*, chs. 1–5 Wanklyn, 'Impact of water transport facilities', pp. 1–6; and Cox, Hussey and Milne, eds, *Database*.

91 It is impossible to confirm whether a reciprocal letpass trade existed between Bristol and Gloucester, although the 1656–57 Gloucester coast book suggests that many petty cargoes were traded in this way: Wakelin, 'Pre-industrial trade', pp. 54–5, 93–4; Andrews, 'Two problems', p. 120; Hussey et al., *Summary*, pp. 40–1. See also the critique of Wakelin's findings in Hussey, 'Coastal trade', pp. 38–9.

92 The 'cardinal point' formed an imaginary line that connected Steep Holm to the river Axe and Flat Holm to Lavernock Point: *CTP*, 1729–30, p. 441.

93 MGRO B/C CH 2, pp. 131–2, 167–8, 173–4.

94 The decay of Cardiff is discussed in *CTP*, 1729–30, p. 441 and MGRO B/C CH 2, pp. 131–2. It is clear from the Treasury warrant that letpasses were already established in part. See Hussey et al., *Summary*, ch. 8 for goods not vitally affected by the change in practice.

95 Willan, *Coasting trade*, p. 5 and Minchinton, 'Port of Bristol', p. 147 acknowledge the change in practice, although both use later data: Willan, *Coasting trade*, pp. 70, 174–5, 177 and Minchinton, 'Metropolis', pp. 70–1. These data reappear in M.D. Lobel and E.M. Carus-Wilson, 'Bristol' in M.D. Lobel, ed., *Historic Towns: maps and plans of towns and cities in the British Isles with historiocal commentaries, from earliest times to 1800* (1970), pp. 5, 15–21;

Walker, *Bristol region*, pp. 181–5, D.H. Sacks, 'Trade, society and politics in Bristol, circa 1500–circa 1650', unpublished Ph.D. thesis, Harvard University, Cambridge, Mass. (1977), pp. 382–4; and Morgan, *Bristol*, p. 99.

96 The Bristol records for 1699 contain 504 shipments (491 voyages) listing 29,532 segments of data. In the same year, 845 voyages cleared regional ports for Bristol, although these carried smaller cargoes.

97 Willan, *Coasting trade*, p. 172.

98 The problems of dealing with coastal port books are covered by Clark, *Guide*, pp. 52–6; Aström, 'English port books', pp. 125–36; Hinton, 'Boston', introduction; Woodward, 'Port books', pp. 147–55; and N. Williams, 'The London port books', *Transactions of the London and Middlesex Archaeological Society*, 18 (1955), pp. 13–26. A discussion of computerisation and data standardisation and exchange is to be found in P. Wakelin, 'Comprehensive computerisation of a very large documentary source: the Portbooks Project at Wolverhampton Polytechnic', in P. Denley eds, and D. Hopkin, eds, *History and computing* (Manchester, 1987), pp. 109–15; Wakelin, 'Pre-industrial trade', ch. 2; Hussey, 'Coastal trade', pp. 41–55; Wakelin and Hussey, 'Investigating regional economies', pp. 14–21; G.J. Milne and M. Paul, 'Establishing a flexible model for port book studies: the recent evolution of the Gloucester port books database', *History and Computing*, 6 (1994), pp. 106–15; and Cox, Hussey and Milne, eds, *Database*, pp. 15–57.

99 See PRO T 64/140 for commissioner Culliford's enquires into abuses in the western ports. J.C.A. Whetter, 'The economic history of Cornwall in the seventeenth century', unpublished Ph.D. thesis, University of London (1965), p. 241, and J. Whetter, *Cornwall in the seventeenth century: an economic survey of Kernow* (Padstow, 1974), pp. 158–9, 176 list some of the abuses discovered in Cornish ports.

100 Somerset RO DD/SF/2769, f. 1, tentatively dated to the late seventeenth century. The document was addressed to Plymouth, Looe, Fowey, Penryn, Truro, Penzance, Padstow, Bideford and Barnstaple.

101 Somerset RO DD/SF/2769, f. 1r. See *CTB*, XV p. 125 and *CTP*, 1697–1701–2, LXXXVIII. 34, pp. 560–1 for measures taken over the proper qualification of customs officers.

102 Wool was noted separately from 1688: P. Bowden, *The wool trade in Tudor and Stuart England* (1961), pp. 200–1. For official reforms to the port book system, see *CTB*, VII, p. 1415; *CTB*, IX, p. 1432.

103 Somerset RO DD/L 1 54/42, Deposition of Mr Webler concerning 1,695 stones of wool shipped from Wales to Minehead, 1713.

104 See Cox, Hussey and Milne, eds, *Database*, Appendix 1.

105 See for example Willan, *Coasting trade*, ch. X and Minchinton, 'Metropolis', pp. 80–4 where samples are used somewhat uncritically.

106 In table 1.2, all double entries associated with the carriage of wool or the occasional multiple cargo have been excluded from the data: Hussey, 'Coastal trade', pp. 58–61; Cox, Hussey and Milne, eds, *Database*, pp. 15–6, 31–3.

107 From 1660 to 1682 and 1702 to 1710 the Bristol record is especially poor. In addition, the Welsh books tail off dramatically from *c.*1712: Williams, *Descriptive list*, I–III; D.T. Williams, 'The port books of Swansea and Neath, 1709–19', *Archaeologia Cambrensis*, XCV (1940)', pp. 192–4.

108 For the use of similar techniques, see J. Stobart, 'An eighteenth-century revolution? Investigating urban growth in north-west England, 1664–1801', *Urban History*, 23, 1 (1996), pp. 30–5.

109 The rationale behind the sampling strategy used here is given in Hussey, 'Coastal trade', pp. 47–55. Gloucester data can be accessed through Cox, Hussey and Milne, eds, *Database* and the ESRC data archive.

110 Barrett, *Bristol*, pp. 57–8, 164 quoting William of Malmesbury.

111 See, for example, Lewis, *Welsh port books*, which reproduces the source verbatim, but fails to analyse the data in any systematic way. Owing to the size of the source, studies of the pre-1640 period remain perhaps the most complete analyses of trade: see Woodward, *Chester*; Hinton, 'Boston'; and Williams, *East Anglian ports*.

112 R.W. Fogel, 'The new economic history: its findings and methods', *EcHR*, 2nd ser. XIX (1966), p. 651.

113 See Williams's critique of the unstatistical nature of certain port book data: *East Anglian ports*, pp. 47–9.

Chapter 2

1 Bettey, *Bristol Observed*, pp. 61–9 and Marcy, 'Eighteenth century views', pp. 13–40 provide a selection of quotations on this subject.

2 See J. Barry, 'The history and antiquities of the city of Bristol: Thomas Chatterton in Bristol', *Angelaki*, 1 (1993/4), pp. 60–3 and Barrett, *Bristol*, ch. 1.

3 Quoted in Martin and Pickard, eds, *Bristol poetry*, p. 6.

4 For a more sympathetic picture of Bristol's cultural history see J. Barry, 'Provincial town culture: urbane or civic?', in J. Pittock and A. Wear, eds, *Interpretation and cultural history* (Basingstoke, 1991), pp. 198–234; Barry, 'Bristol pride', pp. 25–47; and Estabrook, 'Urbane and rustic Bristol', introduction. V. Waite, 'The Bristol Hotwell', in P. McGrath, ed., *Bristol in the eighteenth century* (Newton Abbot, 1972), pp. 109–26 gives a brief but more flattering account of the development of the Hotwell.

5 Minchinton, 'Metropolis', pp. 71–2; Morgan, *Bristol*, p. 33; Minchinton, 'Port of Bristol', pp. 132–3.

6 Williams, 'Port plans', p. 143. For urban zoning in pre-industrial Bristol see Baigent, 'Economy and society', pp. 109–24.

7 See Willan, *Coasting trade*, pp. 174–5 and Minchinton, 'Metropolis, p. 72 (repeated also in Morgan, *Bristol*, p. 99) and critiques in Hussey, 'Coastal trade', pp. 37–40.

8 Somerset RO DD/WY/bx 40 Account book of quay duties at Watchet port, 1708–65.

9 See Williams, *East Anglian ports*, pp. 47–8 for similar techniques.

10 For methodological considerations, see Hussey, 'Coastal trade', pp. 37–40, 58–63; and Cox, Hussey and Milne, eds *Database*, pp. 15–6. It was a legal requirement for wool to be recorded separately from other goods: Bowden, *Wool trade*, pp. 200–1. At ports where wool was a major traded commodity, duplicate voyages represent around 5 per cent of total recorded shipments. Thus, the figures extrapolated by Willan for the south-west, *Coasting trade*, pp. 172–7, are for cargoes, not voyages. Similarly, Minchinton, 'Metropolis', pp. 71–2 specifies voyages when in fact consignments are enumerated.

11 The problems of assessing contemporary tonnage is covered in Davis, *English shipping industry*, pp. 395–406; J.H. Andrews, 'English merchant shipping in 1701', *Mariner's Mirror*, XLI (1955), pp. 232–5; R.C. Jarvis, 'Ship registry, 1707–86', *Maritime History*, II (1972), pp. 151–67; M. Rediker, *Between the devil and the deep blue sea. Merchant seamen, pirates and the Anglo-American maritime world* (Cambridge, 1987), pp. 301–3; and J.J. McCusker,

'The tonnage of ships engaged in British colonial trade during the eighteenth century', *Research in Economic History*, 6 (1981), pp. 73–105.

12 Only Cardiff and Aberystwyth officers continued to note burden tonnage. For earlier assessments, see Hussey et al., *Summary*, pp. 50–2. Overseas port book data are criticised by Morgan, *Bristol*, p. 91.

13 See, J.A. Chartres, 'Road carrying in England in the seventeenth century: myth and reality', *EcHR*, 2nd ser. XXX (1977), pp. 73–94; G.L. Turnbull, 'Provincial road carrying in England in the eighteenth century', *Journal of Transport History*, 2nd ser. IV (1977), pp. 17–39; C.H. Wilson, 'Land carriage in the seventeenth century', *EcHR*, 2nd ser. XXXIII (1980), pp. 92–5; J.A. Chartres, 'On the road with Professor Wilson', *EcHR*, 2nd ser. XXXIII (1980), pp. 92–9; D. Gerhold, 'The growth of the London carrying trade, 1681–1838', *EcHR*, 2nd ser. XLI (1988), pp. 392–410; D. Gerhold, *Road transport before the railways: Russell's London Flying Wagons* (Cambridge, 1993); D. Gerhold, 'Packhorses and wheeled vehicles in England, 1550–1800', *Journal of Transport History*, 14 (1993), pp. 1–26; and D. Gerhold, 'Productivity change in road transport before and after turnpiking, 1690–1840', *EcHR*, XLIX (1996), pp. 491–515.

14 For the trade of Gloucester and the Severn ports, see Cox, Hussey and Milne, eds, *Database*; Hussey et al., *Summary,* and Wakelin, 'Pre-industrial trade', pp. 99–107.

15 The principal ports receiving coastal exports from Liverpool were: London (45 voyages); Chester (38); Mostyn (17); Poolton (15); Lancaster (11); and Yarmouth (9). Coastal imports came from: London (29 voyages); Chester (22); Pielfowdrey (21); and Yarmouth (9). See P.G.E. Clemens, 'The rise of Liverpool, 1665–1750', *EcHR*, 2nd ser. XXIX (1976), pp. 216–18; T.C. Barker, 'Lancashire coal, Cheshire salt and the rise of Liverpool', *Transactions of the Historical Society of Lancashire and Cheshire*, 103 (1951), pp. 83–6; J. Langton, 'Liverpool and its hinterland in the late eighteenth century', in J. Langton, ed., *Commerce, industry and transport: studies in economic change on Merseyside* (Liverpool, 1983); F. Vigier, *Change and apathy: Liverpool and Manchester during the industrial revolution* (Cambridge, Mass., 1971), pp. 36–61; and M. Power, 'Councillors and commerce in Liverpool, 1650–1750', *Urban History*, 24, 3 (1997), pp. 301–23.

16 See chapter 5 below and Hussey 'Coastal trade', pp. 102–82, 245–89; Wakelin 'Pre-industrial trade', pp. 113–18, 170–210; and Hussey et al., *Summary*, pp. 27–39.

17 Wakelin, 'Pre-industrial trade', ch. 3, Hussey et al., *Summary*, pp. 24–39.

18 Data from half-years are used to assess the role of Bristol. See appendix 1.

19 McGrath, *Merchant Venturers of Bristol*, p. 81 indicates the impact of war on the operation of the port of Bristol and the wider Bristol Channel.

20 Between 1680 and 1704, the trade of Newnham and Berkeley was recorded very erratically: Hussey et al., *Summary*, pp. 13, 25–6, 36–7; Cox, Hussey and Milne, eds, *Database*, pp. 9–10.

21 Wanklyn, 'Shrewsbury boats', pp. 34–58; Wanklyn, 'Bridgnorth', pp. 37–64; and Wanklyn, 'Impact of water transport facilities', pp. 1–19.

22 In 1699, 230 voyages were destined for Gloucester; a single voyage bound for Newnham; 23 for the Wye ports; and 29 for Cardiff (14 for the head port, 9 for Caerleon, 4 for Newport, and 2 for Aberthaw). See Wakelin, 'Pre-industrial trade', pp. 99–107 and Willan, *Coasting trade*, pp. 178–9 revised in Hussey, 'Coastal trade', pp. 70–5.

23 Twenty-five voyages discharged for London, eight for Liverpool, seven for Topsham, Exeter's deep-water out-port, and seven for Plymouth. For a comparative impression of trade at Exeter, see Hoskins, *Trade, industry and people* and Clark, *Exe estuary*, pp. 167–87, 220–22.

24 Minchinton, 'Metropolis', pp. 78–80; Willan, *Coasting trade*, pp. 171–8.

25 This is touched on by Grant, 'Devon shipping', pp. 130–8.

26 Jackson, *Hull in the eighteenth century*, pp. 141–2 provides more concrete examples of this trend in rentier shipowning.

27 Somerset RO DD/X/PG/1 W51/3/1, Sealey to Strange 16 December 1701. See also NDRO B69/38 p. 176 for the activities of Strange.

28 S. Ville, 'Total factor productivity in the English shipping industry, the north-east coal trade, 1700–1850', *EcHR*, 2nd ser. XXXIX (1986), pp. 360–1.

29 Armstrong, 'Significance of coastal shipping', pp. 81–2.

30 Jenkins, 'Redbrook', 145–67.

31 For coal see Hussey, 'Coastal trade', pp. 80–4, 290–5; Hatcher, *Coal industry*, pp. 79–83, 135–41, 567–71; Nef, *Coal industry*, pp. 52–6, 369–72; Rees, *Industry*, I, pp. 79–84; Symons, *Llanelli*, pp. 26–38; Trott, 'Neath', pp. 47–74; Willan, *Coasting trade*, pp. 113–18, 143–5; and Cox, Hussey and Milne, eds, *Database*.

32 Llanelli did not record destinations, although examination of the records of importing centres, where these exist, reveals a distinct correlation between the home port of vessels and place of importation.

33 See Nef, *Coal industry*, pp. 88–90.

34 See Nef, *Coal industry*, pp. 96–8, 107–8, 120–3, 442–8; Hatcher, *Coal industry*, pp. 178–81; Wakelin, 'Pre-industrial trade', pp. 135–7; and Wanklyn, 'Bridgnorth', pp. 53–4.

35 Armstrong and Bagwell, 'Coastal shipping', pp. 142–3; B. Dietz, 'The north-east coal trade, 1550–1750: measures, markets and the metropolis', *Northern History*, XXII (1985), pp. 280–94; and Ville, 'Total factor productivity', pp. 355–70.

36 The slight discrepancy between the figures presented here and in tables 2.1 and 2.2 represents delays between the issuing of customs documentation, and the times of clearance and unloading. Bristol, Swansea, Neath, South Burry, Llanelli and Cardiff have been omitted from the analysis because of the absence of inwards data.

37 Willan, *Coasting trade*, pp. 111, 171–80.

38 For comparative costs in the coastal trade see Willan, *Coasting trade*, pp. 17–9; Armstong, 'Significance of coastal shipping', pp. 75–8.

39 PRO E134 23&24 Charles II Hil 28, f. 5v. According to Thomas Games, a former purser to Bridgwater colliers, voyages could be completed in six days 'in seasonable weather', 'very frequently soe to have beene done' in eight days and a fortnight 'att some seasons of the yeare': PRO E134 24 Charles II East 24, f. 2v.

40 PRO C104/12 Pt 2, fos. 233r, 238v. Such provisions were the only items carried by the Company's coal vessels: none were listed in the port books as dutiable goods.

41 Willan, *Coasting trade*, pp. 113–18, 143–5; Dietz, 'North-east coal trade', pp. 280–5; Nef, *Coal industry*, pp. 79–83.

42 See E. Hughes, *Studies in administration and finance 1558–1825, with special reference to the history of salt taxation in England* (Manchester, 1934, repr. Philadelphia, 1980) and chapter 5 below.

43 PRO C104/12 Pt 1, f. 177v Watkins to Himan 20 June 1699.

44 Information from the port books and Somerset RO DD/X/PG/1 W 51/3/1 Sealey to Rogerson 6 January 1703.

45 The duties of the haven master, ballast master and quay warden are described in BRO 05056, fos 5–10r; and McGrath, 'Merchant Venturers and the port of Bristol', pp. 113–14, 121–8. For ballasting on the Severn, see PRO E134 4 William & Mary, Easter 29; PRO E134 10 George I, Easter 2; and Hussey et al, *Summary*, pp. 40–2.

46 Whetter, *Cornwall*, p. 118; J. Rowe, *Cornwall in the age of the industrial revolution* (Liverpool, 1953), p. 19.

47 The Carmarthen port books record the entry of the *Exchange* of Swansea under a coquet dated 9 August 1699 from Bristol to Swansea. See also H. Carter, 'The growth and decline of Welsh towns', in D. Moore, ed., *Wales in the eighteenth century* (Swansea, 1976), pp. 47–62 and Williams, 'Carmarthenshire's maritime trade', pp. 61–70.

48 Overseas figures are taken from Minchinton, ed., *Trade of Bristol*, p. 5; Minchinton, 'Port of Bristol', pp. 131–2; and McGrath, ed., *Merchants*, pp. 280–1. Coastal tonnages are derived from adjusted figures published by Barrett, *Bristol*, pp. 189–91 (coastal craft, 28 tons; Severn trows, 40 tons). See also Trinder, *Industrial revolution in Shropshire*, pp. 104–8 and Hussey, 'Coastal trade', pp. 226–34. Overseas burdens as per area of commerce: Minchinton, ed., *Trade of Bristol*, p. 5; Morgan, *Bristol*, pp. 13–15.

49 Minchinton, ed., *Trade of Bristol*, p. 171; Barrett, *Bristol*, pp. 189–91.

50 No attempt has been made to provide corrective adjustments for the likely omission of letpass cargoes If these factors are included, a further 250 voyages (perhaps 8,200 tons) may be added to the data. An arguably more indicative index of coasting are the Merchant Venturers' Anchorage figures levied on coasters from below the Holms, although these are not available until 1711–12 and survive in continuous series only from 1728–9. See Minchinton, ed., *Trade of Bristol*, p. 177; McGrath, 'Merchant Venturers and the port of Bristol', pp. 113–14.

51 Willan, *Coasting trade*, pp. 53–54, 172–3.

52 See P. Jenkins, 'Times and seasons: the cycle of the year in early modern Glamorgan', *Morgannwg*, XXX (1986), pp. 20–41; W.G. Hoskins, 'Harvest fluctuations and English economic history 1620–1759', *Agricultural History Review*, XVI (1968), pp. 15–31; and A.B. Appleby, 'Grain prices and subsistence crises in England and France, 1590–1740', *Journal of Economic History*, XXXIX (1979), pp. 865–87.

53 See Armstrong, 'Significance of coastal shipping', pp. 84–6.

54 BRO 04437(3) Quarter Sessions Minute Book, 1681–1705, fos 216v, 212r–213v; J.H. Matthews, ed., *Records of the county borough of Cardiff* (Cardiff, 1898–1911), II, p. 371. For wider impacts upon coasting, see J.D. Marshall, ed., *The autobiography of William Stout of Lancaster, 1665–1752* (Chetham Society, 3rd ser., 14, Manchester, 1967), pp. 94–5.

55 C. Wilson, *England's apprenticeship, 1603–1763* (1965), pp. 280–5; J.O. McLachlan, *Trade and peace with old Spain, 1667–1750* (1940), pp. 30–45, and Graph 1; A. Ayo-Ru, 'Anglo-Spanish trade through the port of Bilbao during the second half of the eighteenth century: some preliminary findings', *International Journal of Maritime History*, 4 (1992), pp. 193–217.

56 Somerset RO DD/DN 423, p. 66.

57 PRO C104/12 Pt. 1, fos 65r, 66r, 77v. In 1703, the mayor and magistrates of Bristol were warned that 'noe protections shall be granted to coasters, till one half of the number of seamen belonging to each port' was submitted to the press, BRO 04447(3) 4 Feb. 1703.

58 For a concise account of French privateering see P. Crowhurst, *The defence of British trade, 1689–1815* (1977), pp. 15–31. D.J. Starkey, *British privateering enterprise in the eighteenth century* (Exeter, 1990); J.W. Damer Powell, *Bristol privateers and ships of war* (Bristol, 1930); and Morgan, *Bristol*, pp. 19–22 provide details of regional craft and capital diverted into privateering.

59 BCL 11154 Petition of Merchant Venturers, 1691 fos 35–7; Petition of Merchant Venturers 1692, f. 41. M. Oppenheim, *The maritime history of Devon* (Exeter, 1968), p. 93.

60 PRO C104/12 Pt 2, f. 5r–v. Cockrem intended to deliver salt at Bridgwater, but may have settled for the safety of the convoy to Milford. He loaded coals and culm at Tenby for Ireland on 20 August (ibid., f. 28r).

61 On 19 September 1695 Alloway received £40 from Wheddon 'towards his pt of the ransom of the shipp Sattisfaction lately taken by a French privateere': Somerset RO DD/DN 463, p. 15.

62 Willan, *Coasting trade*, pp. 25–30 details many of the depredations faced by coasters in times of warfare. Nef, *Coal industry*, II, pp. 301–3 and Hatcher, *Coal industry*, pp. 478–81 discuss the effects of war upon prices and unit costs of coal.

63 Some 20 voyages cleared for London, 10 for Topsham, 3 for Falmouth, 2 for Plymouth and 1 for Poole. Nine voyages (8 to Liverpool, 1 to Poolton) were dispatched northwards.

64 BCL B11154, f. 62 and Latimer, *The annals of Bristol in the eighteenth century* (Bristol, 1893), p. 57 record the effects of the Great Storm on Bristol.

65 See Rees, *Industry*, pp. 526–48; Beynon, 'Lead mining industry'; Burt, 'Lead production', pp. 249–68; Lewis, *Lead mining in Wales;* and Lewis, 'Lead-mining in Cardiganshire', pp. 177–90.

66 Clemens, 'Liverpool', pp. 215–16.

67 In 1696, Bridgwater's coastal imports from extra-regional centres were from Liverpool (30 voyages) or Chester (1 voyage). Of the 29 shipments received by Bideford, Liverpool dispatched 25 and Chester 2. All 12 shipments discharging at Padstow in 1696 were from Liverpool.

68 Hughes, *Administration and finance*, pp. 225–40; Barker, 'Lancashire coal, Cheshire salt', pp. 83–8.

69 This was an accepted, if extraordinary, practice: Crouch, *Complete guide*, pp. 18, 38–9.

70 Smith and Buck were important Bideford merchants: NDRO BBT B6/7 f. 3r; NDRO 2379/A/Z/4); Watkins, *Bideford*, pp. 62–5. For Strange see note 26. Wadland was an established Bideford boat master and trader, see also NDRO BBT A1/a/8.

71 Hoon, *English Customs system*, pp. 267–8.

72 In 1700, Smith dispatched 10,900 lb of tobacco and John Daure dispatched, 1,576 lb to Exeter. A further 4,000 lb were also traded to Exeter. A single consignment of 3,000 lb was sent to nearby Clovelly.

73 Between 1722 and 1731, 8,450,427 lbs of tobacco were imported at Bideford (1,486,303 lb retained). In comparison, Barnstaple imported 5,045,377 lb (56,878 lb retained), whilst Bristol imported a massive 41,661,256 lb (25,262,964 lb retained): PRO T 1/278 f. 30 reproduced in Hoskins, *Industry, trade and people*, pp. 160, 162; Minchinton, ed., *Trade of Bristol*, p. 15; and Morgan, *Bristol*, pp. 152–60.

74 H.H. Lamb, *Climate, history and the modern world* (1982), p. 223; J.M. Stratton, *Agricultural records, A.D. 220–1977* (2nd edn, 1977), p. 61.

75 Somerset RO DD/DN 423, pp. 120, 123–4, 143.

76 Hussey, 'Coastal trade', pp. 92–6, 238–45; Minchinton, 'Metropolis', pp. 80–1; Morgan, *Bristol*, pp. 99–101; Sacks, *Widening gate*, pp. 78–9. For fair-related trade see BRO 00120; 00147–9; 00044; 04410; 04411; 04412.

77 PRO E134 23&24 Charles II Hil 18, f. 5v; Hussey, 'Coastal trade', pp. 267–79.

78 Somerset RO DD/DN 423, pp. 62, 107, 111, 125.

79 Hussey et al., *Summary*, p. 21; Barrett, *Bristol*, pp. 102–3; Minchinton, 'Metropolis', pp. 79–80; McGrath, *Merchant Venturers of Bristol*, pp. 70–81.

80 Hatcher, *Coal industry*, pp. 476–8. See also Nef, *Coal industry*, I, pp. 292–4 and, by way of contrast, Chartres's analysis of corn shipments from East Anglia to London: J.A.

Chartres, 'Trade and shipping in the port of London: Wiggins Quay in the later seventeenth century', *Journal of Transport History*, 3rd ser. I (1980), pp. 44–5.

81 See Willan, *Coasting trade*, pp. 35–42, 55–69; Nef, *Coal industry*, pp. 78–100; and Lewis, *Industry*, pp. 70–106. Evans's study is now somewhat dated and his figures are erratic: 'Welsh coal trade' pp. 59–63, 69–75, Appendix A. Symons's examination of Llanelli, though useful, is less concerned with trade: *Llanelli*, Appendix G, pp. 333–8.

82 Hatcher, *Coal industry*, pp. 346–9; Nef, *Coal industry*, I, pp. 136–7. See also Ville's useful comments regarding the linkage between productivity and the improvement of land-based facilities: 'Total factor productivity', pp. 362–5.

83 For the development of the south Wales coalfield see Hatcher, *Coal industry*, pp. 135–41; Nef, *Coal industry*, I, pp. 52–6; John, *South Wales*; Symons, *Llanelli*, pp. 30–6; and Edwards, 'Coal industry in Pembrokeshire', pp. 33–64.

84 Willan, *Coasting trade*, pp. 21–33; Hatcher, *Coal industry*, pp. 476–9.

85 PRO C104/12 Pt 1, fos 76r, 81r, 84r, 93r.

86 See J.F. Rees, *The story of Milford* (Cardiff, 1954), chs 1–2; and George, 'Pembrokeshire sea-trading', pp. 1–24.

87 Edwards, 'Coal industry in Pembrokeshire', pp. 43–4, 52–3.

88 Bettey, *Bristol observed*, pp. 68–9.

Chapter 3

1 See B.J. Atkinson, 'An early example of the decline of the industrial spirit? Bristol enterprise in the first half of the nineteenth century', *Southern History*, 9 (1987), pp. 71–89; C. Harvey and J. Press, 'Industrial change and the economic life of Bristol since 1800', in C. Harvey and J. Press, eds, *Studies in the business history of Bristol* (Bristol, 1988) pp. 1–24; M.J. Daunton, 'Towns and economic growth in eighteenth-century England', in P. Abrams and E.A. Wrigley, eds, *Towns and societies: essays in economic history and historical sociology* (Cambridge, 1978), pp. 266–9; and Morgan, 'Economic development', pp. 64–9.

2 Barrett, *Bristol*, p. 184. See also B. Cottle, 'Thomas Chatterton', in McGrath, ed., *Bristol in the eighteenth century*, pp. 98–9 and Barry, 'History and antiquities', pp. 55–81.

3 Morgan, 'Economic development', pp. 48–75.

4 Defoe, *Tour*, p. 362.

5 Willan, *Coasting trade*, p. 172.

6 Minchinton, 'Metropolis', p. 78.

7 Morgan, *Bristol*, p. 90.

8 Walker, *Bristol region*, pp. 206–8; E.L. Chappell, *History of the port of Cardiff* (Cardiff, 1939), ch. 1; Rees, *Cardiff*, pp. 50–4; Williams, 'Cardiff', pp. 74–97; G.H. Jenkins, *The foundations of modern Wales, 1642–1780. Volume 4* (Oxford, 1987), p. 129; Dawson, *Commerce and customs*, pp. 39–40; Rees, *The story of Milford*; George, 'Pembrokeshire sea-trading', pp. 1–39; Williams, 'Carmarthenshire's maritime trade', pp. 61–70; Williams, 'Economic and social history of Glamorgan', pp. 359–60; Williams, 'Commercial history of Glamorgan'; Williams, 'Further contributions to the commercial history of Glamorgan'; and Whetter, 'Cornish trade', pp. 402–3.

9 Willan, *Coasting trade*, chs V–VII; Nef, *Coal Industry*; and Gras, *English corn market* remain comprehensive overviews of these basic trades. See also Hatcher, *Coal Industry*, and J.A. Chartres, 'The marketing of agricultural produce, 1640–1750', in J.A. Chartres, ed.,

Agricultural markets and trade, 1500–1700: chapters from the agrarian history of England and Wales, 1500–1700, Volume 4 (Cambridge, 1990), pp. 160–255, for more recent revisions.

10 See Chartres, *Internal trade*, pp. 9–13, 34–8; Armstrong and Bagwell, 'Coastal shipping', p. 180; and Gerhold, 'Productivity change', pp. 491–515. For other goods, see Burt, 'Lead production', pp. 249–68; R. Burt, 'The international diffusion of technology in the early modern period: the case of the British non-ferrous mining industry', *EcHR*, 2nd ser. XLIV (1991), pp. 248–71; R. Burt, 'The transformation of the non-ferrous metals industry in the seventeenth and eighteenth century', *EcHR*, XLVIII (1995), pp. 23–45; Weatherill, *Pottery trade;* L.M. Weatherill, 'The growth of the pottery industry in England, 1660–1815: some new evidence and estimates', *Post-Medieval Archaeology*, 17 (1983), pp. 1–22; Grant, *North Devon pottery;* Bettey, 'Livestock trade', pp. 123–8; Woodward, '"Swords into ploughshares"', pp. 175–91.

11 For Cornwall, see M.A. Havinden, J. Queniart and J. Stanyer, eds, *Centre and Periphery: Brittany, Cornwall and Devon compared* (Exeter, 1991), introduction, and Payton, *Cornwall*, pp. 43–70. The undercapitalisation of south-west Wales is emphasised by D.W. Howell, *Patriarchs and Parasites: the gentry of south-west Wales in the eighteenth century* (Cardiff, 1986), pp. 91–110 and is central to Hechter's thesis: *Internal colonialism*. The agricultural and urban basis to Pembrokeshire and Carmarthenshire are covered in Jenkins, *Foundations of modern Wales*, pp. 88–90; Emery, 'Wales', pp. 393–6, 409–17; and Carter, 'Growth and decline of Welsh towns', pp. 47–62.

12 L. Weatherill, *Consumer behaviour and material culture, 1660–1760* (1988), chs 2–4, especially pp. 84–90; L. Weatherill, 'The meaning of consumer behaviour in late seventeenth- and early eighteenth-century England', in J. Brewer and R. Porter, eds, *Consumption and the world of goods* (1993), pp. 206–27; Shammas, *Pre-industrial consumer*, pp. 76–86; C. Shammas, 'Changes in English and Anglo-American consumption from 1550–1800', in Brewer and Porter, eds, *Consumption and the world of goods*, pp. 185–95. See also B. Lemire, 'Consumerism in pre-industrial and early industrial England: the trade in secondhand clothes', *Journal of British Studies*, 27 (1988), pp. 1–24; B. Lemire, *Fashion's favourite: the cotton trade and the consumer in Britain, 1660–1800* (Oxford, 1991), pp. 186–94; and M. Spufford, *The great re-clothing of rural England: petty chapmen and their wares in the seventeenth century* (Cambridge, 1984) for trading networks.

13 Wakelin, 'Pre-industrial trade', pp. 123–69; Wakelin and Hussey, 'Investigating regional economies', pp. 19–21; Wanklyn, 'Shrewsbury boats', pp. 44–53; Wanklyn, 'Bridgnorth', pp. 37–41; Wanklyn, 'Impact of water transport facilities', pp. 1–19; Cox, Hussey and Milne, eds, *Database*.

14 The quote is from Chartres, *Internal trade*, pp. 36–7, 43. See also critiques in Gerhold, 'Productivity change', pp. 491–5; Armstrong, 'Significance of coastal shipping', pp. 71–3; and Jackson, *Hull in the eighteenth century*, pp. 75–6, 84–9 for the comparative role of transport systems. B. Trinder and J. Cox, *Yeomen and colliers in Telford: the probate inventories of Dawley, Lilleshall, Wellington and Wrockwardine 1660–1750* (1980), pp. 20–41 and Weatherill, *Consumer behaviour*, pp. 209–14 indicate the market penetration of such goods.

15 Morgan, *Bristol*, p. 90.

16 Hussey, 'Coastal trade', pp. 104–15; Wakelin, 'Pre-industrial trade', pp. 124–8.

17 Andrews, 'Chepstow', pp. 95–107.

18 See Clemens, 'Liverpool', pp. 211–25; Barker, 'Lancashire coal, Cheshire salt', pp. 83–101; and Power, 'Councillors and commerce', pp. 301–5.

19 Power suggests that an early concentration on transatlantic trade characterised the development of Liverpool, 'Councillors and commerce', pp. 311–15.

20 See R.S. Craig, 'Shipping and shipbuilding in the port of Chester in the eighteenth and early nineteenth centuries', *Transactions of the Historical Society of Lancashire and Cheshire*, 116 (1964); R.S. Craig, 'Some aspects of the trade and shipping of the river Dee in the eighteenth century', *Transactions of the Historical Society of Lancashire and Cheshire*, 115 (1963); Jarvis, 'Head port of Chester', pp. 69–84; R.C. Jarvis, 'Some records of the port of Lancaster', *Transactions of the Lancashire and Cheshire Antiquarian Society*, LVII (1945–6), pp. 117–58; and M. Elder, *The slave trade and the economic development of 18th century Lancaster* (Halifax, 1992).

21 The system is detailed in Hussey, 'Coastal trade', pp. 115–17 and Wakelin, 'Pre-industrial trade', pp. 85–7, 130–3. Ambiguous items such as 'ware', 'all sorts of goods', 'corn etc.', have been excluded. For further thoughts on commodities and data analysis, see Milne and Paul, 'Flexible model', pp. 114–15; N.C. Cox, 'Objects of worth, objects of desire: towards a dictionary of traded goods and commodities, 1550–1800', *Material History Review*, 39 (1994), pp. 24–40; and Cox, Hussey and Milne, eds, *Database*, glossary. The problems of classification are not wholly confined to goods: see J. Stobart, 'Shopping streets as social space: leisure, consumerism and improvement in an eighteenth-century county town', *Urban History*, 25, 1 (1998), p. 21 for a recent attempt to group occupational data.

22 Lignum vitae was the product of the Guaiacum and used extensively for medicinal purposes and as an 'incomparable' material for small turned goods: J. Houghton, *A collection for the improvement of husbandry and trade* (1727–8), III, p. 521.

23 Spanish wool was in great demand by provincial clothiers: Bowden, *Wool trade*, pp. 27, 46–8, 182–3, 216; Mann, *Cloth industry*, pp. 7, 11, 14, 30–1, 266. A different perspective is given by R.P. Carlen, 'The Spanish wool trade, 1500–1780', *Journal of Economic History*, 42 (1982), pp. 775–96, and for a rather earlier period, J.I. Israel, 'Spanish wool exports and the European economy 1610–1640', *EcHR*, 2nd ser. XXXIII (1980), pp. 193–210.

24 Malt (mostly malted barley) was generally carried in conjunction with other crops. Where multiple descriptions occur, as in 'malt, wheat and oats', quantities have been divided equally amongst the main constituents. With measures, evidence suggests that the Winchester bushel was the 'ordinary . . . measure by which corn [was] usually sold by in market' throughout Gloucestershire and the Severn Valley: J. Thirsk and J. P. Cooper, eds, *Seventeenth-century economic documents* (Oxford, 1972), p. 370. None the less, substantial differences existed between regional bushels. Harrison suggests a bushel twice the size of the 56 lb/8 gallon Winchester bushel was in use in Devon: G.V. Harrison, 'Agricultural weights and measures', in J. Thirsk, ed., *The agrarian history of England and Wales. Volume V: 1640–1750. ii: Agrarian change* (Cambridge, 1985), p. 817. Barnstaple, Bideford and Ilfracombe occasionally recorded official 'Winchesters' or 'Winchester measure bushels' separately. At Exeter, the 8 gallon standard was in general force: Houghton, *Husbandry*, I, p. 132. A 21 gallon bushel employed 'usually' at Falmouth may have applied to the Cornish ports, although this again is conjectural: *ibid.* General conversions are taken from R.E. Zupko, *A dictionary of English weights and measures* (Madison, 1968); Harrison, 'Agricultural weights and measures', pp. 815–25; and Houghton, *Husbandry*, I, pp. 132–4, and III, p. 46.

25 Harrison, 'South-west', pp. 365–6; M.A. Havinden and R. Stanes, 'Agriculture in south west England', in Havinden, Queniart, and Stanyer, eds, *Centre and Periphery*, pp. 143–4; Stanes, 'Devon agriculture', pp. 43–65; and N.J.G. Pounds, 'Food production and distribution in pre-industrial Cornwall', in W. Minchinton, ed., *Population and marketing: two studies in the history of the south-west* (Exeter Papers in Economic History, 11, Exeter, 1976), pp. 110–22.

26 See J. Thirsk, ed., *The agrarian history of England and Wales. Volume V: 1640–1750. I: Regional farming systems*; Thirsk, *Agricultural regions*, pp. 10–55; and Overton, *Agricultural revolution*, pp. 46–62. Chartres, 'The marketing of agricultural produce in metropolitan western England'; J.A. Chartres, 'Food consumption and internal trade', in A.L. Beier and R. Finlay, eds, *London 1500–1700: the making of the metropolis* (1986), pp. 168–98; and J.A. Chartres, 'Market integration and agricultural output in seventeenth-, eighteenth-, and early nineteenth-century England', *Agricultural History Review*, 43 (1995), pp. 117–38 indicate the operation of major cities upon patterns of agrarian production and marketing.

27 In 1543, Bristol was allowed by statute (34 & 35 Henry VIII, ch. 9) to engross all supplies of corn carried on the Severn, a contingency only effectively used in times of dearth. See Estabrook, *Urbane and rustic England*, pp. 21–2.

28 See chapter 2 for details of coastal embargo in the Bristol Channel. McGrath, *Merchant Venturers of Bristol*, pp. 80–1 and McGrath, *Records relating to the Society of Merchant Venturers*, pp. 193–8 give examples of requests for convoy protection. Stout indicates that malt was used for the production of domestic spirits: Marshall, ed., *Stout*, pp. 94–5.

29 See Day, *Bristol brass*, pp. 22–6; Day, 'The Costers', pp. 48–58; J. Day, 'Copper, brass, and zinc production', in J. Day and R.F. Tylecote, eds, *The industrial revolution in metals* (1992), pp. 145–63; Jenkins, 'Redbrook', pp. 145–67; C. Hart, *The industrial history of Dean, with an introduction to its industrial archaeology* (Newton Abbot, 1971), pp. 104–12; Burt, 'Lead production, p. 258; Burt, 'Non-ferrous metals industry', p. 35; Hussey, 'Coastal trade', 137–9. Latten, or sheet brass, was a speciality of Redbrook: Cox, Hussey and Milne, eds, *Database*, glossary.

30 For the importance of the midland hardware area see Wanklyn, 'Impact of water transport facilities', pp. 1–9; W.H.B. Court, *The rise of the Midland industries 1600–1838* (Oxford, 1938), pp. 218–20; M.B. Rowlands, *Masters and men in the West Midlands metalware trades before the industrial revolution* (Manchester, 1975), pp. 127–35; M.B. Rowlands, 'Continuity and change in an industrialising society: the case of the West Midlands industries', in P. Hudson, ed., *Regions and industries: a perspective on the industrial revolution in Britain* (Cambridge, 1989), pp. 103–31; and M. Berg, *The age of manufactures: industry, innovation and work in Britain, 1700–1820* (2nd edn, 1994), pp. 255–68. The emergence of Shrewsbury as a centre of leisure is discussed in McInnes, 'Shrewsbury', pp. 53–65. Worcester, which acted in a very similar fashion, awaits further study, but see G. Talbut, 'Worcester as an industrial and commercial centre 1660–1750', *Transactions of the Worcestershire Archaeological Society*, 3rd ser. 10 (1986), pp. 91–102.

31 Grant, *North Devon pottery*. See below for analysis.

32 Woodward, "Swords into ploughshares" and Lemire 'Consumerism', pp. 1–4 indicate the important trade in old metalwares, clothing and rags. J. Thirsk, 'The fantastical folly of fashion: the English stocking knitting industry, 1500–1700', in J. Thirsk, *The rural economy of England* (1984), pp. 235–58 provides a discussion of stocking-knitting. For a wider perspective see Berg, *Age of manufactures*, pp. 66–72.

33 See Wanklyn, 'Shrewsbury boats'; T.C. Mendenhall, *The Shrewsbury drapers and the Welsh wool trade in the sixteenth and seventeenth centuries* (Oxford, 1953); Talbut, 'Worcester', pp. 91–102; and Kerridge, *Textile manufactures*, pp. 21–2, 86–8, 144–8, 182–3.

34 Hoskins, *Industry, trade and people*, pp. 28–44, 62–9; Clark, *Exe estuary*, pp. 96–123; Kerridge, *Textile manufactures*, p. 18.

35 Hart, *Industrial history of Dean*, pp. 322–3, 328; and C.E. Hart, *Royal forest: a history of Dean's woods as producers of timber* (Oxford, 1966), chs 5–7; Chartres, 'Marketing of agricultural produce, 1640–1750', pp. 245–6. Wood and timber was carried on 42 per

cent of voyages entering Gloucester from Chepstow, 73 per cent entering Bridgwater, and on all shipments that discharging at Ilfracombe, Barnstaple, Bideford and Carmarthen. For wood unrecorded and used as ballast see Somerset RO D/B/bw 1895; Q/Rua 12–14; DD/L 1 58/15, pp. 12–4; DD/L 1 55/2; DD/WY bx 41; NDRO BBT B6/7 fos 2v, 3v.

36 As non-dutiable goods, fish did not have to progress under coquet and bond: A. Grant, 'Port books as a source for the maritime history of Devon', in D. Starkey, ed., *Sources for a new maritime history of Devon* (Exeter, 1987), p. 62.

37 See Defoe, *Tour*, p. 242. See also R.P. Chope, ed., *Early tours in Devon and Cornwall* (1918, repr. Newton Abbot, 1967), pp. 178–215, 215–33; Scantlebury, 'Pilchard fishery', pp. 330–59; Whetter, *Cornwall*, pp. 200–6; Whetter, 'Cornish trade', pp. 405–7; Southward, et al, 'Herring and pilchard fisheries', pp. 37–8; and J. Palmer, ed., *Cornwall, the Canaries and the Atlantic. The letter book of Valentine Enys, 1704–1719* (Exeter, 1997), pp. 22–3.

38 The herring barrel usually held 30 gallons, although the ale barrel of 32 gallons was used occasionally. Conversions have followed Zupko, *Dictionary*, pp. 15–16, 96–7, 104, except in the case of the 'last', where Houghton's contemporary conversion of 10 barrels is adopted: *Husbandry*, III, p. 569. Loose fish have been reckoned at 1,000 to a barrel: ibid., I, pp. 132–4.

39 The importance of the trade to Minehead, Watchet and Porlock is revealed in Somerset RO DD/L 1 55/3 petition for extension of quay duties, 1749; Somerset RO T/PH/gc 10; copies of Gloucester RO D1799 E158, f. 1.

40 Plymouth took 1,080 barrels (1,050 from Ilfracombe, 30 from Bideford); Falmouth 932 barrels (622 from Ilfracombe, 250 from Mount's Bay and 60 from Bideford); Looe 447 barrels (from Bideford); Dartmouth 202 barrels (142 from Ilfracombe, 60 from Milford); Exeter 125 barrels (from Milford); London 72 barrels (from Milford); Liverpool 22.5 barrels (from Milford); Whitehaven 5 barrels (from Milford); and Cowes 2 barrels (from Bristol).

41 Whetter, 'Trade of Cornwall', p. 114.

42 PRO C104/12 Pt 1, f. 158r Galpine to Dyer in Barbados. Houghton emphasises that red herring and pilchard were frequently exported to the Mediterranean and 'especially Spain': *Husbandry*, III, pp. 547–9.

43 Latimer, *Bristol in the eighteenth century*, p. 88. The Barnstaple bye-laws of 1690 emphasise that herrings brought by coastal vessels must be retailed directly 'out of the boats' or at the appointed fish market and not until the day after landing: NDRO B1/1603, pp. 9–10. See also W.H. Chaloner, 'Trends in fish consumption', in T.C. Barker, J.C. Mackenzie and J. Yudkin, eds, *Our changing fare: two hundred years of British food habits* (1966), p. 111; J. Rule, 'The home market and the sea fisheries of Devon and Cornwall in the nineteenth century', in W.E. Minchinton, ed., *Population and marketing. Two studies in the history of the south-west* (Exeter Papers in Economic History, 11, Exeter, 1976), pp. 123–39; and W.M. Stern, 'Fish marketing in London in the first half of the eighteenth century', in D.C. Coleman and A.H. John, eds, *Trade, government and economy in pre-industrial England: essays presented to F.J. Fisher* (1976), pp. 68–77.

44 R.G. Lounsbury, *The British fishery at Newfoundland, 1634–1763* (New Haven, 1934), pp. 135–42; Davis, *English shipping industry*, pp. 235–6; H.A. Innis, *The cod fisheries: the history of an international economy* (New Haven and Toronto, 1940), pp. 102–11; J.R. Coull, *The fisheries of Europe: an economic geography* (1972), pp. 75–80; H.E.S. Fisher, 'The south-west & the Atlantic trades, 1660–1760', in H.E.S. Fisher, ed., *The south-west and the sea* (Exeter Papers in Economic History, 1, Exeter, 1968), pp. 7–14; Watkins, *Bideford*, pp. 58–62; and Starkey, 'Newfoundland trade', pp. 163–71.

45 Innes enumerates 207 ships clearing Newfoundland ports in 1698–1701, of which 51 were from regional ports (30 from Bideford; 12 from Barnstaple; 8 from Bristol and a single voyage from Bridgwater). Only five shipments, where destinations were specified, were bound directly for domestic ports, the remainder discharged at Mediterranean ports: *Cod fisheries*, pp. 140–3. Compare tables 22.3 and 22.4 in Starkey, 'Newfoundland trade', pp. 167–8.

46 BRO AC B 64, f. 34 r–v, account book of Anthony Varder, senior; and NDRO B69/38 pp. 1, 45, 144, 162, 171, account book of unnamed London merchant, illustrate the independent nature of the Newfoundland cod trade with Genoa and Leghorn. Hoare and Company maintained a vigorous correspondence with factors in St Johns and Oporto in the trade in fish. PRO C/104/12 Pt 1, fos 154r, 174v, 179r. H.E.S. Fisher, *The Portugal trade. A study of Anglo-Portuguese commerce 1700–1770* (1971), pp. 17–8, 71–6 gives a later perspective of the role of west-country merchants in importing cod. See also F. Braudel, *Civilization and capitalism, fifteenth-eighteenth century. Volume II: the wheels of commerce* (trans. S. Reynolds, 1983), pp. 141, 211–14.

47 Bideford exported 48 barrels to Bristol and 4 to Bridgwater. Of the 282 barrels clearing Bristol, 202 were destined for Severn ports, 60 for Liverpool and London. All conversions are to the herring barrel as above.

48 Minchinton, 'Metropolis', pp. 73–81.

49 See F.J. Fisher, 'The development of the London food market, 1540–1640', *EcHR*, II (1935), pp. 56–7; F.J. Fisher., 'The development of London as a centre of conspicuous consumption in the sixteenth and seventeenth centuries', in E.M. Carus-Wilson, ed., *Essays in economic history*, II (1962), pp. 197–207; E.A. Wrigley, 'A simple model of London's importance in changing English society and economy, 1650–1750', *Past and Present*, 37 (1967), pp. 44–60; Chartres, 'Food, consumption and internal trade', pp. 177–82, 184–6. The political dimension is explored by D.R. Ringrose, 'Metropolitan cities as parasites', in Aerts and Clark, eds. *Metropolitan cities and their hinterlands*, pp. 21–38.

50 J. Latimer, *The annals of Bristol in the seventeenth century* (Bristol, 1900), pp. 72, 365. BRO 04264(8), fos 215r–216r; BRO 64274(2) Book of Ordinances, fos 28, 86, 91.

51 Nef, *Coal industry*, I, pp. 96–98, 107–8, 120–3, 442–8; Hatcher, *Coal industry*, pp. 178–81.

52 Bristol exported 6 tons of tobacco pipe clay to Bridgwater (1 shipment); 6.5 tons to Caerleon (3 shipments); 0.5 ton to Chepstow (1 shipment); 4 tons to Gloucester (2 shipments); and 0.625 tons to Minehead (1 shipment). Some 10 voyages carrying 215 tons cleared Bideford for Bristol and a further 38 tons in two shipments cleared Barnstaple in 1699.

53 R. Plot, *The natural history of Staffordshire* (Oxford, 1686), pp. 121–2; Court, *Midland industries*, pp. 127–8, 130; T.R. Nash, *Collections for the history and antiquities of Worcestershire* (1781–99), II, p. 212; Willan, *Coasting trade*, pp. 155, 173; Rees, *Industry*, II, p. 558. For conversions: Zupko, *Dictionary*, pp. 78–9.

54 Broseley was also a major producer of pipes. Many were shipped on Upton-on-Severn boats to south Wales: Wakelin, 'Pre-industrial trade', pp. 161–3. Barnstaple and to a lesser extent Bideford also maintained a trade in pipes: Grant and Jemmett, 'Pipes and pipe-making in Barnstaple', pp. 439–553. In contrast, the Bristol pipe industry appears to have been geared for the overseas market: J.E. Pritchard, 'Tobacco pipes of Bristol in the seventeenth century and their makers', *TBGAS*, XLV (1924), pp. 165–91; Jackson and Price, 'Bristol clay pipes'; R. Price, R. Jackson and P. Jackson, *Bristol clay pipe makers: a revised and enlarged edition* (Bristol, 1979); I.C. Walker, *Clay tobacco pipes, with particular*

reference to the Bristol industry (Ottawa, 1977). See also R. Jackson, P. Jackson and R. Price, 'Bristol potters and potteries, 1600–1800', *Journal of Ceramic History*, 12 (1982).

55 H.E. Matthews, ed., *Proceedings, minutes and enrolments of the Company of Soapmakers* (BRS, X, 1940); J. Somerville, *Christopher Thomas soapmaker of Bristol: the story of Christopher Thomas & Bros, 1745–1954* (Bristol, 1991); S.J. Diaper, 'Christopher Thomas & Brothers Ltd: the last Bristol soapmakers. An aspect of Bristol's economic development in the nineteenth century', *TBGAS*, CV (1987), pp. 223–32; BRO 64274(2) Book of Ordinances, 1702, 31 n.53.

56 For the trade in Castile and overseas soap, see NDRO B69/38 f. 152r; BRO 04439(3), f. 16r. Levels of domestic demand and hygiene are considered by Houghton, *Husbandry*, I, p. 133.

57 W. St C. Baddeley, 'A glass house at Nailsworth (sixteenth and seventeenth century)', *TBGAS*, XLII (1920), pp. 89–95; F. Buckley, 'The early glass-houses of Bristol', *Journal of the Society of Glass Technology*, 9 (1925), pp. 36–61; A.C. Powell, 'Glass making in Bristol', *TBGAS*, XLVII (1925), pp. 211–57; C. Weeden, 'The Bristol glass industry', *Glass Technology*, 24, 5 (1983), pp. 251–5; C. Weeden, 'Bristol glassmakers: their role in an emergent industry', *Bristol Industrial Archaeological Society Journal*, 17 (1984), pp. 24–5; and C. Witt, C. Weeden and A. P. Schwind, eds, *Bristol glass* (Bristol, 1984).

58 See Zupko, *Dictionary*, pp. 25, 78–9 for conversions.

59 J.H. Bettey, 'A Bristol glassworks in the eighteenth century', in P.V. McGrath, ed., *A Bristol miscellany* (BRS, XXXVIII, 1985), pp. 16–20. For sand as ballast, see Somerset RO DD/WY/BX 40, presentment of Watchet court leet, 1686; NDRO B1/1603, byelaws of Barnstaple Borough council, 1690, p. 7; NDRO BI/2555, Barnstaple Receiver's Account, 1698/9, 3 August 1699; and NDRO 2239/B/add 5/m 1, Northam harbour, p. 2 nos 9–10.

60 Glass bottles were generally traded in dozens. A 'naive' dozen of 12 is adopted for the purposes of conversions. Some 4,722 dozen were dispatched to Severn ports; 3,649 dozen to other regional centres; and 6,329 dozen to extra-regional ports. See Bettey, 'Bristol glassworks', p. 16.

61 H.W. Woodward, 'The glass industry of the Stourbridge district', *West Midlands Studies*, 8 (1976), pp. 36–42.

62 Court, *Midland industries*, p. 124.

63 See E.S. Godfrey, *The development of English glassmaking, 1560–1640* (Oxford, 1975) and D.W. Crossley, 'The performance of the glass industry in sixteenth century England', *EcHR*, 2nd ser. XXV (1972), pp. 421–33 for the impact of distribution and trade upon the early development of the industry.

64 Johnson, 'Foley partnerships', pp. 322–40; B.L.C. Johnson, 'The midland iron industry in the early eighteenth century', *Business History*, 2 (1960), pp. 67–74; B.L.C. Johnson, 'The Stour valley iron industry in the late seventeenth century', *Transactions of the Worcestershire Archaeological Society*, new ser. 27 (1950), pp. 35–46; Johnson, 'Charcoal iron industry', pp. 167–77; G. Hammersley, 'The charcoal iron industry and its fuel, 1540–1750', *EcHR*, 2nd ser. XXVI (1973), pp. 593–613; Rowlands, 'Continuity and change', pp. 113–23; and P. Riden, 'The output of the British iron industry before 1870', *EcHR*, XXX (1977), pp. 442–8.

65 T.S. Ashton, *Iron and steel in the industrial revolution* (Manchester, 1924), p. 242; Minchinton, 'Metropolis', p. 82.

66 Conversions to the standard ton of 2,240 lb have followed Zupko, *Dictionary*. Weights of individual items of ironware are taken from the account books of Abraham Darby

(Shropshire RO, MS329–333); Thomas Goldney (Wiltshire CRO 473/295, esp. fos 1–25, also Stembridge, *Goldney: Bristol merchant dynasty*, pp. 137–42 for transcripts); and Graffin Prankard (Somerset RO DD/DN 423, also J.H. Bettey, 'Graffin Prankard, an eighteenth century Bristol merchant', *Southern History*, 12 (1990), pp. 34–47).

67 Cox, 'Imagination', pp. 132–9.

68 See W.E. Minchinton, *The British tinplate industry* (Oxford, 1957), pp. 16–20 and W.E. Minchinton, 'The diffusion of tinplate manufacture', *EcHR*, 2nd ser. IX (1956–57), p. 352.

69 Hussey, 'Coastal trade', ch. 5.

70 Dean iron was often shipped eastwards through Ashleworth and southwards through Lydney: Johnson, 'The charcoal iron industry in the early eighteenth century', pp. 167–77; Johnson, 'The Foley partnerships', pp. 322–40; Cox, Hussey and Milne, eds, *Database*, pp. 8–9.

71 Somerset RO DD/DN 424, Prankard to Martin, 17 October 1728; Prankard to Mansell, 19 October 1728; Prankard to Machin, 19 November 1728; Prankard to Machin?, 5 December 1728. Beale operated or chartered 12 trows undertaking 46 inwards voyages in 1728. The four main trowmen undertook 31 of these shipments.

72 See Day, *Bristol brass*, pp. 27–34; and W.D. Avery, 'Brass and copper traffic on the river Severn, 1660–1760', unpublished B.A. dissertation, Department of History, University of Birmingham (1990), pp. 42–6. The development of Chepstow as a major shipper of copper is covered by Jenkins, 'Redbrook'; pp. 145–8; Day, 'The Costers'; pp. 47–50; and Day, 'Copper, brass, and zinc production', pp. 145–63.

73 Lewis, *Lead mining in Wales*, pp. 74–91; J.W. Gough, *The mines of Mendip* (Oxford, 1930, repr., Newton Abbot, 1967), pp. 157–205; Burt, 'Lead production', pp. 249–68.

74 Burt, 'Lead production', p. 258; Willan, *Coasting Trade*, pp. 72–3, 181–2; Burt, 'Non-ferrous metals industry', p. 35.

75 Willan remarks that cheese was carried to London in this fashion in the later seventeenth century, *River Navigation*, p. 2.

76 Ponting, *Woollen industry*, pp. 41–5; Mann, *Cloth industry*, ch. 1; Walker, *Bristol region*, pp. 206–12. For forms of Bristol-made and traded textile see Kerridge, *Textile manufacture*, pp. 103–4, 120, 123–4, 145–7.

77 BRO 04264(9), p. 37.

78 Mann, *Cloth industry*, pp. 282–4; J.G. Jenkins, 'The woollen industry', in D. Moore, ed., *Wales in the eighteenth century* (Swansea, 1976), pp. 96–7, 107.

79 All figures are converted from the 'hundred' of 100 items. For the trade in deals see H.S.K. Kent, 'The Anglo-Norwegian timber trade in the eighteenth century', *EcHR*, 2nd ser. VIII (1955–6), pp. 62–74.

80 A.L. Simon, *History of the wine trade in England*, 3 vols, (1906–9); McLachlan, *Trade and peace with old Spain*, pp. 40–2; Fisher, *Portugal trade*, 77–86; G.F. Steckley, 'The wine economy of Tenerife in the seventeenth century: Anglo-Spanish partnership in a luxury trade', *EcHR*, 2nd ser. XXXIII (1980), pp. 335–50; A. Crawford, *Bristol and the wine trade* (BHA, 57, 1984); and Sacks, *Widening gate*, pp. 24–36, 55. See also Braudel, *Wheels of commerce*, p. 229 and F. Braudel, *The Mediterranean and the Mediterranean world in the age of Phillip II* (trans. S. Reynolds, 1972), I, pp. 442–3.

81 Brewing was fairly small-scale at Bristol: P. Mathias, *The brewing industry in England, 1700–1830* (Cambridge, 1959), pp. 193–4; and G. Channon, 'Georges and brewing in Bristol', in C. Harvey and J. Press, eds, *Studies in the business history of Bristol* (Bristol, 1988), pp. 167–71. For spa waters, see T. Fawcett, 'Selling the Bath waters: medicinal

propaganda at an eighteenth century spa', *PSANHS*, 134 (1990), pp. 193–206; R.S. Neale, 'Bath: ideology and utopia' in Borsay, ed., *The eighteenth century town*, pp. 225–7; R.S. Neale, *Bath 1650–1850. A social history, or a valley of pleasure yet a sink of iniquity* (1981), pp. 13–18; B. Cunliffe, *The city of Bath* (Stroud, 1986, repr. 1990), pp, 105–7, 112–3; S. McIntyre, 'Bath: the rise of a resort town', 1660–1800', in P. Clark, ed., *Country towns in pre-industrial England* (Leicester, 1981), pp. 197–249; and S. McIntyre. 'The mineral water trade in the eighteenth century', *Transport History*, II (1973), pp. 12–5. For the link between spa water and the glass industry see Bettey, 'Bristol glassworks', p. 17

82	Quoted in Waite, 'Bristol Hotwell', p. 114 and McIntyre, 'Mineral water trade', pp. 1–2.

83	Somerset RO DD/DN 423, p. 64.

84	Fawcett, 'Selling the Bath waters', p. 195.

85	Data from McIntrye, 'Mineral water trade', pp. 4–5, 12–3. The following conversions, based on the basket of 6 gallons and using volumetric data derived from the port books, apply: bag (0.5 baskets); barrel (5.25); box (3); butt (21); case (3.5); cask (5); crate (3); hamper (1); hogshead (10.5); maund (1.33); rundlet (2); small cask (2.5); and tierce (7). Between 12 and 30 bottles were carried per basket: a median figure of 20 has been applied in all conversions.

86	See above for conversions. Mixed cargoes have been divided into 'naive' halves.

87	Bewdley boats carried over half (412 baskets) the water traded in 1724: Cox, Hussey and Milne, eds, *Database*.

88	Shammas, *Pre-industrial consumer*, pp. 78–81; Shammas, 'English and Anglo-American consumption', pp. 178–85.

89	For domestic production see I.V. Hall, 'A history of the sugar trade in England with special attention to the sugar trade of Bristol', unpublished M.A. thesis, University of Bristol (1925), pp. 50–2, 69–72; I.V. Hall, 'John Knight, Junior, sugar refiner at the Great House on St Augustine's Back (1654–1679), Bristol's second sugar house', *TBGAS*, LXVIII (1949), pp. 110–64; I.V. Hall, 'Temple Street sugar house under the first partnership of Richard Lane and John Hine (1662–78)', *TBGAS*, LXXVI (1957), pp. 118–40; I.V. Hall, 'Whitson Court sugar house, Bristol, 1665–1824', *TBGAS*, LXV (1944), pp. 1–97; I.V. Hall, 'The Daubenys. Part 1', *TBGAS*, LXXXIV (1966), pp. 113–40; and R. Stiles, 'The Old Market sugar refinery: 1680–1908', *Bristol Industrial Archaeological Society Journal*, 2 (1969), pp. 10–12. Morgan, *Bristol*, pp. 184–217; R. Pares, *West India fortune* (1950); R. Pares, 'The London sugar market 1740–69', *EcHR,* 2nd ser. IX (1956–7), pp. 254–70; and J.R. Ward, 'The profitability of sugar planting in the British West Indies, 1650–1834', *EcHR*, 2nd ser. XXXI (1978), pp. 197–213 discuss patterns of overseas trade. For a wider perspective, see T.C. Smout, 'The early Scottish sugar houses 1660–1720', *EcHR*, 2nd ser. XIV (1961–2), pp. 240–69; R. Stein, 'The French sugar business in the eighteenth century: a quantitative study' *Business History*, XXII (1980), pp. 3–17; and Braudel, *Wheels of commerce*, pp. 190–4, 272–80. Mintz's work remains, however, the best overarching analysis of the uptake of sugar: S.W. Mintz, *Sweetness and power: the place of sugar in modern history* (New York, 1985) and S.W. Mintz, 'The changing roles of food in the study of consumption', in J. Brewer and R. Porter, eds, *Consumption and the world of goods* (1993), pp. 260–73. Indices of sugar and rum imports are provided by Shammas, *Pre-industrial consumer,* pp. 81–3.

90	Somerset RO DD/X/PG/1 W51/3/1, 5 January 1702/3, Sealey to Gibbs and Brinley; 15 February 1702/3, Sealey to Gibbs and Brinley; 31 March 1703, Sealey to Bartlett. See also Hall, 'Daubenys: Part 1', pp. 123–4.

91	Conversions are from Hussey, 'Coastal trade', p. 139 and Zupko, *Dictionary*, pp. 33–4, 78–9.

92 See chapter 1. The coastal port books were reorganised in 1692. By 1728 it is likely that the redrawing of the limits of the Severn to non-excisable goods had been adopted informally.

93 For statistics see J.M. Price and P.G.E. Clemens, 'A revolution of scale in overseas trade: British firms in the Chesapeake trade, 1675–1775', *Journal of Economic History*, XLVII (1987), pp. 5, 24–8, 39–40; K.O. Morgan, 'Bristol and the Atlantic trade in the eighteenth century', *English Historical Review*, CVII, (1992) pp. 642–6; Morgan, *Bristol*, pp. 152–60; J. Goodman, *Tobacco in history: the cultures of dependence* (1993), pp. 70–5, 82–3; Wakelin, 'Pre-industrial trade', pp. 211–54; C.M. MacInnes, *The early English tobacco trade* (1926), ch. 4; MacInnes, *Gateway of Empire,* pp. 248–54; Shammas, *Pre-industrial consumer*, pp. 70–8; and Shammas, 'English and Anglo-American consumption', pp. 178–81.

94 Evasion is covered by Nash, 'English and Scottish tobacco trades', pp. 354–372; A. Rive, 'A short history of tobacco smuggling', *EcHR*, I (1929), pp. 544–69; Hoon, *English customs system*, pp. 152–3, 169–70, 261–2; Morgan, *Bristol*, pp. 155–8. Conversions follow Hussey, 'Coastal trade', pp. 139–42, n. 97 and Zupko, *Dictionary*. See also Clemens, 'Liverpool', p. 215; and Price and Clemens, 'Revolution of scale', pp. 25–7.

95 London received 66,194 lb, Liverpool 9,968 lb and Whitehaven 7,442 lb. See Clemens, 'Liverpool', pp. 215–17, 223; J.V. Beckett, *Coal and tobacco: the Lowthers and the economic development of west Cumberland, 1660–1760* (Cambridge, 1981), pp. 104–8; J.E. Williams, 'Whitehaven in the eighteenth century', *EcHR*, 2nd ser. VIII (1956), pp. 393–404; and N. Eaglesham, *Whitehaven and the tobacco trade* (Whitehaven, 1979).

96 NDRO B69/38 Letterbook of an unknown London merchant, 1704–13, p. 129 notes that a cargo of wine and tobacco 'is either gone or [is] to goe to Bristoll to discharge there and the goods to be sent thither' to London by coaster.

97 Hoskins, *Industry, trade and people*, pp. 89–91, 160–2; Clark, *Exe estuary*, pp. 144–5; Watkins, *Bideford,* pp. 66–7.

98 Somerset RO DD/DN 463, pp. 117–20.

99 For Liverpool data see Price and Clemens, 'Revolution of scale', pp. 24–8; Morgan, *Bristol*, pp. 153–5; Clemens, 'Liverpool', p. 223. By 1709 over 3 million lb were imported at Liverpool: Power, 'Councillors and commerce', p. 315.

100 Trends in tobacco marketing are discussed by J.M. Price, *France and the Chesapeake: a history of the French tobacco monopoly, 1674–1791, and of its relationship to the British and American tobacco trades* (Ann Arbor, Michigan, 1973), pp. 509–10; Price and Clemens, 'Revolution of scale', pp. 24–8; and Morgan, *Bristol*, pp. 152–60. The respective attractions of gin versus tobacco and snuff are outlined by Goodman, *Tobacco*, pp. 70–5; and Shammas, 'English and Anglo-American consumption', pp. 178–81.

101 Compare the more aggressive marketing strategies adopted by Glasgow tobacco merchants: T.M. Devine, *The tobacco lords: a study of the tobacco merchants of Glasgow and their trading activities, c. 1740–1790* (Edinburgh, 1975), pp. 65–80 and T.M. Devine, 'The golden age of tobacco', in T.M. Devine and G. Jackson, eds, *Glasgow. Volume I: beginnings to 1830* (Manchester, 1995), pp. 139–83.

102 Morgan, *Bristol*, ch. 6. Morgan, 'Economic development', pp. 56–7, 62–6 stresses business conservatism in the economic stagnancy of Bristol in the later eighteenth century. See also B.W.E. Alford, 'The economic development of Bristol in the nineteenth century: an enigma?', in P.V. McGrath and L. Cannon, eds, *Essays in Bristol and Gloucestershire history* (Bristol, 1976), pp. 252–83; Atkinson, 'Decline of the industrial spirit?', pp. 71–89; and Harvey and Press, 'Industrial change', pp. 1–6 for later perspectives.

103 Shammas, 'English and Anglo-American consumption', pp. 179–83 supplies variable indices of 'mass consumption' in these commodities.

104 Marcy, 'Eighteenth-century views', p. 25.

105 The following discussion is based upon Wakelin, 'Pre-industrial trade', pp. 144–69; Wakelin and Hussey, 'Investigating regional economies', pp. 14–21; Wanklyn, 'Shrewsbury boats', pp. 34–58; Wanklyn, 'Bridgnorth', pp. 37–64; Wanklyn, 'Impact of water transport facilities', pp. 1–19; Hussey, 'Coastal trade', pp. 143–6; and Cox, Hussey and Milne, eds, *Database*.

106 J. Thirsk, 'The South-West Midlands: Warwickshire, Worcestershire, Gloucestershire, and Herefordshire', in Thirsk, ed., *The agrarian history of England and Wales. Volume V: 1640–1750. I: Regional farming systems*, pp. 161–7, 184–7; and Thirsk, *Agricultural regions*, pp. 24, 42–3.

107 See Davies, 'Bewdley', ch. 5; Wakelin, 'Pre-industrial trade', ch. 4.

108 The ports of the Ironbridge Gorge comprised Benthall, Broseley, Buildwas and Madeley. See Wanklyn, 'Bridgnorth', pp. 42–6; Wanklyn, 'Industrial development in the Ironbridge Gorge before Abraham Darby', *West Midlands Studies*, XV (1982), pp. 3–7; Trinder, *Industrial revolution in Shropshire*, pp. 61–6; and Cox, 'Imagination', pp. 130–5.

109 But see also P. Ripley, 'Village and town: occupations and wealth in the hinterland of Gloucester 1660–1700', *Agricultural History Review*, 32 (1984), pp. 170–8 for the importance of the immediate locality.

110 Harrison, 'South-west', pp. 360, 364, 372–3; Kerridge, *Agricultural revolution*, pp. 115–8; Thirsk, *Agricultural regions*, p. 14; M. Thick, 'Market gardening in England and Wales', in Thirsk, ed., *The agrarian history of England and Wales. Volume V: 1640–1750. II: Agrarian change*, p. 507.

111 Between 1695 and 1703, 131,500 cabbage plants were shipped from Bridgwater. Over half (69,500 plants) were destined for Wales, the remainder to Bristol.

112 See M. Thick, 'Garden seeds in England before the late eighteenth century—I, seed growing', *Agricultural History Review*, 38 (1990), pp. 1–13 and 'Garden seeds in England before the late eighteenth century—II, the trade in seeds to 1760', *Agricultural History Review*, 38 (1990), pp. 105–16.

113 Williams, *Somerset Levels*, pp. 110–15.

114 Harrison, 'South-west', p. 377; Bettey, 'Livestock trade'. Trade increased dramatically after the embargo imposed on the import of Irish beasts in 1680: Woodward, 'Anglo-Irish livestock trade'. For local trade, see J.H. Hamer, 'Trading in St White Down Fair', *PSANHS*, CXIII (1973), pp. 61–70; C.M. Gerrard, 'Taunton Fair in the seventeenth century: an archaeological approach to historical data', *PSANHS*, 124 (1984), pp. 65–74; and Chartres, 'Marketing of agricultural produce, 1640–1750', pp. 171–2.

115 For Liverpool-shipped cheese, see W.M. Stern, 'Cheese shipped coastwise to London towards the middle of the eighteenth century', *Guildhall Miscellany*, 4 (1973), pp. 207–21. A mere 4 cwt of Liverpool-shipped cheese reached Somerset via Minehead in 1699.

116 Thirsk, 'English stocking knitting industry', p. 247.

117 Some 4,473 barrels of herring were shipped in 44 voyages in the sample year. Almost three-quarters (3,225 barrels) were traded to Bristol.

118 For serge and perpetuana production, see above and Kerridge, *Textile manufacture*, pp. 118–20, 163–5.

119 Between 1701 and 1703, the Bridgwater merchant William Sealey was supplied directly from Exeter via the carrier John Prickman: Somerset RO DD/X/PG W/51/3 1, Sealey to White, 12 September 1701; 16 September 1701.

120 Harrison, 'South-west', p. 387.

121 See Nix, 'Bideford and Barnstaple', introduction for a survey of the towns' development.

122 Harrison, 'South-west', pp. 362, 375, 383.

123 Both Barnstaple and Bideford were recognised staple ports for Irish wool: Kerridge, *Textile manufacture*, pp. 145–7.

124 PRO C104/12 Pt 1, fos 101v, 106r.

125 See PRO C78 1224/2 for the importance of the fishing trade at Ilfracombe.

126 Watkins, *Bideford*, pp. 74–5. The trade in earthenware is summarised by Grant, *North Devon pottery*. See also Weatherill, 'Growth of the pottery industry: new evidence', pp. 1–22; and Grant and Jemmett, 'Pipes and pipe-making', pp. 439–553.

127 The methodology behind these figures is discussed in Hussey, 'Coastal trade', pp. 154–6.

128 'Dutch mugs' and 'Holland earthenware' represented less than 1 per cent of earthenware shipments clearing Bristol in the period. Such commodities may not of course have originated in the Low Countries but may have been imitative of Dutch ware produced domestically.

129 Conversions are taken from Weatherill, 'Growth of the pottery industry: new evidence', pp. 17–8; volume to ratio measures of wine recorded in the Gloucester port books; Zupko, *Dictionary*, pp. 13–17, 23, 103–4, 115–16. These conversions may underestimate the coastal exports of Bristol, particularly if a heavier crate (which Weatherill suggests was used elsewhere), is adopted.

130 Weatherill, 'Growth of the pottery industry: new evidence', pp. 16–20.

131 The significance of north Devon pipe clay is charted by Rolt, *Potter's field*; Grant and Jemmett, 'Pipes and pipe making', pp. 482–6; and Hussey et. al, *Summary*, pp. 83–6.

132 For copper ore see D.B. Barton, *A history of copper mining in Cornwall and Devon* (Truro, 1968); H. Hamilton, *The English brass and copper industries to 1800* (1926, 2nd edn. 1967) and Day, *Bristol brass*, pp. 20–33.

133 Personal communication from Peter F. Claughton from Cletscher's 'Relation . . . 1696' (from Jenkins's translation in Liverpool University). A slightly different account of Cletscher's activities is presented by Day, *Bristol brass*, pp. 31–2.

134 Whetter, *Cornwall*, pp. 116–8, 121; ch 5.

135 Fisher and Havinden, 'Economy of south-west England', p. 77.

136 St Ives also exported coastally 109 tons of copper ore to Bristol (in 5 shipments); 73 tons to Liverpool (2 shipments); and 16 tons to Neath (1 shipment). Padstow exported 522 tons to Bristol (20 shipments); 54 to Chepstow (2 shipments) and 30 to Neath (1 shipment). In 1699 shipments from St Ives formed over half of Chepstow's imports of copper ore. Some 363 tons were imported from north Cornwall as opposed to 330 tons from Truro and 11 tons transhipped from Bristol. See Day, 'Copper, brass and zinc production', pp. 131–49.

137 In total, 30 tons, 18 cwt was shipped to Bristol; 8 tons, 3.5 cwt to Chepstow; and 8 tons to Liverpool from the north Cornish ports in 1697. All figures have been converted to the standard ton of 20 cwt. Slobs or slabs of tin have been converted using the formula: 1 ton = 8 slobs from multiple measures given in the Padstow and St Ives data. See also Whetter, *Cornwall*, ch. 5 and pp. 188–99.

138 Harrison makes this point strongly: 'South-west', pp. 365–6. See also Fisher and Havinden, 'Economy of south-west England', pp. 77–80; Havinden and Stanes, 'Agriculture in south west England', pp. 143–4; Pounds, 'Food production', pp. 117–22.

139 See chapter 1 above.

140 Although apparently comprehensive, Whetter's figures derived from the regional port books fail to account for under-recording due to letpass shipments: *Cornwall*, pp. 118–20, 200–10.

141 See Rees, *Industry,* I, pp. 79–84 for a description of the coalfield and the types of anthracite and bituminous coals extracted. Nef, *Coal industry,* I, pp. 52–6; Hatcher, *Coal industry,* pp. 135–41; Symons, *Llanelli,* pp. 26–38; and Edwards, 'Coal mining in Pembrokeshire' discuss mining and trade. George, 'Pembrokeshire sea-trading', makes useful additions to Willan's rather bald account of trading, *Coasting trade,* pp. 178–80.

142 Throughout this book coal and culm have been converted to the London measure chaldron of *c.*1.4 tons. No evidence exists to suggests that the Pembrokeshire chaldron of 2 tons as proposed by Nef was used in the coastal trade. See Hatcher, *Coal Industry,* pp. 567–9, 571; Nef, *Coal Industry,* II, pp. 369–72.

143 See Hoskins, *Industry, trade and people,* pp. 103–8, 163–4, 170–4; and Clark, *Exe estuary,* pp. 134–5, 213. Data derived from the Exeter port books and used in both of these works, broadly confirm the trends evident in this survey.

144 Three voyages dispatched 97.3 tons in 1702 and a single voyage in 1703 and 1704 sent 43.4 tons and 49 tons to London respectively.

145 E.G. Bowen, 'The south-west', in E.G. Bowen, ed., *Wales. A physical, historical, and regional geography* (1957), pp. 333–6, 343–4; Emery, 'Wales', pp. 394, 416; Howell, *Patriarchs and parasites,* pp. 50–2, 76–8, 83–4. For discussion of the wider issues of the pays and English farming, see Everitt, 'Country, county, town', pp. 83–115; J. Langton, 'The industrial revolution and the regional geography of England', *Transactions of the Institute of British Geographers,* new ser. 9 (1984), p. 149.

146 See table 3.4.

147 Although Osborne focuses his argument upon the Vale of Glamorgan, his conclusions are equally valid for Carmarthenshire and Pembrokeshire: 'Glamorgan agriculture', pp. 387–405.

148 Chartres, *Internal trade,* pp. 26–7. See also Barrow, 'Corn, carriers and coastal shipping', pp. 9, 12, 19–20 for the long-distance shipment of eggs from Berwick to London in the eighteenth century.

149 Emery, 'Wales', pp. 419–20; Bettey, 'Livestock trade'; Howell, *Patriarchs and parasites,* pp. 88–9; R.J. Colyer, *The Welsh cattle drovers* (Cardiff, 1976); and A.G. Prys-Jones, *The story of Carmarthenshire. Volume 2: from the sixteenth century to 1832* (1972), pp. 291–9.

150 Some 1,140 beasts were shipped to Bridgwater; 890 to Minehead; 575 to Watchet and 100 to Porlock. A further 5 swine were sent to Barnstaple, whilst 49 beasts were bound for an unspecified destination. Multiples have been converted to 'naive' units: dozen equals 12 and score represents 20.

151 Some 30 sheep, 25 cows and oxen, seven cows, two lambs, one horse, and a cow and calf. An additional half a dozen hogs were shipped from Milford to Barnstaple.

152 Zupko, *Dictionary,* p. 14.

153 Bristol took the equivalent of 166 barrels in 11 shipments and London 85 barrels in 3 voyages. Other coastal importers were Barnstaple (14 barrels, 3 shipments); Liverpool (11 barrels; 4 shipments); Lancaster (3 barrels, 1 shipment); Whitehaven (3 barrels, 1 shipment); Bridgwater (2 barrels, 1 shipment); and Plymouth (1 barrel, 1 shipment).

154 The limited and erratically recorded coastal exports of South Burry and Newton have not been summarised here. Both ports dispatched small cargoes of coal to north Devon.

155 The geology and exploitation of the area is outlined in G.M. Howe, 'The south Wales coalfield', in Bowen, ed. *Wales,* pp. 362–4 and Rees, *Industry,* I, pp. 79–93. Glamorganshire coal is described by Nef, *Coal industry,* I, pp. 52–4 and Hatcher, *Coal Industry,* pp. 135–41; see also John, *South Wales,* ch. 1.

156 Plymouth imported 2,637.6 tons (41 per cent of coal shipped to extra-regional ports) in 1701; 2129.4 tons (48 per cent) in 1703; 2,690.8 tons (61 per cent) in 1704; and 2,868.6 tons (59 per cent) in 1705.

157 St Ives supplied the extreme western edge of Cornwall: Palmer, ed., *Cornwall, the Canaries and the Atlantic*, p. 156.

158 H. Mackworth, *The case of Sir Humphry Mackworth, and the Mine-Adventurers with respect to the irregular proceedings of several Justices of the Peace for the County of Glamorgan and of their agents and dependents* (1705), p. 3.

159 See H. Mackworth, *The Mine-Adventure; or an expedient* (1698); H. Mackworth, *An answer to several objections against the Mine-Adventure* (1698); H. Mackworth, *A short state of the case & proceedings of the Company of Mine-Adventurers; with an abstract of the defence of the deputy governor and directors: justified by vouchers* (1710); and H. Mackworth, *The second part of the Book of Vouchers, to prove the case & defence of the deputy governour & directors of the Company of Mine-Adventurers* (1711).

160 Mackworth, *Case of Sir Humphry Mackworth*, p. 3.

161 Mackworth, *Affidavits, certificates, and presentments; proving the facts mentioned in the case of Sir Humphry Mackworth and the Mine-Adventurers with respect to the irregular proceedings of several Justices of the Peace for the County of Glamorgan and of their agents and dependents* (1705), p. 38.

162 Mackworth, *Case of Sir Humphrey Mackworth*, pp. 4–12; Mackworth, *Affidavits, certificates, and presentments*, pp. 24–40. See also Trott, 'Coal mining in Neath', pp. 58–72; S. Evans, 'An examination of Sir Humphrey Mackworth's industrial activities', unpublished M.A. thesis, University of Wales (1950); and PRO C10/303/2; C10/303/5 for Mackworth's activities.

163 Minchinton, *Tinplate industry*, pp. 10–13.

164 Roberts, 'Industrial expansion', pp. 115–6; Roberts, 'The development and decline', pp. 78–115; R.O. Roberts, 'Enterprise and capital for non-ferrous metal smelting in Glamorgan, 1694–1924', *Morgannwg*, 23 (1979), pp. 48–53; Burt, 'Non-ferrous metals industry', pp. 23–45.

165 Rees, *Industry*, II, pp. 521–67; Trott, 'Coalmining in Neath', pp. 47–74; H. Mackworth, *The third abstract of the state of the mines of Bwlchyr Eskir-Hir in the county of Cardigan* (1700), p.4.

166 H. Carter, 'The Vale of Glamorgan and Gower', in Bowen, ed., *Wales*, pp. 420–7; Emery, 'Wales', pp. 397–9, 416–17.

167 See P. Jenkins, *The Making of a ruling class: the Glamorgan gentry, 1640–1790* (Cambridge, 1983), pp. 6–7.

168 Measures have been converted according to Zupko, *Dictionary*, pp. 14–15, 61–2, 132. Plymouth imported 105 cwt, Bridgwater 87 cwt and north Devon 67 cwt from Swansea in 1701.

169 Emery, 'Wales', pp. 399, 414–16; Jenkins, *Making of a ruling class*, pp. 13–15; 50–2; Jenkins, *Foundations of modern Wales*, pp. 88, 92; Osbourne, 'Glamorgan agriculture'. See also M.I. Williams, 'The economic and social history of Glamorgan 1660–1760', in G. Williams, ed., *Early modern Glamorgan from the Act of Union to the industrial revolution*, Glamorgan County History IV (Cardiff, 1974), pp. 321–38 and Williams, 'Southern regions of Glamorgan', pp. 21–40.

170 Willan, *River navigation*, pp. 53–4; Thirsk, 'South-west Midlands', pp. 172–7; Emery, 'Wales', pp. 396–7; R.A. Yates, 'The south-east borderland', in Bowen, ed., *Wales*, pp. 502–3.

171 Thirsk, 'South-west Midlands', pp. 160–2; J. Thirsk, 'Agricultural policy: public debate and legislation, 1640–1750' in J. Thirsk, ed., *Agricultural change: policy and practice,*

1500–1750. Chapters from the agrarian history of England and Wales. Volume 3 (Cambridge, 1990), pp. 303, 310, 345; R. Jenkins, 'Industries of Herefordshire in bygone times', *Transactions of the Newcomen Society*, XVII (1936–7), pp. 184–5.

172 Improvements to the Wye, Lugg and even Bristol Avon were opposed by vested interests claiming potential over-supply of corn from Wales and the borderland: Willan, *River navigation,* p. 46; Andrews, 'Chepstow', pp. 97–9.

173 Somerset RO DD/X/WI 36, 29 February 1693; 28 June 1693.

174 Jenkins, 'Redbrook', pp. 147–56; Day, 'The Costers', pp. 47–52; Hart, *Industrial history of Dean,* pp. 8–15, 104–12; Johnson, 'Foley partnerships', pp. 333–4; Hammersley, 'Charcoal iron industry', pp. 593–613; Jenkins, 'Industries of Herefordshire', pp. 180–4.

175 All three centres exported goods in the period. From 1696, Hanbury was exporting iron and plate from his Pontypool works 'to customers in Bristol, Gloucester, London and the Midlands', presumably via Newport, Minchinton, *Tinplate industry,* pp. 10, 13.

176 Rees, *Cardiff,* p. 204; Dawson, *Commerce and Customs,* pp. 16–48. See also Williams, 'Economic and social history of Glamorgan', pp. 342–3, 348–60; Williams, 'A contribution to the commercial history of Glamorgan'; Williams, 'Further contributions to the commercial history of Glamorgan'; Williams, 'Cardiff, its people and its trade'; Williams, 'Southern regions of Glamorgan', p. 36 which discuss absolute levels of coasting, even though Williams was aware of the erratic nature of the data.

177 Power suggests that the concentration of economic and political power in the hands of Liverpool's 'super' merchants encouraged overseas enterprise at the relative expense of the port's local and Irish trades: 'Councillors and commerce', pp. 310–11.

178 Morgan, 'Bristol and the Atlantic trades', pp. 642–6, and Morgan, *Bristol,* ch. 2. See also Minchinton, 'Port of Bristol', p. 7.

Chapter 4

1 See D. Defoe, *The complete English tradesman* (1727, repr. Gloucester, 1987), p. 5 and Marshall, ed. *Stout,* pp. 24–30 for one such tradesman. H.-C. and L.H. Mui, *Shops and shopkeepers in eighteenth century England,* (1988), ch. 1 and E. Kowaleski-Wallace, *Consuming subjects. Women, shopping and business in the eighteenth century* (New York, 1997), pp. 82–5 supply rather different views.

2 Quoted in Bettey, *Bristol observed,* pp. 58–9. For the activity of lesser traders see Sacks, *Widening gate,* pp. 201–4 and Morgan, *Bristol,* pp. 93–6.

3 See Grassby's reassessment of early work by Westerfield: R. Grassby, 'The personal wealth of the business community in seventeenth-century England', *EcHR,* 2nd ser. XXIII (1970), pp. 220–34; Grassby, *Business community,* esp. pp. 162–3; R.B. Westerfield, *Middlemen in English business: particularly between 1660 and 1760* (1915, repr. New York, 1968), ch. VIII, esp. pp. 351–8, 362–4.

4 M.J. Freeman, 'Introduction', in Aldcroft and Freeman, eds, *Transport in the industrial revolution,* p. 1.

5 Complementary forms of transport are covered by (amongst others) M. Freeman, 'Transporting methods in the British cotton industry during the Industrial Revolution', *Journal of Transport History,* I (1980); J. Langton, *Geographical change and industrial revolution: coalmining in south west Lancashire 1590–1799* (Cambridge, 1979); D. Hey, *Packmen, carriers and packhorse roads: trade and communications in North Derbyshire and South Yorkshire* (Leicester,

1980); Chartres, 'Road carrying', pp. 73–94; Gerhold, 'London carrying trade, 1681–1838', pp. 392–410; Gerhold *Road transport before the railways*; Gerhold, 'Packhorses and wheeled vehicles', pp. 1–26; and Gerhold, 'Productivity change', pp. 491–515.

6 Willan, *Coasting trade*, pp. 34–42. See also Nef, *Coal industry*, pp. 24–41; R. Smith, *Sea coal to London* (1961); and Dietz, 'North-east coal trade', pp. 280–94. W.J. Hausman, 'The English coastal coal trade, 1691–1910: how rapid was productivity growth?', *EcHR*, 2nd ser. XL (1987), pp. 588– 96; S. Ville, 'Defending productivity growth in the English coal trade during the eighteenth and nineteenth centuries', *EcHR*, 2nd ser. XL (1987), pp. 597–602; and Ville, 'Total factor productivity', pp. 355–70 offer interesting insights into the growth of the trade.

7 Willan, *Coasting trade*, pp. 34, 53–4, 171.

8 See Woodward, *Elizabethan Chester*, pp. 26–34, 57–72, 106–24; Jackson, *Hull*, ch. V, esp. pp. 115–20; Hinton, 'Boston'; Metters, 'Kings Lynn'; M. Evans, 'The seaborne trade of the port of Ipswich and its members', unpublished Ph.D. thesis, University of East Anglia (1987); Elder, *Slave trade and Lancaster*, esp. pp. 19–36; and Williams, *East Anglian ports*, pp. 48–65. For an interesting comparison of coastal traders using a single legal quay at the port of London, see Chartres, 'Wiggins Quay', pp. 29–47 and H. Roseveare, 'Wiggins' Key revisited: trade and shipping in the later seventeenth-century port of London', *Journal of Transport History*, 16 (1995), pp. 1–20. Barney's recent study of King's Lynn provides important new light on the role of coastal merchants and shipping in the functioning of the east coast trade in the eighteenth century: 'King's Lynn', pp. 126–40.

9 See McGrath, *Merchant Venturers of Bristol*; McGrath, 'Merchant Venturers and the Port of Bristol'; McGrath, ed., *Records relating to the Society of Merchant Venturers*; and Minchinton, ed., *Politics and the port of Bristol*. The merchant community in Bristol is also covered in P.V. McGrath, *John Whitson and the merchant community of Bristol* (Bristol, 1970); McGrath, ed., *Merchants*; Minchinton, 'Port of Bristol; Minchinton, ed., *Trade of Bristol*; Minchinton, 'Merchants of Bristol', pp. 185–200. See also K. Morgan, 'Bristol West India merchants in the eighteenth century', *TRHS*, 6th ser. 3 (1993), pp. 185–208; Morgan, 'Bristol and the Atlantic trades', pp. 626–50; Morgan, *Bristol*, chs 4–7; and D. Richardson, *The Bristol slave traders: a collective portrait* (BHA, 60, 1985). A rather different perspective is contained in J.A. Press, *The merchant seamen of Bristol, 1746–1789* (BHA, 38, 1976).

10 Sacks, *Widening Gate*. See also Sacks, 'Trade, society and politics', pp. 340–8 and Morgan, *Bristol*, pp. 96–109 for a more general discussion of these themes.

11 Both Westerfield, *Middlemen*, pp. 329–68, 412–16 and T.S Willan, *The inland trade: studies in English internal trade in the sixteenth and seventeenth centuries* (Manchester, 1976) provide a limited overview of the subject. Dr Chartres's work provides the more recent critiques: *Internal trade*; 'Marketing of agricultural produce in metropolitan western England'; 'Food consumption and internal trade', pp. 168–98; 'Marketing of agricultural produce', pp. 220–46; 'City and towns', pp. 138–55; and 'Market integration and agricultural output', pp. 117–35.

12 Willan, *Coasting trade*, pp. 53–4.

13 J.C.A. Whetter, 'Bryan Rogers of Falmouth, merchant, 1632–92', *Old Cornwall*, IV (1965), pp. 347–52; Palmer, ed., *Cornwall, Canaries and the Atlantic*; Bettey, 'Prankard', pp. 34–47; Stembridge, *Goldney: Bristol merchant dynasty*; and Stembridge, 'Bristol-Coalbrookdale connection' provide examples of local studies of merchants involved in the coasting trade.

14 Wakelin's analyses of the salt and tobacco trades come to no firm conclusions regarding cargo ownership as opposed to carriage: 'Pre-industrial trade', pp. 201–10, 247–54. See also Wanklyn, 'Shrewsbury boats', pp. 34–8 and Wanklyn, 'Bridgnorth', pp. 50–1 for local studies. Hussey, 'Coastal trade', pp. 187–8 and Cox, Hussey and Milne, eds, *Database*, pp. 27–30 outline the interpretation of port book data concerning merchant activity.

15 H. Roseveare, ed., *Markets and merchants of the late seventeenth century: the Marescoe-David letters, 1668–1680* (Records of Social and Economic History, new series, XII, Oxford, 1987), pp. 268–9. For the career of Browne, see McGrath, ed., *Merchants*, pp. 68–9, 71 and McGrath, ed., *Records relating to the Society of Merchant Venturers*, pp. 31, 37, 61, 195. A William Browne was recorded as merchant on a cargo of bar iron shipped from Newnham to Bristol in 1666: Cox, Hussey and Milne, eds, *Database*.

16 Cox, 'Imagination', pp. 133–5, 137–8. See also Stembridge, *Goldney: Bristol merchant dynasty*, pp. 17–20 and Minchinton, ed., *Trade of Bristol*, pp. 101–22.

17 See chapter 3 for a discussion of the iron trade.

18 Somerset RO DD/DN 423, 8 August 1715, pp. 81–2. The carriers mentioned are George Bradley, owner of the *Duchess* of Montgomery; William Perkes, owner of the *Society* of Worcester among other trows (the vessel Prankard may be referring to is the *Exchange* of Worcester mastered by Stephen Perkes: it cleared Gloucester on 3 August with 10 tons of iron and ironware on board); and John and Benjamin Beale, who operated the *John and Ann*, *Speedwell*, *Hopewell* and the *William and Thomas,* all of Bewdley. See also PRO C104/12 Pt 1, f. 98v, Smith to Galpine, 20 February 1697 for problems with cargo spoilage associated with open trows.

19 Sacks, *Widening gate*, p. xviii.

20 Woodward, *Elizabethan Chester*, p. 129.

21 For the methodological issues underpinning this research, see Wakelin, 'Pre-industrial trade', pp. 82–90; Wakelin and Hussey, 'Investigating regional economies', pp. 14–21; and Milne and Paul, 'Flexible model', pp. 106–15. Power, 'Councillors and commerce', pp. 303–4 outlines similar issues regarding the merchant community of Liverpool in the seventeenth and eighteenth centuries.

22 For Herle, see PRO E134 5 W&M Mich 52; PRO C104 12 Pt. 1, f. 77r, Cockrem to Galpine, 2 January, 1697; and Whetter, *Cornwall*, pp. 63, 163. Some ten voyages were undertaken between 19 December 1694 and 9 December 1697.

23 Alloway was recorded as merchant at Bridgwater on eight separate occasions, Ilfracombe seven, Minehead four, Gloucester three, and Liverpool two: Somerset RO DD/DN 463, pp. 2–3 and Somerset RO DD/DN 145, will of William Alloway, 1719, proved 1722.

24 This may have been the Sir Edward of Trimsaran, Carmarthenshire, or the Sir Edward of Margam: Jenkins, *Making of a ruling class*, pp. 203–4; D.W. Howell, 'Landlords and estate management in Wales', in Thirsk, ed., *The agrarian history of England and Wales. Volume V: 1640–1750. II: Agrarian change*, pp. 263, 295–7; Lhwyd, *Parochialia*, III, p. 143.

25 Willan, *Coasting trade*, pp. 46–7.

26 NDRO B 1 693, 694, 695, 695a: Barnstaple Coal Warden's accounts, 1670–2, 1678–80. For coal and culm ordered by Hoare and Company see chapter 5.

27 Mackworth, *Affidavits, certificates and presentments*, pp. 24, 28, 38.

28 Wanklyn, 'Bridgnorth', pp. 45–6.

29 Westerfield, *Middlemen*, pp. 229–32; Willan, *Coasting trade*, pp. 34–42; Evans, 'Welsh coal trade', chs 5, 6. See also Nef, *Coal industry*, pp. 87–90; and Hatcher, *Coal industry*, pp. 470–82.

30 Willan, *Coasting trade*, pp. 46, 52–3.

31 Between 1695 and 1704, Isaac Heard of Bridgwater was recorded solely as a merchant in the Bridgwater port books. He appears as a master-merchant in the Bristol records for 1695.

32 Bowden, *Wool trade*, pp. 200–2.

33 See Farr, 'Severn navigation', pp. 71–3, 79–84; Trinder, *Industrial revolution in Shropshire*, pp. 60–3, 71–2.

34 Whetter, *Cornwall*, p. 118; Rowe, *Cornwall*, p. 19.

35 In 1699, Crofts was responsible for cargo discharging at St Ives from Bristol and Liverpool.

36 As in the overseas trades: Davis, *English shipping industry*, pp. 81–90 and Morgan, *Bristol*, pp. 36–8. See chapter 5 below.

37 It is possible that there is more than one John Tyler in the data, particularly the trowman associated with the Tewkesbury boats. The conclusions regarding operational patterns and organisation still stand.

38 In 1713, Penn also mastered the *Hereford* of Bewdley, Samuel Milner merchant, carrying pig iron from Chepstow.

39 The tables includes three return shipments from Gloucester in the *Betty* under John Syner and Syner's two freights in the same boat from Bristol to Gloucester in 1708. For Coster, see Day, *Bristol brass*, pp. 48–53; Jenkins, 'Redbrook', pp. 145–67; Day, 'The Costers', pp. 47–52; Day, 'Copper, brass, and zinc production', pp. 145–63.

40 See Y. Kaukiainen, *A history of Finnish Shipping* (1993), ch. 3 and Y. Kaukiainen, *Sailing into twilight. Finnish shipping in an age of transport revolution, 1860–1914* (Helsinki, 1991). I am indebted to an anonymous referee for drawing my attention to this source.

41 For Juliot and Alloway, see chapter 5.

42 Alloway had shipping concerns at both Minehead and Watchet: Somerset RO DD/DN 463, pp. 60, 117. In 1714 'aged 55' he was mentioned shipping large quantities of wool from Wales in partnership with Christopher Devonshire and Sarah Hayman: Somerset RO DD/L 1 54/42. For John Baston see Somerset RO DD/DN 463 p. 132 and Somerset RO DD/L 1 54/42 wool dockets, 1717.

43 Examples of Cleaveland's role in organising wool shipments to Bridgwater and Minehead are given in Somerset RO DD/DN 463, pp. 111, 116. For the importance of Minehead as a staple port, see Kerridge, *Textile manufacture*, pp. 146–7.

44 McGrath, ed., *Merchants*, p. xix.

45 McGrath, ed., *Merchants*, p. x.

46 For Hackett, see McGrath, *Merchant Venturers of Bristol*, p. 229 and Ralph and Williams, eds, *Inhabitants of Bristol*, p. 164.

47 Hayman acted as merchant to a sole cargo of £500 carried to Falmouth in the *Tiger* of Bristol in September 1688: PRO E190 1144/2. Elton was recorded shipping copper ore from St Ives to Bristol and Chepstow in 1697: see Minchinton, ed., *Trade of Bristol*, pp. 10, 143–4; Jenkins, 'Redbrook', pp. 163–6; and M. Elton, *Annals of the Elton family, Bristol merchants and Somerset landowners* (Stroud, 1994), pp. 12–22. Champion was named as merchant on eight voyages from Bristol to the customs port of Gloucester between 1716 and 1723. Seven of these carried pig iron to Berkeley or Lydney: Cox, Hussey and Milne, eds, *Database*.

48 Minchinton ('Metropolis', pp. 71–80, following Willan, *Coasting trade*, pp. 49–50, 53, 167–80) is rather silent concerning the organisation of Bristol's internal trade networks, despite the fact that several overseas merchants were strongly involved in the domestic

market. In Minchinton, ed., *Trade of Bristol*, pp. 101–22, Prankard's overseas iron dealings are outlined in some detail, but there is scant reference to arguably the core of his business, internal distribution. For a neat juxtaposition of coastal and overseas 'value' see MacInnes, *Gateway of Empire*, pp. 20–1.

49 See Chartres, 'The marketing of agricultural produce, 1640–1750', pp. 237–40; Westerfield, *Middlemen*, pp. 204–7; and Stern, 'Cheese shipped coastwise to London', pp. 207–21 for an overview of this trade.

50 See Power, 'Councillors and commerce', pp. 305–9, 312, 322; C.N. Parkinson, *The rise of the port of Liverpool* (Liverpool, 1952), pp. 68–86; R. Muir and E. Platt, eds, *A history of municipal government in Liverpool* (Liverpool, 1906), pp. 391–4; Hughes, *Administration and finance*, pp. 225–34, 239–42, 394–7; Barker, 'Lancashire coal, Cheshire salt', pp. 89–91; Somerset RO DD/DN 463, pp. 20, 30, 35, 40, 41, 47–8, 52, 61–2, 66, 81, 117–18, 134; BRO 04449 (2), 9/1/1705, 6/12/1704, 10/4/1706, 13/9/1707, and PRO C104/12 Pt 1, f. 19r.

51 PRO C104/12 Pt 1, f. 53v, Warburton to Galpine.

52 See chapter 5 for details of these shipments.

53 See PRO C104/12 Pt 1, f. 111v, Neale to Galpine, 7 May 1697, and f. 272v for the *Providence's* voyage.

54 See McGrath, 'Merchant Venturers and the port of Bristol', pp. 121–8; and McGrath, *Merchant Venturers of Bristol*, pp. 70–7, 161–7 for the duties and fees of Bristol's myriad port officials.

55 PRO E190 1316/7, f. 2v.

56 Tuthill was enrolled as apprentice to Abraham Hooke, Merchant Venturer of Bristol, and Elizabeth, his wife, for seven years in 1693. His father, Francis, was described as an apothecary of Bridgwater: McGrath, ed., *Records relating to the Society of Merchant Venturers*, p. 39. For Hooke's links with Hoare and Company see chapter 5 below.

57 PRO C104/12 Pt. 1, f. 112v, Tuthill to Galpine, 10 May 1697.

58 The *Prosperity* and the *Olive Branch* cleared Bristol for Bridgwater on 2 and 15 June respectively. Both vessels carried 2 tons of hemp each amongst mixed cargoes.

59 McGrath, ed., *Merchants*, pp. xviii–xix; McGrath, ed., *Records relating to the Society of Merchant Venturers*, p. xx; Minchinton, ed., *Trade of Bristol*, p. xvi; Morgan, *Bristol*, p. 5.

60 Information derived from McGrath, ed., *Records relating to the Society of Merchant Venturers*, pp. 30–3, passim; McGrath, *Merchant Venturers of Bristol*, pp. 39–48, 102–23; Minchinton, ed., *Politics and the port of Bristol*, passim; B. Beavan, *Bristol Lists* (Bristol, 1889); J. Latimer, *The history of the Society of Merchant Venturers of Bristol* (Bristol, 1903), passim; Latimer, *Annals of Bristol in seventeenth century*; Latimer, *Annals of Bristol in the eighteenth century*. McGrath's assertion that the Society did not apply a strict religious test in the mid-seventeenth century is borne out by the number of Dissenter merchants who were free: McGrath, ed., *Records relating to the Society of Merchant Venturers*, pp. 97–103. See also Sacks, *Widening Gate*, pp. 270–7.

61 The conversions adopted in the case of the wine gallon have followed Zupko, *Dictionary*, and gallon/volumetric container ratios derived from the Gloucester data: Cox, Hussey, and Milne, eds, *Database*, glossaries.

62 See A. Raistrick, *Quakers in science and industry: an account of the Quaker contribution to science and industry during the seventeenth and eighteenth centuries* (1950, repr. Newton Abbot, 1968) for the careers of Lloyd (pp. 124, 192), Peters (p. 124) and Harford (p. 324). Lloyd's involvement with Darby and the Bristol Brass and Battery Company is outlined by Day, *Bristol brass*, pp. 35–41 and Cox, 'Imagination', pp. 130–1. Harford was refused admittance to the Merchant Venturers in 1711 on the grounds of his Quaker beliefs:

Minchinton, ed., *Trade of Bristol*, pp. 143–4; McGrath, *Merchant Venturers of Bristol*, p. 103. Peters was involved with his fellow Quakers, Prankard and Darby, in the Coalbrookdale iron concern (Somerset RO DD/DN 423, 21 April 1713). See also R. Mortimer, ed., *The Minute Book of the men's meeting of the Society of Friends in Bristol, 1686–1704* (BRS, XXX, 1977), appendix I for biographical details.

63 See Somerset RO DD/X/WI 36; McGrath, ed., *Records relating to the Society of Merchant Venturers*, p. 229; and McGrath, ed., *Merchants*, pp. 163–4.

64 For the activity of Baker, see BRO 04449(2), 6 December 1704 and Somerset RO DD/DN 463, p. 118.

65 BCL B6584, f. 57v.

66 Somerset RO DD/DN 463, p. 47.

67 Somerset RO DD/DN 423, p. 165. For Prankard's other coastal transactions, see ibid., pp. 6, 47, 63, 98–101, 165; BCL B17368, nos 5, 11, 13, 15; Wakelin, 'Pre-industrial trade', pp. 205–6; and Bettey, 'Prankard', pp. 34–47.

68 At Bideford, merchants were only consistently recorded in 1695 and 1699.

69 Wanklyn, 'Shrewsbury boats', pp. 36–7; Wanklyn, 'Bridgnorth', pp. 53–9; Cox, Hussey and Milne, eds, *Database*, pp. 8–9.

70 Somerset RO DD/DN 463, p. 138.

71 Parsons completed 11 voyages in the *Comfort* between December 1697 and September 1698; Vosper 3 shipments at the end of 1698 and the beginning of 1699.

72 See, for example, S. Ville, *English shipowning during the industrial revolution: Michael Henley and Son, London shipowners, 1770–1830* (Manchester, 1987), pp. 55–7.

73 See Willan, *Coasting trade*, pp. 46–54, Appendix 6, 7; and Williams, *East Anglian ports*, pp. 40–4 for an overview of these areas.

74 This is implied by Lewis, *Welsh Port Books*, pp. xxviii–xxix; and Sacks, 'Trade, society, and politics', pp. 742–5. For an account of ship registration, see Jarvis, 'Ship registry', pp. 156–7, 159–61; and Davis, *English shipping industry*, pp. 395–406.

75 Willan, *Coasting trade*, pp. 217–19.

76 Wanklyn, 'Shrewsbury boats', pp. 40–2; Wakelin, 'Pre-industrial trade', pp. 46–8; Hussey, 'Coastal trade', pp. 45–7, 214–16; Cox, Hussey and Milne, eds, *Database*, pp. 26–7.

77 See Barney, 'King's Lynn', pp. 128–30 for similar methodological problems.

78 BRO 04434/3, pp. 156–7, 14 April 1700.

79 See the pro forma entries in Crouch, *Complete guide*, pp. 11–13 and in Somerset RO DD/SF 2769: 'Instructions for the western ports'.

80 Matthews, *Records of Cardiff*, II, pp. 458, 461. Claroe and his regular master, William Jefferies, shipped the equivalent of 204.64 tons of white salt to Cardiff or Cardiff and Newport in eight shipments on board the *Hopewell*, *Francis*, *Elizabeth* and *Success* in 1707 and 93.18 tons in two voyages undertaken by the *Success* to Cardiff in 1708. The final shipment bore a coquet of 15 November, after which Claroe, tellingly, was not recorded until 8 August 1709 when he shipped 60.45 tons of salt on the *Success* for Minehead. Data from Cox, Hussey and Milne, eds, *Database*.

81 Of the 513 voyages of Upton boats from Gloucester over the period, 312 were to the ports of Somerset, north Devon or south Wales.

82 For example, in 1699, the *John and Ann* of Minehead imported 27 tons of white salt under letpass from Minehead to Bridgwater. The boat had previously brought salt from Liverpool.

83 Chartres, *Internal trade*, pp. 44–6.

84 See chapter 1 and NDRO B1 1128; B1 1129.

85 From the Bristol records, 7 boats 'of' either Cardiff, Newport, Caerleon or Aberthaw monopolised the trade to the area. At Minehead, the *Four Sisters* of Aberthaw (24 shipments) and the *Two Brothers* of Cardiff (4 shipments) were the only vessels trading to and from the port jurisdiction, whilst at Gloucester 9 voyages of the *Thomas* of Upton, 2 of the *John and Mary* of Bewdley and 1 of the *Betty* of Bewdley were recorded. At Bideford the *Hopewell* of Northam was involved in 1 voyage in the sample year.

86 Boats either 'of' Swansea, Oystermouth, Port Eynon or Newton were deemed to be local to Swansea.

87 Cockhill was more commonly associated with Liverpool or Bideford ships, including a *True Love* of Liverpool.

88 The three voyages in 1709–13 involved long-distance coasting with Carmarthen, Milford and Bideford. See Cox, Hussey and Milne, eds, *Database*.

89 BL Add. MSS 11256. The figures for coastal trade are reproduced by Willan, *Coasting trade*, pp. 220–2.

90 Andrews, 'English merchant shipping', pp. 232–5.

91 Jarvis, 'Ship registry', pp. 156–7.

92 See Jarvis, 'Ship registry', pp. 159–61; Davis, *English shipping industry*, pp. 395–6, 399, 403–6; D.E. Robinson, 'Half the story of "The rise of the English shipping industry"', *Business History Review*, XLI (1967), pp. 303–8; and D.E. Robinson, 'The secret of British power in the age of sail: Admiralty records of the coasting fleet', *American Neptune*, XLVIII, (1988), pp. 5–21 for assessments and critiques.

93 McCusker, 'Tonnage of ships', pp. 73–105 indicates that in the colonial trade two registered tons were roughly equivalent to three measured tons and to four cargo tons. Davis, *English shipping industry*, pp. 7, 19, 396–406 contends that 'tons burden, deadweight tonnage, carrying capacity . . . was usually about three-quarters of measured tonnage'. See also C.J. French, 'Eighteenth-century shipping tonnage measurements', *Journal of Economic History*, 33 (1973), pp. 434–43; Rediker, *Devil and the deep blue sea*, pp. 301–3; L.A. Harper, *The English navigation laws: a seventeenth-century experiment in social engineering* (New York, 1939), pp. 329, 339; A.P. Usher, 'The growth of English shipping, 1572–1922', *Quarterly Journal of Economics*, XLII (1929), pp. 465–78; C. Lloyd, *The British seaman, 1200–1860* (Rutherford, 1970), pp. 285–6; and S. Ville, 'The problem of tonnage measurement in the English shipping industry, 1780–1830', *International Journal of Maritime History*, I, 2 (1989), pp. 65–84.

94 Barrett, *Bristol*, pp. 189–90.

95 This is more apparent when assessments for other ports are compared. Jackson, for example, indicates that the average tonnage per vessel of coastal craft using Hull in the late eighteenth century was 82 tons: Jackson, *Hull in the eighteenth century*, p. 73; whilst Ville's work suggests that the average size of coasters at Bristol, Hull and Liverpool in 1785 was between 63 and 83 tons: S.P. Ville, 'Shipping in the port of Newcastle, 1780–1800', *Journal of Transport History*, IX (1988), p. 73 discussed in Armstrong, 'Significance of coastal shipping', pp. 74–5.

96 Both Davis, *English shipping industry*, pp. 7, n.1, 395–6 and McCusker, 'Tonnage of ships', pp. 73–105 suggest that carrying capacity, burden tonnage or cargo tons of ships was roughly three-quarters the official measured tonnage. This would mean that 96,254.25 burden tons used Bristol in 1787 at 27.56 tons per vessel. This compares favourably with Chartres's calculations which assessed East Anglian coastal vessels at an average of 42 tons when discharging corn at Wiggins Key in the 1680s: Chartres, 'Wiggins Key', p. 38.

97 For the *Hope*: PRO C104/12 Pt 1, f. 180r, Galpine to Fisher 5 August 1699; f. 183v, Galpine to Fisher, 8 November 1699. For Scott's proposed new ship: ibid., f. 111r, Scott to Galpine, 3 May 1697.

98 Davis, *English shipping industry*, p. 404.

99 PRO C104/12 Pt 1, f. 22r, Francis to Galpine, 1 August 1696. 'Deadweight' was roughly equivalent to burden/cargo tons.

100 See Minchinton, ed., *Trade of Bristol*, pp. 5, 183; McGrath, ed., *Merchants*, pp. 279–81.

101 Williams, 'Cardiff', pp. 93–4.

102 See Appendix 2 for data references.

103 PRO E134 4 W&M, Mich 50, quoted in Thirsk and Cooper, eds, *Seventeenth century economic documents*, pp. 419–20. The three trows completed 25 recorded voyages in 1691 and 19 in 1692: Cox, Hussey and Milne, eds, *Database*. For stowage considerations, see Davis, *English shipping industry*, pp. 178–9.

104 PRO C104/12 Pt 1, f. 98v, Smith to Galpine, 20 February 1697, for problems with cargo spoilage associated with open trows.

105 G. Perry, 'The Severn navigation', *Gentleman's Magazine*, 28 (1758), p. 277. See also Trinder, *Industrial revolution in Shropshire*, pp. 104–6; Farr, 'Severn navigation', p. 72; and Wanklyn, 'Bridgnorth', pp. 43–5 for critiques of these figures.

106 Barrett, *Bristol*, p. 189.

107 The Cardiff port book for June–December 1704 (PRO E190 1288/3) lists Thomas Claroe's trow, the *Thomas* of Upton, at 40 tons burden.

108 Trinder, *Industrial revolution in Shropshire*, pp. 106–8; Wanklyn, 'Bridgnorth', pp. 47–50. The coal trows of the 1720s were capable of carrying up to 25 tons, although the mean size of shipment for the period 1703–24 was 18.9 tons: Cox, Hussey and Milne, eds, *Database*.

109 Wakelin, 'Pre-industrial trade', pp. 106–7. Large Newnham coasters were important vessels in long-distance coasting later in the eighteenth century: N.M. Herbert, 'The Newnham and London traders', *TBGAS*, XCVII (1979), pp. 93–100.

110 Andrews, 'Chepstow', pp. 97–107.

111 Davis, *English shipping industry*, pp. 44–5, 175–6.

112 Davis, *English shipping industry*, p. 399, n.4; Willan, *Coasting trade*, pp. 15–16. For a wider assessment of coasting efficiency see Armstrong, 'Significance of coastal shipping', pp. 73–90.

113 See Jarvis, 'Ship registry', p. 159; Davis, *English shipping industry*, pp. 20, 26–7; Harper, *Navigation laws*, p. 329; and Rediker, *Between the devil and the deep blue sea*, pp. 301–3.

114 PRO C104/12 Pt 1 fos 154r, 160r, 166v, 183v.

115 PRO C104/12 Pt 2, f. 214v.

116 Somerset DD/X/PG/1 W51/3/1, Sealey to White, 22 January 1703; Sealey to White, 26 January 1703; Sealey to White, 2 February 1703; Sealey to White, 22 March 1703.

117 See chapter 3.

118 The inshore fisheries are almost certainly underestimated in the Musgrave figures. In 1709, the only south-western ports with returns are Exeter (764 tons); Dartmouth (14 tons); Fowey (240 tons); Cardigan (240 tons) and Aberdovey (50 tons). BL Add. MSS, fos 2v–3r.

119 See D.T. Williams, 'The port books of Swansea and Neath, 1709–19', *Archaeologia Cambrensis*, XCV (1940), pp. 192–209 and D.T. Williams, 'The maritime trade of the Swansea Bay ports with the Channel Islands from the records of the port books of 1709–19', *Transactions of La Société Guernesaise*, XV (1953), pp. 270–85.

120 For Milford shipping see George, 'Pembrokeshire sea-trading', pp. 1–39.

121 Clemens, 'Liverpool', pp. 211–16; Power, 'Councillors and commerce', pp. 311–21.

122 Piel Island, later Barrow-in-Furness: see Jarvis, 'Head port of Chester', pp. 69–84. Crouch, *Complete view*, p. 248 gives the full administrative division of the area.

123 Willan, *Coasting trade*, pp. 55–69, 111–45; Nef *Coal industry*, II, pp. 380–1 and appendix D; Hatcher, *Coal Industry*, pp. 501–3; Davis, *English shipping industry*, pp. 402–3; and Barney, 'King's Lynn', pp. 128–35. See also Ville's work on productivity and shipping: *English shipowning*, pp. 54–62, 79–80; 'Defending productivity growth', pp. 597–602; and 'Total factor productivity', pp. 355–70.

124 J. Brand, *History of Newcastle* (1789), II, p. 677 discussed in Davis, *English shipping industry*, pp. 402–3. According to Davis's calculations, around 9,000 collier tons were London-owned. Assuming 8 voyages per vessel and an average 248 ton collier in 1701 (Nef, *Coal industry*, I, pp. 390–1), this works out at between 4 and 5 vessels. The figure should perhaps be revised upwards in the light of the smaller vessels operating out of Sunderland. On the same lines, if assumed tonnage for other coastal routes was 6–11,000, and the 8 voyage rule and a smaller coaster of 60 tons (consonant with port book estimates) are applied, a further 13 to 23 coasters may have been London-owned.

125 Andrews, 'English merchant shipping', pp. 232–3.

126 Trinder, *Industrial revolution in Shropshire*, pp. 104–8; Perry, 'Severn navigation' pp. 277–8; Wanklyn, 'Bridgnorth', pp. 43–6.

127 Crowley, 'Of forestallers', in R. Crowley, *The select works of Robert Crowley*, ed. J.M. Cowper (Early English Text Society, extra series 15, 1872), p. 33.

128 Sacks, *Widening gate*, pp. xvi–xvii, 349–51.

Chapter 5

1 See Beavan, *Bristol lists*; Jenkins, 'Redbrook', pp. 163–6; Day, *Bristol brass*, pp. 29–31; BRO 04452(1), p. 80; Minchinton, ed., *Trade of Bristol*, pp. 143–4; Powell, *Privateers*, pp. 90–101; Latimer, *Annals of Bristol in the eighteenth century*, pp. 96, 130, 160, 162; C.H. Cave, *A history of banking in Bristol from 1750 to 1899* (Bristol, 1899), pp. 232–3; and Elton, *Annals of the Elton family* for the career and industrial activities of Sir Abraham Elton.

2 Somerset RO DD/DN 423, Prankard to Owen, p. 58; Prankard to Frye, p. 63; Prankard to Darby, p. 70.

3 Shropshire Borough Library MS 3190, nos 56, 94: Richard Ford to Thomas Goldney, 1 July 1734, 22 Nov. 1735, quoted in Trinder, *Industrial revolution in Shropshire*, p. 61. For Goldney, see Stembridge, *Goldney: Bristol merchant dynasty*, pp. 137–42.

4 The case for these approaches is argued by D. Hancock, *Citizens of the world. London merchants and the integration of the British Atlantic community, 1735–1785* (Cambridge, 1995), pp. 3–5 and with less clarity by Grassby, *Business community*, pp. 1–26. See also Sacks's prefatory essay in *Widening gate*, pp. xv–xxi. J. Agnew, *Belfast merchant families in the seventeenth century* (Dublin, 1996) supplies a practical example of an integrated study of mercantile communities.

5 See Grassby, *Business community*, pp. 261–8 and Armstrong, 'Significance of coastal shipping', pp. 90–3 for examples.

6 Chancery Masters' Exhibits, PRO C104/12. The Company's papers comprise four separate documents: a Letter Book (PRO C104/12 Pt 1, fos 1–187: hereafter *Hoare*

Letter Book); a Waste Book of accounts (PRO C104/12 Pt 1., fos 188–378: hereafter *Hoare Waste Book*); a running Cash Book of credits and debits (PRO C104/12 Pt. 1, fos 379r–438r: hereafter *Hoare Cash Book*); and a Cellar Book of warehoused stock (PRO C104/12 Pt. 2, fos 1–48: hereafter *Hoare Cellar Book*).

7 *Hoare Waste Book*, f. 190r. The Hoare and Balch families, Roberts, Franklin, Galpine and later partners, Thomas Musgrave, Manassee Whitehead and Samuel Codrington were important in the foundation of Bridgwater's early Presbyterian Christ Church: Somerset RO D/N/bw ch ch 1/3/1 and 2/1/4; R.W. Dunning, ed., *The Victoria county history of Somerset. Volume VI. Bridgwater and its neighbouring parishes* (Oxford, 1992), pp. 211, 229, 235.

8 *Hoare Letter Book*, f. 166v, Galpine to Alderman Hoare, 27 March 1699; f. 171v, Galpine to Hoare, 29 April 1699.

9 *Hoare Letter Book*, f. 163v, Galpine to Hoare, 11 March 1699.

10 *Hoare Letter Book*, f. 118v, Galpine to Hoare, 6 April 1698. See also Somerset RO Q/Rua 12.

11 *Hoare Letter Book*, fos 81v–82r, Hoare to Galpine, 14 January 1697; f. 84r, Hoare to Galpine, 16 January 1697. The recoinage crisis severely tested the financial integrity of the Company. For a wider perspective, see D.W. Jones, 'London merchants and the crisis of the 1690s', in P. Clark and P. Slack, eds, *Crisis and order in English towns, 1500–1700* (1972), pp. 311–55.

12 Managed by Galpine's brother, Thomas, and Alexander Wallis: *Hoare Letter Book*, f. 37r, Galpine to Galpine, 1 October 1696; f. 51v, Wallis to Galpine, 5 November 1696; f. 59v, Wallis to Galpine, 24 November 1696; f. 81r, Galpine to Galpine, 12 January 1697; f. 107v, Wallis to Galpine, 13 March 1697. The Ham Mills factory was probably located at Hamp: Somerset RO D/B/bw 570.

13 *Hoare Cash Book*, f. 404r, 13 March 1699.

14 In 1696, Heard was involved in procuring contracts with salt proprietors in Liverpool, Cheshire and Flintshire and in supplying coal for the Ham Mills factory: *Hoare Letter Book*, f. 37r, Galpine to Galpine, 1 October 1696. *Hoare Waste Book*, f. 249r, for Heard's coal ships.

15 *Hoare Letter Book*, f. 1r, Parsons to Drake, 17 March 1696; f. 5r, Cockrem to Drake, 8 June 1696; f. 8v, Higginson to Drake, 19 June 1696; f. 15r, Lockyer to Galpine, 6 August 1696; fos 62r–63r, Drake to Company, 27 November 1696 and 14 November 1696. *Hoare Waste Book*, f. 192v. Drake was involved with Hooke in the chartering of the *Bonavist* of Bristol, in which a quarter share was held on behalf of the Company: *Hoare Letter Book*, f. 9v, Hooke to Drake, 20 June 1696; f. 10r, Hooke to Drake, 7 July 1696, and Hooke to Hoare and Drake, 8 July 1696; f. 81r, Hooke to Drake, no date (January 1697?). For Hooke's later career, see Beavan, *Bristol lists*; Powell, *Privateers*, pp. 90, 100; and Minchinton, ed., *Trade of Bristol*, pp. 143–4.

16 Balch (as mayor), Galpine, Harvey, Greenway and Syms all signed a petition to preserve the Newfoundland fishery in 1709. BL Add MSS 61620, fos 53b–54a.

17 *Hoare Waste Book*, f. 217r, inventory of 'cash, ships, warehouse, cargos, efects [sic], and debts'.

18 Drake purchased Roberts's share: *Hoare Waste Book*, f. 214r.

19 *Hoare Letter Book*, f. 159v, letters to Methwen, February 1699. Methwen also signed the Newfoundland petition in 1709: BM Add MSS 61620 fos 53b–54a. The Company traded with Paul and Ambrose Methwen of Bristol via the agency of William Methwen: *Hoare Waste Book*, f. 349v.

20 *Hoare Letter Book*, f. 152r, Galpine to Hoare, 28 December 1698. In 1701, Ledgingham consigned cargoes imported from overseas coastways.

21 *Hoare Letter Book*, f. 101v, Lowbridge to Galpine, 24 February 1697. Lowbridge planned to be in Bridgwater on 23 and 24 March 1697 to settle his accounts, hoping that 'it will be a convenient time to come to be admitted into your Company'. *Hoare Waste Book*, f. 256r records that Lowbridge paid £300 to be admitted on 31 March 1697. It appears that Lowbridge was based in Exeter, although see Dunning, *VCH Somerset*, VI, p. 228; Somerset RO D/B/bw 2158, 2159. Codrington's admittance is also recorded in *Hoare Waste Book*, f. 295r.

22 *Hoare Letter Book*, f. 157v, Galpine to Hoare, 6 February 1699. The Company appears to have consolidated the type of fractional ownership that was common at the time: Davis, *English shipping industry*, pp. 81–90; Ville, 'English Shipowning', pp. 705–7.

23 *Hoare Letter Book*, f. 160r, Galpine to Hoare, 18 February 1699. Whitehead had already agreed to put in 'two shares being £600 into this joynt stock': *Hoare Letter Book*, f. 159v, Galpine to Whitehead, 15 February 1699. Juliot had part-freighted a voyage to the Straits with the Company: *Hoare Letter Book,* f. 124r, Galpine to Juliot, 27 May 1698.

24 Hoare's will and part of his inventory is detailed in PRO Prob 5/2012.

25 *Hoare Letter Book*, f. 173r–v, Galpine to Fishers, 15 and 17 May 1699; f. 173v, Galpine to Lowbridge, 20 May 1699.

26 *Hoare Cellar Book*, f. 25r.

27 The last entry in the cash book is dated 26 April 1700: *Hoare Cash Book*, fos 425v–426r.

28 The coastal port books indicate that Balch and Company paid duties on tobacco that was imported in May and June 1700 and subsequently shipped coastally to Barnstaple on 31 May 1701. On 17 March 1703, 2 pipes of Canary wine were also shipped to Barnstaple after Balch and Company had paid import duties. The date for this transaction is not specified.

29 Galpine was named as merchant in a voyage from Ilfracombe to Bridgwater in August 1700. On 29 June 1701, the import duties on a consignment of lemons and oranges shipped to Gloucester was secured by Galpine and Company. On the same voyage import duties on 4 pipes of canary wine were certificated by Isaac Heard and Company. Galpine was involved as merchant in three other shipments in 1701 and a further three in 1703. By 1704, Galpine was clearing acting on his own account: PRO SP 34 5/2. See also, *Hoare Letter Book*, fos 184v–187r.

30 Lounsbury, *British fishery*, pp. 135–42; Davis, *English shipping*, pp. 235–6; Innes, *Cod fisheries*, pp. 102–11; Fisher, 'The south-west & the Atlantic trades', pp. 7–14; Starkey, 'Newfoundland trade', pp. 163–71.

31 Coull, *Fisheries of Europe*, pp. 78–80.

32 There were attempts to pass off French bay salt as Spanish using false coquets: BCL B11155, Seizure of the Postillion ketch, 1693.

33 Bristol traded 5.51 tons of French salt in 1695; 7.5 tons of French prize salt in 1695; and 3.6 tons of Lisbon salt in 1701. In 1699–1700 Minehead received 42.11 tons of French and Spanish salt and exported 19.27 tons of Bay salt. At Bideford, 87.89 tons of French and Spanish salt were imported mostly from Plymouth and Penryn in 1699. For conversions, see Hussey, 'Coastal trade', p. 246.

34 For the smaller salt industries see D.A.E. Cross, 'The salt industry of Lymington', *Journal of Industrial Archaeology*, 2 (1965), pp. 86–90; and J. Ellis, 'The decline and fall of the Tyneside salt industry, 1660–1790: a re-examination', *EcHR*, 2nd ser. XXXIII (1980), pp. 45–58. The occasional cargo of salt from Newcastle found its way into the region

through south coast ports: *Hoare Letter Book*, f. 48v, Townson to Smith, 28 October 1696. For Lymington salt, see *Hoare Letter Book*, f. 48v, Cockrem to Galpine, 23 October 1696; f. 67r, Cockrem to Galpine, 15 December 1696.

35 W.H. Chaloner, 'Salt in Cheshire, 1600–1870', *Transactions of the Lancashire and Cheshire Antiquarian Society*, 71 (1961), pp. 61–7.

36 See Wanklyn, 'Shrewsbury boats', pp. 40–4. It is hard to ascertain whether salt from the Broseley and Kingley Wiche saltworks in Shropshire filtered into the river trade: J.M.B. Stamper, 'The Shropshire salt industry', *Transactions of the Shropshire Archaeological Society*, LXIV (1985), pp. 77–82.

37 Barker, 'Lancashire coal, Cheshire salt', pp. 83–8; Hughes, *Administration and finance*, pp. 225–7; Chaloner, 'Salt in Cheshire', pp. 59–60.

38 The salt statutes are summarised in Barker, 'Lancashire coal, Cheshire salt', pp. 90–1 and Hughes, *Administration and finance*, pp. 237, 414–6, 357–64, 366–70. Under 22 Car II c8 s2, the 'Winchester measure, containing eight gallons to the bushel' or 56 lb was to be used for grain and domestic white and refined salt from 29 September 1670. In 1694 rock salt was to be assessed at a far more generous 'double' bushel of 120 lb. The 1696 Act addressed the problems of favourable rock salt drawbacks on duty, whilst from May 1699, the rock salt bushel was reduced to 75 lb, to squeeze a 'farther duty on Rock' (*Hoare Letter Book*, f. 169v, Galpine to Hackett, 18 April 1699). A final Act of May 1702 restricted the refining of rock salt to an area within a 10 mile radius of extraction, established refineries excepted, and further reduced the bushel to 65 lb, a level at which it remained for the rest of the eighteenth century.

39 Marshall, ed., *Stout*, p. 94. See also Chaloner, 'Salt in Cheshire', p. 67. This 'salt upon salt' was stronger, but more expensive than Droitwich and Cheshire white salt: BRO O4449/1, fos 167v, 169v.

40 Barker, 'Lancashire coal, Cheshire salt', pp. 88–92; Hughes, *Administration and finance*, pp. 228–38.

41 The data are from Willan, *Coastal trade*, p. 185. No distinction is made between shipments of white salt and rock salt. If rock salt is included, figures should be adjusted accordingly.

42 For the activities of Steynor and the relative price of Droitwich salt, see Hughes, *Administration and finance*, pp. 225–6; J.W. Willis-Bund and W. Page, eds, *Victoria county history of the county of Worcester. Volume II* (1906), pp. 256–61; E.K. Berry, 'The borough of Droitwich and its salt industry, 1215–1700', *University of Birmingham Historical Journal*, 6 (1957–8), pp. 53, 57–61; and Wakelin, 'Pre-industrial trade', pp. 176–7. Steynor's assertion that the price of salt fell from 1s 6d to 6d a bushel appears to reflect prices at source (Hughes, *Administration and finance*, p. 226). The Bristol Justices fixed the price of wich salt sent down the Severn at between 4s 6d and 4s 8d per Winchester bushel and 'salt made upon salt' at between 5s 6d and 5s 8d per bushel in 1703: BRO 04449/1 fos 167v, 169v.

43 The trade is described in part by Wakelin, 'Pre-industrial trade', pp. 172–81, although data used are discontinuous and no account is made of rock salt. Measures have been converted to the ton after Zupko, *Dictionary*, pp. 25–7, 172–3 and Hussey, 'Coastal trade', pp. 245–56. The data incorporate official changes to the rock salt bushel outlined above.

44 A single shipment of 70 bushels of rock salt was traded from Liverpool in 1684.

45 Berkeley and Newnham maintained an erratic transhipment trade in Cheshire rock salt brought from Liverpool or transhipped via Bristol and Minehead. The very occasional (and very small) cargo of Bay salt was also imported directly from Bristol: Cox, Hussey and Milne, eds, *Database*.

46 Data relating to half-years have been incorporated into figure 5.1 in the form of a running three-year mean.

47 *Hoare Letter Book*, fos 169v–170r; Galpine to Hackett, 18 April 1699.

48 *Hoare Letter Book*, f. 170r, Galpine to Hyde, 19 April 1699.

49 *Hoare Letter Book*, f. 175v, Galpine to Hyde, 6 June 1699.

50 *Hoare Letter Book*, f. 174r, Galpine to Hyde, 24 April 1699.

51 All conversions are to the 2,240 lb ton according to the bushels described above. For the unresolved problems of accurately defining bushel measurements see Willan, *Coasting trade*, pp. 100–2 and Wakelin, 'Pre-industrial trade', pp. 172–81 where the Winchester bushel is universally applied.

52 See BRO 04434/3, pp. 77–8 and 04449(2), 10 April 1706, 11 December 1706, 3 May 1709, 14 March 1711 for the use of the official standard.

53 See P. Linebaugh, *The London hanged: crime and civil society in the eighteenth century* (1991), p. 162 and Morgan, *Bristol*, p. 90 for similar problems in the tobacco trade and in the overseas trade respectively. Divergent measures were used in the port books, notably volumetric hogsheads and barrels (see Wakelin, 'Pre-industrial trade', pp. 172–4 for conversions), but these were quickly supplanted by the officially recognised bushel and ton. Similarly, Hoare and Company note 'heavy' large grained salt that measured the same as the heaped bushel, but weighed somewhat more: *Hoare Letter Book*, f. 92r, Ludlow to Galpine, 31 January 1697 mentions a 92 lb/bushel refined salt; and f. 167r, Galpine to Hackett, 1 April 1699; f. 169r, Galpine to Poole, 12 April 1699 indicates the use of a longer 'merchant ton' weight (21 cwt per ton) in salt negotiations. In all transactions, however, official weights were used. Over measure was also common in the south Wales coalfield: Symons, *Llanelli*, pp. 327–30. For the reform of Britain's erratic metrological standards, see J. Hoppit, 'Reforming Britain's weights and measures', *English Historical Review*, CVIII (1993), pp. 82–104.

54 *Hoare Letter Book*, f. 109r–v, Burnall to Galpine, 26 April 1697.

55 *Hoare Letter Book*, f. 129v, Galpine to Partington and Massy, 6 August 1698.

56 *Hoare Letter Book*, f. 130r–v, Galpine to Massie, 23 August 1698, 27 August 1698.

57 *Hoare Letter Book*, f. 134r–v, Galpine to Massie, 12 September 1698.

58 For Johnson see Power, 'Councillors and commerce', pp. 305–9; Parkinson, *Liverpool*, ch. 7; Barker, 'Lancashire coal, Cheshire salt', pp. 89–91; Hughes, *Administration and finance*, pp. 225–34, 239–42, 394–7; and Muir and Platt, *Liverpool*, pp. 391–4. Warburton claimed to have 'found' rock salt in 1693: *HOC Journals*, XI, p. 102 quoted in Barker 'Lancashire coal, Cheshire salt', pp. 87–8.

59 BRO 04449(2), 6 December 1704. In the corresponding Liverpool port book, Cleaveland was named as the sole merchant.

60 Hughes, *Administration and finance*, pp. 225, 237, 390, 395–6; Barker, 'Lancashire coal, Cheshire salt', pp. 86, 89, 93–4.

61 For Houghton and Haydock, see Hughes, *Administration and finance*, pp. 393, 395–7, 404 and Marshall, ed., *Stout*, pp. 124, 262.

62 Nixon defaulted on excise payment in 1708: Hughes, *Administration and finance*, p. 391. Slyford was one of the earliest pioneer entrepreneurs of the rock salt interest and the extension of the Weaver navigation: ibid., pp. 225, 229–31, 233, 255– 60. In 1707 he unsuccessfully petitioned for letters patent for 'a new way of making salt from the brine of the natural salt-springs and of the rock-salt of England without the use of any fewell or fire': ibid., p. 428 and BL Add MSS 61620, f. 17r.

63 A 'gentleman refiner', Hughes, *Administration and finance*, p. 237; Barker, 'Lancashire coal, Cheshire salt', p. 91 n.4.

64 See Jackson, *Hull in the eighteenth century*, pp. 140–3 and Armstrong, 'Significance of coastal shipping', pp. 90–1 for further examples of this type of organisation.

65 Internal evidence suggests that the partnership may have been in at least informal operation by 1695 if not earlier. Writing from London in September 1696, Hoare reported that he 'had the good fortune to gett the majority of the Board [of Excise] on my side to allow so much salt duty free that was lost in the Providence last year'. *Hoare Letter Book*, f. 53r, Hoare to Galpine, 7 September 1696.

66 *Hoare Waste Book.* fos 190r, 192v. Burnall regularly sailed as supercargo in the *Blessing*: *Hoare Letter Book*, f. 66v, Cockrem to Galpine, 24 November 1696.

67 *Hoare Waste Book*, fos 190r, 196r. Heard was a co-partner, holding two shares in the new Company in September 1696: *Hoare Waste Book*, f. 217r.

68 The *Blessing* with Robert Hyde acting as merchant completed a shipment of salt on 20 February 1696, five days before being sent north by the Company. The *Exchange* was frequently chartered by the Company throughout its operation: *Hoare Letter Book*, f. 5r, Cockrem to Drake, 8 June 1696; f. 66r, Cockrem to Galpine, 19 November 1696; f. 66v, Cockrem to Galpine, 24 November 1696. The *Hannah* completed a voyage with mostly rock salt on 24 March 1696. All vessels were later to ship goods exclusively for Hoare and Company.

69 *Hoare Letter Book*, f. 1v, Currant to Hoare, 8 April 1696; f. 3r, Minshall to Company, April 1696. *Hoare Waste Book*, f. 197r. Currant acted as supercargo for the voyage; Nathaniel Hatherly appears in the Bridgwater port book as master.

70 *Hoare Letter Book*, f. 4r, Neale to Galpine, 31 May 1696; f. 5r, Cockrem to Drake, 8 June 1696; f. 7r, Cockrem to Galpine, 11 June 1696; Neale to Company, 12 June 1696. *Hoare Waste Book*, fos 199v–200v.

71 *Hoare Letter Book*, fos 7v, 9v, 13v, 17v, Pettitt to Company; fos 8r, 9r, 11r, 17v, Higginson to Company; f. 23r; Thomas Webb to Galpine. The *Mary and Elizabeth* broke bulk on 7 September; the *Blessing* on 10 October. *Hoare Waste Book*, fos 202r, 203r, 209r–v.

72 *Hoare Letter Book*, f. 14v, Page to Galpine; fos 19r–20v, Currant to Galpine; fos 19v, 21r, Warburton to Hoare. *Hoare Waste Book*, f. 203v, 20 August 1696.

73 The five-twelfths share in the *Hannah* was sold for £110 6s 8d on 19 October: *Hoare Waste Book*, f. 221r.

74 *Hoare Letter Book*, fos 33r, 44r, Hyde to Company; f. 33v, Baldwin to Company; f. 39v, Warburton to Galpine. The cargo was sold on 3 December: *Hoare Waste Book*, p. 233r.

75 *Hoare Letter Book*, f. 39v, Warburton to Company, 28 September 1696. *Hoare Waste Book*, fos 226v–227r.

76 *Hoare Letter Book*, fos 37v, 42r, Neale to Galpine; f. 50v, Webb to Hoare.

77 *Hoare Letter Book*, f. 61r, Neale to Galpine, 16 November 1696. The cargo of 1,936 bushels and 13 lb (48.41 tons) was sold by 8 January 1697: *Hoare Waste Book*, f. 242r–v.

78 *Hoare Letter Book*, fos 45r, 50r, Higginson to Galpine; f. 50v, Webb to Hoare. *Hoare Waste Book*, f. 225r. For Nathaniel Ludlow's salt, see *Hoare Letter Book*, f. 91r, Ludlow to Galpine, 31 January 1697; *Hoare Waste Book*, f. 262v.

79 Higginson's salt was not completely offloaded until 4 January 1697. *Hoare Waste Book*, f. 240r.

80 Salt may also have been procured from Edward Wheeler, a Droitwich salter: *Hoare Letter Book*, f. 42v, Lowbridge to Galpine, 7 October 1696; f. 47r, Lowbridge to Galpine, 21 October 1696; Hughes, *Administration and finance*, p. 379, n. 1456.

81 *Hoare Waste Book*, fos 211v–212r. For the replacement of wood-fired lead pans by coal-fired iron pans see Hughes, *Administration and finance*, pp. 384, 403–5. Berry, 'Borough of

Droitwich', pp. 49–51 and Wakelin, 'Pre-industrial trade', p. 177 are convinced of the full-scale use of iron pans at this time.

82 *Hoare Letter Book*, f. 57v, Padmore to Galpine, 12 November 1696. Padmore had important links with Cheshire factors: H.J. Hodson, *Cheshire 1660–1780: restoration to industrial revolution* (Chester, 1978), p. 143.

83 *Hoare Letter Book*, f. 57v, Padmore to Galpine, 12 November 1696: 'I have now sent Geo Pyrks about the same quantity as he had last voyage'. *Hoare Waste Book*, f. 232v.

84 *Hoare Waste Book*, f. 236v.

85 The *Endeavour* cleared Liverpool on 6 July 1696 discharging ten days later: *Hoare Waste Book*, f. 199r. Two cwt and 36 lb recorded in the port books were not traded to Hoare and may have represented the crew's salt allowance. In September, Chinn angrily claimed that discounted bills and referred bank notes had represented a loss on the deal 'which ought to be yours': *Hoare Letter Book*, f. 30v, Chinn to Hoare, 4 September 1696.

86 *Hoare Letter Book*, f. 14r, Hyde to Galpine, 28 July 1696; f. 55v, Partington to Methwen, 9 November 1696. *Hoare Waste Book*, f. 222v.

87 *Hoare Waste Book*, fos 220r, 230v.

88 *Hoare Letter Book*, f. 48v, Cockrem to Galpine, 23 October 1696.

89 With 1,546 bushels (38.65 tons) of white salt loaded in January: *Hoare Letter Book*, f. 83r, Burnall to Hoare, 10 January 1697.

90 Carrying 2,608 bushels (65.2 tons). *Hoare Letter Book,* f. 94r–v, Higginson to Galpine, 8 and 9 February 1697. *Hoare Waste Book*, f. 249r.

91 The *Providence* shipped 1,970 bushels of white salt (49.25 tons) from Liverpool in March: *Hoare Letter Book*, f. 104r, Neale to Galpine, 3 March; f. 105v, Neale to Galpine, 5 March. See also *Hoare Waste Book*, f. 253r, 17 March.

92 *Hoare Letter Book*, f. 85r, Cockrem to Galpine, 16 January; f. 86r, Cockrem to Galpine, 21 January; f. 92r, Cockrem to Galpine, 7 February. See *Hoare Waste Book*, f. 272r–v for the full itinerary of the *Exchange* in 1696 and 1697.

93 This was the assessment of John Scott of Fowey: *Hoare Letter Book*, f. 111r, Scott to Galpine, 3 May 1697. Nathaniel Dowdridge, a merchant of Plymouth and factor for Neale's salt, reckoned that peace would bring cheap supplies of French salt: *Hoare Letter Book*, f. 108v, Dowdridge to Galpine, 25 April 1697. Burnall finally discharged at Fowey, Higginson at Dartmouth, and Neale at Plymouth: *Hoare Letter Book*, f. 110v, Burnall to Galpine, 3 May 1697; f. 111v, Neale to Galpine, 7 May 1697; *Hoare Waste Book*, f. 272v, itinerary of the *Providence*; f. 278v, itinerary of the *Mary and Elizabeth*.

94 *Hoare Letter Book*, f. 92r, Dashwood to Galpine, 5 February 1697; f. 100r, Dashwood to Galpine, 15 February; f. 107r, Dashwood to Galpine, 6 March 1697. *Hoare Waste Book*, f. 262v.

95 *Hoare Waste Book*, fos 262v, 271r. The boat was purchased by Currant in February 1697, a three-quarter share of which was held by the Company: *Hoare Waste Book*, f. 248v.

96 *Hoare Waste Book*, f. 298r, completion of the *Hope*, 27 September; f. 308v, completion of the *Michael,* 8 December.

97 *Hoare Waste Book*, f. 313v, account of the *Exchange,* 14 January 1698. The Company may have had interests in two further shipments in the *Hannah* of Bridgwater, and the *Rebecca* of Liverpool mastered by Higginson.

98 *Hoare Letter Book*, f. 83v, Lowbridge to Galpine, 16 January; f. 95v, Lowbridge to Galpine, 9 February; f. 101v, Lowbridge to Galpine, 24 February. Corker's shipments, disbursements and the sale of salt brought on his trows are listed in *Hoare Waste Book*, fos 244r–v, 251r, 255r–v, 256v, 260r, 278r, 290v, 294v.

99 *Hoare Waste Book*, fos 275r–276r, 282r, 307v.

100 *Hoare Waste Book*, f. 310v.

101 See *Hoare Waste Book*, f. 320r–v. For Steynor, see Hughes, *Administration and finance*, pp. 225–36, 378–9; Berry, 'Borough of Droitwich', pp. 46–50.

102 For the career of Edward, William, Thomas and Samuel Jackson, see Wanklyn, 'Bridgnorth', pp. 47–8, n.39 and Wakelin, 'Pre-industrial trade', pp. 202–4.

103 The *Charles* entered Bridgwater on 7 January 1698 carrying 40 tons of salt (39.75 tons were sold to regular customers): *Hoare Waste Book*, f. 320 r–v. A further 35 tons of salt were delivered in March (*Hoare Waste Book*, f. 328r) and a final consignment of 19 tons and 18 cwt was discharged on the account of the Company from a cargo of 41 tons on 5 April (*Hoare Waste Book*, f. 337v).

104 *Hoare Waste Book*, fos 331v–332r. Steynor sent 39 tons and 17 cwt (2 cwt overweight) which was discharged 'out off Owner Chance['s] trow' by 17 March.

105 *Hoare Waste Book*, fos 326v, 358v, 363r. See also *Hoare Letter Book*, f. 133r, Galpine to Padmore, 7 September 1698.

106 *Hoare Letter Book*, f. 129v, Galpine to Padmore, 17, 18 August 1698; f. 132r–v, Galpine to Padmore, 5 September 1698.

107 *Hoare Waste Book*, fos 369r, 372v, 375v. *Hoare Letter Book*, f. 145r, Galpine to Herbert, 19 November 1698; *Hoare Cash Book*, f. 388v records 1 ton, 3 cwt of clod salt delivered to cellar K. Clod salt was made from the residue of the boiling process: Plot, *Staffordshire*, pp. 93–6; Wakelin, 'Pre-industrial trade', p. 171.

108 *Hoare Letter Book*, f. 122v, Galpine to Hoare, 18 May 1698.

109 The Company bought 20.45 tons of salt from Claroe on 9 May, selling it on by 14 May: *Hoare Waste Book*, fos 344r, 345r.

110 The *Elizabeth* was recorded as carrying 36 tons in the Bridgwater port book. In the accompanying wool coquet, William Smith was named as the merchant: *Hoare Waste Book*, f. 355r.

111 *Hoare Letter Book*, f. 144v. The Norris family were to rise to some importance. Thomas and Richard Norris were listed as Droitwich salt proprietors in Cardonel's list of 1732: Hughes, *Administration and finance*, p. 379, n.1456. A James Norris was also freighting salt vessels to Bristol in 1733. Wakelin conjectures a familial link with the Droitwich producers: 'Pre-industrial trade', p. 207.

112 For the prior activity of Throgmorton's steward, see *Hoare Letter Book*, f. 129v, Galpine to Padmore, 17 August 1698; *Hoare Waste Book*, f. 365v.

113 *Hoare Waste Book*, fos 370v, 375v–376r. The Bridgwater port book records the second of these shipments bearing coquet of 24 November from Gloucester twice. Only one shipment has been accounted for in the text and data.

114 *Hoare Letter Book*, f. 147r, Galpine to Norris, 7 December 1698.

115 During 1698, the *Fly* was occupied in a voyage to Waterford and the Canaries, returning home via France; the *Mary and Elizabeth* was dispatched to Virginia on two occasions; the *Hope* to Bilbao; the *Friendship* to Spain and France; the *Betty* to the West Indies; and the *Michael* to Newfoundland.

116 *Hoare Waste Book*, fos 339v, 350v. *Hoare Letter Book*, f. 122r, Galpine to Hoare, 14 May 1698; f. 123r Galpine to Hoare, 21 May 1698.

117 *Hoare Letter Book*, f. 129r, Galpine to Partington and Massy, 6 August 1698; f. 130v, Galpine to Massie, 27 August 1698; f. 131r, Galpine to Vinecott, 28 August 1698; f. 134r–v, Galpine to Massie, 12 September 1698. The voyage ended on 29 October: *Hoare Waste Book*, f. 372r.

118 Hyde and Hoare and Company were recorded as merchants in the port books: *Hoare Letter Book*, f. 130r, Galpine to Hyde, 23 August 1698. *Hoare Waste Book*, fos 368r–v, 371v.

119 *Hoare Cash Book,* f. 402r, 28 February 1699 records Oakes being paid for freight and Norris for 211 tons 15 cwt of salt to be delivered at Bridgwater.

120 *Hoare Letter Book*, f. 169r, Galpine to Poole, 12 April 1699; *Hoare Cash Book*, fos 414v–415r notes salt purchased out of Clarke's trow, 26 May 1699, and payment to Norris on the same date.

121 *Hoare Cash Book*, f. 402r, 7 March 1698. The *Samuel* arrived in Bridgwater on 3 March.

122 *Hoare Letter Book*, f. 150r, Galpine to Padmore, 17 December 1698; f.153v, Galpine to Hall, 28 December 1698, reveal that Padmore and Hall's contract was continued. Padmore was reimbursed for weighing out 46 tons of white salt at Worcester on 7 March and Corker for freight on 14 April: *Hoare Cash Book*, fos 403r, 404r.

123 *Hoare Letter Book*, f. 169r, Galpine to Hall and Penrice, 12 April 1699; Hughes, *Administration and finance*, pp. 379–80.

124 On 5 July the *Success* with John Beale as merchant discharged 5 tons of white salt. It returned on 19 August with 40 tons and was again in Bridgwater on 21 September with 35 tons: *Hoare Cash Book*, fos 409r–411r.

125 It is likely that the Company was also involved in the two voyages undertaken by Jackson on the *Prosperity* of Bridgnorth towards the end of the year, although the records tail off at this point.

126 The *Hope* was dispatched in November 1698: *Hoare Letter Book*, f. 150v, Galpine to Hyde, 17 December; f. 151r, Galpine to Hyde, 26 December; f. 151v, Galpine to Currant, 28 December 1698; f. 152r, Galpine to Hyde, 28 December. Hoare appeared as the merchant in the port book.

127 Heard was still a member of the Company when the coquet for the *Elizabeth* was granted (10 December 1698), although it is clear that by February he was anxious to quit: *Hoare Letter Book*, f. 160v, Galpine to Hoare, 18 February 1699.

128 The *Speedwell* set off on 20 February: *Hoare Letter Book*, f. 160v, Galpine to Partington. On 17 March Galpine ordered Massey and Partington to load rock and white, specifying mostly rock in a letter dated twelve days later: *Hoare Letter Book*, fos 165r, 166v. Galpine's final order was that if Partington had not forwarded rock salt 'nor yett freighted for us . . . dispatch the *Speedwell* with white salt': *Hoare Letter Book*, f. 168v, Galpine to Partington, 10 April. The *Speedwell* had completely discharged by 26 May: *Hoare Cash Book*, f. 415r.

129 *Hoare Letter Book*, f. 155r, Galpine to Hyde, 16 January 1699.

130 *Hoare Letter Book*, f. 170r, Galpine to Hyde, 19 April 1699; f. 171r, Galpine to Currant, 28 April 1699; f. 173r, Galpine to Currant, 9 May 1699; f. 174r–v, Galpine to Hyde, 24 May 1699; *Hoare Cash Book*, fos 416r, 418r. The *Michael* discharged at Bridgwater with Hoare and Company as the acting merchant in the port books.

131 The Company was aware of the impending legislation by January 1699: *Hoare Letter Book*, f. 153v, Galpine to Hoare, 11 January 1699.

132 *Hoare Letter Book*, f. 167r, Galpine to Hackett, 1 April 1699; f. 175r, Farewell to Fishers, 3 June reports that Galpine has been in Bristol buying rock salt and was indebted to Abraham Elton on a bill of £100.

133 See S.C. Morland, ed., *Somersetshire Quarterly Meeting of the Society of Friends, 1668–99* (Somerset Record Society, 75, 1978) for Alloway's religious activities. Details of Alloway's commercial career are provided by his Irish partner, Joseph Pike (*Some account of the life of Joseph Pike of Cork in Ireland who died in the year 1729, written by himself* (1837), pp. 121–2) and also by Dunning, *VCH Somerset*, VI, p. 200 and J.H. Bettey, 'From Quaker traders to

Anglican gentry: the rise of a Somerset dynasty', *PSANHS*, 135 (1992), pp. 1–2. Alloway's Account Book survives for 1695–1704 Somerset RO DD/DN 463 1695–1704 (hereafter, *Alloway Account Book*).

134 Alloway possessed controlling interests in rock salt works at Bridgwater, Taunton, Shepton Mallet and Port Isaac in Cornwall: *Alloway Account Book*, pp. 40, 54–5, 59, 64, 84.

135 The Lynmouth fishery was inherited from his father, William Alloway senior of Minehead (Somerset RO DD/DN 462, f. 1r–v): *Alloway Account Book*, pp. 100, 134.

136 Hughes, *Administration and finance*, pp. 225–41, 394–7; Barker, 'Lancashire coal, Cheshire salt', pp. 86–90; Chaloner, 'Salt in Cheshire', p. 68; Power, 'Councillors and commerce', pp. 305–9. Johnson was described as 'Mr. Allaway's friend in Liverpool': *Hoare Letter Book*, f. 19r, Currant to Galpine, 7 August 1696. For return journeys organised by Alloway for Johnson, see *Alloway Account Book*, pp. 81, 118.

137 *Alloway Account Book*, p. 2. Wheddon was a major merchant and landowner in Watchet: Somerset RO DD/L2 19/110 (Box 128), assessment of Watchet 1708. See also Wheddon's account of shipping in Somerset RO DD/WY bx 40, Account Book of duties at Watchet Quay, 1708–1764. The *Satisfaction* was often described as 'of' Minehead. The three-eighths share in the *Robert and Thomas* was probably increased after 1696, especially as the boat's regular shipper, Thomas Anstice, was more directly involved in goods shipped on board the vessel: *Alloway Account Book*, p. 41.

138 *Alloway Account Book*, pp. 1, 6–7, 15, 20, 23–4. The *Satisfaction* was taken to St Malo in September and not ransomed until October.

139 *Alloway Account Book*, pp. 7–8, 17, 20, 23, 25.

140 *Alloway Account Book*, p. 30.

141 The vessel arrived in Liverpool by mid-December 1695, clearing the following February: *Alloway Account Book*, p. 30.

142 *Alloway Account Book*, p. 41. The vessel was fully discharged by 10 May 1696.

143 *Alloway Account Book*, pp. 39, 41. *Hoare Letter Book*, f. 3r, Minshall to Hoare, 23? May 1696. Minshall supposed that Holmes's loading was on the Company's account.

144 *Alloway Account Book*, p. 48. *Hoare Letter Book*, f. 17v, Pettitt to Hoare, 2 August 1696 reports on Holmes's arrival in Liverpool; f. 19r, Currant to Galpine, 7 August indicates the problems of procuring a loading.

145 In the port books, Hyde appeared as merchant and Thomas Fisher as master. Anstice acted as supercargo: *Alloway Account Book*, pp. 48–9. See also *Hoare Letter Book*, f. 4r, Higginson to Hoare, 1 June 1696 at Oberson travelling in convoy to Hoylake; f. 7v, Neale to Company, 19 June at Liverpool in convoy with the *Robert and Thomas*.

146 *Alloway Account Book*, pp. 52–3.

147 *Alloway Account Book*, pp. 66–7.

148 *Alloway Account Book*, p. 142.

149 *Alloway Account Book*, pp. 56, 62, 80.

150 Alloway appeared as merchant in the Bridgwater port book. *Alloway Account Book*, p. 81.

151 *Alloway Account Book*, p. 134.

152 *Alloway Account Book*, p. 117. Simon Hayman and Alloway's brother Joseph, merchants of Minehead, were paid cellarage for this salt in December 1698.

153 Bridgwater corporation's Exchequer suit claimed that Richard Bobbett consistently defied custom by not paying town duties, keelage, pontage and the right of first sale to freemen on cargoes of coal 'and other merchandizes' shipped 'in small boates' to Ham Mills. PRO E134 23&24 Chas 2, Hil. 18, esp. f. 5r–v depositions; PRO E134 24 Chas 2,

East. 24, fos 2r–3r. The map was produced by Martin Roberts using software supplied by 'Digital Map Data © Bartholomew 1999'.

154 These were major installations. In September 1698, Galpine entreated John Padmore to 'provide . . . a well made pan of 12 foott'. This was ready by December when a further '3 or 4 plates to mend the old one' were required. *Hoare Letter Book*, f. 132r, Galpine to Padmore, 5 September 1698; f. 150r, Galpine to Padmore, 17 December 1698. Padmore also dispatched an experienced pan setter and salt maker: *Hoare Letter Book*, f. 154v, Galpine to Padmore, 14 January 1699.

155 For inland traders rock salt may also have been used in its unprocessed or crushed form as cattle lick: Chaloner, 'Salt in Cheshire', p. 59.

156 These were the first roads to be turnpiked in the area: E. Pawson, *Transport and economy: the turnpike roads of eighteenth-century Britain* (1977), p. 140. Kirby was also used by Prankard to convey tallow from Bridgwater to Langport: Somerset RO DD/DN 423, p. 47.

157 PRO E134 23&24 Chas 2, Hil 18, f. 5v.

158 The *Waste Book* only recorded regular agents and not the eventual users who often contracted carriers to supply them. Some idea of the range of the Company's salt dealings can be gathered from *Hoare Cash Book*, fos 16r–18r.

159 Morland, ed., *Somersetshire quarterly meeting*, pp. 7, 43.

160 For Boldy's activities, see Somerset RO Q/Rua 12, loose leaf account 20 August 1700 – 4 February 1701 and Somerset RO D/B/bw 1524, Accounts of money from Vinsin Bolding of Langport, 1716–19. See also *Hoare Waste Book*, fos 319v, 332r. The Parrett and Tone were only effectively made navigable to Taunton after the gradual enforcement of successive improvement Acts in the early eighteenth century: Willan, *River Navigation*, pp. 31, 48, 56, 155.

161 *Alloway Account Book*, pp. 7–8, 17, 31, 40; *Hoare Waste Book*, f. 199v.

162 *Hoare Letter Book*, f. 81r, Thomas Galpine to Nathaniel Galpine, 12 January 1697; f. 81v, Hoare to Galpine, 12 January 1697.

163 *Hoare Letter Book*, fos 113v–114r, Account of Robert Bobbett, 1697–8; f. 114r, Roberts to Galpine, 18 September 1698.

164 *Alloway Account Book*, pp. 16, 17, 40, 48, 57.

165 *Hoare Letter Book*, fos 125r–126r; Company to Methwen, Chanler, Town, Smith, Lloyd, Barnsdale and Bailey. *Hoare Waste Book*, f. 348v.

166 *Hoare Waste Book*, f. 374r–v.

167 *Hoare Letter Book*, f. 155r, Galpine to Hackett, 14 January 1699.

168 *Hoare Waste Book*, fos 249r, 252r, 253v, 287r, 294r, 369r. *Hoare Letter Book*, f. 126r, Galpine to Hyde, 15 June 1698; f. 138r, Galpine to Stonard, 15 October 1698. Neither the Company nor its officials appeared as merchants in the respective port books.

169 See *Hoare Letter Book*, f. 41r, Mackworth to Hoare, 2 October 1696; Mackworth to Company, 9 December 1696 (loose leaf insert); Trott, 'Coalmining in Neath', pp. 47–74; and Rees, *Industry,* pp. 88–9, 109–110, 523–5. Between 1698 and 1700, Mackworth had extensive dealings with the bankers Hoare and Company of London: R.O. Roberts, 'Financial developments in early modern Wales and the emergence of the first banks', *Welsh Historical Review*, 16 (1993), pp. 300–1.

170 The Company also dealt with an Evans of Neath, and James Phillips of Tenby: *Hoare Letter Book*, f. 28r, Cockrem to Galpine, 28 August 1696; f. 176r, Galpine to Hyman, 6 June 1699. *Hoare Waste Book*, fos 190r, 319v. See also Hatcher, *Coal industry*, p. 139; Rees, *Industry,* pp. 538–40.

171 *Hoare Letter Book*, f. 84v, Thomas Galpine to Nathaniel Galpine, 19 January 1697; f. 93r, Galpine to Galpine, 13 February 1697.

172 Writing from Dublin in 1696, John Neale claimed that Milford culm outsold Tenby culm by a shilling a ton, whilst the inferior Saundersfoot culm he was carrying could only be sold for almost 3 shillings a ton less than Tenby culm: *Hoare Letter Book*, f. 33v, Neale to Galpine, 10 September 1696; f. 37v, Neale to Galpine, 25 September 1696. The price differential between the three types of coal varied according to the level of supplies, season and credit extended to the customer. In January 1697, Swansea hearth coal sold at between 34s 2d and 36s 2d per wey, 'Abbey' or Neath coal at between 25s 2d and 27s 2d per wey, and Milford culm at a more consistent 27s 2d per wey, *Hoare Waste Book*, fos 259v–260r. See also Nef, *Coal Industry*, pp. 116–17.

173 Nef, *Coal industry*, pp. 373–4; Rees, *Industry*, pp. 129–32; Symons, *Llanelli*, pp. 324–30.

174 Hatcher, *Coal industry*, p. 571.

175 Nef, *Coal industry*, p. 370; Willan, *Coasting trade*, pp. 208–9.

176 This implies that the London measure was used throughout the region, which Rees seems to suggest at least for overseas trade: *Industry*, p. 131. See also 6/7 Wil. & Mar., c.10 and Hatcher, *Coal industry*, p. 559.

177 Hatcher, *Coal industry*, pp. 559–69 dismisses the Pembrokeshire chaldron by omission, concentrating upon the London and Newcastle standards.

178 *Hoare Waste Book*, f. 204v. If a wey measured 5 tons, a quarter 6 cwt (Nef, *Coal industry*, p. 373), and a bushel 56 lb, 530.45 tons of coal were sold by Wallis in 1696.

179 *Hoare Waste Book*, fos 204v–237v.

180 *Hoare Letter Book*, f. 81r, Galpine to Galpine, 12 January 1697; f. 93r, Galpine to Galpine, 13 February 1697.

181 The details of shipments are gained from the port books and *Hoare Waste Book*, fos 241r–296r.

182 Some 182 tons of culm and 60 barrels (8 tons: Nef, *Coal Industry*, pp. 371–2) were transported on board the *Two Sisters* in 1697. The vessel may well have been operating for the Company in the previous year, although there is no direct evidence tying the eleven shipments undertaken with coals received by the factory or dispensed at the quayside.

183 By 1698, Wallis's contract with the Company to freight the *William and Richard* had expired; *Hoare Waste Book*, f. 321v.

184 *Hoare Waste Book*, fos 317r–377v.

185 *Hoare Letter Book*, f. 176r, Galpine to Hyman, 6 June 1699.

186 The vessel cleared Gloucester on 30 October ostensibly for Bridgwater and Newport carrying chairs and pins alongside Smith's malt (measured at 5 weys) and wool (444 tods of 28 lbs) and 20 hogsheads of Company salt. Smith was named as merchant on the wool coquet. *Hoare Waste Book*, f. 233r.

187 The *Thomas* cleared Gloucester for Bridgwater on 30 December 1695, 4 March 1696 and 2 September with very similar cargoes.

188 *Hoare Letter Book*, f. 75r, Smith to Hoare, 28 December 1696; f. 82v, Smith to Hoare, 11 January 1697; f. 84v, Smyth to Galpine, 16 January 1697; f. 98v, Smith to Galpine, 20 February 1697. The *Thomas* finally cleared Gloucester on 9 February 1697. Her loading brought only 1,627 bushels of grain specifically for Smith and Hoare, some was freighted for Joseph Hunt of Upton. In addition, Smith ventured 18 bags of wool (from a total of 53 bags) on his own account to be delivered to Charles Cork of Taunton.

189 *Hoare Letter Book*, f. 92v, Smith to Galpine, 8 February 1697. For the importance of the marlstone uplands surrounding Banbury as a grain producing area, see J.R. Wordie, 'The South: Oxfordshire, Buckinghamshire, Berkshire, Wiltshire, and Hampshire', in Thirsk, ed., *The agrarian history of England and Wales. Volume V: 1640–1750. I: Regional farming systems*, pp. 317–20.

190 *Hoare Waste Book*, fos 275r–276r. A further 36 tods (at 28 lb per tod) were carried by the *Thomas*.

191 For details of the Company's contract with Smith, see *Hoare Waste Book*, fos. 275r–276r, 282r, 283v–284r, 290v, 293r–v.

192 The Company weighed out 1,187 bushels of wheat and malt. Some was accounted 'lost' and some may have been distributed as freight. Smith appeared as merchant on the wool coquet, although his loading amounted to only 85 per cent of the wool carried by the *Success*. The grain was dispatched to Exeter via the Cullompton carrier: *Hoare Waste Book*, fos 286v–287r.

193 *Hoare Waste Book*, f. 284r. All measures have been converted to the Winchester bushel as outlined in chapter 3 and, with modifications, Wakelin, 'Pre-industrial trade', pp. 141–2 and n.28. There is some discrepancy between the Company's accounts and the Bridgwater port books. The Company itemised 36 bags carried on the *John and Elizabeth* and not 34. This probably indicates a scribal error in the coquet (the same amount appears in the outwards section of the Gloucester port book). The research has standardised upon the port book enumeration.

194 *Hoare Waste Book*, fos 290v, 293r–v, 301v. The *Elizabeth* cleared Gloucester on 5 October. It was back in the Severn by 3 November to ship another wool cargo to Bridgwater, although it is not clear whether this was for Smith and Hoare.

195 *Hoare Waste Book*, f. 255r.

196 *Hoare Letter Book*, f. 27v, Smyth to Galpine, 29 August 1696; f. 28r, Cockrem to Galpine, 20 August 1696. See also Chartres, 'Marketing of agricultural produce, 1640–1750', p. 224.

197 *Hoare Waste Book*, f. 326r.

198 In 1697, 25,767.5 bushels of grain and cereal crops were imported coastally at Bridgwater, compared to a mere 1,661 bushels in 1696 and 2,832 bushels in 1698.

199 Hoskins, 'Harvest fluctuations, 1620–1759', pp. 22, 24, 30. See also T.S. Ashton, *Economic fluctuations in England, 1700–1800* (Oxford, 1959); E.L. Jones, *Seasons and prices. The role of weather in agricultural history* (1964); Chartres, 'Marketing of agricultural produce, 1640–1750', pp. 205–16; and Jenkins, 'Times and seasons', pp. 21–2. Climatic change may also have been a factor: see Lamb, *Climate*, p. 219; E. Le Roy Ladurie, *Times of feast, times of famine: a history of climate since the year 1000* (New Jersey, 1971), pp. 118–20; and J. de Vries, 'Measuring the impact of climate on history: the search for appropriate methodologies', in R.I. Rotberg and T.K. Rabb, eds, *Climate and history* (Princeton, 1981), pp. 38–50.

200 Chartres, 'Marketing of agricultural produce, 1640–1750', pp. 208–9.

201 The seventeenth- and early eighteenth-century business community of Bristol remains a woefully under-researched area. See C.E. Harvey J. and Press, eds, *Studies in the business history of Bristol* (Bristol, 1988) and their later methodological work: 'The business elite of Bristol: a case study in database design', *History and Computing*, 3 (1991), pp. 1–11 and 'Relational data analysis: value, concepts and methods', *History and Computing*, 4, 2 (1992), pp. 98–109 for later comparisons.

202 The Dickenson papers provide an unrivalled insight into the organisation of trade in the 1730s and 1740s: Somerset RO DD/DN 424–444.

203 BRO 04434/3, pp. 77–8. The Liverpool port book records Thomas Hinde as merchant.
204 BRO 04434/3, pp. 83–5, 92. Trewell was ordered to be distrained on 21 September 1699. Hollidge was a member of the Society of Merchant Venturers in 1690, warden in 1695–6 and eventually mayor in 1708: McGrath, ed., *Records relating to the Society of Merchant Venturers*, pp. 33, 257–60; Beavan, *Bristol lists*. See also Ralph and Williams, eds, *Inhabitants of Bristol*, p. 191 and Minchinton, ed., *Trade of Bristol*, p. 7.
205 BRO 04449(2), 9 January 1705. For Nixon and Woodruffe, see Hughes, *Administration and finance*, p. 391.
206 BRO 04449(2), 13 August 1707.
207 BRO 04449(2), 10 April 1706.
208 BRO 04449(2), 11 December 1706, 3 May 1709.
209 See note 1. Elton also brought overloads of foreign salt to Bristol from Falmouth on board the *John* of Falmouth in 1701: BRO 04434/3, pp. 137–8.
210 Scandrett freighted large cargoes of rock and white salt on the *Mary and Martha* of London; the *John and Mary*; the *Globe* of Milford; and the *Endeavour* of Bideford: BRO 04434/3, pp. 122–3, 162–3, 163–4, 176–7.
211 BRO 04434/3, pp. 144–5. Bearpacker appears to have generally acted as a factor. In 1696 and 1697 he dealt with Hoare and Company in goods imported on the *Bonavist*: *Hoare Letter Book*, f. 81r, Hooke to Drake, ?12 January 1697. A John Beerpacker was living in All Saints parish, Bristol, with his wife and five children in 1696: Ralph and Williams, eds, *Inhabitants of Bristol*, p. 9.
212 BRO 04449(2), 6 December 1704. Alloway dispatched peas ordered by Thomas Johnson to Baker in 1699: *Alloway Account Book*, p. 119.
213 Wakelin, 'Pre-industrial trade', pp. 201–10; Hughes, *Administration and finance*, p. 379, n. 1456.
214 BRO 04434/3, pp. 119, 151–2, 170, 189–90.
215 BRO 04434/3, p. 130; BRO 04449(1), f. 98r. For Lane, see Hughes, *Administration and finance*, pp. 244, 379.
216 BRO 04434/3, pp. 83–5.
217 BRO 04434/3, pp. 94–5. Lewis was recorded as master and merchant in the Gloucester port book.
218 Lewis and the *Hester* cleared Gloucester on 15 August with 15 hogsheads of rock salt.
219 Burnall was 'captain' to the *Blessing* mastered by Giles Vinecott on her voyage from Liverpool to the south coast of Cornwall: *Hoare Letter Book*, f. 83r, Burnall to Hoare, 10 January 1697; f. 110v, Burnall to Galpine, 3 May 1697.
220 *Hoare Waste Book*, f. 320r.
221 Defoe, *English tradesman*, p. 8.
222 Willan, *Coasting trade*, pp. 43–6.
223 PRO Prob 5 2012, Roger Hoare, inventory and schedule of debts, 1699. The sum, paltry compared to London merchants, does not appear to account for most of Hoare's commercial transactions or stock. See P. Earle, *The making of the English middle class. Business, society and family life in London, 1660–1730* (1989), pp. 36–42 and Grassby, *Business community*, pp. 247–57 for comparative, if highly metrocentric, data. Hoare's son, also Roger, died a very comfortable Somerset gentleman in 1728: PRO PROB 3 27/221.
224 Somerset RO DD/SP 1716/17, inventory of John Syms, merchant of Bridgwater. Syms had half-shares in the *Prosperity* of Bridgwater, the *Hopewell* of Bridgwater, and the *John and Henry* of Bridgwater, a three-eighths share in the *Exeter Merchant* of Bridgwater, and a third-share in the *Betty* of Bridgwater, in total worth £285. His house possessed

fashionable furniture, glass and earthenware, pictures, books, looking glasses, a clock, and a shovelboard room.

225 See Somerset RO DD/DN 145, certificate of marriage, William Alloway and Hannah Anderson, 1686; will of William Alloway, 1719, proved 1722. PRO PROB 4 2773, will of William Alloway the elder, 1686. A very short biographical account is given in Bettey, 'Quaker traders', pp. 1–9.

Conclusion

1 See MacInnes, *Gateway of Empire* and discussions in Sacks, *Widening gate*, pp. 348–53 and Morgan, *Bristol*, pp. 9–13.

2 See McGrath, ed., *Merchants*; McGrath, *Merchant Venturers of Bristol*, pp. 49–101, 124–69; McGrath, ed., *Records relating to the Society of Merchant Venturers*; Minchinton, *Politics and the port of Bristol*; and Minchinton, 'Merchants of Bristol', pp. 185–200. For individual studies, see McGrath, *John Whitson*; Elton, *Annals of the Elton family*; P. K. Stembridge, *Goldney, a house and family* (Bristol, 1969, 4th edn 1982); and Pares, *A West-India fortune*.

3 *The Journal of Samuel Curwen, Loyalist*, 6 September 1777, quoted in Morgan, *Bristol*, p. 9.

4 Estabrook, *Urbane and rustic England*, pp. 67–82.

5 Minchinton, 'Metropolis', pp. 69–89.

6 Minchinton, ed., *Trade of Bristol*, pp. xiv–xv; Minchinton, 'Port of Bristol', pp. 132–3.

7 See B.J.L. Berry and W.L. Garrison, 'The functional bases of central-place hierarchy', in H.M. Mayer and C.F. Kohn, eds, *Readings in urban geography* (Chicago, 1959), pp. 218–27; A. Lösch, *The economics of location* (New Haven, 1954), introduction; and critiques in Beavon, *Central place theory*, pp. 10–22.

8 Morgan, *Bristol*, pp. 152–60; Price, *France and the Chesapeake*, pp. 509–10; Price and Clemens, 'Revolution of scale', pp. 24–8; Goodman, *Tobacco*, pp. 70–5; and Devine, 'Golden age of tobacco', pp. 139–83.

9 Morgan, 'Economic development', p. 66; Walker, *Bristol region*, pp. 229–30.

10 C. Morris, ed., *The illustrated journeys of Celia Fiennes c. 1682–c. 1712* (1984), p. 193; Nef, *Coal industry*, I, pp. 65, 97, 360.

11 Quoted in Martin and Pickard, eds, *Bristol poetry*, p. 6.

12 Williams, 'Port plans', pp. 138–88.

13 See Willan, *Coasting trade*, chs 5–6; Willan, *River navigation*, pp. 2–5; Chartres, *Internal trade*, pp. 43–6; and Armstrong and Bagwell, 'Coastal shipping', pp. 152–3.

14 For discussions of some of these 'consumer-inspired' goods see Weatherill, *Consumer behaviour*; Weatherill 'The meaning of consumer behaviour', pp. 206–27; Shammas, *The pre-industrial consumer*; and Shammas 'Changes in English and Anglo-American consumption', pp. 185–95.

15 Somerset RO DD/DN 423, pp. 92, 94, 97. Prankard's father-in-law, William Alloway, had earlier adopted a far more rigorous line with regard to such 'superfluous garnishing': Pike, *Life of Joseph Pike*, p. 66.

16 *Hoare Letter Book*, f. 112v, Tuthill to Galpine, 10 May 1697.

17 Minchinton, 'Port of Bristol', p. 132 gives details of these later services.

18 BCL B11153 (2), Abraham to Southwell, Banbury, 19 May 1684. Vickers, a freeman of Tewkesbury, made 21 voyages in 1683 and 10 in 1684: Cox, Hussey and Milne, eds, *Database*.

19 Chartres, *Internal trade*, p. 46. See also Willan, *Coasting trade*, pp. 13–20; Davis, *English shipping industry*, pp. 76, 194–5, appendix A; and Ville, 'Total factor productivity', pp. 358–62.

20 Willan, *Coasting trade*, pp. 34, 53–4.

21 *Hoare Letter Book*, fos 125r–126r, Company to Methwen, Chanler, Town, Smith, Lloyd, Barnsdale and Bayly, 10–11 June 1698. *Hoare Letter Book*, fos 144v–145v, Company to Hoare, Padmore, Herbert, Lloyd and Hall, 19–29 November 1698.

22 Willan, *Coasting trade*, pp. 46–7.

23 See Power, 'Councillors and commerce', pp. 305–9 for details of the Liverpool mercantile elite.

24 D. Defoe, *A plan of the English commerce* (1728, repr. Oxford, 1928), p. 1.

25 John Man to Joseph Williamson, Swansea, 30 September 1678: PRO SP 29 406, p. 224 (*CSPD*, 1678, p. 434); Willan, *Coasting trade*, p. 193.

Bibliography

Manuscript sources

Bristol Central Library

B4939	Oaths, list of members and accounts: Mercers and Linendrapers Company, 1647–1729.
B6584	Actions in Tolzey and Pie Poudre Courts, 1725–7.
B11153	Southwell Papers: Romsey and Knight papers.
B11154	Southwell Papers: Henley and Merchant Adventurers papers, 1690–1709.
B11155	Southwell Papers: seizure of the Postillion ketch, 1693–7.
B17368	John Galton and Graffin Prankard, bills and manuscripts, 1740–2.

Bristol Record Office

00044	St Paul's Fair: agreement for stands, 1723.
00120	St Paul's Fair: agreement for stands, 1673.
00147	St Paul's Fair: agreement for stands, 1705.
00148	St Paul's Fair: agreement for stands, 1719
00149	St Paul's Fair: agreement for stands, 1720.
04264	Common Council proceedings [(7) 1675–87; (8) 1687–1702; (9) 1702–22].
04274(2)	Book of Ordinances, 1702.
04410	Whitson Court Book, 1629–53.
04411	Piepowdre Court Book, 1656.
04412	Piepowdre Court Book.
04434	Orders and recognisances of Tolzey Court [(2) 1688–93; (3) 1693–1703].
04439	Deposition books [(3) 1657–61; (4) 1661–7].
04447(3)	Quarter Sessions minute book, 1681–1705.
04449	Quarter Sessions doggett books and papers, [(1) 1695–1703; (2) 1703–12].
04452(1)	Quarter Sessions convictions, 1695–1728 (Back).
04452(1)	Grand Jury presentments, 1676–1700 (Front).
05056	Orders and recognisances of Tolzey Court, 1703–16.
09701	Richard Haynes, letters, 1690–1722.
11109(11)	Account of James Charles (pilot), 1733.
11109(8)	List of dues payable to quaywarden, 1716.

29587(1)	Accounts of a timber merchant, 1691–2.
32835/AC/B64	Anthony Varder senior, account book, 1697–1713.
36074(58)	Loss of cargo from ship being piloted in Kingroad, seventeenth century.

British Library, Additional Manuscripts

11255	Musgrave lists of shipping, 1709–51.
28879	Letters of Roger Hoare of Bridgwater, MP
28880	Letters of Roger Hoare of Bridgwater, MP
47151	Letters of Roger Hoare of Bridgwater, MP
61611	Blenheim Papers: information vs customs officials at Bristol, 1718.
61620	Blenheim Papers: petitions to Queen Anne, 1709.

Devon Record Office, Exeter

D3/169	Cash book of Exon quay, 1701–16.
D3/173	Accounts of town duty, Exeter, 1716–22.
P1/Box 1	Legal papers Glyde vs Sandford; Glyde vs Northcote, 1693.
61/6/1	Jeffery family, merchants of Exeter, ledger book, 1689–1739.
956 M/T 36	Assignment of property: Thomas Atkin & Cornelius Parminter, bankrupt salt boilers, 1711.
1522 Z/Z 1–3	Letters concerning transport and shipping of goods to and from Topsham, 1699–1700.
3219 B/1	John Redwood/John Wolston of Exeter, account books, 1676–1725.

Mid-Glamorgan Record Office

CL MS 4.266	Port of Cardiff: letter book of John Bird, comptroller, 1647–80.
B/C CH 1	Port of Cardiff: reports inwards of ships, 1686–1765, and reports outwards, 1727–67.
B/C CH 2	Port of Cardiff: outgoing letter book, 1732–46.
D/D MG 1 (part)	Port of Swansea: port book, August-December 1685.

National Library of Wales

LL/C/P/Acct 486a	Zipporah Yeomans, account book.
Powis Castle 1251	Petition for Customs House to be moved from Aberdovey to Aberystwyth.
Powis Castle 21102–4	Trade at Aberdovey.

North Devon Record Office

B1/332	Licences for boats and barges, 1700.
B1/693–5	Barnstaple, coal warden's accounts, 1670–80.
B1/1128	Barnstaple, seizure of soap cargo at Appledore, 1738.
B1/1299	As above, 1738–9.
B1/1603–5	Barnstaple, copy of borough byelaws, 1690.

B1/2303	Certificate of loss of salt cargo, 1735.
B1/2555	Barnstaple, receiver's accounts, 1698.
B1/2556	Barnstaple, mayoralty accounts, 1698–1700.
B1/3033	Barnstaple, receiver's accounts, 1701–2.
B9/18/30(b)	Legacy receipt under will of John King, Northam, 1717.
B10/BWO/14	Deeds and leases, house in Ilfracombe, 1688–1728.
B69/37	Benjamin Smale, account book, 1687–90.
B69/38	Letter book of a London merchant, 1704–6.
B69 Add 3/1	Account book of a London merchant, ?Martyn, 1704/5–11.
BBT A1/a/8	Bideford Bridge Trust: list of old and new feoffees, 1832
BBT A1/b/32	Bideford Bridge Trust: Trust rents in Bideford town, 1693–.
BBT A1/6/40	Bideford Bridge Trust: houses in Bideford.
BBT B6/1	Bideford Bridge Trust: ledger or Account Book, 1688–1738.
BBT B6/7	Bideford Bridge Trust: Long Bridge day book, 1693–1769.
BBT B11/2	Bideford Bridge Trust: annual bridge warden's accounts, 1701–3.
BBT C8/8	Bideford Bridge Trust: petition opposing plans to scour the Torridge, 1727.
1064/Q/SO 1	Bideford, Quarter Sessions book, 1659–1709.
1142B/L27/L20	Lease, Fremington, n.d.
1142B/T20/139	Agreement, tithes West Down, 1690.
1142B/T22/110	Premises in Fremington.
1142B/T22/279A	Property at Fremington.
1843/A/PF 73	Northam parish register: trust deed.
1843/A/PR 3	Northam parish register: erection of a quay etc. at Northam, 1601.
2008 B/LI	Land in Appledore, 1712.
2239/B/add5/m1	Transcript of dispute over rights of the manor of Northam, 1716.
2379/A/Z 4	Bideford Court of Record and Minute Book, 1709–15.
3479M/L6	Parties to lease, Barnstaple, 1714.
4227m/T2	Bonds, 1701.

Public Record Office

C10/303/2	Burgesses of Neath vs Sir Humphrey Mackworth and others, Neath 1705.
C10/303/5	Burgesses of Neath vs Thomas Hakins and others (answers), Neath 1705.
C78 1224/2	Chancery Decree Rolls, Ilfracombe 13 William III: Harris vs Somers.
C104/12	Roger Hoare and Company, letter book, waste book and cash book, 1696–1713.
E134	Exchequer depositions by commission.
E190	Exchequer port books: Barnstaple; Bridgwater; Bristol; Cardiff; Carmarthen; Chepstow; Gloucester; Exeter; Ilfracombe; Lancaster; Liverpool; Looe; Minehead; Milford; Mount's Bay; Padstow; Plymouth and Fowey; Poole; Portsmouth; St Ives; Southampton; and Swansea and Neath coastal port books.
Prob 3, 4, 5	Prerogative Court of Canterbury: wills and inventories.
SP	State papers.

T64 139–140	William Culliford on customs frauds, 1681–4.
T64 142	Correspondence and report of complaints against tide surveyor, Bristol, 1718.
T64 143	Revenue frauds: London and the western ports, 1723–32.
T64 145	Seizures of tobacco, 1723–32.

Shropshire Record Office

| MS 329–333 | Abraham Darby I and II, account books. |

Somerset Record Office

D/B/bw 570	Leases of land at Hamp, nr Bridgwater, 1698–1712.
D/B/bw 1521	Bridgwater water bailliff's account, 1652.
D/B/bw 1524	Account of money due from Vinsin Bolding of Langport, 1716–19.
D/B/bw 1525	Accounts of moorage and landing fees, Bridgwater, 1716–17.
D/B/bw 1636–1638	Bridgwater receivers' accounts.
D/B/bw 1645	Accounts of moorage, measurage and pontage, Bridgwater, ?1716–20.
D/B/bw 1664	Accounts of pontage dues, Bridgwater, 1716–20.
D/B/bw 1864	Petition for making river Weaver navigable to Frodsham, 1728.
D/B/bw 1870	Accounts of stones landed at the quay, Bridgwater, eighteenth century.
D/B/bw 1895	Bridgwater quay accounts.
D/B/bw 1896	Disbursements on Bridgwater quay and Langport slip, 1714.
D/B/bw 2052	Messuages on quay, Bridgwater.
D/B/bw 2119	Accounts of stones landed at Bridgwater quay.
D/B/bw 2159	Lease of waterworks, Bridgwater, 1709
D/D/Cd/108 19	Depositions concerning Roger Hoare junior, 1696
D/N/bw.ch.ch.	Papers relating to Christ church, Bridgwater, 1699
DD/BR/gr 10	Table of fees payable to searcher at port of Bristol, 1670
DD/DN 118, 127, 129, 149	Deeds: Bridgwater and Weston Zoyland
DD/DN 145	Deeds and certificates, seventeenth to eighteenth centuries.
DD/DN 423–4	Dickenson Papers, Graffin Prankard, letter books, 1712–18, 1728–32.
DD/DN 444	Dickenson Papers, Graffin Prankard, cash books and salt accounts, 1742.
DD/DN 461–63	William Alloway, senior and junior, journals and ledgers, 1683–1704.
DD/L 1 54/42	Papers relating to weighing of wool at Minehead, *c.*1714–68.
DD/L 1 55/1–5 (Box 106)	Papers relating to Minehead harbour, sixteenth to eighteenth centuries.
DD/L 1 58/15 (Box 109)	Surveys, particulars and maps of Minehead harbour, 1701.
DD/L 2 19/110\ (Box 128)	Agreements concerning the rebuilding of Minehead pier, 1665; Proposals and orders concerning Watchet harbour, 1665.

DD/L P 30/105	Quay duties accounts, Minehead, 1648.
DD/SF 2769	Notes concerning registration of shipping, seventeenth century.
DD/SP 341	Accounts of St Botolph's and St Thomas' fairs, Taunton, 1694.
DD/SX 9/3(b)	Sketch map of river Parrot and landing berths at Bridgwater, *c*.1730.
DD/WY BX 10 E3/1,2	Deeds re harbour, manor and borough of Watchet, 1528–1665.
DD/WY BX 23	Legal papers concerning Lord's Bushel of salt, Watchet, 1634.
DD/WY BX 40	Account books of Watchet quay duties, 1708–65; Schedule of harbour dues, *c*.1700; Harbour trust deeds, 1665; Presentment harbour trustees, 1685.
DD/WY BX 41	Accounts of quay duties, Watchet, 1712–17; Legal papers concerning quay, *c*.1720.
DD/X/AUS 40	Abstract of deeds concerning profits of landing cattle at Weston-super-Mare.
DD/X/KLT 1	Letter concerning estimate for new dock, Bridgwater, 1728.
DD/X/HYN 1	George Hayman of Minehead, account book, 1685–7.
DD/X/PG/I W 51/3/1	William Sealy of Bridgwater, letter book, 1701–3.
DD/X/WI 36	Edward Martindale of Bristol, letters.
T/PH/gc 10	Proposals concerning port charges, Porlock, *c*.1700.
T/PH/gc 11	Agreement for erection of sea walls, Porlock, 1714.
Q/Rua 12–14 1706–12.	Quay accounts: accounts for harbour, Bridgwater, 1697–1704;

Wiltshire County Record Office

473/295	Thomas Goldney, day book, 1741–62.

Printed primary sources

Place of publication is London unless otherwise stated

Barrett, W., *The history and antiquities of the city of Bristol* (Bristol, 1789, repr. Gloucester, 1984).

Bettey, J., 'A Bristol glassworks in the eighteenth century', in P.V. McGrath, ed., *A Bristol miscellany* (BRS, XXXVIII, 1985), pp. 15–20.

Brand, J., *History of Newcastle*, 2 vols (1789).

Calendar of State Papers Domestic.

Calendar of Treasury Books, ed. W.A. Shaw et al. (1904–23).

Calendar of Treasury Papers, ed. J. Redington (1868–89).

Cox, N.C., Hussey, D.P. and Milne, G.J., eds, *The Gloucester port books database, 1575–1765, on CD-ROM* (1998).

Crouch, H., *A complete view of the British Customs* (1725).

Crouch, H., *A complete guide to the officers of His Majesty's Customs in the outports* (1732).

Crowley, R., *The select works of Robert Crowley*, ed. J.M. Cowper (Early English Text Society, extra series, 15, 1872).

Defoe, D., *A tour through the whole island of Great Britain* (1724–6, repr. 1974).

Defoe, D., *The complete English tradesman* (1727, repr. Gloucester, 1987).

Defoe, D., *A plan of the English commerce* (1728, repr. Oxford, 1928).

Eden, F.M., *The state of the poor*, 3 vols (1797).

Felix Farley's Bristol Journal (1752).

Goldwin, W., *A poetical description of Bristol* (1712).

Hinton, R.W.K., ed., *The port books of Boston, 1600–1640* (Lincoln Record Society, 50, 1956).

Houghton, J., *A collection for the improvement of husbandry and trade*, 4 vols (1727–8).

Hyde, R., *A prospect of Britain: the panoramas of Samuel and Nathaniel Buck* (1994).

Jarvis, R.C., ed., *Customs letter-books of the port of Liverpool, 1711–1813* (Chetham Society, 3rd ser., 6, 1954).

Lewis, E.A., ed., *The Welsh port books, 1550–1603* (Cymmrodorion Record Series, 12, 1927).

Lewis, E.A., 'The port books of Cardigan in Elizabethan and Stuart times', *Cardigan Antiquarian Society*, VII (1930), pp. 21–49; VIII (1931), pp. 36–62; XI (1936), pp. 83–114.

Lhwyd, E., *Parochialia, being a summary of answers to parochial queries*, vol. III, ed. R.H. Morris (1911).

McGrath, P., ed., *Merchants and merchandise in seventeenth century Bristol* (BRS, XIX, 1955).

McGrath, P., ed., *Records relating to the Society of Merchant Venturers in the City of Bristol in the seventeenth century* (BRS, XVII, 1952).

Mackworth, Sir H., *The Mine-Adventure; or an expedient* (1698).

Mackworth, Sir H., *An answer to several objections against the Mine-Adventure* (1698).

Mackworth, Sir H., *The third abstract of the state of the mines of Bwlchyr Eskir-Hir in the county of Cardigan* (1700).

Mackworth, Sir H., *The case of Sir Humphry Mackworth, and the Mine-Adventurers with respect to the irregular proceedings of several Justices of the Peace for the County of Glamorgan and of their agents and dependents* (1705).

Mackworth, Sir H., *Affidavits, certificates, and presentments; proving the facts mentioned in the case of Sir Humphry Mackworth and the Mine-Adventurers with respect to the irregular proceedings of several Justices of the Peace for the County of Glamorgan and of their agents and dependents* (1705).

Mackworth, Sir H., *A short state of the case & procedings of the Company of Mine-Adventurers; with an abstract of the defence of the deputy governor and directors: justified by vouchers* (1710).

Mackworth, Sir H., *The second part of the Book of Vouchers, to prove the case & defence of the deputy governour & directors of the Company of Mine-Adventurers* (1711).

Marshall, J.D., ed., *The autobiography of William Stout of Lancaster, 1665–1752* (Chetham Society, 3rd ser., 14, Manchester, 1967).

Martin, E. and Pickard, B., eds, *Six hundred years of Bristol poetry* (Bristol, 1973).

Matthews, H.E., ed., *Proceedings, minutes and enrolments of the Company of Soapmakers* (BRS, X, 1940).

Matthews, J.H., ed., *Records of the county borough of Cardiff*, 6 vols (Cardiff, 1898–1911).

Minchinton, W.E., ed., *The trade of Bristol in the eighteenth century* (BRS, XX, 1957).

Minchinton, W.E., ed., *Politics and the port of Bristol in the eighteenth century: the petitions of the Society of Merchant Venturers, 1698–1803* (BRS, XXIII, 1963).

Moore, J.S., ed., *The goods and chattels of our forefathers: Frampton Cotterell and district probate inventories, 1539–1804* (1976).

Morland, S.C., ed., *Somersetshire quarterly meeting of the Society of Friends, 1668–99* (Somerset Record Society, 75, 1978).

Morris, C., ed., *The illustrated journeys of Celia Fiennes c. 1682–c. 1712* (1984).

Mortimer, R., ed., *The minute book of the men's meeting of the Society of Friends in Bristol, 1686–1704* (BRS, XXX, 1977).

Nash, T.R., *Collections for the history and antiquities of Worcestershire* (1781–99).

Palmer, J., ed., *Cornwall, the Canaries and the Atlantic. The letter book of Valentine Enys, 1704–1719* (Exeter, 1997).

Perry, G., 'A description of the Severn', *Gentleman's Magazine*, XXVIII (1758), pp. 277–8.

Perry, G., 'The Severn navigation', *Gentleman's Magazine*, XXVIII (1758), p. 277.

Pike, J., *Some account of the life of Joseph Pike of Cork in Ireland who died in the year 1729, written by himself* (1837).

Plot, R., *The natural history of Staffordshire* (Oxford, 1686).

Quinn, D.B. and Ruddock, A.A., *Port books of Southampton* (Southampton Record Society, 37–8, 1937–8).

Ralph, E. and Williams, M.E., eds, *The inhabitants of Bristol in 1696* (BRS, XXV, 1968).

Rees, W., 'The port books for the port of Cardiff and its member ports, Swansea and Neath, 1606–10', *South Wales and Monmouthshire Record Society*, 3 (1954), pp. 69–91.

Richardson, D., ed., *Bristol, Africa and the eighteenth century slave trade to America. Volume I: the years of expansion, 1698–1729* (BRS, XXXVIII, 1986).

Richardson, D., ed., *Bristol, Africa and the eighteenth century slave trade to America. Volume II: the years of ascendancy, 1730–1745* (BRS, XXXIX, 1987).

Richardson, D., ed., *Bristol, Africa and the eighteenth century slave trade to America. Volume III: the years of decline, 1746–1769* (BRS, XLII, 1991).

Roseveare, H., ed., *Markets and merchants of the late seventeenth century: the Marescoe-David letters, 1668–1680* (Records of Social and Economic History, new series, XII, Oxford, 1987).

Score, R., *A guide to the customers and collectors clerks or a new index to the Book of Rates* (1699).

Stembridge, P.K., *The Goldney family: A Bristol merchant dynasty* (BRS, XLIX, 1998).

Thirsk, J. and Cooper, J.P., eds, *Seventeenth-century economic documents* (Oxford, 1972).

Trinder, B. and Cox, J., *Yeomen and colliers in Telford: the probate inventories of Dawley, Lilleshall, Wellington and Wrockwardine 1660–1750* (1980).

Vanes, J., *Documents illustrating the overseas trade of Bristol in the sixteenth century* (BRS, XXXI, 1979).

Watkins, J., *An essay towards a history of Bideford* (Exeter, 1792).

Secondary works

Place of publication is London unless otherwise stated

Abrams, P. and Wrigley, E.A., eds, *Towns in societies: essays in economic history and historical sociology* (Cambridge, 1978).

Aerts, E. and Clark, P., eds, *Metropolitan cities and their hinterlands in early modern Europe* (Tenth Economic History Conference, Leuven, 1990).

Agnew, J., *Belfast merchant families in the seventeenth century* (Dublin, 1996).

Aldcroft, D.H., and Freeman, M.J, eds, *Transport in the industrial revolution* (Manchester, 1983).

Alford, B.W.E., 'The economic development of Bristol in the nineteenth century: an enigma?', in P.V. McGrath and L. Cannon, eds, *Essays in Bristol and Gloucestershire history* (Bristol, 1976), pp. 252–83.

Andrews, J.H., 'The customs ports of Sussex, 1680–1730', *Sussex Notes and Queries*, XIV (1954), pp. 1–3.

Andrews, J.H., 'The port of Chichester and the grain trade, 1650–1750', *Sussex Archaeological Collections*, 92 (1954), pp. 93–105.

Andrews, J.H., 'The Thanet seaports, 1650–1750', *Archaeologia Cantiana*, 66 (1954), pp. 37–44.

Andrews, J.H., 'Chepstow: a defunct seaport of the Severn estuary', *Geography*, XL (1955), pp. 97–107.

Andrews, J.H., 'English merchant shipping in 1701', *Mariner's Mirror*, XLI (1955), pp. 232–5.

Andrews, J.H., 'The trade of the port of Faversham, 1650–1750', *Archaeologia Cantiana*, 69 (1955), pp. 125–31.

Andrews, J.H., 'Two problems in the interpretation of the port books', *EcHR*, 2nd ser. IX (1956), pp. 119–122.

Appleby, A.B., 'Grain prices and subsistence crises in England and France, 1590–1740', *Journal of Economic History*, XXXIX (1979), pp. 865–87.

Armstrong, J., 'The significance of coastal shipping in British domestic transport', *International Journal of Maritime History*, III (1991), pp. 63–94.

Armstrong, J. and Bagwell, P.S., 'Coastal shipping', in D.H. Aldcroft and M.J. Freeman, eds, *Transport in the industrial revolution* (Manchester, 1983), pp. 142–76.

Ashton, T.S., *Iron and steel in the industrial revolution* (Manchester, 1924).

Ashton, T.S., *The coal industry of the eighteenth century* (Manchester, 1929).

Ashton, T.S., *Economic fluctuations in England, 1700–1800* (Oxford, 1959).

Aström, S.-E., 'The reliability of the English port books', *Scandinavian Economic History Review*, XVI (1968), pp. 125–36.

Atkinson, B.J., 'An early example of the decline of the industrial spirit? Bristol enterprise in the first half of the nineteenth century', *Southern History*, 9 (1987), pp. 71–89.

Avery, W.D., 'Brass and copper traffic on the river Severn, 1660–1760', unpublished B.A. dissertation, Department of History, University of Birmingham (1990).

Ayo-Ru, A., 'Anglo-Spanish trade through the port of Bilbao during the second half of the eighteenth century: some preliminary findings', *International Journal of Maritime History*, 4 (1992), pp. 193–217.

Baddeley, W. St C., 'A glass house at Nailsworth (sixteenth and seventeenth century)', *TBGAS*, XLII (1920), pp. 89–95.

Baigent, E., 'Bristol society in the later eighteenth century with special reference to the handling by computer of fragmentary historical sources', unpublished D.Phil. thesis, University of Oxford (1986).

Baigent, E., 'Economy and society in eighteenth-century English towns: Bristol in the 1770s', in D. Denecke and G. Shaw, eds, *Urban historical geography. Recent progress in Britain and Germany* (Cambridge, 1988), pp. 109–24.

Bairoch, P., 'Urbanization and the economy: the findings of two decades of research', *Journal of European Economic History*, 2 (1989).

Bairoch, P. and Goertz, G., 'A note on the impact of large cities on the surrounding cities, Europe 1500 to 1800', in E. Aerts and P. Clark, eds, *Metropolitan cities and their hinterlands in early modern Europe* (Tenth Economic History Conference, Leuven, 1990), pp. 48–57.

Barker, T.C., 'Lancashire coal, Cheshire salt and the rise of Liverpool', *Transactions of the Historical Society of Lancashire and Cheshire*, 103 (1951), pp. 83–101.

Barney, J., 'Shipping in the port of King's Lynn, 1702–1800', *Journal of Transport History*, 20 (1999), pp. 126–40.

Barrow, T., 'Corn, carriers and coastal shipping: the shipping and trade of Berwick and the borders, 1730–1830', *Journal of Transport History*, 21 (2000), pp. 6–27.

Barry, J., 'The cultural life of Bristol, 1640–1775', unpublished D.Phil. thesis, University of Oxford (1986).

Barry, J., 'Provincial town culture: urbane or civic?', in J. Pittock and A. Wear, eds, *Interpretation and cultural history* (Basingstoke, 1991), pp. 198–234.

Barry, J., 'The history and antiquities of the city of Bristol: Thomas Chatterton in Bristol', *Angelaki*, 1 (1993/4), pp. 55–81.

Barry, J., 'Bristol pride: civic identity in Bristol, c.1640–1775', in M. Dresser and P. Ollerenshaw, eds, *The making of modern Bristol* (Tiverton, 1996), pp. 25–47.

Barton, D.B., *A history of copper mining in Cornwall and Devon* (Truro, 1968).

Beavan, B., *Bristol lists* (Bristol, 1889).

Beavon, K.S.O., *Central place theory: a reinterpretation* (1977).

Beckett, J.V., *Coal and tobacco: the Lowthers and the economic development of west Cumberland, 1660–1760* (Cambridge, 1981).

Beier, A.L. and Finlay, R., eds, *London 1500–1700: the making of the metrolpolis* (1986).

Berg, M., *The age of manufactures: industry, innovation and work in Britain, 1700–1820* (1985, 2nd edn 1994).

Berry, B.J.L. and Garrison, W.L., 'The functional bases of central-place hierarchy', in H.M. Mayer and C.F. Kohn, eds, *Readings in urban geography* (Chicago, 1959), pp. 218–27.

Berry, E.K, 'The borough of Droitwich and its salt industry, 1215–1700', *University of Birmingham Historical Journal*, 6 (1957–8), pp. 39–61.

Bettey, J.H., 'The livestock trade in the west country in the seventeenth century', *PSANHS*, 127 (1984), pp. 123– 8.

Bettey, J.H., *Bristol observed. Visitors' impressions of the city from Domesday to the Blitz* (Bristol, 1986).

Bettey, J.H., 'Graffin Prankard, an eighteenth century Bristol merchant', *Southern History*, 12 (1990), pp. 34–47.

Bettey, J.H., 'From Quaker traders to Anglican gentry: the rise of a Somerset dynasty', *PSANHS*, 135 (1992), pp. 1–9.

Beynon, O., 'The lead mining industry of Cardiganshire from 1700 to 1800', unpublished M.A. thesis, University of Wales (1937).

Borsay, P., *The English urban renaissance: culture and society in the English provincial town, 1660–1770* (Oxford, 1989).

Borsay, P., ed., *The eighteenth century town, 1688–1820* (1990).

Bowden, P., *The wool trade in Tudor and Stuart England* (1961).

Bowen, E.G., 'The regional divisions of Wales', in E.G. Bowen, ed., *Wales. A physical, historical, and regional geography* (1957), pp. 267–9.

Bowen, E.G., 'The south-west', in E.G. Bowen ed., *Wales. A physical, historical, and regional geography* (1957), pp. 329–52.

Braudel, F., *The Mediterranean and the Mediterranean world in the age of Phillip II*, 2 vols, trans. S. Reynolds (1972).

Braudel, F., *Civilization and capitalism, fifteenth-eighteenth century. Volume I: the structures of everyday life*, (Paris, 1979, trans. S. Reynolds, 1983).

Braudel, F., *Civilization and capitalism, fifteenth-eighteenth century. Volume II: the wheels of commerce* (Paris, 1979, trans. S. Reynolds, 1983).

Braudel, F., *Civilization and capitalism, fifteenth-eighteenth century. Volume III: the perspective of the world* (Paris, 1979, trans. S. Reynolds, 1983).

Breen, T.H., 'An empire of goods: the anglicization of colonial America 1690–1776', *Journal of British Studies*, XXV (1986), pp. 467–99.

Breen, T.H., '"Baubles of Britain": the American and consumer revolutions of the eighteenth century', *Past and Present*, CXIX (1988), pp. 73–104.

Brookfield, H.C., 'Three Sussex ports, 1850–1950', *Journal of Transport History*, II (1955), pp. 34–50.

Buckley, F., 'The early glass-houses of Bristol', *Journal of the Society of Glass Technology*, 9 (1925), pp. 36–61.

Burt, R., 'Lead production in England and Wales, 1700–1770', *EcHR*, XXII (1969), pp. 249–68.

Burt, R., 'The international diffusion of technology in the early modern period: the case of the British non-ferrous mining industry', *EcHR*, 2nd ser. XLIV (1991), pp. 248–71.

Burt, R., 'The transformation of the non-ferrous metals industry in the seventeenth and eighteenth century', *EcHR*, XLVIII (1995), pp. 23–45.

Burton, V., 'Liverpool's mid-nineteenth century coasting trade', in V. Burton, ed., *Liverpool shipping, trade and commerce* (Liverpool, 1989), pp. 26–66.

Carlen, R.P., 'The Spanish wool trade, 1500–1780', *Journal of Economic History*, 42 (1982), pp. 775–96.

Carter, H., 'The Vale of Glamorgan and Gower', in E.G. Bowen, ed., *Wales. A physical, historical, and regional geography* (1957), pp. 401–30.

Carter, H., 'The growth and decline of Welsh towns', in D. Moore, ed., *Wales in the eighteenth century* (Swansea, 1976), pp. 47–62.

Cave, C.H., *A history of banking in Bristol from 1750 to 1899* (Bristol, 1899).

Chalklin, C., *The provincial towns of Georgian England* (1974).

Chaloner, W.H., 'Salt in Cheshire, 1600–1870', *Transactions of the Lancashire and Cheshire Antiquarian Society*, 71 (1961), pp. 58–74.

Chaloner, W.H., 'Trends in fish consumption', in T.C. Barker, J.C. Mackenzie and J. Yudkin, eds, *Our changing fare: two hundred years of British food habits* (1966).

Channon, G., 'Georges and brewing in Bristol', in C. Harvey and J. Press, eds, *Studies in the business history of Bristol* (Bristol, 1988).

Chappell, E.L., *History of the port of Cardiff* (Cardiff, 1939).

Chartres, J.A., 'The marketing of agricultural produce in metropolitan western England in the late seventeenth and eighteenth centuries', in M. Havinden, ed., *Husbandry and marketing in the south-west, 1500–1800* (Exeter Papers in Economic History, 8, Exeter, 1973), pp. 63–74.

Chartres, J.A., *Internal trade in England, 1500–1700* (1977).

Chartres, J.A., 'Road carrying in England in the seventeenth century: myth and reality', *EcHR*, 2nd ser. XXX (1977), pp. 73–94.

Chartres, J.A., 'Trade and shipping in the port of London: Wiggins Quay in the later seventeenth century', *Journal of Transport History*, 3rd ser. I (1980), pp. 29–47.

Chartres, J.A., 'On the road with Professor Wilson', *EcHR*, 2nd ser. XXXIII (1980), pp. 92–9.

Chartres, J.A., 'Food consumption and internal trade', in A.L. Beier and R. Finlay, eds, *London 1500–1700: the making of the metropolis* (1986), pp. 168–98.

Chartres, J., *Agricultural markets and trade, 1500–1750: chapters from the agrarian history of England and Wales 1500–1750. Volume 4* (Cambridge, 1990).

Chartres, J.A., 'The marketing of agricultural produce, 1640–1750', in J.A. Chartres, ed., *Agricultural markets and trade, 1500–1700: chapters from the agrarian history of England and Wales, 1500–1700. Volume 4* (Cambridge, 1990), pp. 160–255.

Chartres, J.A., 'City and towns, farmers and economic change in the eighteenth century', *Historical Research*, LXIV (1991), pp. 138–55.

Chartres, J.A., 'Market integration and agricultural output in seventeenth-, eighteenth-, and early nineteenth-century England', *Agricultural History Review*, 43 (1995), pp. 117–38.

Chope, R.P., ed., *Early tours in Devon and Cornwall* (1918, repr. Newton Abbot, 1967).

Clark, E.A.G., *The ports of the Exe estuary, 1660–1860: a study in historical geography* (1960).

Clark, G.N., *Guide to English commercial statistics, 1696–1782* (1938).

Clark, P., *The English county town* (Leicester, 1982).

Clark, P., ed., *The transformation of English provincial towns, 1600–1800* (1984).

Clemens, P.G.E., 'The rise of Liverpool, 1665–1750', *EcHR*, 2nd ser. XXIX (1976).

Cole, W.A., 'Trends in eighteenth-century smuggling', in W.E. Minchinton, ed., *The growth of English overseas trade in the seventeenth and eighteenth centuries* (1969), pp. 121–43.

Colyer, R.J., *The Welsh cattle drovers* (Cardiff, 1976).

Corfield, P.J., 'A provincial capital in the late seventeenth century: the case of Norwich', in P. Clark and P. Slack, eds, *Crisis and order in English towns 1500–1700* (1972), pp. 263–310.

Corfield, P.J., *The impact of English towns, 1700–1800* (1982).

Cottle, B., 'Thomas Chatterton', in P. McGrath, ed., *Bristol in the eighteenth century* (Newton Abbot, 1972), pp. 89–108.

Coull, J.R., *The fisheries of Europe: an economic geography* (1972).

Cox, N.C., 'Imagination and innovation of an industrial pioneer: the first Abraham Darby', *Industrial Archaeology Review*, XII (1990), pp. 127–44.

Cox, N.C., 'Objects of worth, objects of desire: towards a dictionary of traded goods and commodities, 1550–1800', *Material History Review*, 39 (1994), pp. 24–40.

Craig, R.S., 'Some aspects of the trade and shipping of the river Dee in the eighteenth century', *Transactions of the Historical Society of Lancashire and Cheshire*, 115 (1963), pp. 99– 128.

Craig, R.S., 'Shipping and shipbuilding in the port of Chester in the eighteenth and early nineteenth centuries', *Transactions of the Historical Society of Lancashire and Cheshire*, 116 (1964), pp. 36–68.

Crawford, A., *Bristol and the wine trade* (BHA, 57, 1984).

Cross, D.A.E., 'The salt industry of Lymington', *Journal of Industrial Archaeology*, 2 (1965), pp. 86–90.

Crossley, D.W., 'The performance of the glass industry in sixteenth century England', *EcHR*, 2nd ser. XXV (1972), pp. 421–33.

Crowhurst, P., *The Defence of British trade, 1689–1815* (1977).

Cunliffe, B., *The city of Bath* (Stroud, 1986, repr. 1990).

Daunton, M.J., 'Towns and economic growth in eighteenth-century England', in P. Abrams and E.A. Wrigley, eds, *Towns and societies: essays in economic history and historical sociology* (Cambridge, 1978).

Davies, S.W., 'An economic history of Bewdley before c.1700', unpublished Ph.D. thesis, University of London (1981).

Davis, R., *The rise of the English shipping industry in the seventeenth and eighteenth centuries* (1962).

Davis, R., *The trade and shipping of Hull, 1500–1700* (1964).

Davis, R., 'English foreign trade, 1660–1700', in W.E. Minchinton, ed., *The growth of English overseas trade in the seventeenth and eighteenth centuries* (1969), pp. 78–98.

Davis, R., 'English foreign trade, 1700–74', in W.E. Minchinton, ed., *The growth of English overseas trade in the seventeenth and eighteenth centuries* (1969), pp. 99–119.

Dawson, J.W., *Commerce and customs - a history of the ports of Newport and Caerleon* (Cardiff, 1932).

Day, J., *Bristol brass: the history of the industry* (Newton Abbot, 1973).

Day, J., 'The Costers: copper smelters and manufacturers', *Transactions of the Newcomen Society*, 47 (1974–6), pp. 48–58.

Day, J., 'Copper, brass, and zinc production', in J. Day, and R.F. Tylecote, eds, *The industrial revolution in metals* (1992), pp. 145–63.

Devine, T.M., *The tobacco lords: a study of the tobacco merchants of Glasgow and their trading activities, c. 1740–1790* (Edinburgh, 1975).

Devine, T.M., 'The golden age of tobacco', in T.M. Devine and G. Jackson, eds, *Glasgow. Volume I: beginnings to 1830* (Manchester, 1995), pp. 139–83.

de Vries, J., 'Measuring the impact of climate on history: the search for appropriate methodologies', in R.I. Rotberg and T.K. Rabb, eds, *Climate and history* (Princeton, 1981), pp. 19–50.

de Vries, J., *European urbanization, 1500–1800* (1984).

de Vries, J., 'Problems in the measurement, description, and analysis of historical urbanization', in A. van der Woude, A. Hayami and J. de Vries, eds, *Urbanization in history* (Oxford, 1990), pp. 43–60.

Diaper, S.J., 'Christopher Thomas & Brothers Ltd.: the last Bristol soapmakers. An aspect of Bristol's economic development in the nineteenth century', *TBGAS*, CV (1987), pp. 223–32.

Dietz, B., 'The north-east coal trade, 1550–1750: measures, markets and the metropolis', *Northern History*, XXII (1985), pp. 280–94.

Duffy, M., Fisher, S., Greenhill, B., Starkey, D.J. and Youings, J., eds. *The new maritime history of Devon. Volume I: from early times to the late eighteenth century* (Exeter, 1992).

Dunning, R.W., ed., *The Victoria county history of Somerset. Volume V* (Oxford, 1985).

Dunning, R.W., ed., *The Victoria county history of Somerset. Volume VI: Bridgwater and its neighbouring parishes* (Oxford, 1992).

Eaglesham, N., *Whitehaven and the tobacco trade* (Whitehaven, 1979).

Earle, P., *The making of the English middle class. Business, society and family life in London, 1660–1730* (1989).

Edwards, G., 'The coal industry in Pembrokeshire', *Field Studies*, 1, 5 (1963), pp. 33–64.

Edwards, P.R., 'The cattle trade of Shropshire in the late sixteenth and seventeenth centuries', *Midland History*, VI (1981), pp. 72–94.

Elder, M., *The slave trade and the economic development of 18th century Lancaster* (Halifax, 1992).

Ellis, J., 'The decline and fall of the Tyneside salt industry, 1660–1790: a re-examination', *EcHR*, 2nd ser. XXXIII (1980), pp. 45–58.

Elton, M., *Annals of the Elton family, Bristol merchants and Somerset landowners* (Stroud, 1994).

Emery, F., 'Wales', in J. Thirsk, ed., *The agrarian history of England and Wales. Volume V: 1640–1750. I: Regional farming systems* (Cambridge, 1985), pp. 393–428.

Estabrook, C.B., 'Urbane and rustic Bristol: social spheres and cultural ties in an English city and its hinterland: 1660–1780', unpublished Ph.D. thesis, Brown University (1992).

Estabrook, C.B., *Urbane and rustic England: cultural ties and social spheres in the provinces, 1660–1780* (Manchester, 1998).

Evans, B.M., 'The Welsh coal trade during the Stuart period, 1603–1709', unpublished M.A. thesis, University of Wales (1928).

Evans, M., 'The seaborne trade of the port of Ipswich and its members', unpublished Ph.D. thesis, University of East Anglia (1987).

Evans, N., 'Two paths to economic development: Wales and the north-east of England', in P. Hudson, ed., *Regions and industries: a perspective on the industrial revolution in Britain* (Cambridge, 1989), pp. 201–27.

Evans, S., 'An examination of Sir Humphrey Mackworth's industrial activities', unpublished M.A. thesis, University of Wales (1950).

Everitt, A., 'Country, county and town: patterns of regional evolution in England', in P. Borsay, ed., *The eighteenth century town, 1688–1820* (1990), pp. 83–115.

Farr, G.E., 'Severn navigation and the trow', *Mariner's Mirror*, XXXII (1946), pp. 66–95.

Farr, G.E., 'Bristol Channel pilotage, historical notes on its administration and craft', *Mariner's Mirror*, XXXIX (1953), pp. 27–44.

Fawcett, T., 'Selling the Bath waters: medicinal propaganda at an eighteenth century spa', *SANHS*, 134 (1990), pp. 193–206.

Fisher, F.J., 'The development of the London food market, 1540–1640', *EcHR*, II (1935), pp. 46–64.

Fisher, F.J., 'The development of London as a centre of conspicuous consumption in the sixteenth and seventeenth centuries', in E.M. Carus-Wilson, ed., *Essays in economic history*, II (1962), pp. 197–207.

Fisher, H.E.S., 'The south-west & the Atlantic trades, 1660–1760', in H.E.S. Fisher, ed., *The south-west and the sea* (Exeter Papers in Economic History, 1, Exeter, 1968), pp. 7–14.

Fisher, H.E.S., *The Portugal trade. A study of Anglo-Portuguese commerce 1700–1770* (1971).

Fisher, S., 'Devon's maritime trade and shipping, 1680–1780', in M. Duffy, S. Fisher, B. Greenhill, D.J. Starkey, and J. Youings, eds, *The new maritime history of Devon. Volume I: from early times to the late eighteenth century* (Exeter, 1992), pp. 232–41.

Fisher, S. and Havinden, M., 'The long-term evolution of the economy of south west England, from autonomy to dependence', in M.A. Havinden, J. Queniart and J. Stanyer, eds., *Centre and periphery: Brittany, Cornwall and Devon compared* (Exeter, 1991), pp. 76–85.

Fleming, P., 'The emergence of modern Bristol', in M. Dresser and P. Ollerenshaw, eds, *The making of modern Bristol* (Tiverton, 1996), pp. 1–24.

Fogel, R.W., 'The new economic history: its findings and methods', *EcHR*, 2nd ser. XIX (1966), pp. 642–56.

Freeman, M., 'Transporting methods in the British cotton industry during the industrial revolution', *Journal of Transport History*, I (1980), pp. 59–74.

Freeman, M.J., 'Introduction', in D.H. Aldcroft and M.J. Freeman, eds, *Transport in the industrial revolution* (Manchester, 1983), pp. 1–31.

French, C.J., 'Eighteenth-century shipping tonnage measurements', *Journal of Economic History*, 33 (1973), pp. 434–43.

French, C.J., '"Crowded with traders and a great commerce": London's domination of English overseas trade, 1700–1775', *London Journal*, 17 (1992), pp. 27–35.

George, B.J., 'Pembrokeshire sea-trading before 1900', *Field Studies*, 2, 1 (1964), pp. 1–39.

Gerhold, D., 'The growth of the London carrying trade, 1681–1838', *EcHR*, 2nd ser. XLI (1988), pp. 392–410.

Gerhold, D., 'Packhorses and wheeled vehicles in England, 1550–1800', *Journal of Transport History*, 14 (1993), pp. 1–26.

Gerhold, D., *Road transport before the railways: Russell's London Flying Waggons* (Cambridge, 1993).

Gerhold, D., 'Productivity change in road transport before and after turnpiking, 1690–1840', *EcHR*, XLIX (1996), pp. 491–515.

Gerrard, C.M., 'Taunton Fair in the seventeenth century: an archaeological approach to historical data', *PSANHS*, 124 (1984), pp. 65–74.

Godfrey, E.S., *The development of English glassmaking, 1560–1640* (Oxford, 1975).

Goodman, J., *Tobacco in history: the cultures of dependence* (1993).

Gough, J.W., *The mines of Mendip* (Oxford, 1930, repr. Newton Abbot, 1967).

Grant, A., *North Devon pottery: the seventeenth century* (Exeter, 1983).

Grant, A., 'Port books as a source for the maritime history of Devon', in D. Starkey, ed., *Sources for a new maritime history of Devon* (Exeter, 1987).

Grant, A., 'Devon shipping, trade, and ports, 1600–1689', in M. Duffy, S. Fisher, B. Greenhill, D.J. Starkey and J. Youings, eds, *The new maritime history of Devon. Volume I: from early times to the late eighteenth century* (Exeter, 1992), pp. 130–8.

Grant, A. and Jemmett, D., 'Pipes and pipe-making in Barnstaple, Devon', in P. Davey, ed., *The archaeology of the clay tobacco pipe. Volume IX* (British Archaeological Reports, British Series, 146, ii 1985), pp. 439–553.

Gras, N.S.B., 'Memorandum on the port books', *First Report of the Royal Commission on the Public Records*, Appendix IV (16), Parliamentary Papers 1912–13, XLIV (1913), pp. 125–7.

Gras, N.S.B., *The evolution of the English corn market, from the twelfth to the eighteenth century* (1915).

Gras, N.S.B., *The early English Customs system* (1918).

Grassby, R., 'The personal wealth of the business community in seventeenth-century England', *EcHR*, 2nd ser. XXIII (1970), pp. 220–34.

Grassby, R., *The business community of seventeenth century England* (Cambridge, 1995).

Gribble, J.B., *Memorials of Barnstaple* (Barnstaple, 1830).

Hall, I.V., 'A history of the sugar trade in England with special attention to the sugar trade of Bristol', unpublished M.A. thesis, University of Bristol (1925).

Hall, I.V., 'Whitson Court sugar house, Bristol, 1665–1824', *TBGAS*, LXV (1944), pp. 1–97.

Hall, I.V., 'John Knight, Junior, sugar refiner at the Great House on St Augustine's Back (1654–1679), Bristol's second sugar house', *TBGAS*, LXVIII (1949), pp. 110–64.

Hall, I.V., 'Temple Sreet sugar house under the first partnership of Richard Lane and John Hine (1662–78)', *TBGAS*, LXXVI (1957), pp. 118–40.

Hall, I.V., 'The Daubenys. Part 1', *TBGAS*, LXXXIV (1966), pp. 113–40.

Hamer, J.H., 'Trading in St White Down Fair', *SANHS*, CXIII (1973), pp. 61–70.

Hamilton, H., *The English brass and copper industries to 1800* (1926, 2nd edn 1967).

Hammersley, G., 'The charcoal iron industry and its fuel, 1540–1750', *EcHR*, 2nd ser. XXVI (1973), pp. 593–613.

Hancock, D., *Citizens of the world. London merchants and the integration of the British Atlantic community, 1735–1785* (Cambridge, 1995).

Harper, L.A., *The English navigation laws: a seventeenth-century experiment in social engineering* (New York, 1939).

Harrison, G.V., 'Agricultural weights and measures', in J. Thirsk, ed., *The agrarian history of England and Wales. Volume V: 1640–1750. II: Agrarian change* (Cambridge, 1985), pp. 815–25.

Harrison, G.V., 'The south-west: Dorset, Somerset, Devon, and Cornwall', in J. Thirsk, ed., *The agrarian history of England and Wales. Volume V: 1640–1750. I. Regional farming systems* (Cambridge, 1985), pp. 358–389.

Hart, C.E., *Royal forest: a history of Dean's woods as producers of timber* (Oxford, 1966).

Hart, C.E., *The industrial history of Dean, with an introduction to its industrial archaeology* (Newton Abbot, 1971).

Harvey, C.E. and Press, J., 'Industrial change and the economic life of Bristol since 1800', in C. Harvey and J. Press, eds, *Studies in the business history of Bristol* (Bristol, 1988), pp. 1–32.

Harvey, C.E. and Press, J., eds, *Studies in the business history of Bristol* (Bristol, 1988).

Harvey, C.E. and Press, J., 'The business elite of Bristol: a case study in database design', *History and Computing*, 3 (1991), pp. 1–11.

Harvey, C.E. and Press, J., 'Relational data analysis: value, concepts and methods', *History and Computing*, 4, 2 (1992), pp. 98–109.

Hatcher, J., *The history of the British coal industry. Volume 1: before 1700* (Oxford, 1993).

Hausman, W.J., 'The English coastal coal trade, 1691–1910: how rapid was productivity growth?', *EcHR*, 2nd ser. XL (1987), pp. 588–96.

Havinden, M.A., Queniart, J. and Stanyer, J., *Centre and periphery: Brittany, Cornwall and Devon compared* (Exeter, 1991).

Havinden, M.A. and Stanes, R., 'Agriculture in south west England', in M.A. Havinden, J. Queniart, and J. Stanyer, eds, *Centre and periphery: Brittany, Cornwall and Devon compared* (Exeter, 1991), pp. 143–52.

Hechter, M., *Internal colonialism: the Celtic fringe in British national development, 1536–1966* (1975).

Herbert, N.M., 'The Newnham and London traders', *TBGAS*, XCVII (1979), pp. 93–100.

Hey, D., *Packmen, carriers and packhorse roads: trade and communications in North Derbyshire and South Yorkshire* (Leicester, 1980).

Hodson, H.J., *Cheshire 1660–1780: restoration to industrial revolution* (Chester, 1978).

Hoon, E.E., *The organisation of the English Customs system, 1696–1786* (1938, repr. Newton Abbot, 1968).

Hoppit, J., 'Reforming Britain's weights and measures', *English Historical Review*, CVIII, (1993), pp. 82–104.

Hoskins, W.G., *Industry, trade and people in Exeter, 1688–1800* (Manchester 1935, 2nd edn. Exeter, 1968).

Hoskins, W.G., 'Harvest fluctuations and English economic history 1620–1759', *Agricultural History Review*, XVI (1968), pp. 15–31.

Howe, G.M., 'The south Wales coalfield', in E.G. Bowen, ed., *Wales. A physical, historical, and regional geography* (1957), pp. 353–400.

Howell, D.W., 'Landlords and estate management in Wales', in J. Thirsk, ed., *The agrarian history of England and Wales. Volume V: 1640–1750. II: Agrarian change* (Cambridge, 1985), pp. 252–97.

Howell, D.W., *Patriarchs and parasites: the gentry of south-west Wales in the eighteenth century* (Cardiff, 1986).

Hughes, E., *Studies in administration and finance 1558–1825, with special reference to the history of salt taxation in England* (Manchester, 1934, repr. Philadelphia, 1980).

Hussey, D.P., 'Re-investigating coastal trade: the ports of the Bristol Channel and the Severn Estuary, c.1695–c.1704', unpublished Ph.D. thesis, University of Wolverhampton (1995).

Hussey, D.P., Milne, G., Wakelin, A.P. and Wanklyn, M.D.G., eds, *The Gloucester coastal port books, 1575–1765: a summary* (Wolverhampton, 1995).

Innis, H.A., *The cod fisheries: the history of an international economy* (New Haven and Toronto, 1940).

Israel, J.I., 'Spanish wool exports and the European economy 1610–1640', *EcHR*, 2nd ser. XXXIII (1980), pp. 193–210.

Jackson, G., *Hull in the eighteenth century: a study in economic and social history* (1972).

Jackson, G., *The trade and shipping of eighteenth-century Hull* (York, 1975).

Jackson, G., 'The ports', in D.H. Aldcroft and M.J. Freeman, eds, *Transport in the industrial revolution* (Manchester, 1983).

Jackson, R.G., Jackson, P. and Price, R.H., *Bristol clay pipe makers* (Bristol, 1981).

Jackson, R.G., Jackson, P. and Price, R., 'Bristol potters and potteries, 1600–1800', *Journal of Ceramic History*, 12 (1982).

Jamieson, A.G., 'Devon and smuggling, 1680–1850', in M. Duffy, S. Fisher, B. Greenhill, D.J. Starkey and J. Youings, eds, *The new maritime history of Devon. Volume I: from early times to the late eighteenth century* (Exeter, 1992), pp. 244–50.

Jarvis, R.C., 'Some records of the port of Lancaster', *Transactions of the Lancashire and Cheshire Antiquarian Society*, LVII (1945–6), pp. 117–58.

Jarvis, R.C., 'The head port of Chester; and Liverpool, its creek and member', *Transactions of the Historical Society of Lancashire and Cheshire*, CII (1950), pp. 69–84.

Jarvis, R.C., 'Sources for the history of ports', *Journal of Transport History*, 3 (1957–8), pp. 76–93.

Jarvis, R.C., 'The appointment of ports', *EcHR*, 2nd ser. XI (1958), pp. 455–66.

Jarvis, R.C., 'Critical historical introduction' to E.E. Hoon, *The organisation of the English Customs system, 1696–1786* (Newton Abbot, 1968), pp. vii-xxvii.

Jarvis, R.C., 'Ship registry, 1707–86', *Maritime History,* II (1972), pp. 151–67.

Jenkins, G.H., *The foundations of modern Wales, 1642–1780. Vol.4* (Oxford, 1987).

Jenkins, J.G., 'The woollen industry', in D. Moore, ed., *Wales in the eighteenth century* (Swansea, 1976), pp. 89–108.

Jenkins, P., *The making of a ruling class: the Glamorgan gentry, 1640–1790* (Cambridge, 1983).

Jenkins, P., 'Times and seasons: the cycle of the year in early modern Glamorgan', *Morgannwg,* XXX (1986), pp. 20–41.

Jenkins, R., 'Industries of Herefordshire in bygone times', *Transactions of the Newcomen Society,* XVII (1936–7), pp. 175–89.

Jenkins, R., 'The copper works at Redbrook and Bristol', *TBGAS,* LXIII (1942), pp. 145–67.

Jenkins, T.J., *The herring and the herring fisheries* (1924).

John, A.H., *The industrial development of south Wales, 1750–1850: an essay* (Cardiff, 1950).

Johnson, B.L.C., 'The Stour valley iron industry in the late seventeenth century', *Transactions of the Worcestershire Archaeological Society,* new ser. 27 (1950), pp. 35–46.

Johnson, B.L.C., 'The charcoal iron industry in the early eighteenth century', *Geographical Journal,* 117 (1951), pp. 167–77.

Johnson, B.L.C., 'The Foley partnerships: the iron industry at the end of the charcoal era', *EcHR,* 2nd ser. IV (1952), pp. 322–40.

Johnson, B.L.C., 'The midland iron industry in the early eighteenth century', *Business History,* 2 (1960), pp. 67–74.

Jones, D.W., 'London merchants and the crisis of the 1690s', in P. Clark and P. Slack, eds, *Crisis and order in English towns, 1500–1700* (1972), pp. 311–55.

Jones, E.L., *Seasons and prices. The role of weather in agricultural history* (1964).

Jones, G.M. and Scourfield, E., *Sully: a village and parish in the Vale of Glamorgan* (1986).

Jones, S.J., 'The growth of Bristol', *Transactions of the Institute of British Geographers,* XI (1954), pp. 55–83.

Kaukiainen, Y., *Sailing into twilight. Finnish shipping in an age of transport revolution, 1860–1914* (Helsinki, 1991).

Kaukiainen, Y., *A history of Finnish shipping* (1993).

Kent, H.S.K., 'The Anglo-Norwegian timber trade in the eighteenth century', *EcHR,* 2nd ser. VIII (1955–6), pp. 62–74.

Kerridge, E., *The agricultural revolution* (1967).

Kerridge, E., *Textile manufactures in early modern England* (Manchester, 1985).

Knight, F.A., *The sea-board of Mendip* (1902, 2nd edn 1988).

Kowaleski-Wallace, E., *Consuming subjects. Women, shopping and business in the eighteenth century* (New York, 1997).

Lamb, H.H., *Climate, history and the modern world* (1982).

Langton, J., *Geographical change and industrial revolution: coalmining in south west Lancashire 1590–1799* (Cambridge, 1979).

Langton, J., 'Liverpool and its hinterland in the late eighteenth century', in J. Langton, ed., *Commerce, industry and transport: studies in economic change on Merseyside* (Liverpool, 1983), pp. 1–25.

Langton, J., 'The industrial revolution and the regional geography of England', *Transactions of the Institute of British Geographers,* new ser. 9 (1984), pp. 145–67.

Large, P., 'Urban growth and agricultural change in the West Midlands during the seventeenth and eighteenth centuries', in P. Clark, ed., *The transformation of English provincial towns* (1984), pp. 169–89.

Latimer, J., *The annals of Bristol in the eighteenth century* (Bristol, 1893).

Latimer, J., *The annals of Bristol in the seventeenth century* (Bristol, 1900).

Latimer, J., *The history of the Society of Merchant Venturers of Bristol* (Bristol, 1903).

Le Roy Ladurie, E., *Times of feast, times of famine: a history of climate since the year 1000* (New Jersey, 1971).

Lemire, B., 'Consumerism in pre-industrial and early industrial England: the trade in secondhand clothes', *Journal of British Studies*, 27 (1988), pp. 1–24.

Lemire, B., *Fashion's favourite: the cotton trade and the consumer in Britain, 1660–1800* (Oxford, 1991).

Lewis, W.J., 'Some aspects of lead-mining in Cardiganshire in the sixteenth and seventeenth centuries', *Ceredigion*, I (1951), pp. 177–90.

Lewis, W.J., *Lead mining in Wales* (Cardiff, 1967).

Linebaugh, P., *The London hanged: crime and civil society in the eighteenth century* (1991).

Lloyd, C., *The British seaman, 1200–1860* (Rutherford, 1970).

Lloyd, L., 'The ports and shipping of Cardigan Bay', *Maritime Wales*, 4 (1979), pp. 33–61.

Lobel, M.D. and Carus-Wilson, E.M., 'Bristol', in M.D. Lobel, ed., *Historic towns: maps and plans of towns and cities in the British Isles with historical commentaries, from earliest times to 1800* (1970).

Lösch, A., *The economics of location* (New Haven, 1954)

Lounsbury, R.G., *The British fishery at Newfoundland, 1634–1763* (New Haven, 1934).

McCusker, J.J., 'The tonnage of ships engaged in British colonial trade during the eighteenth century', *Research in Economic History*, 6 (1981), pp. 73–115.

McGrath, P.V., 'The Society of Merchant Venturers and the port of Bristol in the seventeenth century', *TBGAS*, LXXII (1953), pp. 105–28.

McGrath, P.V., *John Whitson and the merchant community of Bristol* (BHA, 25, 1970).

McGrath, P.V., ed., *Bristol in the eighteenth century* (Newton Abbot, 1972).

McGrath, P.V., *The Merchant Venturers of Bristol: a history of the Society of Merchant Venturers of the City of Bristol from its origins to the present day* (Bristol, 1975).

McInnes, A., 'The emergence of a leisure town: Shrewsbury 1660–1760', *Past and Present*, 120 (1978), pp. 53–87.

MacInnes, C.M., *The early English tobacco trade* (1926).

MacInnes, C.M., *Bristol: a gateway of empire* (Bristol, 1939, repr. Newton Abbot, 1968).

MacInnes, C.M. and Wittard, W.F., eds, *Bristol and its adjoining counties* (1955, 2nd edn 1973).

McIntyre, S., 'The mineral water trade in the eighteenth century', *Transport History*, II (1973), pp. 1–19.

McIntyre, S., 'Bath: the rise of a resort town', 1660–1800', in P. Clark, ed., *Country towns in pre-industrial England* (Leicester, 1981), pp. 197–249.

McKendrick, N., Brewer, J. and Plumb, J.H., eds, *The birth of a consumer society: the commercialisation of eighteenth-century England* (1982).

McLachlan, J.O., *Trade and peace with old Spain, 1667–1750* (1940).

Mann, J. de L., *The cloth industry in the West of England from 1640 to 1880* (Oxford, 1971, repr. Gloucester, 1987).

Marcy, P.T., 'Bristol's roads and communications on the eve of the industrial revolution, 1740–1780', *TBGAS*, LXXXVII (1969), pp. 149–72.

Marcy, P.T., 'Eighteenth-century views of Bristol and Bristollians', in P. McGrath, ed., *Bristol in the eighteenth century* (Newton Abbott, 1972), pp. 11–40.

Mathias, P., *The brewing industry in England, 1700–1830* (Cambridge, 1959)

Mendenhall, T.C., *The Shrewsbury drapers and the Welsh wool trade in the sixteenth and seventeenth centuries* (Oxford, 1953).

Metters, G.A., 'The rulers and merchants of Kings Lynn in the early seventeenth century', unpublished Ph.D. thesis, University of East Anglia (1982).

Milne, G.J. and Paul, M., 'Establishing a flexible model for port book studies: the recent evolution of the Gloucester port books database', *History and Computing*, 6 (1994), pp. 106–15.

Minchinton, W.E., 'Bristol—metropolis of the west in the eighteenth century', *TRHS*, 5th ser. 4 (1954), pp. 69–89.

Minchinton, W.E., 'The diffusion of tinplate manufacture', *EcHR*, 2nd ser. IX (1956–57), pp. 349–58.

Minchinton, W.E., *The British tinplate industry* (Oxford, 1957).

Minchinton, W.E., *The port of Bristol in the eighteenth century* (Bristol, 1962).

Minchinton, W.E., ed., *The growth of English overseas trade in the seventeenth and eighteenth centuries* (1969).

Minchinton, W.E., 'The port of Bristol', in P. McGrath, ed., *Bristol in the eighteenth century* (Newton Abbot, 1972), pp. 125–60.

Minchinton, W.E., 'The merchants of Bristol in the eighteenth century', in *Sociétés et groupes sociaux en Aquitaine et en Angleterre*, Fédérations Historiques du Sud-ouest (Bordeaux, 1979), pp. 185–200.

Mintz, S.W., *Sweetness and power: the place of sugar in modern history* (New York, 1985).

Mintz, S.W., 'The changing roles of food in the study of consumption', in J. Brewer and R. Porter, eds, *Consumption and the world of goods* (1993), pp. 260–73.

Morgan, K.O., 'Bristol and the Atlantic trade in the eighteenth century', *English Historical Review*, CVII, (1992), pp. 626–50.

Morgan, K.O., *Bristol and the Atlantic trade in the eighteenth century* (Cambridge, 1993).

Morgan, K.O., 'Bristol West India merchants in the eighteenth century', *TRHS*, 6th ser. 3 (1993), pp. 185–208.

Morgan, K.O., 'The economic development of Bristol, 1700–1850', in M. Dresser and P. Ollerenshaw, eds, *The making of modern Bristol* (Tiverton, 1996), pp. 48–76.

Mott, R.A., 'The London and Newcastle chaldrons for measuring coal', *Archaeologia Aeliana*, 4th ser. XL (1962), pp. 227–39.

Mowl, T., *To build the second city: architects and craftsmen of Georgian Bristol* (Bristol, 1991).

Mui, H.-C. and L.H., *Shops and shopkeepers in eighteenth century England* (1988).

Muir, R. and Platt, E., eds, *A history of municipal government in Liverpool* (Liverpool, 1906).

Muldrew, C., 'Interpreting the market: the ethics of credit and community relations in early modern England', *Social History*, 18 (1993), pp. 163–84.

Nash, R.C., 'The English and Scottish tobacco trades in the seventeenth and eighteenth centuries: legal and illegal trade', *EcHR*, 2nd ser. XXXV (1982), pp. 354–72.

Neale, R.S., *Bath 1650–1850. A social history, or a valley of pleasure yet a sink of iniquity* (1981).

Neale, R.S., 'Bath: ideology and utopia', in P. Borsay, ed., *The eighteenth century town, 1688–1820* (1990), pp. 223–42.

Nef, J.U., *The rise of the British coal industry*, 2 vols (1932, repr. 1966).

Newton, R., *Eighteenth century Exeter* (Exeter, 1984).

Nix, M., 'A maritime history of the ports of Bideford and Barnstaple, 1786–1841', unpublished Ph.D. thesis, University of Leicester (1991).

O'Brien, P., 'European economic development: the contribution of the periphery', *EcHR*, XXXV (1982), pp. 1–18.

Oppenheim, M., 'Maritime history', in W. Page, ed., *The Victoria history of the county of Cornwall. Volume I* (1906), pp. 475–511.

Oppenheim, M., *The maritime history of Devon* (Exeter, 1968).

Osborne, B., 'Glamorgan agriculture in the seventeenth and eighteenth centuries', *National Library of Wales Journal*, 20 (1977–8), pp. 387–405.

Overton, M., *Agricultural revolution in England. The transformation of the agrarian economy, 1500–1850* (Cambridge, 1996).

Pares, R., *A West-India fortune* (1950).

Pares, R., 'The London sugar market 1740–69', *EcHR*, 2nd ser. IX (1956–7), pp. 254–70.

Parkinson, C.N., *The rise of the port of Liverpool* (Liverpool, 1952).

Pawson, E., *Transport and economy: the turnpike roads of eighteenth-century Britain* (1977).

Payton, P., *The making of modern Cornwall: historical experience and the persistence of 'difference'* (Redruth, 1994).

Phillips, E., *Pioneers of the south Wales coalfield* (Cardiff, 1925).

Ponting, K.G., *A history of the west of England cloth industry* (1957).

Ponting, K.G., *The woollen industry of south west England* (Bath, 1971).

Pounds, N.J.G., 'Food production and distribution in pre-industrial Cornwall', in W. Minchinton, ed., *Population and marketing: two studies in the history of the south-west* (Exeter Papers in Economic History, 11, Exeter, 1976), pp. 107–22.

Powell, A.C., 'Glass making in Bristol', *TBGAS*, XLVII (1925), pp. 211–57.

Powell, J.W.D., *Bristol privateers and ships of war* (Bristol, 1930).

Power, M., 'Councillors and commerce in Liverpool, 1650–1750', *Urban History*, 24, 3 (1997), pp. 301–23.

Press, J.A., *The merchant seamen of Bristol, 1746–1789*, (BHA, 38, 1976).

Price, J.M., *France and the Chesapeake: a history of the French tobacco monopoly, 1674–1791, and of its relationship to the British and American tobacco trades*, 2 vols (Ann Arbor, Michigan, 1973).

Price, J.M. and Clemens, P.G.E., 'A revolution of scale in overseas trade: British firms in the Chesapeake trade, 1675–1775', *Journal of Economic History*, XLVII (1987), pp. 1–43.

Price, R., Jackson, R. and Jackson, P., *Bristol clay pipe makers: a revised and enlarged edition* (Bristol, 1979).

Prior, M., *Fisher Row: fishermen, bargemen and canal boatmen in Oxford 1500–1900* (Oxford, 1982).

Pritchard, J.E., 'The great plan of Bristol, 1673', *TBGAS*, XLIV (1922), pp. 203–20.

Pritchard, J.E., 'Tobacco pipes of Bristol in the seventeenth century and their makers', *TBGAS*, XLV (1924), pp. 165–91.

Prys-Jones, A.G., *The story of Carmarthenshire. Volume 2: from the sixteenth century to 1832* (1972).

Quilici, R. H., 'Turmoil in a city and empire: Bristol's factions, 1700–1775', unpublished Ph.D. dissertation, University of New Hampshire, (1976).

Raistrick, A., *Quakers in science and industry: an account of the Quaker contribution to science and industry during the seventeenth and eighteenth centuries* (1950, repr. Newton Abbot, 1968).

Ramsey, G.D., 'The smuggler's trade: a neglected aspect of English commercial development', *TRHS*, 5th ser. II (1952), pp. 131–57.

Rediker, M., *Between the devil and the deep blue sea. Merchant seamen, pirates and the Anglo-American maritime world* (Cambridge, 1987).

Rees, J.F., *The story of Milford* (Cardiff, 1954).

Rees, W., *Industry before the industrial revolution: incorporating a study of the Chartered Companies of the Society of Mines Royal and of Mineral and Battery Works*, 2 vols (Cardiff, 1968).

Rees, W., *Cardiff, a history of the city* (Cardiff, 1969).

Richardson, D., *The Bristol slave traders: a collective portrait*, (BHA, 60, 1985).

Riden, P., 'The output of the British iron industry before 1870', *EcHR*, XXX (1977), pp. 442–59.

Ringrose, D.R., 'Metropolitan cities as parasites', in E. Aerts and P. Clark, eds, *Metropolitan cities and their hinterlands in early modern Europe* (Tenth Economic History Conference, Leuven, 1990), pp. 21–38.

Ripley, P., 'Trade and social structure of Gloucester, 1600–1700', *TBGAS*, XCIV (1976), pp. 117–23.

Ripley, P., 'The economy of Gloucester 1660–1740', *TBGAS*, XCVIII (1980), pp. 135–53.

Ripley, P., 'Village and town: occupations and wealth in the hinterland of Gloucester 1660–1700', *Agricultural History Review*, 32 (1984), pp. 170–8.

Rive, A., 'A short history of tobacco smuggling', *EcHR*, I (1929), pp. 554–69.

Roberts, R.O., 'The development and decline in the non-ferrous metal smelting industries in south Wales', *Transactions of the Honourable Society of Cymmrodorion*, 52 (1956), pp. 78–115.

Roberts, R.O., 'A further note on Dr. John Lane', *Gower*, 22 (1971), pp. 22–5.

Roberts, R.O., 'Industrial expansion in south Wales', in D. Moore, ed., *Wales in the eighteenth century* (Swansea, 1976), pp. 109–26.

Roberts, R.O., 'Enterprise and capital for non-ferrous metal smelting in Glamorgan, 1694–1924', *Morgannwg*, 23 (1979), pp. 48–82.

Roberts, R.O., 'Financial developments in early modern Wales and the emergence of the first banks', *Welsh Historical Review*, 16 (1993), pp. 291–307.

Robinson, D.E., 'Half the story of "The rise of the English shipping industry"', *Business History Review*, XLI (1967), pp. 303–8.

Robinson, D.E., 'The secret of British power in the age of sail: Admiralty records of the coasting fleet', *American Neptune*, XLVIII (1988), pp. 5–21.

Rolt, L.T.C., *The potters' field: a history of the south Devon ball clay industry* (Newton Abbot, 1974).

Roseveare, H., 'Wiggins' Key revisited: trade and shipping in the later seventeenth-century port of London', *Journal of Transport History*, 16 (1995), pp. 1–20.

Rowe, J., *Cornwall in the age of the industrial revolution* (Liverpool, 1953).

Rowlands, M.B., *Masters and men in the West Midlands metalware trades before the industrial revolution* (Manchester, 1975).

Rowlands, M.B., 'Continuity and change in an industrialising society: the case of the West Midlands industries', in P. Hudson, ed., *Regions and industries: a perspective on the industrial revolution in Britain* (Cambridge, 1989), pp. 103–31.

Rule, J., 'The home market and the sea fisheries of Devon and Cornwall in the nineteenth century', in W.E. Minchinton, ed., *Population and marketing. Two studies in the history of the south-west* (Exeter Papers in Economic History, 11, Exeter, 1976), pp. 123–39.

Sacks, D.H., 'Trade, society and politics in Bristol, circa 1500–circa 1650', unpublished Ph.D. Thesis, Harvard University, Cambridge, Mass. (1977).

Sacks, D.H., *The widening gate: Bristol and the Atlantic economy, 1450–1700* (Berkeley and Los Angeles, 1991).

Scantlebury, J., 'The development of the export trade in pilchards from Cornwall during the sixteenth century', *Journal of the Royal Institution of Cornwall*, X (1989), pp. 330–59.

Shammas, C., *The pre-industrial consumer in England and America* (Oxford, 1990).

Shammas, C., 'Changes in English and Anglo-American consumption from 1550–1800', in J. Brewer and R. Porter, eds, *Consumption and the world of goods* (1993), pp. 185–95.

Simon, A.L., *History of the wine trade in England*, 3 vols (1906–9).

Skeel, C., 'The cattle trade between Wales and England from the fifteenth century to the eighteenth century', *TRHS*, 4th ser. IX (1926).

Smith, R., *Sea coal to London* (1961).

Smout, T.C., 'The early Scottish sugar houses 1660–1720', *EcHR*, 2nd ser. XIV (1961–2), pp. 240–69.

Somerville, J., *Christopher Thomas soapmaker of Bristol: the story of Christopher Thomas & Bros, 1745–1954* (Bristol, 1991).

Southward, A., Boalch, G., and Maddock, L., 'Climatic change and the herring and pilchard fisheries of Devon and Cornwall', in D.J. Starkey, ed., *Devon's coastline and coastal waters* (Exeter Maritime Studies, 3, Exeter, 1988), pp. 33–58.

Southward, A.J. and Boalch, G.T., 'The marine resources of Devon's coastal waters', in M. Duffy, S. Fisher, B. Greenhill, D.J. Starkey and J. Youings, eds, *The new maritime history of Devon. Volume I: from early times to the late eighteenth century* (Exeter, 1992), pp. 51–60.

Spufford, M., *The great re-clothing of rural England: petty chapmen and their wares in the seventeenth century* (Cambridge, 1984).

Stamper, J.M.B., 'The Shropshire salt industry', *Transactions of the Shropshire Archaeological Society*, LXIV (1985), pp. 77–82.

Stanes, R.G.F., 'Devon agriculture in the mid-eighteenth century: the evidence of the Milles enquiries', in M.A. Havinden and C.M. King, eds, *The south-west and the land* (Exeter Papers in Economic History, 2, Exeter, 1969), pp. 43–65.

Starkey, D.J., ed., *Devon's coastline and coastal waters: aspects of man's relationship with the sea*, (Exeter Maritime Studies, 3, Exeter, 1988).

Starkey, D.J., *British privateering enterprise in the eighteenth century* (Exeter, 1990).

Starkey, D.J., 'Devonians and the Newfoundland trade', in M. Duffy, S. Fisher, B. Greenhill, D.J. Starkey and J. Youings, eds, *The new maritime history of Devon. Volume I: from early times to the late eighteenth century* (Exeter, 1992), pp. 163–71.

Steckley, G.F., 'The wine economy of Tenerife in the seventeenth century: Anglo-Spanish partnership in a luxury trade', *EcHR*, 2nd ser. XXXIII (1980), pp. 335–50.

Stein, R., 'The French sugar business in the eighteenth century: a quantitative study' *Business History*, XXII (1980), pp. 3–17.

Stembridge, P.K., *Goldney: a house and family* (Bristol, 1969, 4th edn, 1982).

Stembridge, P.K., 'A Bristol-Coalbrookdale connection: the Goldneys', *Bristol Industrial Archaeological Society Journal*, 19 (1986), pp. 14–20.

Stephens, W.B., 'The west-country ports and the struggle for the Newfoundland fisheries in the seventeenth century', *Transactions of the Devonshire Association*, LXXXVIII (1956), pp. 90–101.

Stephens, W.B., *Seventeenth-century Exeter: a study of industrial and commercial development 1625–1688* (1958).

Stephens, W.B., 'The Exchequer port books as a source for the history of the English cloth trade', *Textile History*, 1 (1969), pp. 206–13.

Stephens, W.B., 'Trade trends at Bristol, 1600–1700', *TBGAS*, XCIII (1974), pp. 156–61.

Stern, W.M., 'Cheese shipped coastwise to London towards the middle of the eighteenth century', *Guildhall Miscellany*, 4 (1973), pp. 207–21.

Stern, W.M., 'Fish marketing in London in the first half of the eighteenth century', in D.C. Coleman and A.H. John, eds, *Trade, government and economy in pre-industrial England: essays presented to F.J. Fisher* (1976), pp. 68–77.

Stiles, R., 'The Old Market sugar refinery: 1680–1908', *Bristol Industrial Archaeological Society Journal*, 2 (1969), pp. 10–17.

Stobart, J., 'An eighteenth-century revolution? Investigating urban growth in north-west England, 1664–1801', *Urban History*, 23, 1 (1996), pp. 26–47.

Stobart, J., 'Shopping streets as social space: leisure, consumerism and improvement in an eighteenth-century county town', *Urban History*, 25, 1 (1998), pp. 3–21.

Stratton, J.M., *Agricultural records, A.D. 220–1977* (2nd edn, 1977).

Stuckey, P., *The sailing pilots of the Bristol Channel* (Newton Abbot, 1977).

Symons, M.V., *Coal mining in the Llanelli area. Volume one: sixteenth century to 1829* (Llanelli, 1979).

Talbut, G., 'Worcester as an industrial and commercial centre 1660–1750', *Transactions of the Worcestershire Archaeological Society*, 3rd ser. 10 (1986), pp. 91–102.

Thick, M., 'Market gardening in England and Wales', in J. Thirsk, ed., *The agrarian history of England and Wales. Volume V: 1640–1750. II: Agrarian change* (Cambridge, 1985), pp. 503–32.

Thick, M., 'Garden seeds in England before the late eighteenth century—I, seed growing', *Agricultural History Review*, 38 (1990), pp. 1–13.

Thick, M., 'Garden seeds in England before the late eighteenth century—II, the trade in seeds to 1760', *Agricultural History Review*, 38 (1990), pp. 105–16.

Thirsk, J., *Economic policy and projects: the development of a consumer society in early modern England* (Oxford, 1978).

Thirsk, J., 'The fantastical folly of fashion: the English stocking knitting industry, 1500–1700', in J. Thirsk, *The rural economy of England* (1984), pp. 235–58.

Thirsk, J., ed., *The agrarian history of England and Wales. Volume V: 1640–1750. I: Regional farming systems* (Cambridge, 1985).

Thirsk, J., 'The south-west Midlands: Warwickshire, Worcestershire, Gloucestershire, and Herefordshire', in J. Thirsk, ed., *The agrarian history of England and Wales. Volume V: 1640–1750. I: Regional farming systems* (Cambridge, 1985), pp. 159–193.

Thirsk, J., *Agricultural regions and agrarian history in England, 1500–1750* (Cambridge, 1987).

Thirsk, J., ed., *Agricultural change: policy and practice, 1500–1750. Chapters from the agrarian history of England and Wales. Volume 3* (Cambridge, 1990), pp. 135–215.

Tracy, J.D., ed., *The rise of merchant empires: long-distance trading in the early modern world, 1350–1750* (Cambridge, 1990).

Trinder, B.S., *The industrial revolution in Shropshire* (Chichester, 1973, 2nd edn 1981).

Trott, C., 'Coalmining in the borough of Neath in the seventeenth and eighteenth centuries', *Morgannwg*, 13 (1969), pp. 47–74.

Turnbull, G.L., 'Provincial road carrying in England in the eighteenth century', *Journal of Transport History*, 2nd ser. IV (1977), pp. 17–39.

Usher, A.P., 'The growth of English shipping, 1572–1922', *Quarterly Journal of Economics*, XLII (1929), pp. 465–78.

van der Woude, A., Hayami, A. and de Vries, J., 'The hierarchies, provisioning, and demographic patterns of cities', in A. van der Woude, A. Hayami, and J. de Vries, eds., *Urbanization in history* (Oxford, 1990), pp. 1–19.

Vanes, J., *The port of Bristol in the sixteenth century* (Bristol, 1977).

Vigier, F., *Change and apathy: Liverpool and Manchester during the Industrial Revolution* (Cambridge, Mass., 1971).

Ville, S., 'Total factor productivity in the English shipping industry: the north-east coal trade, 1700–1850', *EcHR*, 2nd ser. XXXIX (1986), pp. 355–70.

Ville, S., 'Defending productivity growth in the English coal trade during the eighteenth and nineteenth centuries', *EcHR*, 2nd ser. XL (1987), pp. 597–602.

Ville, S., *English shipowning during the industrial revolution: Michael Henley and Son, London shipowners, 1770–1830* (Manchester, 1987).

Ville, S.P., 'Shipping in the port of Newcastle, 1780–1800', *Journal of Transport History*, IX (1988), pp. 60–77.

Ville, S., 'The problem of tonnage measurement in the English shipping industry, 1780–1830', *International Journal of Maritime History*, I, 2 (1989), pp. 65–84.

Waite, V., 'The Bristol Hotwell', in P. McGrath, ed., *Bristol in the eighteenth century* (Newton Abbot, 1972), pp. 109–26.

Wakelin, P., 'Comprehensive computerisation of a very large documentary source: the Portbooks Project at Wolverhampton Polytechnic', in P. Denley and D. Hopkin, eds, *History and computing* (Manchester, 1987), pp. 109–15.

Wakelin, A.P., 'Pre-industrial trade on the river Severn: a computer-aided study of the Gloucester port books, *c.*1640–*c.*1770', unpublished Ph.D. thesis, CNAA, Wolverhampton Polytechnic (1991).

Wakelin, A.P. and Hussey, D.P., 'Investigating regional economies: the Gloucester port books database', in C.E. Harvey and J. Press, eds, *Database systems and historical research* (1996), pp. 14–21.

Walker, F., *The Bristol region* (1972).

Walker, I.C., *Clay tobacco pipes, with particular reference to the Bristol industry* (Ottawa, 1977).

Wanklyn, M.D.G., 'Industrial development in the Ironbridge Gorge before Abraham Darby', *West Midlands Studies*, XV (1982), pp. 3–7.

Wanklyn, M.D.G., 'The Severn navigation in the seventeenth century: long-distance trade of Shrewsbury boats', *Midland History*, XIII (1988), pp. 34–58.

Wanklyn, M.D.G., 'Urban revival in early modern England: Bridgnorth and the river trade', *Midland History*, XVIII (1993), pp. 37–64.

Wanklyn, M.D.G., 'The impact of water transport facilities on English river ports, *c.*1660–*c.*1760', *EcHR*, XLIX (1996), pp. 1–19.

Ward, J.R., 'The profitability of sugar planting in the British west indies 1650–1834', *EcHR*, 2nd ser. XXXI (1978), pp. 197–213.

Watkins, C.M., *North Devon pottery and its export to America in the seventeenth century*, (US Natural Museum Bulletin 225, Washington D.C., 1960).

Weatherill, L., *The pottery trade and north Staffordshire 1660–1760* (Manchester, 1971).

Weatherill, L., 'The growth of the pottery industry in England, 1660–1815: some new evidence and estimates', *Post-Medieval Archaeology*, 17 (1983), pp. 1–22.

Weatherill, L., *Consumer behaviour and material culture, 1660–1760* (1988).

Weatherill, L., 'The meaning of consumer behaviour in late seventeenth- and early eighteenth-century England', in J. Brewer and R. Porter, eds, *Consumption and the world of goods* (1993), pp. 206–27

Wedlake, W., *A history of Watchet* (Williton, 1955).

Weeden, C., 'The Bristol glass industry', *Glass Technology*, 24, 5 (1983), pp. 251–5.

Weeden, C., 'Bristol glassmakers: their role in an emergent industry', *Bristol Industrial Archeological Society Journal*, 17 (1984), pp. 24–31.

Westerfield, R.B., *Middlemen in English business: particularly between 1660 and 1760* (1915, repr. New York, 1968).

Whetter, J.C.A., 'Cornish trade in the seventeenth century' *Journal of the Royal Institution of Cornwall*, new ser. IV, 4 (1964).

Whetter, J.C.A., 'The economic history of Cornwall in the seventeenth century', unpublished Ph.D. Thesis, University of London (1965).

Whetter, J.C.A., 'Bryan Rogers of Falmouth, merchant, 1632–92', *Old Cornwall*, IV (1965), pp. 347–52.

Whetter, J.C.A., 'The rise of the port of Falmouth, 1600–1800', in H.E.S. Fisher, ed., *Ports and shipping in the south-west* (Exeter Papers in Economic History, 4 , Exeter, 1970), pp. 1–32.

Whetter, J.C.A., *Cornwall in the seventeenth century: an economic survey of Kernow* (Padstow, 1974).

Wiggs, J.L., 'The seaborne trade of Southampton in the second half of the sixteenth century', unpublished M.A. thesis, University of Southampton (1955).

Willan, T.S., 'Bath and the navigation of the Avon', *PSANHS, Bath and District Branch* (1936), pp. 139–40.

Willan, T.S., *River navigation in England 1600–1750* (Manchester, 1936, repr. 1964).

Willan, T.S., 'The river navigation and trade of the Severn valley, 1600–1750', *EcHR,* VIII (1937), pp. 68–79.

Willan, T.S., *The English coasting trade 1600–1750* (Manchester, 1938, repr. 1967).

Willan, T.S., *The inland trade: studies in English internal trade in the sixteenth and seventeenth centuries* (Manchester, 1976).

Williams, A.F., 'Bristol port plans and improvement schemes of the eighteenth century', *TBGAS,* LXXXI (1962), pp. 138–88.

Williams, D.T., 'The port books of Swansea and Neath, 1709–19', *Archaeologia Cambrensis,* XCV (1940), pp. 192–209.

Williams, D.T., 'The maritime trade of the Swansea Bay ports with the Channel Islands from the records of the port books of 1709–19', *Transactions of La Société Guernesaise,* XV (1953), pp. 270–85.

Williams, J.E., 'Whitehaven in the eighteenth century', *EcHR,* 2nd ser. VIII (1956), pp. 393–404.

Williams, M., *The draining of the Somerset Levels* (Cambridge, 1970).

Williams, M.I., 'Some aspects of the economic and social life of the southern regions of Glamorgan, 1600–1800', *Morgannwg,* III (1959), pp. 21–40.

Williams, M.I., 'A contibution to the commercial history of Glamorgan', *National Library of Wales Journal,* XI (1959–60), pp. 330–60.

Williams, M.I., 'Further contributions to the commercial history of Glamorgan', *National Library of Wales Journal,* XII (1962), pp. 354–66.

Williams, M.I., 'Cardiff, its people and its trade, 1660–1720', *Morgannwg,* VII (1963), pp. 74–97.

Williams, M.I., 'The port of Aberdyfi in the eighteenth century', *National Library of Wales Journal,* XVIII, i (1973), pp. 95–134.

Williams, M.I., 'The economic and social history of Glamorgan 1660–1760', in G. Williams, ed., *Early modern Glamorgan from the Act of Union to the industrial revolution*, Glamorgan County History IV (Cardiff, 1974), pp. 311–73.

Williams, M.I., 'Carmarthenshire's maritime trade in the sixteenth and seventeenth centuries', *The Carmarthenshire Antiquary,* 14 (1978), pp. 61–70.

Williams, N., 'The London port books', *Transactions of the London and Middlesex Archaeological Society,* 18 (1955), pp. 13–26.

Williams, N., *Contraband cargoes: seven centuries of smuggling* (1959).

Williams, N.J., *Descriptive list of Exchequer, Queen's Remembrancer, Port Books, Parts 1–111: 1565–1700; 1700–1799 (1960)*.

Williams, N.J., *The maritime trade of the East Anglian ports, 1550–1590* (Oxford, 1988).

Willis-Bund, J.W. and Page, W., eds, *Victoria county history of the county of Worcester. Volume II* (1906).

Wilson, C., *England's apprenticeship 1603–1763* (1965).

Wilson, C.H., 'Land carriage in the seventeenth century', *EcHR,* 2nd ser. XXXIII (1980), pp. 92–5.

Witt, C., Weeden, C. and Schwind, A.P., eds, *Bristol glass* (Bristol, 1984).

Wolf, E., *Europe and the people without history* (Berkeley, 1982),

Woodward, D.M., 'Short guides to records 22: port books', *History*, 55 (1970), pp. 207–10.

Woodward, D.M., *The trade of Elizabethan Chester* (Hull, 1970).

Woodward, D.M., 'The Anglo-Irish livestock trade of the seventeenth century', *Irish Historical Studies*, XVIII (1972–3), pp. 484–523.

Woodward, D.M., 'The port-books of England and Wales', *Maritime History*, III (1973), pp. 147–65.

Woodward, D.M., '"Swords into ploughshares": recycling in pre-industrial England, *EcHR*, XXXVIII (1985), pp. 175–91.

Woodward, H.W., 'The glass industry of the Stourbridge district', *West Midlands Studies*, 8 (1976), pp. 36–42.

Wordie, J.R., 'The South: Oxfordshire, Buckinghamshire, Berkshire, Wiltshire, and Hampshire', in J. Thirsk, ed., *The agrarian history of England and Wales. Volume V: 1640–1750. I: Regional farming systems* (Cambridge, 1985), pp. 317–57.

Wrigley, E.A., 'A simple model of London's importance in changing English society and economy, 1650–1750', *Past and Present*, 37 (1967), pp. 44–60.

Wrigley, E.A., 'Metropolitan cities and their hinterlands: stimulus and constraints to growth', in E. Aerts and P. Clark, eds, *Metropolitan cities and their hinterlands in early modern Europe* (Tenth Economic History Conference, Leuven, 1990), pp. 12–21.

Wrigley, E.A., 'Urban growth and agricultural change: England and the continent in the early modern period', in P. Borsay, ed., *The eighteenth century town, 1688–1820* (1990), pp. 39–82.

Wrigley, E.A. and Schofield, R.S., *The population history of England 1541–1871* (Cambridge, 1981).

Yates, R.A., 'The south-east borderland', in E.G. Bowen, ed., *Wales. A physical, historical, and regional geography* (1957), pp. 486–513.

Zahedieh, N, 'London and the colonial consumer in the late seventeenth century', *EcHR*, XLVII (1994), pp. 239–61.

Zupko, R.E., *A dictionary of English weights and measures* (Madison, 1968).

Index

Aberdovey, 4, 6, 10, 33, 45, 100, 111, 123, 143; trade in goods, 58–60
Aberthaw, 10, 13, 101
Aberystwyth, 4, 10
Adams, John, 180
ale, 59, 98
Alloway, Joseph, 120
Alloway, William, xvi, 42, 86, 110, 120, 132, 136, 192, 193, 194–5; fishery at Lynmouth, 152–3, 176, 183; salt trade, 161, 167, 174, 175–9, 180, 182; trade with Bristol, 126
America, xiv, 40, 92, 104, 178, 196
Amsterdam, 146
Andrews, J.H., 141
Anstice, Robert, 176
Anstice, Thomas, 180, 182, 192
Anthony, John, 125
Anthony, Thomas, 125
apothecary ware, 67
Appledore, 9, 10
apples, 75
Ashton, Richard, 191
Aust, 13–14
Avon, River (Bristol), 1, 2, 4, 22, 50
Avon, River (Warks), 3–4, 10, 23, 144–5, 187, 199, 200
Axe, River, 10
Aymes, John, 176

bacon, 140, 171, 205
Bailey, Henry, 118, 188
Bailey, William, 114
Baker, Anthony, 180
Baker, Stephen, 125, 165, 191
Balch, George, 152, 183, 195
Balch, Robert, 153
Balch and Company, 154
Baldwin, Hugh, 168
ball clay *see* tobacco pipe clay
Banbury, 188, 199, 200
Barbados *see* West Indies
bark *see* timber trade

barley, *see* grain trade
Barnstaple, 4, 6, 23, 30–1, 37; boats, 134, 138–9, 154, 197; customs administration, 9–10, 14–15; 'home' port, 142–3, 146–7; organisation of trade, 108–9, 113; trade in goods, 58–63, 92–5; shipping patterns, 25–6, 35–8; *see also* coal trade: south Wales ports; grain trade
Barrett, William, 55, 141–4
Bartlett, George, 31
Baston, John, 120, 180
Bath, 2
Bath spa water, 82–4, 127
Baugh, Joseph, 125
Bay of Biscay *see* salt trade
bay yarn, 81; *see also* textile trade
Bayley, Richard, 125
bays, 69, 92; *see also* textile trade
Beachley, 10, 13–14
Beale, Benjamin, 115
Beale, John (jun.), 128
Beale, John (sen.), 79, 106, 114, 115–17, 128, 151, 193
beans, 188
Bearpacker, John, 191, 194
Beaumaris, 169
Beaver, William, 180
bedding, 56
beer, 98
beeswax, 59, 75
bell metal, 119
Benbow, John, 117
Benthall, 118
Berkeley, 13, 23
Bewdley, 4, 27, 67, 69, 75, 77, 79, 81, 90, 116, 135, 183; boats, 82, 115–7, 124, 169, 171, 173–4, 188, 193; *see also* Gloucester
Bickclish, Thomas, 191
Bideford, 4, 6, 30–1, 37; boats, 30–1, 134, 137–9, 154, 168, 173, 197; customs administration, 9–10, 14; 'home' port, 142–3, 147–8; organisation of trade, 108–9, 113, 120,

287

tobacco pipes, 75, 93, 205
tobacco stems, 205
tobacco trade, xiii, xiv, 59, 205; Barnstaple and
    Bideford, 6, 67, 86, 197; Bideford, 46–7, 92;
    Bristol, 8, 30, 67, 86–9; 91, 125, 126–7, 197;
    disruption, 41
Tone, River, 3
Topsham, 33, 146, 178; trade with Bristol, 42, 47,
    148; *see also* Exeter
Torbay, 146
Torridge, River, 6, 64
train oil, 30, 81, 183, 205
Trent, River, 3
Trewell, William, 190
Trinder, B.S., 149
Truro, 33, 95, 107, 110, 170
Turner, John, 180
Turner, Thomas, 111
Tuthill, Richard, 123
Tyler, Humphrey, 129
Tyler, John, 115–17
Tyler, Peter, 79
Tyler, William, 118

Uphill, 14, 179, 180, 181
Upton-on-Severn, 4, 27, 90, 135; boats 136–7,
    169, 171–3, 187–8, 192; *see also* Gloucester
Usk, River, 3

Vale of Evesham, 3
Vale of Glamorgan, 5, 101
Vale of Taunton Deane, 5, 91
Vaughan, William, 111
Vickers, Richard, 199
Ville, Simon, 31
Vinecott, Giles, 167, 172, 187, 193
Vinecott, John, 170, 173, 180, 182, 186, 193
vinegar, 183, 205
Virginia *see* America
Vosper, Nathaniel, 132, 187
Voss, Philip, 178

Wadding, Peter, 190
Wadebridge, 10
Wakelin, A.P., 191
Wallis, Alexander, 153, 179, 180, 182, 185–6, 187
Walpole, Horace, xiv
Wanklyn, M.D.G., 149
war *see* coastal trade: impact of war
Warburton, Thomas, 122, 160, 165, 168–9, 174
Ward, Dr Samuel, 82
Washer, Francis, 187
Watchet, 4, 42, 146, 180, 181; boats, 168, 170,
    177; customs administration, 10–12; shipping
    patterns, 12, 22, 137; trade, 91, 110; *see also*
    coal trade: south Wales ports; Minehead
Watkins, J., 93
Watts, Henry, 125
wearing apparel, 30, 69

Weatherill, Lorna, 93
Webb, Thomas, 168, 169
Webber, Amos, 146
Wellington, 181–2; fair, 123
Wells (Norfolk), 33
Wells (Somerset), 180, 181
Welshpool, 3
West Indies, xiv, 40, 84, 92, 104, 145, 154, 178, 196
Westerfield, 111
Weymouth, 33
wheat *see* grain trade
Wheddon, John, 42, 176, 180, 183
Wheeler, John, 116
White, James, 118
White, Samuel, 153
Whitehaven, 23, 86–8, 197
Whitehead, Henry, 191
Whitehead, Manassee, 153
Whitson, John, 196
Whittington, Richard, 118
Whittuck, Thomas, 125
Willan, T.S., 17, 40, 55–6, 105, 110, 111–12, 145,
    149, 184, 194
Willett, James, 118
Williams, Aaron, 125
Williams, John, 111
Williams, Thomas, 106
Williams, William (s.), boat master of Cardiff,
    114
Williams, William, boat master of Newnham,
    170
Williams, William, crewman, *Hannah* of
    Bridgwater, 146
wine trade, 59, 92, 183, 205; Bristol, 30, 67, 81–2,
    91, 117, 125
wire, 3, 5, 119
wood *see* timber trade
wood ashes, 73, 76, 91, 136
Woodbury, Hugh, 179–80
Woodruffe, Dr, 190
Woodward, D., 107
Woodward, Oliver, 180
wool, 5–6, 60, 73, 98, 101, 114, 117, 164, 172,
    174, 187–8, 199, 200, 205; Irish 6, 64, 91, 120,
    178; Spanish merino, 64: Welsh, 124
woollens *see* textile trade
Worcester, 4, 27; 67, 75, 81, 86, 90, 135, 144, 171;
    boats, 118, 133, 136–7, 144, 171, 188, 191–2;
    broad cloth, 69; *see also* Gloucester; salt trade
Wye, River, 3, 10, 24, 33, 55, 144–5, 197–8;
    tramping, 131; *see also* Chepstow
Wyre Forest, 69–70, 90

Yarcombe, 181–2
Yarmouth, 33, 45, 140
yarn, 172, 205; *see also* textile trade
Youghall, 191
Young, Peter, 125